THINKING THROUGH CRISIS

FORDHAM UNIVERSITY PRESS   NEW YORK 2020

COMMONALITIES
Timothy C. Campbell, series editor

THINKING THROUGH CRISIS

Depression-Era Black Literature,

Theory, and Politics

JAMES EDWARD FORD III

Fordham University Press gratefully acknowledges financial assistance and support provided for the publication of this book by Occidental College.

Earlier versions of the Introduction, Notebook 1, and Notebook 3 were published in *Rethinking Marxism, Novel, and Cultural Critique.*

Fordham University Press has no responsibility for the persistence or accuracy of URLs for external or third-party Internet websites referred to in this publication and does not guarantee that any content on such websites is, or will remain, accurate or appropriate.

Fordham University Press also publishes its books in a variety of electronic formats. Some content that appears in print may not be available in electronic books.

Visit us online at www.fordhampress.com.

Library of Congress Cataloging-in-Publication Data available online at https://catalog.loc.gov.

Printed in the United States of America

22 21 20   5 4 3 2 1

First edition

To K, To T, To A, To W,
The Lost and The Found

CONTENTS

Acknowledgments. ix

Introduction: From Being to Unrest,
from Objectivity to Motion. 1

Notebook 1 Down by the Riverside: Richard Wright,
the 1927 Flood, and the Citizen-Refugee 35

Notebook 2 "Crusade for Justice": Ida B. Wells and
the Power of the Multitude 74

Notebook 3 W. E. B. Du Bois's *Black Reconstruction*:
Theorizing Divine Violence. 123

Notebook 4 Zora Neale Hurston's *Moses, Man of the
Mountain*: An Anthropology of Power 193

Notebook 5 The New Day: Notes on Education and
the Dark Proletariat 244

Conclusion: From Being to Unrest,
from Objectivity to Motion—A Race
for Theory. 291

Notes 299

Index 333

ACKNOWLEDGMENTS

I have received immense support over the years. During my graduate training at Notre Dame, Ivy Wilson, David Ruccio, and the late Joseph Buttigieg helped me turn my broad ideas into a concrete project. Joe, though I miss our conversations, I'm heartened by your influence gracing this entire book. Thanks to Sandra Gustafson, Stephen Fredman, Graham Hammill, Glenn Hendler, Luke Gibbons, and other English faculty for their generosity. Richard Pierce and Dianne Pinderhughes made Africana Studies a second home. Seth Markle, Jessica Graham, and Shana Redmond modeled what cutting-edge scholarship can do.

At Occidental, Deans Jorge Gonzalez and Wendy Sternberg provided funds for my book's publication. I have learned so much from Warren Montag, Dolores Trevizo, Leila Neti, John Swift, Sharla Fett, Gretchen North, Amy Lyford, Dan Fineman, Eric Newhall, John Lang, Regina Freer, Movindri Reddy, Amy Tahani, Paul Nam, Kristi Upson-Saia, and Michael Gasper. Thank you, Courtney Baker and Erica Ball, for being institution-builders. Krystale Littlejohn, Ross Lerner, Ainsley Lesure, Kelema Moses, Mijin Cha, Jane Hong, and Zinzi Clemmons have shown me how new faculty can revitalize academic spaces.

The special collections at Tuskegee University, University of Chicago, UMASS-Amherst, and the New York Public Library supported my research. Nahum Dimitri Chandler, Stephanie Leigh Batiste, Brent Edwards, Robin D.G. Kelley, and Fred Moten have been wonderful mentors. This book grew out of a vibrant discourse involving Jill Richardson, Rizvana Bradley, Ashon Crawley, the "PRG" (Ryan McCormick and Matt Brown), Shadee Malaklou,

Regina Bradley, Taryn Jordan, Seulghee Lee, Jarvis McCinnis, Erica Edwards, and many others.

I'm most grateful to my family and community. Kwanda, thank you for sharing so many victories with me. Ajana, your courage paved the way. Trinity, may the best in me inspire the best in you. When you returned, I lifted you from the car seat and said, "I told you we'd get you back. Daddy kept his promise." That will be true for every lifetime. Every. One. I learned to believe in myself because my mother and grandparents believed in me first. To my aunts, uncles, cousins, and now second-cousins: Catch y'all in 407. Papa, I still miss you. HD, Denaro, Aaron, Ifeuro, Ikechi, Stuart, Lorme, Zahid, Ravi: Seeing us flourish is a blessing. Baba Amos, Marvin Jackson, Alex Yoo, and Cynthia Keith, thanks for the insights. To Andrew, JD, Ami, Mestre Themba, Adam, CM Versatil, CM Muito Tempo, all of Batuque; the LA Angoleiros, CECA, CM Chorao, CM Jurandir, and Justin Eumeka: *Capoeira de Angola mandou me chàma. Vamos Vadiar camará!*

THINKING THROUGH CRISIS

INTRODUCTION

From Being to Unrest, from Objectivity to Motion

> What matters is the life earned when it plunges into the inexplicable and
> emerges from it.
>
> —DAVID MARRIOTT, HAUNTED LIFE

Black radicalism demonstrates that decisions can be made in undecidable
situations, that possibility can be culled from petrification, and that force
is not an exclusive property of the privileged. Black radicalism contests the
assumption that overwhelming experience necessarily hinders thought and
action. The spiritual strivings, the *conatus* in black life, suggests much more
is afoot. The African American saying "make a way out of no way" is a plati-
tude when it is divorced from the lives and art forms that forged it in racialized, gendered, and classed contexts. When that saying gets restored to
those lives, art forms, and contexts, a theory of crisis emerges. Making a way
out of no way wrestles with "the contemporary persistence of black social
death" and the "insistence of black social life."[1] This theory of crisis—which
one can also call a materialist theory of trauma—develops in the encounter
between black radical aesthetics, trauma theory, Marxist thought, and leftist political philosophy at large. Black radicalism's exorbitance to conventional intellectual boundaries requires this traversal of disciplines.[2]

That exorbitance makes a theory of crisis elusive. That elusiveness
prompts reading to become a self-aware practice producing knowledge in
the nexus of visions, blindness, voices, silences, and gestures brought to
texts. Self-aware reading means judging the shortcomings one sees in texts

but also judging "the sight itself. . . . Nonvision is therefore inside vision, it is a form of vision."[3] To judge what one sees in a text without judging how one sees inevitably pushes less understood forms of agency into partial invisibility and inaudibility.[4] Far from a neutral technique of fact-finding, reading involves Du Boisian second-sight in all its rich, surreal implications, so lives haunting and haunted come into view and earshot at unexpected angles, unsettling well-worn critical vocabularies and the traditions in which they find their canonical formulations.[5]

Engaging several texts from these fields can provide the critical terminology and central themes for a theory of crisis. The challenge is to employ a strategy of inversion through a "stratified, dislodged and dislodging writing" that "brings low what was high" in "the irruptive emergence of a new 'concept,' a concept that can no longer be and never could be, included in the previous regime."[6] Western thought cannot venture into any investigation that must bear witness to black suffering. The phrase does not necessarily mean the actual physical or emotional difficulties of recently African-descended populations but refers to the *fantasies thrust on them.* Such projections stem from an anxiety over losing (access to) the privileges of "European Man"—the image of thought, affective regime, and institutional impulse of the Enlightenment project in the West. For many, losing political, economic, gender, and racial privileges means becoming black, if "black" here means falling into utter disrepair, condemnation, dishonor, nonvalue, formlessness, powerlessness, and immorality. The premise of European Man promises that its faithful adherents will never experience such loss or will see their loss redeemed in the end.

This leads to a "negative categorical imperative"—"above all, don't be black."[7] This projection is so seductive that many will deny the abuse they have undergone in fitting into Eurocentric standards. They will go through rhetorical acrobatics to pull back from their research findings and alter their argumentative direction in fear of getting close to the nonvalue they associate with blackness, as if European Man's definition of blackness is correct, as if blackness really is nothingness, as if the very normality bleeding this group dry will save them.

Thinking Through Crisis covers the writings of Richard Wright, Ida B. Wells, W. E. B. Du Bois, Zora Neale Hurston, and Langston Hughes in the 1930s to illustrate that on the hither side of losing (or never having) Europe's privileges lies other forms of living. Blackness is not merely suffering but the life lived in spite of suffering. Black radical artistry in the Great Depression has much to teach us about the "second Great Depression" that has persisted from Hurricane Katrina to the close of President Barack Obama's second administration.

I begin this work with three vignettes illustrating how thinkers drawing on the European tradition compromise brilliant, impassioned, and urgent theoretical work out of the fear that they will transgress the limits of European thought, and yet, much of this work instrumentalizes blackness as a foil. Thus, blackness becomes a tool for theory but not a companion in thinking with its own insights, terms, and models to share. The first vignette pushes the slave's (more than) supplemental role in Marx's *Capital* to its limit, altering Marx's theory of the labor process in unexpected ways. The second vignette questions Giorgio Agamben's truncated idea of political decision. Agamben finds himself among strange ideological company because of his misreading of Abraham Lincoln's Emancipation Proclamation. This misstep, intrinsic to his juridical methodology, shows the need for an overdetermined understanding of political decision derived from an ante-juridical outlook. The third and longest vignette turns to trauma theory's tendency toward ethical indecision out of nostalgia for the triumphalist European subject. I then offer preliminary statements on the "dark proletariat" as an alternate subjectivity to the colonial features of European Man. Finally, I close the notebook with a note on critical narrative, which includes a summary of the project and its mode of composition.

ON THE FIGURE OF THE SLAVE IN KARL MARX'S *CAPITAL*

The first work of slavery is to mar and deface those characteristics of its victims which distinguish men from things, and persons from property.

Frederick Douglass, Lecture, December 1850

One of the striking features of *Capital* is how frequently Karl Marx references the slave without making this figure central among his "dramatis personae."[8] Marx considers the slave tangential to capitalism's structure and attendant bodies of knowledge even though this figure recurs in almost all of *Capital*'s chapters. Marx will not acknowledge the slave's agency in a way that is directly incorporable into *Capital* or articulate the relationship between slave and wage laborer in struggles against economic exploitation. Unable to jettison or accept the slave, Marx instead constrains this figure to haunt his formulations.

The rebellious slave, as a worker, performs an exorbitance that provokes classical metaphysics to deform itself and take account of blackness. This other metaphysics would account for an "ontological totality" that "never allowed property in either the physical, philosophical, temporal, legal, social, or psychic senses," as Cedric Robinson has claimed.[9] Robinson considers this agency an underexamined *surplus* in black life. "We are not the subjects of or the subject formations of the capitalist world-system," Robinson says. "It is merely one condition of our being."[10] This surplus manifests itself in Marx's *Capital* through textual supplements—footnotes, excised notes, appendices, analogies, foils, etc. Said differently, the Eurocentric and black radical perspectives value the supplements differently. The Eurocentric view treats footnotes as detachable from an otherwise self-sufficient text. What Eurocentrism considers empty, the black radical tradition treats as surplus, which means the footnotes are surprisingly central to the text's effects. A new conclusion can be drawn from this attention to surplus. Unrest, rather than objectified being, becomes the new focal point of labor in the slaves' fight against capitalist exploitation.

Marx places his theoretical presupposition regarding the slave in footnote 18 in the chapter "The Labor Process and the Valorization Process." Marx quotes Marcus Terentius Varro to conceptualize the slave as the "speaking implement" (*instrumentum vocale*) existing between the beast of burden (the "semi-mute instrument") and the mute instrument.[11] That Marx takes this ontological account unchallenged from antiquity might suggest that slaves are among *Capital*'s marginalia. However, the term "speaking implement" encapsulates questions about discourse, practice, and consciousness central to *Capital* despite Marx making the wage laborer his priority.

"Speaking implement" designates the slave as a foil for analyzing the wage laborer. The slave is central to the exploitation of the nineteenth-century wage laborer and to Marx's theorization of the wage laborer's plight. The labor process and the theorizing of that process each instrumentalize the slave. The oft-mentioned contrast between the slave and the wage laborer concerns the former being sold altogether while the latter sells its labor power over time. But in Marx's "Additional remarks on the formal subsumption of labor under capital," he also compares forms of "existence": "In contrast to the slave, [the wage laborer's] labor becomes more intensive, since the slave works only under the spur of external fear but not for his existence which is guaranteed even though it does not belong to him. The free worker, however, is impelled by his wants."[12] Yet accounts of starvation and sexual/reproductive violence suggest slavery does not even respect biological need. This is the slaveowner's "voracious appetite for surplus labor."[13]

Studying the slaveowner's appetite for labor alongside "The Working Day" chapter in *Capital* suggests the "overworking of the Negro" has an unacknowledged rhetorical impact and structural presence in Marx's analysis. In one example, Marx writes: "As soon as peoples whose production still moves within the lower forms of slavery . . . are drawn into a world market dominated by the capitalist mode of production . . . the civilized horrors of over-work are grafted onto the barbaric horrors of slavery, serfdom, etc."[14] "Consumption" of the overworked Negro's "life in seven years of labor, became a factor in a calculated and calculating system" rather than an extraordinary occurrence.[15] In another example, Marx sees the overworked slave as a relevant stand-in for the British capitalist system. Marx quotes other texts that call the treatment of the capitalist labor market a "traffic in human flesh" operating as successfully "as slaves are sold to the cotton-grower in the United States":[16]

> Considerations of economy . . . [justify] racking the uttermost toil of the slave; for, when his place can at once be supplied from foreign preserves, the duration of his life becomes a matter of less moment than its productive-ness while it lasts. . . . It is accordingly a maxim of slave management . . . that the most effective economy is that which takes out of the human chattel in the shortest space of time the utmost amount of exertion. It is in tropical culture, where annual profits often equal the whole capital of plantations, that negro life is most recklessly sacrificed.[17]

After this, Marx says, "*Mutato nomine de te fibula narratur*," or "The name is changed, but the tale is told of you." He warns, "For slave trade, read labour-market, for Kentucky and Virginia, Ireland and the agricultural districts of England, Scotland and Wales, for Africa, Germany."[18]

In both these examples, despite the tentative freedoms of wage-labor, economic systems subsumed under capitalism remain closely linked to slavery. The first example, which discusses the slave's connection to a predominantly capitalist world market, should suggest that "the barbaric horrors" of plantation labor are *compounded* by the "civilized horrors" of capitalist development. Instead, Marx guarantees the slave's existence to avoid theorizing the wage laborer's and the slave's precarity under capitalism. Marx does not distinguish slavery from capitalism in the second example but writes captivatingly about capitalism's avoidance of these ethical concerns. In what reads like moving oratory, Marx points to "this throng of people" consisting of "generations of stunted, short-lived and rapidly replaced human beings, plucked, so to speak, before they were ripe."[19] It is difficult not to imagine someone speaking with the same fervor, if not the same words, against slavery. Beyond his rhetoric, Marx does not address how capitalist dealings in labor markets appropriated and revised slavery's strategies for finding or replacing labor. Nonetheless, textual evidence suggests the real subsumption of labor under capital raises rather than dispels the specter of slavery. Marx's equivocations about the slave's existence under capitalist demands for profit suggest another meaning to the phrase "speaking implement."

Although Marx celebrated slave revolts in his journalism and correspondence, his acceptance of capitalism's ontological premises (in order to defeat classical economists on their own terms) leaves no space to consider the slave's capacity for speech. Nor does this move leave Marx room to evaluate his (in)ability to hear the slave's own critique of capitalism. A brief passage from Frederick Douglass's famous slave narrative *My Bondage and My Freedom* (1855) will serve as an example. In the following quotation, Douglass has escaped slavery and given antislavery lectures throughout the United States with other abolitionists: "Many came . . . from curiosity to hear what a negro could say in his own cause. I was generally introduced as a 'chattel'—a 'thing'—a piece of southern 'property'—the chairman assuring the audience that it could speak."[20] Douglass's abolitionist comrades are fine with calling him nominally free, but they adamantly remind their audiences that Douglass does not inhabit the same world they do. Douglass does not acquiesce to their misrepresentations of him. However, he was pressed to find ways of inhabiting an antiblack context promoting abolition without a sense of contradiction.

The tensions surrounding the development and reception of Douglass's critiques of slavery are common in fugitive discourse, a form of critique coming from a subject who is not supposed to exist aside from being instrumentalized for another's use (in this case, the theorization of the slave/wage laborer's vulnerability to exploitation, whether by capitalists, Marx, or white abolitionists). Fugitive discourse is vulnerable to disqualification *because* it is compelling, since the slave should not be able to speak cogently about slavery's violence. Such a person could never have been a slave, so this perspective went. Douglass's fellow abolitionists walked into this trap. They admonished Douglass to water down his speeches to "simple narrative." One abolitionist told him, "Give us the facts . . . we will take care of the philosophy." His colleagues felt it would be "better [for Douglass to] have a little of the plantation manner of speech than not; 'tis not best that you appear too learned"; otherwise his audience would doubt his slave past, discrediting his abolitionist goals.[21] These abolitionists muffle Douglass's critical voice by calling him "property" after having escaped that condition and by separating his narrative from the philosophy it carries. They reproduce the distinction between human and slave they claim to abolish.

One finds a similar disavowal of slave agency—as Fred Moten does—embedded in Marx's *Capital*.[22] When the "chairman" introducing Douglass says, "it could speak," he echoes Marx's parodic discussion of the commodity who speaks "through the mouth of the economist": "If commodities could speak, they would say this: our use-value may interest men, but it does not belong to us as objects. What does belong to us, however, is our value. Our own intercourse as commodities proves it. We relate to each other merely as exchange-values."[23] In Marx's estimation, exchange-value is no less socially produced than use-value. He is countering the classical economist's empiricist mode of reading that treats the evidence as transparent. The slave demonstrates, through fugitive discourse despite being instrumentalized in Marx's *Capital*, that commodities speak, bringing Marx's own reading of the slave into question. Instead of assuming the speaking commodity's impossibility, Marx might have explored the "intercourse" between commodities and avoided equivocating on the slave's subterranean existence. Marx might have stood more solidly on the side that the slave's tale of suffering is told for the wage laborer, not just as a frightening analogy, but to show their linked economic plights. A form of collectivity and individuation lurks in the intercourse Marx parodies.

Commodity fetishism only emerges through social relations. The intercourse among supposed commodities suggests other forms of critical consciousness emerging in the interstices of modernity. Nineteenth-century capitalism's great critics and proponents ignored that commodities spoke and therefore disavowed these forms of critical consciousness. Marx participates in such a disavowal to the extent that he associates the slave with a natural attitude that is not adapted and perhaps not adaptable to capitalist transformations. Of course, this move does not allow him to question his own natural attitude toward the slave: alongside guaranteeing the slave's existence, he claims the slave's means of subsistence are mere "*naturalia*" while the free worker earns exchange-values; the slave "needs a master" in contrast to the free worker who "learns to control himself"; "slave labor" is "utterly monotonous and traditional" in comparison to the free worker's "versatility"; the slave's plight, like that of "the beast of burden," "merely befalls him, [is] something forced on him, it is the mere-activation of his labor-power."[24] Marx's assumption about the slave's natural, unevolved status stems from the German idealist philosophical tradition, which deems the New World slave of African descent a natural remainder from a previous epoch.

Pondering the New World African's role as product and producer of modernity gives readers a new task: reconsidering the black slave's ontological status so as to identify their critiques of and efforts to overthrow exploitative economic structures. This wrings a new sound from Marx's claim that the commodity's "value . . . does not have its description branded on its forehead; it rather transforms every product of labor into a social hieroglyphic."[25] The black speaking commodity *is* branded, literally and figuratively, which marks it, its labor, and its products as a "social hieroglyphic" whose decipherment is suppressed by Eurocentrism's natural attitude toward the slave. Just as Douglass's words run astray from William Lloyd Garrison's agenda, so a fugitive discourse inhabits *Capital*, specifically Marx's description of the general tendency of the labor process. "During the labor process," he says, "the worker's labor constantly undergoes a transformation, from the form of unrest into that of being, from the form of motion into that of objectivity."[26] Marx offers this as a general description of the labor process. But the regular functioning of modern economies, as informed by and informing the ontology mapped out so far, tends to objectify the slave. Just as the "commodity who speaks" disturbs assumptions about where consciousness emerges, so inverting the labor process can aid in comprehending the slave's critiques and methods of resistance. The slave moves from "being" to "unrest," from "objectivity" to "motion." The goal is to recover slaves' anarchic response to their supposedly natural position in society, their escape from that position, and their destruction of the system that maintains and is maintained by that position. But this does not simply mean war or an ethical free-for-all. It means exploring the slave's potential for "versatility," something Marx restricts to the wage laborer's reaction to capitalism's technological and organizational advances. Versatility can also be synonymous with improvisation—that is, a rigorous engagement with and revision of law in its aesthetic, political, and ethical senses.

Such improvisatory responses may be destructive, but that destruction is not directed primarily at people. Rather, it is directed at exploitative labor conditions. With that in mind, the remainder of the footnote inspiring my analysis can be read in greater detail. It is Marx quoting a passage from F. L. Olmsted: "I am here shown tools that no man in his senses . . . would allow a laborer, for whom he was paying wages, to be encumbered with . . . and I am assured that, with the careless and clumsy treatment they always must get from the slaves, anything lighter or less rude could not be furnished them with good economy."[27] This passage, even more than the one on the speaking commodity, exposes how Marx's framework cannot see the slave's resistance effectively. By sharing Frederick Olmsted's "window" and scene of writing about slavery, Marx inadvertently takes on Olmsted's rhetoric of efficiency. Granted, Marx says the slave "takes care to let both beast and implement feel that he is none of them, but rather a human being." But Marx fails to acknowledge the slave's sociality or question his own complicity in suppressing that underground way of being.[28]

The footnote insinuates that if this unproductive form of labor disappeared then so would the slave, as if the slave is another outdated tool outside Olmsted's window. Marx's use of Olmsted's window, his scene of writing, and then its place in a footnote suggest Marx's apprehension at taking a position. But this is why the supplement proves so necessary yet risky, even for a radical like Marx. "The dangerous supplement breaks with nature," and yet *Capital* diminishes the slave to uneventful natural existence.[29] What is for sure, in *Capital*, Marx does not join Frederick Douglass in forthrightly challenging slavery's tendency to reduce humans to things for capitalism's benefit.

In sum, the problem is in the sight itself, not what is seen. Looking at the same phenomena, Douglass would likely see everyday antidisciplinary tactics and the kernel of a collective project to end chattel slavery. Though these daily forms of sabotage in themselves were not enough to overthrow slavery, they signal a persistent unrest across the US South. To understand how local sabotage developed into revolt on a national scale, one would have to inhabit the intercourse between commodities, in the sense of political deliberation animated by emancipatory desire—in short, a form of sociality developing where it should not exist. Far from competing with animals and tools, slaves challenge their conditions to better preserve their underground sociality *already in existence*.[30] Understanding that sociality requires a plunge underground.

STATE OF EXCEPTION

The slave's exploitation and unrest fade more completely from view in Giorgio Agamben's *State of Exception* (2005) than in Marx's *Capital*. In shifting from Marx's wayward footnotes to Agamben's wayward curiosities, I ponder how the slave's agency gets suppressed under a strict preoccupation with exceptional legal circumstances and specifically the decision of the sovereign. Agamben calls "the state of exception" a "crisis," a "no-man's land between public law and political fact," "situated—like civil war, insurrection and resistance—in an 'ambiguous, uncertain, borderline fringe, at the intersection of the legal and the political.'"[31] The most incisive limit Agamben places on his monograph, which carves out its unique object of inquiry and its contribution to several disciplinary fields, has to do with the thinking of crisis in relation to juridical-constitutional theory. With this limit, Agamben sees the state of exception's long genealogy and its cloaked centrality to contemporary democracies and tyrannies alike. This thesis brings him to bare life, the figure that could be simultaneously the protagonist and the utter absence of a protagonist to his theory, a central figure so stripped of political features to be, in a way, nonexistent.

Analogies, which often serve as near-synonymous terms or foils for Agamben's main explanations, have unexpected effects on his primary object of study. Reconsider the previous quote from *State of Exception*: "like civil war, insurrection and resistance." "Civil war" is the most important analogous term in *State of Exception* for its frequent occurrence in the text and its linkage to Hannah Arendt's and Carl Schmitt's writings, as well as its exceptional status in ancient and contemporary constitutional law. But the same cannot be said of "insurrection and resistance." These terms recur without receiving their own elaborations, as if their bracketing guarantees an effective conceptualization of the state of exception. Such bracketing risks endorsing an emanationist approach to law—that is, an approach that operates as if political changes in the world inevitably and directly reflect legal changes. Evidence beyond the sight of the law sits beyond the researcher's eye as well. Agamben's critical appropriation of Carl Schmitt brings him to this methodological error. Granted, Agamben places Schmitt's theory among the "fallacious" ones.[32] Still, Agamben has to inhabit Schmitt's position at certain places in order to further his own investigation, as when he speaks of the *iustitium* as "an absolute non-place with respect to the law."[33] This last prepositional phrase indicates his interpretive lens and its limits. The fact that the law has to control what is unthinkable "at all costs," and that Schmitt, who endorses this view, turns to the *iustitium* to support his cause, suggests that the law is not the automatic foundation many wish it to be—that it is actually an ontology attempting to manage what it cannot or will not see.[34] The question is how the collective agency of the slave, the ultimate nonprotagonist, has undeniable effects on the political and on Agamben's arguments.

Answering that question requires understanding crisis as more than the manifestations of aporias in the law. An ante-juridical approach to law, in which the law is "permanently subordinate to the relations of force" in a historical conjuncture, allows for a more overdetermined analysis that reopens the possibility for understanding civil war, insurrection, and resistance during a crisis on their own terms and not just as analogues. Agamben's "Brief History of the State of Exception," in which he discusses the US Civil War as a "conflict over sovereign decision" reveals the need for this ante-juridical approach.[35] He notes, quite confidently, that Abraham Lincoln "acted as an absolute dictator," emancipating the slaves "on his authority alone" and then "generalized the state of exception throughout the entire territory of the United States," becoming "the holder of the sovereign decision on the state of exception."[36]

This is a most curious example of dictatorship. Nowhere else in *State of Exception* does Agamben call someone a dictator for helping to free four million people from being bare life, so they may clothe themselves with rights; nowhere else does Agamben call someone a dictator for stopping nine million others from keeping the emancipated in a position denuded of all rights, forever. Agamben must account for turning the greatest proponents of bare life into the greatest victims in the situation. It is stunning to read Agamben's assertion that Lincoln's Emancipation Proclamation to free slaves "generalized the state of exception" in nineteenth-century America, rather than the previous decades of laws expanding slavery, including the Missouri Compromise and the Fugitive Slave Laws. Confederates wielded this oft-utilized argument against emancipation before, during, and after the Civil War. Agamben would undoubtedly shudder if he realized that he stepped into such ideological territory. But this obscene conclusion is the logical outcome of naturalizing slavery, which means only an all-powerful dictator, and not the multigenerational efforts of the slaves themselves, could achieve abolition. Thus, the once-enslaved become useful instruments to Lincoln's sovereign will and Agamben's theoretical matrix, but not agents modeling a nation's or a political philosopher's most generative options, in their time or a sesquicentennial later.

One might counter that Lincoln's specific decision matters less than his sovereign right to decide. But substantial evidence from before the Civil War up to within a year of the Emancipation Proclamation indicates that Lincoln, as sovereign decision maker, had no intention of freeing the slaves. He doubted that the enslaved would ever seriously pursue freedom. He could not imagine a critical mass of slaves willfully leaving plantations forever. He believed that arming the slaves would fail—that being faithful speaking instruments, they would give their weapons to their masters. Add to this several factors: the South did not want to end slavery; the North could hardly be a consistent foe of slavery after years of admiration for Southern aristocracy and only a mild dislike of or indifference to slavery itself; Northern white workers generally feared black competition for jobs; and the wealth of slaves funded a range of institutions, including the nation's oldest universities. This evidence provides little reason for Lincoln, as *the* decider in Agamben's analysis, to make the decision that went against his and his supporters' attitudes. Even this cursory list of details suggests Agamben's image of Lincoln-the-absolute-dictator is too reductive for the crisis he describes.

At this point, Agamben's study no longer inhabits the "no-man's land between public law and political fact." He places both feet squarely in public law, because the political facts of the situation would require him to think differently of the slave population. Other forces pushed Lincoln to act, the most unexpected being the slaves pursuing their own freedom, although this fact was ignored as long as possible by Lincoln, the Union Army, the Confederacy, and now Agamben. This force—the dark proletariat escaping, fighting, even dying for freedom—could not be understood within juridico-constitutional limits, because that legal order presumed that black life could never be a constituting force for nationhood.[37] Emancipation was not the aftereffect of legal changes; quite the contrary, public law responded to political fact. Although "in the ears of the world," Lincoln freed the slaves single-handedly, W. E. B. Du Bois says, "the truth [about Lincoln's heroism] was less than this." Lincoln's proclamation only freed slaves below the border states, while "hundreds of thousands of such slaves *were already free by their own action* and that of the invading armies. . . . *Lincoln's proclamation only added possible legal sanction to an accomplished fact.*"[38] Sixty years before, Du Bois anticipates Agamben's own description of revolution in *State of Exception*, when "law is suspended and obliterated in fact."[39] Agamben placed emancipation under the rubric of oppressive exception, when it epitomizes the "inverse movement" of revolution that he decided not to analyze. *Thinking Through Crisis* studies this inverse movement, by journeying through the subterranean passageway that reveals slaves-turned-fugitives-turned-freedpersons holding the decision in an undecidable moment when law fades into fact, or said differently, life.

THE CRISIS IN TRAUMA THEORY

Trauma studies both desires and denies a theory of crisis. Similar to Marx's or Agamben's failures to theorize the slave, Cathy Caruth's and Shoshana Felman's groundbreaking books miss the racialized history of "crisis" in their work. Pursuing that theory would push this field to confront the nothingness typically projected onto black social life. Unable to surmount this projection, trauma theory cannot conceptualize the ethical action it promises, a problem troubling the now-canonical texts of that field, especially Caruth's *Unclaimed Experiences* (1996) and Felman and Dori Laub's *Testimony* (1992). This surmounting cannot occur because trauma theory, as a reading practice, remains wedded to the cultural-epistemological limit of the bourgeois modern European subject, European Man, misrepresented as modern subjectivity in general. Despite how frequently Caruth and Felman both deploy the term "crisis"—in *Testimony* alone, Felman speaks of an "existential crisis," a "crisis of witnessing," a "crisis of history," a "crisis of literature," a "crisis of evidence," a "crisis of truth," a "crisis in the witness," an "archetypical testimonial crisis," a "crisis of verse"—its relation to "trauma" remains vague.[40] That vagueness stems from the theory's nostalgia, which hinders its forward movement. I support my critique by tracing Caruth's and Felman's works back to their roots in interwar-period European philosophy in the constructs of Edmund Husserl, through one of the oldest thematizations of crisis—the life-or-death decision to find a medicine for the sick, dying body. This thematization is the predecessor for Antonio Gramsci's formulation of crisis, that the old is dying but the new cannot be born.[41] I will examine Gramsci's formulation elsewhere; here, after exploring the current reading of Felman, Caruth, and Husserl, I turn to Aimé Césaire's approach to this theme.

Felman's essay "Education and Crisis" is the self-proclaimed core of *Testimony*. Felman's thesis seems compelling initially for heralding pedagogy's significance. She says that "teaching . . . takes place precisely through a crisis: if teaching does not hit upon some sort of crisis, [some] . . . critical and unpredictable dimension, it has perhaps *not truly taught*." But the critical dimension drops out when Felman discusses a graduate course on the Holocaust that "broke out into a crisis."[42] In the following passage, one hears Felman's empiricist reading try to fill in the *apparently* vacated "site of silence."[43] After screening an interview with a Holocaust survivor, Felman's "eloquent" students were "inarticulate and speechless," then the silence "fermented into endless and relentless talking. . . . Students of my class who met in other classes could only talk about the session and could focus on no other subject. . . . They were set apart and *set themselves apart* from others who had not gone through the same experience."[44] After holding half-hour "crisis-sessions" with the students, Felman concludes "that a resolution had been reached," indicated by the "amazingly articulate, reflective and profound statement of the trauma they had gone through and of the significance of their assuming the position of the witness."[45] Felman becomes the "subject presumed to know," whose highly controlled teaching environment manages to remove and then restore the coherence of the student witnesses.[46]

Within Felman's psychoanalytic pedagogy one still finds the theory of Marxian labor process, which moves from being to unrest back to being—that is, a return to normalcy—if one listens for her students' transitions from "eloquence" to "silence" to "relentless talking" to "amazing articulation." The pedagogue does not critique but facilitates the sickened individual's movement from emotional disturbance to equilibrium, to avoid enduring the weight of silence, the dissonance of nonstop chatter, or the risk of a new sociality of feeling set apart. Amazing articulation refers to placing oneself back in the most conventional grammar available. But equilibrium is not synonymous with equity. Felman does not consider that, like the Lafargue mental health clinic said of its Negro clients in 1940s Harlem, working through racial trauma entails refusing racist standards of normality, "transform[ing] despair not into hope, but determination" to alter social conditions.[47] Felman offers no evidence that the students realized a need to intervene structurally at their institution. No doubt the visuals of horrific death and unexpected survival touched them. But the pedagogical model directed them back to a routine that, institutionally speaking, reproduces racialized, classed, gendered, and sexualized wounding, not just alienation.

Felman's pedagogical decision saves students from the "critical and unpredictable dimension" that, I think, parallels the "plunge into the inexplicable" in my epigraph from Marriott. I trace the reason for Felman's dodge to the chapter "Traumatic Awakenings" in Caruth's *Unclaimed Experience*, which deals with another sick body. By "relating trauma to the very identity of the self and to one's relation to another," "traumatic sight reveals at the heart of human subjectivity not so much an epistemological, but rather what can be defined as an *ethical* relation to the real."[48] Caruth formulates her ethics by rereading Jacques Lacan's lecture in *The Four Fundamental Concepts of Psycho-analysis* on the story of a father and his recently deceased boy from Freud's *Interpretation of Dreams*:

A father had been watching beside his child's sick-bed for days and nights on end. After the child had died, [the father] went into the next room to lie down, but left the door open so that he could see from his bedroom into the room in which his child's body was laid out. . . . An old man had been engaged to watch over it, and sat beside the body murmuring prayers. After a few hours' sleep, the father had a dream that *his child was standing beside his bed, caught him by the arm and whispered to him reproachfully: 'Father, don't you see I'm burning?'* He woke up, noticed a bright glare of light from the next room, hurried into it and found that the old watchman had dropped off to sleep and that . . . one of the arms of his beloved child's dead body had been burned by a lighted candle that had fallen.[49]

Caruth extrapolates from the father-son relation a general claim about ethical relationality. The passage depicts the "impossible responsibility of consciousness in its own originating relation to others. . . . As an awakening, the ethical relation to the real is the revelation of this impossible demand at the heart of human consciousness."[50] If it is the case that consciousness is first and foremost an awakening to an insistent, impossible ethical demand, no wonder Felman omits details about her students' experience. The model takes this demand and awakening for granted. Trauma awakens by transferring one's suffering to another, like the father who wakes from a dream of his son to find the son's body literally burning. True learning, for Felman and Caruth, depends on the revelation that comes from receiving another's suffering.

Yet Lacan's passage does not support this thesis about consciousness being an awakening to a general ethical demand. If anything, the passage testifies to how ethical demands are overdetermined by other factors, so that those in obvious need are left with no witness to stand beside them. Felman says her students' traumatic experience went beyond her classroom. No evidence in the chapter suggests other students, faculty, or administrators awoke to the demand that shook her students to their core. Felman's students *withdrew* from others around them on Yale's campus because other students could not or would not relate. Similarly, in Caruth's example, the witness, who had promised to watch over the son, *sleeps next to the burning body and through the father's awakening.* Instead of confirming a general ethical principle of awakening, the scene raises doubts that even the self-proclaimed witness, only a room away, will share in the father's sorrow.

Furthermore, these difficulties to witnessing occur in examples of *claimed* experiences, and not unclaimed ones, if by "claimed" one means tragedies in which the wounded or recently deceased fit into some widely recognized social structure. Despite the traumatization of her students, Felman suggests that "resolution" could be found in restoring their routine relation to the school and that she could do so through her role as professor. Even though the witness sleeps while the boy's body burns, the boy is still in the care of his father. The unclaimed, those who are marginalized in institutions and society, remain ignored. Ralph Ellison writes of the unclaimed in a letter to Richard Wright on November 3, 1941, after the publication of *12 Million Black Voices* (1941). "We need to enter a period of public testimony," Ellison says, and surely Caruth and Felman would agree. Then Ellison says: "We are the ones who had no comforting amnesia of childhood and for whom the trauma of passing from country to the city of destruction brought no anesthesia of unconsciousness, but left our nerves peeled and quivering. We are not the numbed, but the seething. God!"[51] On the hither side of trauma theory's cultural-epistemological limit, one finds a tradition of texts grappling with being conscious of the traumas they experience and of the watchman sleeping as others burn. Ellison does not deny the unconscious so much as expand its reach into consciousness through the dreamwork of culture, where one culture's anxious response to phobia becomes another's living nightmare, in which real-life watchmen give the keys to the mob and other watchmen sit idly by the literally burning, lynched body; the suspicious suicide in the cell; the battered body in back of the squad car; and other instances of witnesses sleeping in eyeshot of the suffering for the socially unclaimed. Restoring the normal cuts off this hither side to European Man and how the unclaimed and their experiences contest a violent society. Edmund Husserl's Vienna lectures, I argue, set an important precedent for this return to normativity in trauma theory, to which I now turn.

THE CRISIS OF EUROPEAN MAN

Of the several texts Petar Ramadanovic mentions in his genealogy of trauma theory, Edmund Husserl's Vienna lecture, "The Crisis of European Humanity and Philosophy" (1935) proves most relevant to this study.[52] Trauma theory shares several of the presuppositions Husserl promoted in his lecture, most especially a fervent desire to restore European Man's primacy. Despite being hounded by the Nazis because of his Jewish heritage, Husserl argues for a "European humanity" as *the* revolutionary option for saving a Europe devastated by world war and racism. Husserl's longing for European subjectivity anticipates trauma theory's troubling nostalgia. Caruth and Felman substitute claimed experiences for unclaimed ones, because otherwise they would have to go beyond (the ruins of) European Man for a different account of agency, belonging, and thought—the very spaces where black radicalism finds momentum.

In the Vienna lecture, Husserl bemoans a sick Europe.[53] The crisis may conclude "in ruin of a Europe alienated from its rational sense of life" or "the rebirth of Europe from the spirit of philosophy."[54] Husserl's argument depends on a disturbing Eurocentrism. He leaves no doubt that despite the current "inimical" attitude Europeans have toward each other, their shared "spirit" "transcend[s] national differences." He says shockingly little to support his claim for European superiority, besides noting "something unique, which all other human groups, too, feel with regard to us, something that . . . becomes a motivation for them—despite their determination to retain their spiritual autonomy—constantly to Europeanize themselves, whereas we, if we understand ourselves properly, will never, for example, Indianize ourselves."[55] Husserl separates the "theoretical" from the "practical attitudes" at his speech's outset, creating a dualism incapable of accounting for European colonialism's impact on the colonized. Strangely, he uses the sick body to thematize a disembodied account of Europe's theoretical attitude, allowing him to minimize power relations. Hence his vague reference to the "determination [of colonized groups] to retain their spiritual autonomy" despite the urge to "Europeanize," an urge forced on the non-European by colonialism's naked violence.

Husserl's idea of Europe's spiritual mission depends less on global intellectual tasks and more on immediate geographical identifications. Husserl never squares how the world's majority, mired in practical tasks, as he sees it, can take up Europe's infinite task of producing theoretical knowledge. The intellectual subdisciplines may serve as a bridge between Europe and the Europeanized, but Husserl's speech does not say how. These infinite tasks become an intellectual dead end. The lecture's purpose is not found in its program but in its mode of address. Herein lies Husserl's influence on trauma theory. Pronouns do an unreasonable amount of work in the lecture, like the "we" who do not "Indianize"; like the us/them logic separating Europe from "the Eskimos," "Indians," and "Gypsies"; or when he says "*we* feel (and in spite of all obscurity this feeling is probably legitimate) that an entelechy is inborn in our European civilization."[56] These are not just rhetorical ploys to keep the audience interested. They cultivate an affective orientation that supports racial distinctions reiterating European superiority. Baruch Spinoza's theory of the imitation of the affects, which highlights affect's complex interaction with rationality, proves helpful here. Spinoza recognizes affect as a social force in its own right that is transferable and sharable. Spinoza gives "hate" major attention because it spreads so quickly in society, turning powerlessness, gratuitous violence, and self-destruction into virtues.[57] At its worst, imitating this affect leads to attacking oneself as one's persecutor would do. It also urges one to identify with and justify the persecutor's actions, thereby associating the victimizer with goodness and the victim with evil. Self-hatred ceases one's ability to act or to live virtuously, because it negates one's ability to act at all.[58]

The silences in Husserl's lecture accommodate the hatred mounting across Europe. He calls Europe a "supranationality."[59] The term suggests spiritual unity at the very moment Europe is tearing itself apart; when Husserl, like millions of others, faces Nazi persecution; and when Europeanization reaches a fever pitch *within Europe*. Husserl fails to call this racist persecution as such. He stresses the non-European's desire to be like "us." He is not among the persecuted, so his speech suggests, but is among the privileged bringing misguided European xenophobes back to their senses while ushering the non-European into the "European way of life"—an odd hospitality, to say the least. World war, scapegoating, and the stripping of citizenship from millions of people are unable to disrupt Husserl's fetishization of white inclusiveness. Rather than identify European Man as the source of the misery, Husserl calls Europeanization the road less traveled, so as to avoid appearing reactionary. The lecture sides with those who would harm him. Regrettably, his support of Europeanization did nothing to stop fascism's spread or temper its ferocity. Recommitting to European Man fueled the flames of prejudice and tied the hands of the oppressed in one stroke.

Spinoza would call this being overcome with sad passions—that is, being dominated by a reactive existence.[60] Fortunately, Felman and Caruth do not vie for European Man's "rebirth." Nevertheless, *Testimony* and *Unclaimed Experiences* orbit around the loss of the image Husserl enshrined. Caruth and Felman ultimately, if inadvertently, abide by the limits European Man has set. They do not minimize suffering like Husserl does. But they make suffering infinitely transferable without examining the institutions that systematically produce suffering. Trauma theory's and Husserl's lecture's shortcomings are attempts to avoid the dangers of leaving European Man behind. Even huddling around the loss of this figure would be better than stepping away from that ruined, blood-stained space to face a void, so it seems. But that decision also means accepting the violence guaranteed by European Man's endurance. By transgressing this cultural-epistemological limit, trauma theory would join black thought in making the underground its province. In the underground, cutting through the territory Eurocentrism tries to monopolize, one finds those who contend with the conscious and unconscious aspects of overwhelming experience, those who consider the "reclamation of the critical edge" essential to sharing in suffering, those who explore routine life as the site of subjection and upheaval, and those who see the intellectual's pedagogical role to be "the living site of a significant intervention."[61] On this latter score, perhaps pedagogy would strive to bring students to evaluate their thoughts, affects, and actions while they critique the context that perpetuates racial, gender, class, and other forms of oppression. Perhaps it would lead to a different sociality, since returning to the ruins of European Man provides no salvation, only agents of violence and drowsy watchmen sleeping peacefully while another awakens to the burning body.

AFTER EUROPEAN MAN . . .

Nevertheless, a fugitive discourse runs astray in Husserl's central theme, spinning it out of Europeanization's orbit and into black radical possibilities. In that fugitive discourse, Husserl proffers a "new sort of praxis" that seeks to "transform [mankind] from the bottom up into a new humanity." Achieving this new transformation requires a "universal critique of all life and life-goals, all cultural products and systems, . . . and thus it also becomes a critique of mankind itself and of the values which guide it explicitly or implicitly."[62] Had the Vienna lecture, *Testimony*, or *Unclaimed Experiences* enacted this new praxis, then European Man would be the primary target of critique. Readers of Frantz Fanon, Sylvia Wynter, and their commentators are familiar with this motif in black radicalism. To put Husserl's idea into the parlance of Alexander Weheliye, the "new humanity" Husserl speaks of involves "different modalities of the human" enacted "by those subjects excluded from" European Man's privileged sites."[63] Had Husserl carried out this new praxis, he might have anticipated Aimé Césaire's *Discourse on Colonialism* (1955), which responds term for term to Husserl's lecture.

Césaire directs readers to the literal body lost in Husserl's theorization:

> We must study how colonization works to *decivilize* the colonizer, to *brutalize* him . . . to degrade him. . . . We must show that each time a head is cut off or an eye put out in Vietnam and in France they accept the fact, each time a little girl is raped and in France they accept the fact, each time a Madagascan is tortured and in France they accept the fact, civilization acquires another dead weight, a universal regression takes place, a gangrene sets in, a center of infection begins to spread. . . . At the end of all these treaties that have been violated, all these lies that have been propagated, all these punitive expeditions that have been tolerated, all these prisoners who have been tied up and "interrogated," all these patriots who have been tortured, at the end of all the racial pride that has been encouraged . . . a poison has been instilled into the veins of Europe and, slowly but surely, the continent proceeds toward *savagery*.[64]

Césaire's shuttling between Vietnam and France and Madagascar indicates a different "we" in each location in the text. His "we" consists of non-Europeans and Europeans, cuts through Husserl's privileged "supernational," and mobilizes people in spaces broken and reorganized by European imperialism. Césaire models a politics of "detour" that looks beyond one's immediate locality to find the "principle of domination."[65] His description of Europe's *de*civilization and slide toward savagery suggests that a political detour would work somewhat differently for the colonizers. Césaire's reference to "poison" reminds one of Spinoza's discussion of a dialectical relationship between two entities that leads to "mutual decomposition."[66] Europe's civilizing mission is such a poison. After turning its colonial tools of physical violence, legal loopholes, extracted resources, and unbearable indebtedness on itself, Europe cannot understand its traumas without learning from the colonized. Overcoming this self-colonizing impulse requires Europe to abolish its imperial missions and decolonize its culture by following the lead of anticolonial movements.

Had Husserl considered such a lesson in his day, he might have admitted that Europe was undergoing a "universal regression" and not a new phase of unification. European Man had become the regressive force it would exorcise from humanity. Césaire's proof is the physical, mental, and emotional violence of Europeanization omitted from Husserl's speech: "Between colonizer and colonized there is only room for forced labor, intimidation . . . the police, taxation, theft, rape, compulsory crops, contempt, mistrust, arrogance, self-complacency, swinishness, brainless elites, degraded masses."[67] Exploration and cross-cultural contact never satisfied the colonizer's voracious hunger for "punitive expeditions" around the world, suddenly aimed at home, from becoming a "gangrene" attacking Europe's connective tissue. The metaphor of the sick body suggests a decline of European power and marks the pathology harbored in Europe's methods of purifying foreign culture—a pathologization to which Europe should have always been immune, were the premise of European Man half as true as its claims to be.

Husserl only recognizes corporeality when it threatens European spirit, not other cultures. Still, he backpedals from his admission when he says European spirit "transcend[s]" national differences, no matter how "inimical" they are to each other.[68] "Inimical" is a charged term, bespeaking the right to annihilate anyone threatening the nation-state-empire framework. Conventionally, the term *inimicus* has been reserved for an unjust enemy disrupting nation-state-empire formation and international economic integration. The *inimicus* deserves whatever fate it receives. Scholars have revealed that from Thomas Hobbes's *Leviathan* to Hugo Grotius's *The Rights of War and Peace* to Immanuel Kant's *Metaphysics of Morals*, the would-be colonized are increasingly labeled the *inimicus*.[69] Husserl, working hard to recover European Man, does not question the term's shift in geographical locus, now referring to Europe itself during the 1930s.

Césaire offers a fascinating answer to this question. When Europeans begin to apply their hatred and colonialist procedures to themselves, they become their own *inimicus*, hunting internal enemies, leading to what Césaire calls a "reverse shock":

> The gestapos are busy, the prisons fill up, the torturers around the racks invent, refine, discuss. People are surprised, they become indignant. They say: "how strange! But never mind—it's Nazism, it will pass!" And they wait and they hope; and they hide the truth from themselves . . . that they tolerated Nazism before it was inflicted on them, that they absolved it, shut their eyes to it, legitimized it, because, until then, it had been applied only to non-European peoples. . . . What [the European] cannot forgive Hitler for is not *crime* in itself . . . it is the crime against the white

man, the humiliation of the white man, and the fact that he applied to Europe colonialist procedures which until then had been reserved exclusively for the Arabs of Algeria, the coolies of India, and the blacks of Africa.[70]

Césaire maps the conditions fostering a critical perspective on suffering and the factors producing it. In doing so, he distinguishes himself from Husserl by identifying Europe's "crimes" as such. The Eurocentric position considers the "crime in itself," the techniques of colonial domination, no crime at all when applied to its proper targets, people of color. From that same view, these techniques become heinous war crimes when applied in Europe. And yet the criminal and victim are the same in this setup. For Europeans, to acknowledge this crime is to acknowledge complicity. Husserl, too, fails to address this complicity, which proves a barrier to the new humanity he would explore. Césaire observes Europeans becoming the unjust enemies threatening their own nation-state-empire framework for the sake of an imperial supremacy divorced from reality. He spurns colonial normalcy and the self-harm it perpetuates. No writing back into equilibrium will suffice.

Césaire's observations are no less trenchant today. In recent years, Europe has entered a new stage of autocolonization brought on by a supernational arrangement placing power in the hands of an economic elite using indebtedness and a core-periphery model to undermine democracy. While drawing on the same thematization of crisis explored in this introduction, Etienne Balibar gave an interview in which he said, "All sorts of pathological phenomena are emerging, because the old order is not working, in particular the European Union in the form it's been given since 1990," with no general alternative available, which explains "why we face the pathology of rising nationalisms, popular moral despair, disgust with politics, etc."[71] Maurizio Lazzarato considers this the outcome of a continental debtor economy dominated by guilt, designed to produce widespread precarity so that surplus value goes to a select few countries, and a select few elite in those countries, while framing any protest as ungratefulness from below. The United States also participates in this autocolonization today through its exploitation of the middle class, working class, working poor, and those who are unable to work; increasing militarization of local law enforcement; hundreds of police-involved and vigilante killings during the 2000s; a $1.3 trillion student debt that, at the time of this writing, balloons to ever-larger proportions that no previous generation has experienced; and the ongoing violence of the American classroom, from discriminatory practice in the classroom to unpunished abuse and sexual assault. Europe and the United States, among other locales, pay dearly for being so unwilling to plunge into the inexplicable that goes beyond black suffering to join black life.

IN SEARCH OF THE DARK PROLETARIAT; OR, BLACK WRITING IN THE "SECOND GREAT DEPRESSION"

As these theoretical vignettes suggest, the inability to think about the black—whether as the slave who was a potential ally to the nineteenth-century wage laborer, the freedperson whose decision pushed the hand of a president, the student who cannot overcome traumatization by return to normal campus life, the black migrant moving from the rural farms to the metropolis, the colonized who cannot find safety in Europeanization, and many others who live outside the parameters of European Man—has hindered the search for adequate theorizations of crisis. More than that, whether symbolized by depths to be plumbed or a naked declivity to be traversed, fear of approaching limits to European thought compromises otherwise brilliant, impassioned, and urgent theoretical work and instrumentalizes the black once again, now for theory's sake, without considering the insights black thought produces. Failing to confront material history and one's own inhibitions distracts one from black culture's ingenious responses to such suffering and the intellectual tradition that has recorded and analyzed this emancipatory project's evolution. In European theory's political unconscious, the black is "the absence" and "negation of values," "a corrosive element, destroying everything within his reach, a corrupting element, distorting everything which involves aesthetics or morals." The black, as a sick body, is "incurable" to the Eurocentric. Joining black life would mean entering a valueless "no-man's land."[72]

From a black radical perspective, only in that unclaimed and unclaimable space can an "authentic upheaval" occur.[73] The myriad pathologies projected onto black culture have distracted from one of the key features of black radical thought—namely, the "transvaluation of pathology itself," answering "the need to affirm affirmation through negation . . . not as a moral imperative . . . but as a psychopolitical necessity."[74] If the black is not only pathologized but pathology itself, then there are two options: (1) The black may work harder to obtain the cure of Europeanization, as Husserl prescribes. Yet Césaire persuasively argues that the effort to escape stereotypical images will not get rid of Europeanization's *need* for stereotyping. (2) The black can transvaluate pathology by rejecting the Europeanized terms of "sickness" and "cure" to begin crafting a new form of empowerment, new terms, and a new ethics. An excess lingers in the Eurocentric's fatal diagnosis of blackness, such that what has been called sick may actually affirm living. Lingering in the pathologized space to reimagine knowledge, connectedness, and empowerment amounts to turning a cold shoulder on Europe's illusory moral high ground. I call the population willing to linger in this space the "dark proletariat."

"Proletariat" has always been associated with decomposition, with *what* and *who* is leftover after an economy's destructive forces finish their work for the benefits of the few. The *proletarius* originally designated a heterogeneous, propertyless group of the Roman Empire's lowest class who contributed to the state only by increasing the population. In the mid-nineteenth century, Marx makes this derogatory term into the name of a world-changing agency. Balibar observes that the proletariat consistently designates a population living in "general insecurity," under the threat of "legally normalized" violence, in conditions that are "historically untenable," which begs for "another transition" beyond capitalism.[75] Marx and his fellow travelers never concluded whether the proletariat maintained a "negative" relation to politics, meaning the proletariat would tear down the state altogether, or a "positive" relation to politics, meaning it would take over and redirect state institutions in noncapitalist directions. Marx and his cohort could not locate "the boundary line between the 'compromise' with the existing state forms and their revolutionary 'use' against the ruling class."[76] Increasing use of the term "working class" did not solve the problem. This theoretical difficulty suggests that activists can draw this line only in specific contexts, not beforehand. In the 1930s, black writers struggled with how to aesthetically convey drawing this line between compromise and revolutionary use. I follow Barbara Foley, Bill Mullen, William Maxwell, James Smethurst, Alan Wald, and Michael Denning in recovering the complex relationship between literary and political radicalism in the 1930s.[77] I join a second generation of scholars, like Sonnet Retman in *Real Folks* (2011) and Stephanie Leigh Batiste in *Darkening Mirrors* (2012), who query orthodoxies of the field, including the romanticizing of categories like "the folk" and the frequent juxtaposition of black "others" to white "selves," even in studying black literature. Taking heed of these warnings against endlessly romanticizing or othering the proletariat, I study this group's role in social reconstruction and how 1930s writers conveyed this effort in poetry, short fiction, novels, autobiography, and other genres.

Blackness's unwieldy persistence makes it something more than the unending negation feared by European Man. I call the proletariat "dark" because interrogating black radical culture leads to a metonymic rather than metaphoric relation. Rather than standing in place of another, one stands with another, sharing spaces that would appear irrelevant to the colonist's gaze and grip on power.

In "Dear Lovely Death," the titular poem for one of Langston Hughes's volumes, death "taketh all things under wing—/Never to kill—/Only to change/Into some other thing."[78] Barely two pages later, another poem, "Demand," speaks of "my body of utter death" being touched by a "dream of utter aliveness."[79] One inhabits black thought to nurture the critical knowledge, optimism of the will, affective fortitude, and vulnerability to confront social death because of the utter aliveness beyond that naked declivity. However, Hughes does not restrict this point to phenotypically black people. While Hughes's poems like "Always the Same" speak specifically of the black diaspora—"On the docks at Sierra Leone/In the cotton fields of Alabama . . . The Banana Lands of Central America"—poems like "Open Letter to the South" invite white workers to unite with black "to smash the old dead dogmas of the past."[80] Hughes's poem agrees with Du Bois's first chapter of *Black Reconstruction*, which makes the "Black Worker" the extreme example to prove a general rule of freedom for laboring humanity: "The emancipation of man is the emancipation of labor and *the emancipation of labor is the freeing of the basic majority of workers who are yellow, brown, and black.*"[81]

I join scholars like Michelle Stephens and Brent Edwards, who assert black radicalism's "autonomy" as a tradition, with its own "concept-metaphors, statements, and elaborations" with intriguing points of convergence and divergence with other leftist traditions, including Marxism.[82] I go farther than my counterparts in challenging the long-held view, popularized by Harold Cruse, that black artists and activists in the 1930s simply parroted European radical dogmas and, as a consequence, missed the opportunity for revolution or a better place for black people in New Deal politics.[83] Black writers of the 1930s considered social reconstruction an ongoing process of affirmation, negation, and transformation rather than a mere stop-gap measure. Whether it is Richard Wright's proposal in "Blueprint for Negro Literature" to "say no and depict the horror of capitalism upon the human being" and "to say yes and depict the faint stirrings of a new emerging life,"[84] or W. E. B. Du Bois's proposal for a "negative program of protest" alongside a "positive program of construction and inspiration,"[85] 1930s writers accentuate the *labor for emancipation*, not as a single day of cultural reckoning based on one individual's miracle but as an ongoing collective project, full of suspense, disruption, progress, and retrogression.[86] These authors placed immense pressure on the messianisms of their day by recovering several events and eras in their literature, including the 1927 Mississippi River Flood, anti-lynching and prison abolition protests in the 1890s, the counterrevolution of 1876, the Reconstruction Era, the Civil War, and even the Haitian Revolution.

Black writers composed such compelling literature about social reconstruction because they saw themselves as part of a global array of artists, activists, and intellectuals rethinking the political *as such*. Though some may claim that the global economy or certain regions of it have recovered from the 2008 crash, few could persuasively argue that the common terms of national or global politics are not being challenged, considering the resurgence of far-right groups, the newly found street presence of far-left groups, the crowding in of fainthearted liberal groups, and the scrambling of politicians seeking to position themselves advantageously in the fray. The 1930s provides great insight into such difficulties, and black radical writing in the United States is central to this conversation. An incomprehensive list of 1930s texts rethinking the political includes Antonio Gramsci's *Prison Notebooks* (1929–1937), Georges Bataille's "Notion of Expenditure" (1934), Carl Schmitt's *The Concept of the Political* (1932), Alexandre Kojeve's *Introduction to the Reading of Hegel: The Phenomenology of Spirit* (1933–1939), George Padmore's *How Britain Rules Africa* (1936), Mao Tse Tung's "On Contradiction" (1936), Leo Strauss's *The Political Philosophy of Hobbes* (1936), Walter Benjamin's "The Work of Art in the Age of Mechanical Reproduction" (1936), C. L. R. James's *The Black Jacobins* (1937), Martin Buber's *I and Thou* (1937), Emmanuel Levinas's *On Escape* (1937), and Sigmund Freud's *Moses and Monotheism* (1938)—not to mention the extensive work of surrealists, including Andre Breton's Parisian inner circle in *La Surrealiste Revolution* and later in *Minotaure* to his critics in *Documents*; the much broader surrealist artistry featured in periodicals like *Legitime Defense*,

L'Estudiant Noir, the *Negro Worker, Le Cris de Negro*; and individual artistic productions like Césaire's *Return to My Native Land* (1938). Throughout *Thinking Through Crisis,* I place 1930s black radical writing in this "global context of cultural production."[87]

A NOTE ON CRITICAL NARRATIVE

Thinking Through Crisis is an excursion into "performative writing." Della Pollock explains that performative writing does not just describe or itemize, but enacts. Performative writing abides "with logics of possibility" instead of the logics of "validity or causality" that typify normative writing.[88] The challenge here is to sustain a space for academic discourse to impact and be impacted by the dark proletariat. This critical narrative seeks to convey the dark proletariat's development as a material process to locate the generativity in trauma and to disabuse scholarship of its passive spectator's position.

Performative writing is restless. To write about the shift from being to unrest and from objectivity to motion, one must "cross various stories, theories, texts, intertexts, and spheres of practice, unable to settle into a clear, linear course." Each notebook covers texts that "confound normative distinctions between critical and creative."[89] Pollock says such writing is "neither willing nor able to stop moving" and calls it "transient and transitive, traversing spatial and temporal borders." Performative writing puts unusual pressure on intellectual discourses that find their stability in assuming that black subjects are little else than enchained. If one imagines these subjects as part of a more complicated process of breaking those chains, then writing performatively about their experiences becomes "unwriting": unlearning conventional theses about blackness frees up insights pinned down by academic norms, unleashing a range of texts, concepts, and movements that are part of the dark proletariat's material history. That is to say, performative writing is metonymic, advancing "toward engaged, embodied, material ends," dodging "both the siren's song of textual self-reference and the equally dangerous, whirling drain of unreflexive commitment."[90]

Performative writing's mix of evocation, restlessness, and metonymy instantiates a different grammar—namely, "free indirect discourse"—where third- and first-person narration constantly interact. In *Signifying Monkey,* Henry Louis Gates Jr. associated this aesthetic technique with the "speakerly text," in which black culture's orality infuses literary composition.[91] For Gates, this technique granted black writers and readers the interiority of liberal individuals within the multiculturalist framework of late twentieth-century America. As Gramsci might put it, Gates's work linked the "immanent grammars" of black people to the "unitary," "normative" grammar of mainstream American politics.[92] But political power obtained collectively cannot be sustained individually. This move from collective endeavor to individual accomplishment could not combat the concerted effort of ultraconservative backlash in terms of retrogressive policy, vigilante and state-sanctioned violence, and the attack on education intensifying from the 1980s to the present.

Yet Gates's model does not exhaust free indirect discourse's complexities. Far from artistically representing liberal assimilation, free indirect discourse linguistically performs the "last" becoming "the first" that Frantz Fanon describes in *Wretched of the Earth* (1961).[93] Liberalism's unitary grammar operates through the first- and second-person grammatical positions. Roberto Esposito says the first- and second-person structure is "not a pluralization, since a *unicum* cannot multiply itself," but adds to its membership in an illusory way, forcing others to fit this mirror reflection.[94] It conceives of an "I" with "audacious dreams" to "preside over capitalism's work ethic." Most of all, the unitary structure devises "a defense against *things and all that is unforeseeable in them*."[95] Western eyes prefer to hold the third person at a distance as a nonperson, no different than William Lloyd Garrison and his disciples saying "I" and "you" to majority-white abolitionist audiences but calling Douglass an "it." They would champion his freedom while they set him apart in the same, eardrum-grating breath.

No matter: *Thinking Through Crisis* infrequently uses the liberal positioning of the "I," at most. As Della Pollock notes, "positioning the self" is no primary goal of performative writing when, actually, the challenge is to question those fixities and foreswear their allure.[96] The third person cannot assimilate to the "I-you" specular relationship. The third person functions as supplement barred from full inclusion, securing the "I-you" relationship from the outside. The third person's aesthetic and political potential lies in the fact that it does not *need* that specular relationship. From the third person's view, that first-second person structure is a meantime measure, not the *telos* of living. But the third person has greater things to do. The third person secures but threatens the "I-you" relationship from the outside, warning the subjects that they might fall from favor. The third person unsettles or even undoes the "I-you" relationship from within by "play[ing] havoc with conventional grammar and syntax" and "contaminat[ing] by attraction verbs outside the statement, or grammatical monstrosities may occur that nevertheless are stylistically effective and logical."[97] The third person's immanent grammar consists of singularities or combinations which "show a remarkable variety in the sequence of tenses . . . [and] enjoy an almost absolute syntactical liberty."[98] Sacrificing this absolute liberty for the mainstream specular relationship would lead to losses that black radicalism ought not risk.

Making free indirect discourse the grammar of the dark proletariat means the third person's magnetic, contaminative, unsettling, singular-plural style of life opens a new aesthetic terrain that recasts proletarian, modernist, and surrealist artistry. Free indirect discourse also means proletarian writing should feature metropolitan factory workers as well as the working poor, the homeless, the refugee, and other waged and wageless figures. Modernism takes a more anarchist orientation in this context. Gerald Bruns calls it "conceptual art, which argues that in order to experience a thing as art, we need to have developed or have in hand a *conceptual context*," in which "*freedom* rather than truth, beauty or goodness had become the end of art." Blackness resides at the heart of the aesthetic-political experimentation in a modernism defined "not just [as] a cognitive problem about strange objects making aesthetic claims" but as "a hermeneutical problem of *how to enter the form of life in which these objects are at home, recognized and accepted by those who live with them* (as if they were persons and not just mere things)."[99] *Thinking Through Crisis* modifies Bruns's fascinating account of modernism in one significant way—namely, that blackness conveys being *away* from home with people mistaken for things, so that a different form of freedom can redefine truth, beauty, and goodness. Broaching this hermeneutical problem runs directly into surrealism, in which "new social relationships, new ways of living and interacting, new attitudes toward work and leisure and community" become an aesthetic intervention in themselves. Surrealism inheres in "an international revolutionary movement concerned with the emancipation of thought" even more than achieving beauty. It opens the marvelous space where fantasy and reality converge, with second-sight as its primary guide.[100] Unavoidably, these grammatical and aesthetic extravagances push the dark proletariat into constant transmutations, shifting "between selves/structures projecting in turn alternative figures of social relation," from the sharecropper to the underground railroad conductor to the student activist and more.[101]

In Notebook 1 of *Thinking Through Crisis*, I situate Richard Wright as a theorist of possibility during social breakdown, like the sort portrayed in his novella "Down by the Riverside," from his collection *Uncle Tom's Children* (1938), inspired by the 1927 Mississippi River Flood, the largest flood in US history, only recently surpassed by Hurricane Katrina. A close reading of the novella in relation to several journalistic and government documents about the flood reveals a politics of abandonment: the "relief" effort, though framed as humanitarian intervention, actually intended to restore the Mississippi delta's sharecropping economy for the benefit of the plantation owners. At the same time, Wright's novella highlights the critical intelligence of the black worker in social upheaval and the spark of a collective consciousness in the Event—that is, the break with an affective regime stabilized by fear and guilt from racial violence and indebtedness.

Notebook 2, "Crusade for Justice: Ida B. Wells and the Power of the Multitude," considers how this new sense of empowerment, when fear and guilt no longer dominate, turns into a collective consciousness that historicizes its own political movement. Wells has often identified herself and been identified as a lone voice protesting lynching. But in her final work, *Crusade for Justice: The Autobiography of Ida B. Wells* (1970), Wells melds first-person autobiography with the biography of the movements she led. In other words, she frames her legacy in terms of collective movement and institution building. *Crusade* provides the key for reinterpreting her earlier anti-lynching pamphlets as instances of collective organization, enacting a concept of tradition for the dark proletariat based not on conservative notions of sameness but on a radically moveable archive remixable in response to contemporary questions, so the past remains available to enable present-day action.[102] Wells teaches that movements protecting black life must write their own histories or risk their enemies claiming the story. Wells says a sense of "pride" animates this project, which I translate into what Cedric Robinson calls "the shared sense of obligation to preserve the collective being, the ontological totality."[103]

In Notebook 3, "W. E. B. Du Bois's *Black Reconstruction*: Theorizing Divine Violence," I turn to several of Du Bois's writings, moving from *Souls of Black Folk* to *John Brown* and finally to *Black Reconstruction*. After finding the dark proletariat's spark of collective consciousness and its self-contextualization, I explore its different forms of force capable of altering society. Earlier notebooks attend to mythic violence and the guilt it induces as an agent binding black lives to the law. But here, I attend to what Du Bois calls the "Coming of the Lord," when the dark proletariat throws off metaphysical guilt and undoes the system oppressing it. I study this concept by framing Du Bois's historiography of Emancipation through two songs that he quotes in *Black Reconstruction*, "John Brown's Body" and Schiller's "Ode to Joy." Du Bois sees the former as a mistranslation of the latter, and that patriotic mistranslation reveals how mainstream American cultural history misunderstands and contravenes the labor for emancipation. Du Bois's free indirect style deconstructs the messianism associating Emancipation with a wide cast of white saviors—Abraham Lincoln, abolitionists, Northern industrialists, Union soldiers, etc. Only by accepting that the freedpersons freed themselves, becoming a vanguard for national progress in a decentralized organizational structure, can today's dark proletariat look back for a model of collective agency and look forward to undoing mythic violence's current expressions.

I study Zora Neale Hurston's *Moses, Man of the Mountain* to further my critique of messianism in Notebook 4. Few scholars have noted that Hurston published *Moses* as the first installment of an incomplete, long-term project tracing the theological-political development of the West. Even fewer know Hurston's longstanding interest in Spinoza's philosophy. Spinoza's materialist account of belief and the political informs Hurston's retelling of the Exodus story, which she uses to critique reactive tendencies in the "long civil rights movement." Her critique centered around the themes of chosenness, which justifies persecution; sacrifice, which confuses self-renunciation with moral transcendence; and sovereign miracle, which transfers the surplus labor of the dark proletariat to an undeserving single leader. This notebook distinguishes the radical Hurston from the Hurston associated with the worst dimensions of Booker T. Washington's politics, which would epitomize the reactive tendency that leads to self-renunciation, not self-determination, in *Moses*.

In Notebook 5, "The New Day: Notes on Education and the Dark Proletariat," I argue that the current narrative of educational decline in the United States rings too nostalgic for the industrial era of education, with its segregationist leanings. Nostalgia of this sort offers no alternative to what Carter G. Woodson famously called "mis-education," a term that I make a general heading for how multiple black thinkers alongside Woodson interrogated the histories of exploitation in educational institutions. Langston Hughes's 1930s journalism and poetry offer a chilling critique of mis-education at the university level. Beyond this, I claim that mis-education is merely the reaction to something prior—the black's underground drive for education, stirred by an ecstasy that will pursue education at all costs, modeled compellingly by the freedpersons establishing multiracial educational institutions across the post–Civil War South in spite of hostility from the white poor and elite alike. This prior drive, which I call the "New Day," brings the underground educational effort aboveground to alter mainstream America's educational landscape. In other words, I am arguing that although the proletarianization of academic labor signals general insecurity, that insecurity *returns* us to the originary conditions of reconstructing education in America. Nostalgia should not distract us from this unexpected opportunity to rethink education with the dark proletariat's youth (and older learners) at its center.

The performative writing in *Thinking Through Crisis* takes the form of "crisis notebooks." The notebook is an important creative and critical form in the 1930s, as texts like Césaire's *Notebook on a Return to My Native Land* (1939), Gramsci's *Prison Notebooks* (1929–1935) or Mary Low's and Juan Brea's *Red Spanish Notebook* (1937) illustrate. The notebook recognizes the fragment as a sign of breakdown and the starting point for reconstruction. Thetic reverberations and thematic echoes traverse the notebooks that come along with studying free indirect discourse's aesthetic and political implications. The notebook's form allows one to think of the event "in the duration of its happening." As a result, notebooks tend to characterize thought as "pending" or "indeterminate," which complicates the desire for final determinations but reaffirms the chance for effective direct action. Pending thought "cannot seek grounding in familiar categories of knowledge and be adequate to understand that with which it is occurring, that which is imminent."[104] The notebook is more amenable to the fits and starts of collective consciousness. Recall Harriet Jacobs's *Incidents in the Life of a Slave Girl* (1861), written at "irregular intervals."[105] The irregular interval structure partially stems from Jacobs's predicament, doing abolitionist work as a fugitive slave and then domestic laborer in the US North. While one should be wary of people claiming to face Jacobs's specific challenges, it would be even more disingenuous to think that today we have fully transcended her general situation. Despite some changes, many Americans live viscerally torn between freedom and unfreedom. Jacobs's "irregular intervals" prefigures the proletariat's syncopated rhythm as it cultivates a collective critical consciousness in this fugitive state.

With this expository mode, *Thinking Through Crisis* delinks the notebook, as a form, from Antonio Gramsci's concept of hegemony. Frank Wilderson says the dissonant character of black life "places hegemony in a structurally impossible position because . . . our presence works back on the grammar of hegemony and threatens it with incoherence."[106] I heed Wilderson's warning. The concept of hegemony fits too easily into the first-person grammar of exclusivity and segregation. Nevertheless, Wilderson's critique applies more to Gramsci's scholarship than to Gramsci himself. In Southern Italian communities, then in parliament, and finally in Mussolini's prisons, Gramsci often played a dissonant, fugitive role in Italian politics (using notebooks and books smuggled from libraries; changing names to avoid further persecution by the jailers; and suffering from racism as a Southern Italian and ableism because of a spinal injury in his infancy). Reading Gramsci for what is exorbitant to the concept of hegemony reveals an underground, third-person relation useful to theorizing from the dark proletariat's perspective:

> This movement from the particular to the general characterizes countless notes in the *Quaderni.* . . . When fragments, or particular pieces of information or specific observations lead to some general or generalizing insight, the generalization does not acquire the status of an overarching theory which endows the particulars with a stable meaning. . . . The generalizations or concepts are themselves never complete or completed, they are always in a fluid, increasingly complex relation to other generalizations or concepts; they always point to different synthetic combinations but without ever settling into a final definitive synthesis, and they always call for a return to the particular details, the fragments which retain their historical specificity even as they induce new and more complex concepts that are linked to one another in an increasingly denser and ever more extensive shifting network of relations.[107]

The notebook's shuttling between specificity and generality presumes the unrest and motion inspiring *Thinking Through Crisis*. The goal is to produce a matrix of concepts from reading 1930s black literature that provides an auto/biography of today's black radical movements and the experimental, surreal experience of making a way out of no way.

NOTEBOOK 1

DOWN BY THE RIVERSIDE

Richard Wright, the 1927 Flood,
and the Citizen-Refugee

The water was risin' up at my friend's door
The water was risin' up at my friend's door
The man said to his women folk, "Lord we'd better go"
You know I can't stay here,
I'll go where it's high boy,
I would go to the hilly country
But, they got me barred

          —CHARLEY PATTON, "HIGH WATER EVERYWHERE"

Mmmm, I can't move no more
Mmmm, I can't move no more
There ain't no place for a poor old girl to go
When it thunders and lightnin' and when the wind bout to blow
When it thunders and lightnin' and when the wind bout to blow
There's thousands of people ain't got no place to go

          —BESSIE SMITH, "BACK WATER BLUES"

THE CITIZEN AND THE REFUGEE

Many Americans pondered how US citizens could become refugees in an instant back in August and September 2005, when Hurricane Katrina hit the Gulf Coast and government on all levels failed to protect the public.

"Refugee" and "looter" jumped from the lips of journalists, politicians, and television viewers. This seemingly spontaneous change in civic identity raises questions about the quotidian relationship between citizen, refugee status, and the state. The ease with which the change occurred suggests that citizenship already carries within it the threat of refugee status. The citizen-refugee not only identifies the onrush of a politics of abandonment, it also bespeaks the disciplinary procedures of mainstream institutions and economies while it lurches into new possibilities of self-organization. To think through this issue, I turn to Richard Wright's novella "Down by the River-side" in his classic *Uncle Tom's Children* (1938). Wright composed the novella while reflecting on what would eventually be known as the precursor to Hurricane Katrina—namely, the 1927 Mississippi River Flood, another instance when the same convoluted debates over citizenship, refugee status, and the state dominated popular discourse.

Wright's novella focuses on the tribulations of Brother Mann; his pregnant wife, Lulu; their son Peewee; and Grannie, Lulu's mother. They will all drown if they remain in their home. Unfortunately, the shock of the flood put Lulu into labor four days earlier, and she has yet to give birth. It is incumbent on Brother Mann to find a boat and row through the racist township to the relief camp to save Lulu and their unborn child. In the 1930s, Wright looks back at the mistreatment of 1927 flood survivors to see, in microcosm, the racialized exclusions that would burden the country's most disadvantaged populations. Wright read Trigant Burrows's *The Social Basis of Human Consciousness* (1925), which urges psychology to give primacy to the social over the individual and revels in humans banding together. Burrows's book triggered a "whole train of thought" for Wright: "I decided to use the flood to show the relationship between the two races in the South in a time of general tragedy."[1] Race complicated recovery efforts in the Mississippi delta. In Wright's hands, those efforts serve as a synecdoche for the nation's racialized response to the Great Depression.

By analyzing Wright's novella to study this citizen-refugee structure, I veer from his claim in *Black Boy* that *Uncle Tom's Children* moves dialectically from unsuccessful individual revolt to multiracial working-class solidarity.[2] Based on this logic, the second story of the collection, "Down by the Riverside," should be read primarily for shortcomings or for its pessimism, an immature stage in Wright's literary apprenticeship that reached its destination with the realism of *Native Son* (1940) two years later. When read strictly as Wright's preparation for *Native Son*, "Down by the River-side's" own formal and intellectual intervention falls from view. No wonder early reviewers called the narrative an unconvincing set of coincidences. Abdul R. JanMohammed's contests this dismissal and instead considers "Down by the Riverside" to be an account of death-bound subjectivity. But JanMohammed removes it from any specific time or place, despite Wright's emphasis on historical and geographical particularity for every story in *Uncle Tom's Children*.[3] Cheryl Higashida asserts that *Uncle Tom's Children* "does not merely subordinate the Woman Question to other political themes" but "insists that issues of gender—especially those pertaining to African American working-class women—are integral to conceptualizing revolutionary praxis and subjectivity."[4] Feeling that "Down by the Riverside" is the least successful of the stories in promoting this view, she condemns the novella's focus on hypermasculine revolt.

In contrast, I read the novella as a theorization of political possibility opened in the unexpected relationship between citizenship and refugee status. Granted, the novella does not overtly portray collective revolt. But when restored to the context of mass-media and government documents about the 1927 flood, the novella identifies two components for concerted action: it asserts the critical intellectual and performative capacity within the dark proletariat, and it captures the Event—namely, when the dark proletariat confronts, works through, and comes out on the hither side of the fear of actual death, triggering an internal transformation that grants the courage to risk changing society. These elements are essential to any break with the petrification that comes from racial violence, economic exploitation, and gendered discrimination, ironically placed under the heading of "relief." By making Lulu the novella's ethical center, Wright distinguishes this narrative from his other, more disconcerting representations of women characters. Her going through labor to give birth in the flood metaphorizes the story's greatest challenge: restoring the pre-flood debtor's economy or establishing a new, more egalitarian structure in the delta region. With this thesis, I can detail how the narrative says no to the sharecropping economy and says yes to "the faint stirrings of a new and emerging life."[5]

Far from simply being Wright's training ground for *Native Son*, *Uncle Tom's Children* frames the most precarious forms of life as capable of collectively resisting the politics of abandonment troubling late nineteenth- and early twentieth-century American life. The literary and philosophical entry points for such a project can be found where life no longer poses a technical problem for representation but an ethical problem for a "process of becoming."[6] The fragility of mainstream representations of citizenship and their institutional supports marks a larger process of social transformation requiring an alternative vocabulary that focuses on singularities, multiplicity, and the commons, rather than the individual, the subject, and property. It would also pay attention to the microworlds that authors place within the space of "domestic realism" so that the former challenges the naturalness of the latter; thus, naturalism questions the structures realism takes for granted.[7]

SHARECROPPING, GUILT, AND INDEBTED MAN(N)

"Down by the Riverside" initiates an "ontological reframing" that "open[s] the field from which the unexpected can emerge, while increasing our space of decision and room to move as political subjects."[8] Readers unaccustomed to this ontological reframing may expect a realist story that, in its effort to assert its technical accuracy, turns *a* reality into the *only possible* reality. Possibility tends to connote available options made in the likeness of what is already considered "real," thereby reducing futurity to the logical extension of the status quo.[9] The story's events become horrific coincidences designed to elicit sympathy for flood victims who should have known better. But Wright accepts the task of presupposing contingency and the restlessness carried by humans mistaken for inanimate objects, even in the Mississippi delta.[10] He does not just add one more likely possibility among others. He offers readers an altogether different orientation to possibility.

In the epigraph to *Uncle Tom's Children*, Wright calls into question the common viewpoints shaping and being shaped by the Mississippi delta region's daily operation. The epigraph comes from a Southern song, which asks, "Is it true what they say about Dixie?" After describing the South in pastoral terms, the song concludes: "If it's true, that's where I belong."[11] In Wright's hands, the conditional clause undoes the song's self-assured descriptive function, which renders ontology a function of technical representation. With "Down by the Riverside," the conditionality inscribed within the epigraph gets transferred to Brother Mann's waterlogged home. The song's failure to account for conditions in the flooded delta region admits the limits of domestic realism. Brother Mann's precarious home environment indicates its inability to frame the narrative that follows. This soon-to-be collapsed home calls into question the Manns' belonging in the delta and unsettles the politics of conventional realism grounded in property: "Each step [Mann] took the old house creaked as though the earth beneath the foundations were soggy. He wondered how long the logs which supported the house could stand against the water. [The steps] might wash away at any moment . . . then they would be trapped. . . . Through a dingy pane he saw yellow water swirling. . . . It was about six feet deep and still rising; it had risen two feet that day."[12] Those who live on the edges of realist depiction often get blamed for not conforming to that aesthetic framework's rules, when aesthetic conformity yields diminishing political returns. This realism has real-life consequences, especially when considering the condemnations hurled at the survivors of the 1927 flood and Hurricane Katrina. On May 23, 1927, H. L. Mencken, columnist for the Baltimore *Evening Sun*, explains the mere trickle of donations for victims of the recent flood. Framing his entire argument in terms of domestic realism, he claims that the United States has "no longer house[d] a happy family" ever since Southern backwardness began to weaken national solidarity. Mencken failed to understand that his comments presuppose that some people deserve to perish because of where they live and who they are. "Most of those who have lost their lives [in the 1927 flood] . . . might have escaped without difficulty," Mencken says. "They were warned weeks in advance and high ground was nearly always well within their reach. But thousands of them remained. . . . It is hard to work up any very active sympathy for such people."[13]

What stinging irony to read Mencken saying that New Orleans is the exception to his rule about the South: "The destruction of New Orleans would have put a far different aspect upon the matter, for New Orleans is a civilized city and everyone who has ever been there cherishes a pleasant memory of it. . . . If the city had suffered any serious damage, contributions for its relief would be pouring in today."[14] Hurricane Katrina demonstrated that New Orleans was no less vulnerable to realist condemnations. Many objected strenuously to Mencken's harshness, but few exposed the limits of his realist account, which functioned as if the victims should have already known how to survive a flood that swallowed an entire region of the country—as if people who, in some cases, had never left the city limits or their farms should magically know to leave the city and have the resources to do so; as if those with the most precarious relation to citizenship would not be taking a greater risk by leaving their homes to face armed vigilantes, the police, and military than by staying put; as if Southern infrastructure could support such mass evacuations, which it cannot.

Only when the Manns—and by extension Wright's readers—abandon the home can a new narrative take shape by challenging assumptions about the collective potentials and risks of departure. But Wright refuses to dispatch Brother Mann to face peril alone. Wright's free indirect discourse weaves back and forth between first- and third-person points of view, making the reader his unwilling companion on a journey common enough to people like the Manns but not one many readers would experience otherwise. Free indirect discourse offers a way of reading literature for signs of "transindividuality," which provides access to the interiority of an "alternate social body" irreducible to the relation between "individual and state."[15]

The main character and the narrator seem to blend at crucial moments of the novella, thinking and acting in unison. This narrative style includes forms of life that cannot consistently say "I" in ways supported by mainstream political, civic, and economic institutions. With thought and action being coextensive in this social body, they mark a potentiality not found in liberal subjecthood. The liberal subject's privileges and protections come from (the fantasy of) resigning its force over to the state. The alternate social body lacks these privileges and protections but maintains its force, which remains a constant threat to politics as usual. "Down by the Riverside" introduces readers to this simultaneous threat and potentiality for those excluded from liberal protections.

Wright reminds readers of the experience of the excluded—and the chance that their numbers can increase rapidly with the slightest change in environmental and political factors—through the frequent refrain from the narrator and Brother Mann, "Ef only tha levee don break!"[16] In each case, the narrator speaks of a collective vulnerability that is never reduced to Brother Mann's individual plight. Wright does not begin with a triumphant hero but with an ambivalent, fearful, feverish, guilty man. Brother Mann admits guilt for not leaving as soon as the government provided boats for this purpose. Mencken would take this admission at face value and pronounce Brother Mann's fate as sad but well deserved. That judgment would protect the liberal equation of the individual with the state from the charge of racial bias. But when Wright has Brother Mann admit that he stayed to get a head start on other sharecroppers by planting seed in the floodwaters, Wright displaces personal recrimination for another form of guilt that brings political structures and civil society into account. The archive of the 1927 flood—government documents, autobiographical sources, newspaper exposés, editorials, and correspondence—confirms Wright's effort. In *The Mississippi Valley Flood Disaster of 1927: Official Report of the Relief Operations* (1928), the American Red Cross explains that sharecroppers learned the technique of "*mudding in*" so that they could plant during floods rather than waste time waiting for the floodwaters to recede.[17] This information begs the question of why sharecroppers would learn to plant during a flood if it were in their rational self-interest to leave. Here we find a fugitive discourse, in which the truth runs astray from the report's desire to reaffirm forcing flood survivors into submissive subjects of economy, law, and a racialized civil-society. Similarly, this fugitive discourse strays from the terms that are now popular for understanding life outside these structures.

"Bare life" cannot account for this situation. Instead of relating that concept to the broken link between birth and nationhood in which some develop into citizens according to the logic of the *bildungsroman* and others do not, Wright's economically vulnerable population suffers from a link between *birth* and *labor* that only contingently touches on citizenship. One must have had citizenship to lose it. Wright's figuration of the black worker can be compared to Marx's account of *vogelfrei*, meaning "free as a bird" but "outside the human community and therefore unprotected and without legal rights."[18] Whereas Marx described the violent dissolution of an agrarian economy in Europe, Wright exposes the violent perpetuation of an agrarian economy in the United States—a bird chained to the land by debt and physical threat who escapes to freedom but finds few legal protections. The rest of this notebook explores how race adds another dimension to the *vogelfrei* Marx speaks of, and what agency can come from the indebted despite the risks of seeking freedom.

In a sharecropper's economy, the need to repay one's debt will always trump the need to escape. Sharecropping, as Saidiya Hartman has argued, is a moral economy based on multigenerational guilt, which made departure unacceptable to the sharecroppers themselves even in life-or-death circumstances. Hartman points out that sharecropping was the economic aspect of a political, legislative, and cultural program intent on perverting the positive effects of Emancipation on African Americans. Confederates claimed they sacrificed to achieve Emancipation for the freedpersons who now owed the South repayment for such a gracious gift.[19] Hartman's historiography suggests that during the late nineteenth and early twentieth centuries, sharecropping turned an opportunity to recognize the laborer's needs and capacities in all their living complexity into a new form of dead labor, which reduced humanity to the one-dimensional logic of exchange-value backed by guilt.[20] After the amazing triumph of Emancipation, the Long Depression took hold, national support for the black worker's citizenship waned, and the recently defeated Confederacy was given back the reins of Southern labor.

Becoming the indebted subject of a newly rebuilt plantation system hamstrung the black worker's drive for normative citizenship.[21] The worker brought labor-power, but the tools, land, home, and clothing all belonged to the planter. No harvest, however successful, would pay off the debt. This debtor relationship was accompanied by financial speculation whereby one planter sold a sharecropper's debt to another planter. In that process, the sharecropper, often illiterate and lacking access to paperwork or legal recourse, would have to accept a new level of debt created from thin air by the second planter. Sheriffs, acting as muscle for the sharecroppers, threatened debtors with the chain gang or worse if they tried to escape across state lines.[22] Thus, in Wright's early texts, he brings attention to the making of European Man by its underside, the making of Indebted Man, which he so boldly states with a sharecropping protagonist named Brother Mann. European Man and all who partake in its greatest privileges depend on an indebted subject, who "labors" upon himself, carrying out a "self-torture" based on infinite guilt.[23] Not only does this indebtedness ensure an impossible level of debt that can never be repaid, it also compromises futurity itself through the promise to repay the impossible. As Maurizio Lazzarato says, "The system of debt must therefore neutralize time, that is, the risk inherent to it."[24] Such an approach necessarily undermines the risk needed for individual and collective development. But that is part of the point for this debtor's society—"reducing what will be to what is, that is, reducing the future and its possibilities to current power relations," thereby "pre-empt[ing] non-chronological time, each person's future as well as the future of society as a whole."[25] This produces a never-ending guilty present—the temporality of Indebted Man.

As W. E. B. Du Bois has explained, allowing economic exploitation for one population does not protect other populations from the same. It brings all people closer to that extreme suffering.[26] Hurricane Katrina's occurrence decades later compounds the significance of the economic exploitation portrayed in "Down by the Riverside." Using Wright's novella to understand the 1927 flood and Hurricane Katrina raises a disturbing question of economy. Neoliberalism has adopted and expanded the tactics that targeted the black peasantry after the Civil War. A backwater system of exploitation has become the dominant structure of global governance, turning entire countries into debtors.[27] Wright's novella highlights the risks of sharecroppers staying in and departing from these impossible labor obligations. The question of "departure" is paramount, not just for leaving immediate dangers, but also for escaping an entire mode of governance that depends on guilt for its operation.

TOWARD A CRITIQUE OF VIOLENCE; OR, THE GUNSHOT HEARD ACROSS THE DELTA

Wright positions the reader to join the Manns in the potential for escape, as Brother Mann tilts "his head, listening" for conflict in the distance.[28] What readers hear, with Brother Mann, marks the limit point of the sharecropping economy, the emergency economy, and the protagonist's worldview as he seeks a way out of this high-pressure environment. At this limit to lived experience, one can begin to understand the theories implied by the conflicts in "Down by the Riverside." For 1930s black radical writing, the sounds that Mann hears will inspire a critique of violence that parses out the forces necessary to founding, sustaining, and ending different state formations.

I use the title from Walter Benjamin's famous essay "A Critique of Violence" to bring attention to a research question explored through critical and creative works of black intellectuals since the eighteenth century, at least. But I also hope that drawing on Benjamin's essay will continue the comparative analyses of theory started in the introduction. While several of Benjamin's terms are useful, he, too, restricts his study to "European conditions" when a critique of violence requires a politics of detour through the colony; the sharecropper's farm; the camp's barbed wire fence; or, in this case, the muddy brown waters over which gunshots echo:

It seemed he had heard the sound of a shot. There it was again. . . . Mus be trouble, mus be trouble somewhere. He had heard that the white folks were threatening to conscript all Negroes they could lay their hands on to pile sand- and cement-bags on the levee. And they were talking about bringing in soldiers, too. They were afraid of stores being looted. Shucks, in times like these they'll shoota nigger down just lika dog n think nothin of it. Tha shooting might mean anything. But likely as not its just some po black man gon.[29]

Wright uses free indirect discourse to render a group's past and present exposure to violence during social upheaval, not just Brother's Mann's own vulnerability. The Manns find this out directly when Bob warns them against crossing town to reach the relief camp. Bob admits that it was impossible to sell one of Brother Mann's cows and use the money to purchase a boat: no one would buy the cow at price, and boat owners raised the price of their boats to unreasonable levels. So Bob stole the white boat from Heartfield, the town postmaster, because he thought no one would see the Manns in it. But crossing town means they will inevitably be seen in it. Bob says:

Mann, Ahm mighty scared yull git in trouble takin the boat thu town. Ah stole tha boat from the Pos Office. Its ol man Heartfiels, n yuh know how he hates niggers. Everybody knows his boat when they see it; its white n yuh couldn't get erway wid it. N lissen, theres trouble a-startin in town, too. . . . They done put ever nigger they could fin on the levee by the railroad. . . . They drivin em like slaves. . . . Everywhere Ah looked wuznt nothin but white men wid guns. They wuz a-waiting fer the soljers when Ah lef, n yuh know whut tha means.[30]

That means that martial law will add yet another set of justifications for vigilante and state violence against black bodies. Brother Mann's/the narrator's thoughts and Bob's comments call for a study of the interrelation between vigilante, state, and economic violence targeting racialized bodies.

To follow Wright's theorization, one must remember that in "Blueprint for Negro Literature," he emphasized Christianity's impact on the black Southerner's and migrant's outlook. Thus, Wright chooses "Down by the Riverside" as his novella's title to advocate for a more dynamic understanding of the "theological imaginary." Beyond the title, Wright plots the story so the Manns' departure for the relief camp happens just after a prayer from Elder Murray, who visits to check on Lulu's condition: "Lawd Gawd Awmighty in Heaven, wes a-bowin befo Yuh once ergin, humble in Yo sight, a-pleased fer forgiveness and mercy! . . . Today wes callin on Yuh . . . n today wes believ n waitin fer yuh t hep us! No soften the hard hearts of them white folks there in town, Lawd! Purify their hearts! . . . n save our souls for Jesus sake! Ahmen." Murray then stands up and begins to sing. The others chime in softly:

Ahm gonna lay down mah sword n shiel
Down by the Riverside . . .
Ah ain gonna study war no mo
Ah ain gonna study war no mo
Ah ain gonna study war no mo
Ah ain gonna study war no mo
Ah ain gonna study war no mo
Ah ain gonna study war no mo[31]

JanMohamed calls this a "political catechism through which Mann ritualistically reinforces his subjugation to and subjection by Jim Crow society."[32] It is not surprising that a study of death-bound subjectivity arrives at this conclusion. But Wright also found that religion, despite its limits, could "create emotional attitudes which are conducive to action."[33] Rather than decide for or against religion, it is important to recognize that the "theological imagination" has a dual role in justifying oppression and enabling "a democratic vision of society and of justice," though *Thinking Through Crisis* ultimately takes an *a*theological position, which challenges the Judeo-Christian content in African American literature as well as in political philosophy and aesthetics.[34] Taken to its logical end, a death-bound subjectivity carries no meaningful risk, making it incompatible for a story that compels by strategically loading the narrative with imminent danger and potentials for successful escape. Hence my claim that Wright is a thinker of possibility, not because he understates the threats posed to black life but because he saves space for a surplus in black life that constant threats cannot consistently contain.

Brother Mann's thoughts and Bob's comments, heard against the gunshot over the waters and Elder Murray's hymn, bring up two different assessments of violence that this book will tease out. I follow Benjamin in calling them "mythic violence" and "divine violence." Mythic violence requires force to produce subjects bound to the law and civil society through (their potential to bear) guilt. As Brother Mann's and Bob's comments illustrate, however, this guilt precedes any wrongdoing. It creates the ideal liberal subject, with certain protections and privileges grounded in property relations, alongside a host of less ideal or even pathological subjects, with progressively fewer protections. Racialization, among other factors, tempers this guilt so that white liberal subjects are most often considered innocent until due process indicates otherwise. Racialization tends to make blacks guilty without investigation or with investigations coordinated to confirm the initial prejudice. This makes the black available for immediate violent judgment. This makeshift judge—a teacher, a police officer, a farm overseer, a vacationer at a swimming pool, the neighborhood watch, whoever—expects to carry out violent punishment with impunity. More than that, the guilty figure is not worthy of being mourned. Black diasporic thinkers and artists have many names and images for the black who accepts this fate of being unfairly blamed, abused, even killed, only to be judged guilty retroactively, but not mourned. Frederick Douglass called this "soul murder." Frantz Fanon called it "petrification," a description similar to Walter Benjamin's allusion to the figure of Niobe turning into stone after she angered the gods and they massacred her village. For sure, sharecropping in the delta is one iteration of mythic violence.

Another version of force, divine violence, breaks the cycle of soul murder, expiates unjustified guilt, and overturns the state structure depending on these actions and affects. Divine violence invokes a subjectivity that cannot be individuated into liberal personhood, though individuation occurs nonetheless, on other terms. The very agency that cannot be transferred to the state becomes the basis for this revolutionary power. One cannot see this divine violence at play in "Down by the Riverside." But the story makes legible several conditions of possibility for the concept of divine violence as it plays out in the other writings that receive attention in *Thinking Through Crisis*. The question in the rest of this notebook is how the fictional Manns and the actual black survivors of the 1927 flood demonstrate the potential for this radical force, moving from being to unrest, from objectivity to motion, even out of the very situations meant to ensure their petrification.

Mythic violence first sounds its presence in "Down by the Riverside" through the gunshot Brother Mann hears from his flooding home. As the narrative continues, mythic violence expresses itself through the risk the Manns take in loading into Heartfield's boat to face the torrent and reach the relief camp. Wright tempts readers to accept the realist reading, which would affirm normative property relations, leading to the conclusion that the Manns and any other family too poor to pay inflated prices for boats deserve whatever treatment they receive for traveling in a "stolen" boat. But the narrative sides with the Manns by revealing how the seemingly ethically neutral logic of supply and demand helps pathologize the poor at the outset. Their will to live becomes a crime, even when unprecedented disasters destabilize the rule of law and forestall formal legal judgment. For support of the claim that this stigma attaches itself to specific populations and not others and has the effect of law even when law has been suspended, one need reflect on the archive of the 1927 flood. Planter and Vicksburg relief camp director William Percy, for instance, says in his autobiography that the first thing he does to stop looting is to steal boats: "Our first acts, though *in defiance of all law*, were effective: we seized and manned all privately owned motor boats, skiffs, pleasure craft, wagons and trucks. . . . We confiscated all stocks of food . . . in the local stores."[35] And so, theft itself is not the issue. *Who* has the right to steal is the issue. Race, class, gender, location, and institutional sanction all contribute to who occupies this privilege to thieve without being called a thief and has the authority to punish others for doing the same. Petrification, at its most lethal, would mean that the Manns would accept this guilt, merely waiting for the flood to rip their home from its foundations with them still in it, while others take the resources they need to survive. The Manns' effort to live marks the beginnings of a different force, which does not cohere around pathologizing others for surviving.

According to Cedric Robinson, "Wright intended that his writing engage and confront a political reality of movement." He took on the "task" of "com[ing] to terms with the character of social change and agencies that emerged to direct that chance."[36] Despite mythic violence's frequent attempts to petrify the indebted black worker, Wright activates a concept of possibility that puts its hopes in emergent life with the Mann family's boat ride. Lulu's reproductive labor occurs in the tension between conveying that emergent life or reproducing capital's oppressive relation to labor. But I would also insist, along with Robinson, that Wright uses Lulu to complicate the double bind that condemns Brother Mann to two impossible alternatives by transforming our understanding of it. Instead of confronting us with a choice between two impossible options, the Lulu plot urges readers to see those options as two different concepts of possibility. One concept is "active"—favoring difference, multiplicity, and becoming. While this option affirms emergent life, the other is "reactive"—favoring homogeneity, teleology, and stasis.

The leap from reactive to active possibilities is a precondition for divine violence to disrupt mythic violence.[37] This leap requires a rethinking of contingency, which can be sources of danger and empowerment. Wright makes this point in the novella by way of the accidental "swerves and spins" that interrupt the Mann family's voyage to the Red Cross camp.[38] The Manns' uncharted boat ride enables Wright to identify a kernel of creative and critical thinking within this population that might someday prove capable of imagining and enacting alternatives to the structures oppressing them. "Darkness" also serves as a motif reminding the reader to approach contingency in an active manner. Enlightenment thought typically associates darkness with the absence of agency or with moral pathology.

For Wright, darkness contains nonhierarchical forms of differentiation and the potential to choose between positive and negative forms of labor. These contingencies force Brother Mann to break out of habitual thought patterns and continually think anew. At one point in their journey, for example, the Mann family finds themselves "ringed in by walls of darkness" just before the boat swerves and begins to spin. Brother Mann "grabbed something. . . . He breathed hard, trying to build in his mind something familiar around the cold, wet, smooth pieces of wood. . . . A series of pictures flashed through his mind, but none fitted." But when Mann stops trying to force experience into familiar patterns and lets the environment speak to him, he finds he can understand it: "He could feel the tugging and trembling of the current vibrating through his body as his heart gave soft, steady throbs. He breathed hard, trying to build in his mind something familiar around the cold, wet, smooth pieces of wood. . . . He groped higher, thinking with his fingers. . . . Suddenly, he saw the whole street: sunshine, wagons, and buggies tied to a water trough. This is old man Toms sto. And these were the railing that went around the front porch."[39] Wright associates passive force with idealism that reduces thinking to the matching of physical objects to mental images, as if thought occurred at a remove from physical experience. Here, the breakdown of social patterns requires his protagonist to adapt to an environment in flux—precisely an environment that idealism cannot deal with. Wright suggests in this passage that active force is embodied thought, as when Mann tries "thinking with his fingers," but this form of thought does not stop at his fingertips. Embodiment reaches out into the environment, as when Mann feels "the current vibrating through his body" and beats in time with his throbbing heart. Under such circumstances, knowledge does not occur outside and above experience but is part and parcel of material events. Here, moreover, Mann's thinking is informed and not hindered by his desire to save his family; in embodied thought, they are one entity. Indeed, Wright's odd placement of the narrative voice between the third and first person draws the reader into Mann's active thought as well.

Method proves crucial here. Passive thinking can be traced back to the Cartesian model, inasmuch as it sees method in terms of negotiating options that inevitably repeat that which is already familiar. But active thinking, as Wright construes it, treats method as the pathway by which an idea takes shape. According to this model, even if Mann were to encounter the same landmarks in the same boat at another moment in time, the encounter between embodied subject and object would not produce the same idea. Method does not exist outside and before what is being thought, as if it were possible to constrain thought before it emerges as such. Crises may well undo some forms of difference altogether. But more consistently they shake up how the hierarchy orders and values differences in particular ways. As goes hierarchy, so goes the tribunal of reason that depends on hierarchy to operate. This scene of Brother Mann's boat ride demonstrates that especially under catastrophic situations one can detect nascent elements of collective thought among the sharecroppers despite Jim Crow's attempts to crush it.

"Down by the Riverside" also demonstrates what happens when passive thinking informs Brother Mann's decisions, through two examples. Where darkness held forth new possibilities for imagining one's relationship to the material environment, these instances of passive thinking are brought on by light and the imposition of oppositional thinking. In the first instance, Brother Mann unintentionally rows to the home of Heartfield, the man who owns the boat Mann needs if he is to save his family. He almost turns away from that house, but as the narrator explains, the "soft, yellow glow" of the lights "was in his mind. They helped him, those lights. For awhile he rowed without effort. Where there were lights there were people, and where there were people there was help." He "steered for the lights" and yelled, "Mah wifes sick! Shes in birth!" The Heartfields respond to Mann's pleas first by identifying the man in need of help as a criminal—"That's our boat, Father! Its *white*!" yells Heartfield's son—and then with lethal violence. Mann kills Heartfield in self-defense.[40]

This is neither coincidence nor fate nor a completely irrational response from Heartfield. Heartfield's violence supports my argument that the refugee is punished not for looting but for threatening the very idea of property and its privileged relationship to whiteness. As I state earlier, Brother Mann's use of Heartfield's boat is, in terms of use-value, what any other person would do to avoid drowning—use whatever boat you can find, of course. In terms of exchange-value and the symbolism that exchange carries, however, the boat represents all the reasons why Brother Mann does *not* have the same right to survive as Heartfield. In fact, the moment Brother Mann reveals the willpower to survive, Heartfield still does not see it as an equality of sorts. Heartfield believes his family's safety is threatened by the Mann family's will to live. Frantz Fanon calls this *negrophobogensis*, the sense that black people are phobia-incarnate and the one who feels such fear is justified in doing absolutely anything to quell this threat. Moreover, this threat need not appear in one's immediate space. Evidence of black people being threatening in any time or place seems to confirm for Heartfield that Brother Mann cares more about doing harm to the Heartfields than about saving his own family. When fear gets sucked into this fantastical logic, violence against the innocent is acceptable, even required, since no black person can truly be innocent.[41] This is the logic that rationalizes Heartfield feeling justified in attacking a man asking for help; shooting at an unarmed pregnant woman, grandmother, and young child; and trying to kill the people who might have helped him. Were he to kill Brother Mann, Heartfield would still have no chance of using the boat to save his own family. If he recognized this, he might have regarded Brother Mann's cry for help as a sincere opportunity for the two families to save each other. But to imagine this possibility would be to acknowledge the shared humanity of black and white, and Heartfield would rather kill or die than entertain this option.

The second instance of reactive thinking occurs when the Manns arrive at the Red Cross relief camp. The Red Cross report describes the relief camp as a modernization project in the reform tradition, proclaiming that with the 1927 flood's "loss of life, suffering and tremendous property destruction, are involved many significant advances, in the public health service and the promotion of social and economic welfare."[42] But the Mann family's experience of the camp exposes an underside to such projects, placing Wright among a chorus of critics that challenge the camp's humanitarian purpose. At the camp's entrance, Wright introduces readers to the violence of discipline that will characterize the camp experience: Mann "pulled the oars. A *glare of light* shot from a second-story porch and made him blink. Two white soldiers in khaki uniforms leaned over the banisters. . . . He could see the *dull glint of steel* on the tips of their rifles."[43] Operating in concert with the hostile military posture of the soldiers, the light targets him, interpellating the weatherworn family as criminals before the fact.

This act of interpellation redefines the categories of race, class, and gender that organize the Manns' daily life outside the camp. "Where you going, nigger?" one of the guards asks. Mann replies:

"Ahm takin mah wife t the hospital, suh. She in birth, suh! . . ."
    "You got a pass?"
    "Nawsuh"
    "Where you bring that boat from?"
    "The South En, suh."
    "You *rowed* here?"
    "Yessuh"
    The soldiers laughed at each other.
    "Well, I'll be Goddamned! Nigger, you take the prize! . . . I never thought anybody was fool enough to row a boat against that current . . ."
    "I got a nigger here who beat everybody. He rowed from the South End, against the current. Can you beat that?"
    [Another soldier replies] "Well, what you want us to do about it? Give im a medal?"
    "Naw; his bitch is sick. Having a picaninny. Shoot em over to the Red Cross hospital."[44]

Even though he killed Heartfield to protect his family, Mann knows the soldiers would as soon lynch him as send him and his family to the hospital.

Gender discrimination collaborates with racism here. In undermining the manhood evident in Mann's feat of rowing the boat against the current, the soldiers establish theirs. Their description of Lulu as "sick" denies her the dignity of motherhood and renders her barely human with the insult "bitch." Since Wright has placed the reader in the boat as well, the reader shares this insult with Brother Mann and Lulu. The question is how Wright's story reveals something in excess of the insults hurled at Lulu, Brother Mann, and all others who share the exclusions made lethal by the flood.

LULU'S LAMENT; OR, THE RELIEF CAMP AND ITS DISCONTENTS

The second phase of this notebook attends to the Manns' excruciating experience of a relief camp designed to relieve the collapsing economic system rather than its exploited workers. Many would like to assume that during catastrophes people will overcome their prejudices and unify for human survival—this is a beautiful dream but a problematic theoretical assumption for thinking through social breakdown. These breakdowns reveal the ethical, political, and cultural allegiances and hostilities that informed day-to-day activity but were easily ignored or deemed exceptional because they spoke to more complicated realities. The relief project is indispensable proof that times of crisis reveal, but do not automatically overcome, the social and institutional inequities that dominate more mundane situations. Understanding this relief project's unethical program requires close attention to Lulu Mann as a fictional character pushed to the limits of what women experienced in the historic 1927 flood. While feminist scholars rightly question Wright's characterizations of women in his writings in general, and Lulu's silence and inaction in particular, I would argue that she is absolutely essential to the concern with social reconstruction in "Down by the Riverside." According to the Red Cross report, the shock of the 1927 flood sent many women into labor. While attending not at all to Lulu's personal experience, Wright turns the historical impact of the flood on women's reproductive labor into *the* animating tension of the novella. Lulu's struggle to give birth also serves as Wright's metaphor for his personal difficulty—and that of others claiming a radical stance—in imagining an alternative way of life in a time of social breakdown. He acknowledges that delta labor relations cannot be rethought without addressing the question of reproductive labor. Lulu's plight calls for an examination of the 1927 flood's archive alongside the several groups reimagining the delta, including the planter class and their loyal white workers; the black intellectuals, ranging from radical to conservative; and the federal government's interest in rebuilding the economy but not dealing with race.

In this light, the family name "Mann" is both exact and a cruel joke. It acknowledges their membership in the human species but accents their exclusion from the Enlightenment ideal of humanity, European Man. Lulu's character most intensely conveys a spectrality enveloping the entire family. Black feminist scholar Hortense Spillers has said much regarding this virtual space for the black family, in which black husbands and fathers fall from "mimetic view," meaning that black husbands and fathers rarely fit into how American culture *imagines* family, social development, gender identity, and other factors. To say instead that the black family is matriarchal would *misname* the situation. It would overstate black women's political and civic standing while understating the brutality levied against them for simply being black women and being sisters, partners, wives, mothers, and guardians. But Spillers finds an amazing opportunity in this virtual space. The black female, "*in the flesh*, both mother and mother-dispossessed," has a chance to enter a new, "*insurgent*" space of subjectivity. The black male "has been touched" by the black mother in a distinctive way, based on how she can "break in upon [his] imagination," making him one of the "*only* American community of males" with the chance "to learn *who* the female is within itself, the infant child who bears the life against the could-be fateful game, against the odds of pulverization and murder, including her own."[45] Precisely because certain social protections and assumptions have been withheld from black femininity, the black male may witness a (noneconomic) value others have yet to see and affirm femininity in a more genuine and sophisticated way.

Placing Lulu in a seemingly virtual space between life and death poses the question of whether her arrival at the relief camp will realize the dream that out of catastrophe can come some drastic transformation of the South. To address that question, we must consider the narrative form "Down by the Riverside" takes to make this point effectively. To describe this aspect of the free indirect discourse I have associated with Wright's story, one must remember Maurice Blanchot's description of a similar narrative style, which he called "spectral, ghostlike, not that it comes from beyond the grave" or "represent[s] a completed whole, once and forever achieved," but because it affirms "the forces of life" by placing narrative itself in a "hazardous space."[46] "Down by the Riverside" occupies such a hazardous space, offering readers a story where the delta is never completely constructed, where the perfect witness to the worst of the flood and the camps is the one who, paradoxically, does not live to tell the story. Perhaps Wright wagers that by pulling the main characters, and most especially Lulu, into this spectrality, readers will see a fuller range of the perils taking lives and the new(er) forms of life evolving to survive the unpredictable. In other words, this spectral space is not where death is sovereign and the wise merely embrace their fate—it is not a space of pure natural selection. In this space, life persists even as older forms of existence lose primacy and new ones emerge, precisely because those old forms never fully disappear.[47]

Looking at Brother Mann, Lulu, and their relationship in this frame, it would be misguided to think Brother Mann's attempt to save his wife is individualist machismo. It would be even more problematic to think that Brother Mann would treat Lulu like Bigger Thomas treated female characters in *Native Son*. Even Lulu's spectral position between life and death does not curb Brother Mann's persistence. Quite the contrary, Brother Mann esteems Lulu's life in its specificity and its reference to life in general. To borrow from Nietzsche, Brother Mann "say[s] Yes to life even in its strangest and most painful episodes," when "even pain still has the effect of a stimulus," and, most specifically, the "pangs of the woman giving birth consecrate all pain; and conversely all becoming and growing—all that guarantees a future—involves pain."[48] Brother Mann affirms Lulu in a way the entire relief camp structure refuses to do, in a way others deem foolish. Wright's version of the story opens this insurgent space, although it falls short of imagining how Lulu or other women might act within it. Nevertheless, Lulu's plight sparks unrest within Brother Mann, who risks himself to save her and their unborn child. In addition, looking at their story helps us think more broadly about the relief camps as a site of unrest, coming from different racialized, gendered, economic, and political agendas. The issue is whether these different agendas seek to use the unrest to restore old forms of sociality in the delta or foster new ones. Lulu's presence as a woman in labor shows us how the relief camps put black men in subordinate positions by denying them the power to take care of their families. As a substitute for reconstruction, "relief" only restores the exploitative system that was washed away. The drive for full citizenship becomes lost in the collective fantasy of getting back to normal, which converts the possibilities for change that open up during disaster back into reactive formations characterized by economic and moral indebtedness. In the process, we will see the camp as a site of tension between relief and reconstruction.[49]

Americans gave millions of dollars to the Red Cross to aid the flood survivors, a gift that might have improved conditions for workers across the South. As donations poured in from around the country, African American intellectuals debated for months in newspapers, magazines, and symposia. As Robert Russa Moton, president of the Tuskegee Institute and chair of the Hoover-selected Colored Advisory Commission (CAC) for the relief project, put it, "We were face to face with one of the greatest labor questions of America. . . . [The sharecroppers] felt that the flood had emancipated them from a condition of peonage." Moton concluded that these workers "ought not to be permitted to go back to this hopeless situation . . . if there is rehabilitation." "Rehabilitation" in Moton's vocabulary has virtually the same meaning as "reconstruction" in mine, because he associates it with a "regeneration" of the delta so the black flood survivors will be "healthier and happier, and economically more independent."[50] Moton and other black intellectuals, like W. E. B. Du Bois and Walter White of the NAACP as well as Ida B. Wells with the *Chicago Defender*, were aware that the flood brought them an opportunity to reconstruct the delta, with millions of dollars available to bring those ideas to fruition.

Anyone familiar with these leaders knows that a shared desire for reconstruction in the delta does not equate to a shared method or set of concrete goals. Despite their differences and similarities, their distinct positions all testify to the importance of a black public sphere for debating reconstruction.[51] The issue was whether Moton and the Tuskegee machine, White and Du Bois of the NAACP, or Wells and the *Chicago Defender* could find "the boundary line between 'compromise' with the existing state forms and their revolutionary 'use' against the ruling class," as I mentioned in the Introduction.[52] Answers to this question would influence how the gift economy resulting from the 1927 flood would lead to a more egalitarian delta or devolve into debt peonage once again. Coupling this 1927 flood archive material with "Down by the Riverside" enriches our understanding of *why* Wright has the Manns enter the camp and confront so many difficulties in a space where they should find comfort.

Moton succeeded Booker T. Washington at Tuskegee Institute and, for more than a decade, continued much of Washington's brand of conservative leadership. One must keep in mind that by that time, Tuskegee leadership had a long history of serving in advisory roles. At the turn of the twentieth century, as Roderick Ferguson notes, "Booker T. Washington locates the emergence of a new, modern, nationalized and moralized African American subject as the effect of U.S. imperialism," as in the Spanish-American War.[53] With this position held consistently over several decades, it was no wonder that some black intellectuals feared that Moton and his colleagues would merely accommodate a half-hearted attempt at post-flood relief by the US government.

This pessimistic viewpoint proved to be correct. But why, considering that Moton believed the 1927 flood was the chance to change the delta? Moton hoped to convince Hoover that this reconstructive work would win black support for Hoover's presidential campaign and for the Republican Party in general. Moton tried to strike a delicate balance between critiquing the camps, offering locally specific suggestions for camp improvement, and winning Hoover over to the idea of an egalitarian new delta. But two things were lacking from Moton's and the CAC's vision: a theory of exploitation and the forms of discipline that make people conform to that exploitation, and a hope that fails to become optimism.

By a theory of exploitation, I mean a perspective that can examine the structural ways that resources and profits are distributed unfairly so that those who do the least to develop or obtain the resources and profits actually take in the lion's share. As Ryan McCormick has noted, Marx's point goes beyond economic efficiency and enters the realm of ethics.[54] A theory of exploitation exposes the unethical practices that are hidden from and by the law. This is because law has been and is being constituted from the same perspective that enables exploitation in economic production. Without a theory of exploitation, the CAC mistakes structural inequalities being recreated by the relief project for unintentional, ephemeral errors of judgment with no relevance to the pre-disaster status quo. By a hope that fails to become optimism, I mean that the CAC fails to find the beginnings of this new delta within the ideas and practices common to the sharecropping folk. In the archival materials, one finds a consistent return to the idea that the potential for rebuilding comes strictly from the federal government in all aspects because of the dearth of agency among the flood survivors. Consequently, the CAC sees a small window of opportunity for change, but its orientation assumes one must wait for a vision of reconstruction and plan of implementation from the government.

Take, for instance, CAC member T. M. Campbell's field report on several relief camps. Campbell is quite aware of how overwhelming the flood has been for the survivors. "I was never so impressed by the intense excitement and fear caused by this terrible catastrophy [sic] as I was when I saw these people. . . . Men, women, and children were all dazed from the intense strain which they had undergone while fleeing for their lives."[55] Campbell agrees with Moton's observation in a related document, saying "We found a class of people who were . . . practically helpless without initiative and with little self-control and self-reliance."[56] While in the Baton Rouge relief camp, Campbell inspected "whether guards were stationed there to keep the refugees in or to keep the public out." Campbell concludes:

> I confess that when I first saw this, it did look a little too militaristic for these suffering people. And then, to make the thing a little worse, I saw a guard with fixed bayonet bring a young colored boy down through the camp to the headquarters. On inquiry though, I found that this young fellow had attempted to cut another refugee in the camp and he was simply brought in for the offense. Then a thought occurred to me to drive around to the white refugee camp to see what was going on there, and to my surprise the uniformed guards were guarding the white camps the same as the colored. When I reported this to those of the colored citizens the remark was, "well, it is all right then if they are doing that for the whites." . . . I heard some complaints which I was not able to verify, that there was some discrimination on the part of the Red Cross . . . in giving the [black] refugees clothing. This may or may not be true, but all the people I saw had on some clothes. Everywhere I went I found white and colored working side by side in a very unselfish manner.[57]

In another instance, Campbell appears all too eager to gratify the relief camp directors despite the testimony of black flood survivors:

> Most of [the refugees Campbell interviewed] spoke very praiseworthy of the treatment which they had been given since they had been concentrated. Talking with one rather level-headed farmer, he said "We ain't got no complaint to make about our treatment here, only they are making

all the men unload boats at the river and work on the levees and ain't said nothing about paying us. Course we're getting a place to eat and sleep, but it looks like we ought to get some pay for our work." He said, "We'd a been much better off if the white people had let us pack [before evacuating]. They made us work on the levees down in the delta, up to the last minute, tellin' us that the levee wasn't going to break and then when it did break, we didn't have time to do nothing but save our families. That's the biggest complaint we got."[58]

One is taken aback by how superficially Campbell examines the refugee camps and how eagerly he praises the camp's officers in the face of consistent complaints about racially discriminatory treatment and economic exploitation (unpaid levee work and camp work). To say that there is no racial discrimination in distribution of clothing because black people all have on clothes is nearly laughable. Although there are numerous instances where the CAC's critiques help correct camp conditions, their effectiveness in other aspects does not make up for the oversights mentioned above.

These oversights stem from the assumption on the part of Campbell and his colleagues that there is something fundamentally wrong with the flood survivors themselves. A second look at Campbell's reference to the "level-headed farmer" indicates a mistrust of flood survivor testimony, as if the other testimonies are untrue for not being even-keeled. And yet, must the testimony to surviving the nation's largest flood be judged primarily by its restrained, self-possessed character? Furthermore, Campbell misses the point of the level-headed farmer's testimony. While the CAC understands the need for reconstructing the delta for a dispossessed population, they do not see how reconstruction requires embracing dispossession, not as a personal deficiency but as an alternative outlook on the emergency. In other words, I find the weakness of the CAC position on reconstruction in Moton saying that "the American people and the South owe it to this faithful, hard-working group of Negroes to give them for their own contentment and fairness a better home-life to the end that they may be healthier and happier, and economically more independent."[59] Of course, the South owed the Negro for decades of economic, intellectual, artistic, and emotional labor. Stating that truth is no weakness. The weakness stems from assuming that the flood survivors would have to wait on the South to "give" it as if the rest of the South fully possesses contentment, fairness, health, and independence. This passive position allows for hope but not optimism. Optimism assumes that the agency of the dispossessed must be cultivated knowing full well that the South has acted unjustly, whether or not the South tries to right its wrongs. By looking to Herbert Hoover to set this agenda, Moton missed the chance to lead delta reconstruction, though he offered important suggestions for immediate relief after the flood.

The NAACP and the *Chicago Defender* represent the other two facets of this debate. (Their respective critiques overlap in several key ways and so, for now, I will toggle between their positions to continue analyzing this intellectual debate and Wright's "Down by the Riverside." Later in my analysis, however, I will distinguish between the *Chicago Defender* and the NAACP on a crucial point.) In contrast to the CAC, the NAACP and the *Chicago Defender* reveal the relief camp's exploitative tendencies in a more thoroughgoing manner. In the pages of the *Chicago Defender*—and those of *Crisis* magazine and the *Nation*—the paper and the NAACP find fault with the relief process based on widespread segregation; the flouting of local, state, and federal law at the expense of black flood survivors; the threat of violence for those who would challenge this state of affairs; and economic abandonment. On July 30, 1927, Ida B. Wells said it best: "Why are [there] Colored camps? Why are hundreds of thousands of our people herded in camps, instead of being provided for in houses, where they and their families can be helped as are the white refugees, and live together as families should do? . . . And why can't the Race, who are 90 per cent of the actual flood sufferers, share in that $14,000,000 relief fund which the country sent freely to the flooded district?"[60] These questions from the black public sphere place a magnifying glass on the transformation of a gift economy into the basis for a debtor's society. Well's critique of the flood response touches local, state, and national levels. The need for critique on the national level stems from Herbert Hoover's mistaken decision to "avoid entanglement in race."[61] The federal government's decision left it unable to foresee and forbid the segregated distribution of donations at every other level of government. The plantation owners who profited the most from the sharecropping system that had just been washed away are put in charge of the Red Cross relief camps. The planters fear nothing more than losing their black laborers. As one planter puts it, "If the government takes our Negroes and our mules, they might just as well take our land."[62] Where workers' migrations to the North had threatened the antediluvian sharecropping system, the planters' control of the Red Cross camps gives them a captive labor force. They segregated the relief camps and placed National Guardsmen around black survivors, who could leave the camps only with a pass, and they saw to it that no one could inspect the camps without a planter's consent. In my view, the donations were misused to revive a dying aristocracy, halt the emancipation of once-indebted laborers, and recreate the South in the likeness of recently decimated sharecropping traditions.

This information gives us cause to follow Wright in questioning the Red Cross report's celebration of its modernizing approach to flood relief. In 1927, Wright was in Memphis reading the *Crisis*, the *Nation*, and the *Chicago Defender* and associated presses, all of which exposed the underside of these procedures and the benefits planters received from the relief camp structure.[63] The camps prepared the labor force for conditions rebuilt to reflect the delta before the flood. Vaccinations and rations alone do not illustrate the extent to which the pre-1927 flood conditions were being reproduced. Recreating discriminatory racial and class relations in the delta required regulation of gender and sexual relations.[64] If the Red Cross is "the agent of the American people" that provides "sympathy," as Calvin Coolidge says,[65] then the medical examination scene in "Down by the Riverside" suggests that the level of national sympathy is proportional to America's ability to contain the problem at a level below national threat. Wright first questions the level of national sympathy by marking the medical examination room with the ultimate sign of Jim Crow America: "FOR COLORED." With this sign, Wright typographically links the hospital to resegregation, which singles out the population most vulnerable to mistreatment, accusation, and the assignation of guilt, so that even accepting the "sympathy" of the camp counts as a moral debt to be repaid.

When Mann opens the examination door, he is dazed, "blinking in a blaze bright lights," which represent another scene of interpellation, just like the entrance into the camp. Mann begs a nurse for help—"Please, Mam . . . Mah wife . . . She sick!"—the nurse checks "Lulu's pulse" and then "look[s] searchingly at Mann" before she calls Dr. Burrows. After Burrows realizes Lulu is dead, he looks up and stares at Brother Mann "quizzically."[66] In *The Birth of the Clinic* (1973), Michel Foucault says, "The observing gaze refrains from intervening: it is silent and gestureless. Observation leaves things as they are."[67] If Foucault is correct about medical perception, then the nurse changes expression between looking at Lulu and Brother Mann. She looks at Lulu without feeling for a moment but searches Mann's face in an accusatory manner, as if to say, "Don't you know she's already dead? Why didn't *you* . . . ?" Dr. Burrows vocalizes what the nurse will not, which sets off a scene of the most perverted sympathy:

"Well, boy, it's all over. . . . Maybe if you could have gotten her here a little sooner we could have saved her. The baby, anyway."

Mann stared at the thin, black face; at the wet cloths, at the arm hanging still and limp. His lips moved, but he could not speak. Two more white nurses and another white doctor came and stood. Grannie ran to the table.

"Lulu!"

"Its awright, Aunty," said the doctor, pulling her away.

Grannie sank to the floor, her head on her knees.

"Lawd . . ."

Mann stood like stone now. Lulu dead? He seemed not to see the white doctors and nurses gathering, looking at him. He sighed and the lids of his eyes drooped half-way down over the pupils.

"Poor nigger," said a white nurse.

Blankly, Mann stared at her. He wet his lips and swallowed. Something pressed against his knee. . . . Peewee was clinging to him, his little black face tense with fear. He caught Peewee by the hand, went over to the wall and stood above Grannie, hesitating. His fingers touched her shoulders.

"Awright," said the doctor. "Roll her out."

. . . A white nurse giggled, nervously. Mann stood squeezing his blistered palms, taking out of the intense pain a sort of consolation, a sort of forgetfulness. . . . Somewhere a bell tolled, faint and far off.

Crash!

Everybody jumped. One of the nurses gave a short scream.

"What's that?"

"Aw, just a chair fell over. That's all . . ."

"Oh!"

The doctors looked at the nurses and the nurses looked at the doctors. Then all of them laughed, uneasily.[68]

I quote this passage at length for several reasons. This scene confirms one of my original points. Unlike *Native Son*, in which main character Bigger

Thomas kills and disposes of a black woman's body for his selfish gain, "Down by the Riverside" features a main character doing all he can to save his wife. Brother Mann provides a much-needed counterpoint to Bigger Thomas in Wright's fiction. The passage also demonstrates the complexities of mourning that are discussed in the introductory notebook. Recall Cathy Caruth's ethical theory, which uses Sigmund Freud's anecdote about the deceased son, the mourning father, and the watchman who falls asleep and lets a candle burn the boy's body as proof of an ethical relation founding human consciousness. I point out that Caruth looks past the watchman when actually his negligence raises multiple questions about why some do and others do not share our losses, mourn with us, or share our pain. How can a study of bearing witness to trauma be properly delineated without exposing failed instances of witnessing?

This scene in the segregated hospital is further support for my critique. Indeed, the ethical relation between Brother Mann and Lulu requires the utmost attention and cannot be fully understood without examining how and why the nurses founder at bearing witness to the Mann family's loss. The nurse and doctor coldly blame Brother Mann for Lulu's death, which ignores his hands, blistered, splintered, and bleeding from rowing for hours, and his typhoid-like symptoms—basically everything that would emphasize Brother Mann's efforts and humanize the family. Once the medical personnel finally realize the depth of the Mann family's loss, the personnel can barely tolerate it. Mourning with the Manns would imply an equality that would decry all the mistreatment in the camps up until this point. Faux-sympathetic lines like "poor nigger" acknowledge Brother Mann's pain and minimize its value at the same time. Any distraction, from rain pelting the roof to the crash of a chair, deserves more attention than sharing the family's shock.

But maybe that is Wright's point. In their survival and their death, the Manns assert a life that exceeds the ideas of personhood, citizenship, family, and labor forming the premise for the relief camps. Proof that positive social transformation is happening would mean that the medical personnel can sympathize with *this* family, which points to a life that has hitherto been pathologized and targeted for functioning outside "normal" patterns (not to mention that the very notion of normal is already premised on excluding such a life). The spectral character of this family, sitting between life and death, increases the likelihood of its alienation and makes it a constant target of neglect, whether malicious or benign. Then again, this spectral character makes Lulu and others in similar vulnerable positions the true measure of transformation for the relief camp. One reason Brother Mann's actions should not be likened to the mainstream machismo of 1930s labor movement imagery is because he offers slight hints as to what this new form of interaction looks like. The slightest groan, whether it indicates Lulu's slide toward death or her enlivening, reinvigorates fatigued Brother Mann to row on toward the hospital. When at the hospital, he lingers with his son and mother-in-law, nearly petrified by the shock of Lulu's passing (rather than looking for a distraction from it). Mann does not become fully numb to his wife's mistreatment in the camps or her death, since his physical pain becomes his "consolation." One cannot fully be sure of what Brother Mann forgets as he faces his pain, but I believe that in coupling forgetting with consolation, Brother Mann rebuffs the guilt imputed to him by the medical personnel. Still, this scene illustrates how medical administration reinstates racial divides and pulverizes kinship relations already strained by sickness, injury, fear, disillusionment, and death.

With this scene, Wright joins black newspapers in rebutting mainstream news outlets lauding the relief effort. Major newspapers agreed with the Red Cross report's claim that black women and men found stability through domestic training and manual labor, respectively.[69] On June 11, 1927, the *Chicago Defender* disclosed the real terms under which black flood survivors did such work in the camps. Those who found outside jobs and wanted to stay in the camps would receive no rations and would have to put up a month's savings. Black single mothers and their children received rations only if they were attached to a man with a job in the camp, whether they knew him or not. Sharecropping required a black nuclear family to reproduce itself and take on multigenerational debt once again. This rule strips black workers of familial relationships, as if the wives, husbands, parents, and other loved ones who lost their lives before or during the flood are interchangeable with the survivors. Their interchangeability makes these workers disposable, even as they become subjects of debt in perpetuity. Lulu's suffering encapsulates the logic of disposability enabled by the rhetoric of relief. In light of this historical information, the breaking up of the Mann family says more about the violence dealt out by the camps than about the uneven effects of natural disaster.

Relief for the victims of the 1927 flood restored the capacity for indebtedness among sharecropping families, but it did not restore the debt itself. Since there were laws in the delta that canceled debts in the event of natural disaster, how was the debt restored?[70] Planters could not justify keeping black workers captive without indebting them. NAACP inspector Walter White's investigation later uncovered evidence that planters assigned black men to the harshest work around the camps and assigned black women to domestic work for little to no wages. Planters supplied these workers with the food, clothing, and other rations paid for by national donations, which the planters treated as loans. Thus donations that might have transformed the crumbling sharecropping system instead revitalized it by recapturing the sharecroppers' labor. Wright's rendering of this process is richly allusive, drawing on literature from Dante's *Divine Comedy* and Milton's *Paradise Lost* to Muriel Rukeyser's *Book of the Dead*. After Lulu's death, Brother Mann is on a boat taking him to join the sandbagging team: "Mann could see long, black lines of men weaving snake-fashion about the levee-top. . . . The levee was a ridge of dry land between two stretches of black water. The men on the levee-top moved slowly, like dim shadows. They were carrying heavy bags on their shoulders and when they reached a certain point the bags were dumped down. They returned slowly, with bent backs, going to get more bags. . . . At the water's edge men unloaded boats; behind them stood soldiers with rifles."[71] Just as darkness became the space for thinking anew during the Mann family boat ride, so the darkness that saturates this scene of levee-labor paradoxically sheds light on the situation. Wright shows the dedication of the relief project organizers to such an exploitative system in their willingness to rebuild it even on the tiniest "ridge of dry land" that remains above water. At last, Mann and the reader understand the absurdity of a labor system that places these workers in danger at precisely the moment when they should be evacuating the area.

This insight emerges from exceptional circumstances to characterize the sharecropping system itself as a deathly system, even under normal conditions. Indeed, all the elements of everyday work reappear in this description. The organization of laborers based on segregation, labor that could kill a human being from strain alone, harsh conditions where the gains never outweigh the dangers—all this indicates a system driven by disposable labor. The laborers face "soldiers with rifles" if they try to escape dangerous working conditions, which means the laborers are already disposed of, as Wright suggests by referring to them as "dim shadows." Working them to death would be like killing no one at all, from the planter's perspective.

Although these dim, shadowy men will be washed away much as Lulu was earlier on in the novella, there is, I believe, a crucial difference between them. Lulu died when the Mann family left their home behind. In departing, they took a risk, certainly, but there was a chance that Lulu would survive, and none if they stayed. The outcome was not predetermined. By returning to the sharecropping system, on the other hand, the shadow men consign themselves to two options—the crushed levee or the rifle—with no possibility of survival. At the same time, if this history repeats itself, then the sharecropping system will be washed away again, and the Gulf Coast remains a place of darkness out of which new possibilities can emerge.

A brief moment of insight occurs as the guards march Brother Mann to his death at the edge of the camp. On that long walk, he passes through the black section of the camp and, for the first time, understands himself as part of a collective: Soldiers "led him among the tents. . . . The black faces he passed were blurred and merged one into the other. And he heard tense talk, whispers. For a split second he was there among those blunt and hazy black faces looking silently and fearfully at the white folks take some black man away. Why don they hep me? Yet he knew that they would not help him, even as he in times past had not helped other black men being taken by the white folks to their death."[72] Whereas the narrator has oscillated between first- and third-person narrative so that we can see Brother Mann from both the inside and the outside of his character, this is the first time that Wright shifts Brother Mann's first-person perspective so he imagines himself from another black person's viewpoint. One minute he looks at faces that "blurred and merged one into the other," and the next instant he is "among those blunt and hazy faces" trying to understand why they do not rise up and save him. The answer comes neither from them nor from himself alone but from his identification with them. This mutual recognition is coterminous with his death. The remainder of this chapter considers the several meanings of his death for Wright's story as well as for flood survivors of the historic 1927 flood.

Although neither Mann nor the other black folk in the camp turn into a "we" capable of decisive action against the planters' army, Wright does hint that Brother Mann's death might be the disruption that initiates collective self-reflection and communal action. Wright calls attention to the potential for such action in stressing that the black folks' inability to act as one seals Mann's fate. Wright uses free indirect discourse again to reject the notion that black rebellion against white exploiters alone was sufficient to resolve the problem. In "Blueprint for Negro Literature," he explains that any rebellion must rise "not only against the exploiting whites, but against all of that within his own race that retards decisive action and obscures clarity of vision."[73] In short, this novella mounts a critique of reactive forces, which I understand as the first stage of a labor for emancipation requiring freedom of the mind, the body, and the collective as well.[74]

With this in mind, I must note that Wright's novella exaggerates the passivity of relief camp prisoners in order to place some of the blame on collective inaction. There was actually much more resistance in the camps than he lets on. At one point, the *Chicago Defender* called for an underground railroad to rescue survivors, not from the flood, but from the camps. Newspaper exposés and eyewitness accounts indicate that many people actually fought in the camps, escaped, and made it as far as Chicago, Washington D.C., and New York City. By organizing, moreover, black intellectuals and activists did succeed in reforming some camps and extricating their loved ones, though their reconstruction of the South did not take the shape some of them expected.

In this way, the *Chicago Defender* distinguishes itself from the NAACP. By the 1927 flood, the *Chicago Defender* had already been the loudest voice in print for black migration from the South. No wonder Ida B. Wells's boldest critique of the CAC has a strong geographical inflection. While Du Bois doubts that the CAC will do more than accommodate Hoover's relief camp agenda, based on his decades-long opposition to the Tuskegee program, Wells's argument is that the CAC *has no choice* in the matter. The geographical location of the main members of the CAC makes it practically impossible for them to express sharper critiques of Jim Crow practices. Wells notes the disingenuousness of Hoover's appointments to the CAC and suggests that the most effective critique of the relief project must come from outside the South.

Wells's emphasis on the most effective location for critique also renews interest in the politics of cultural and demographic movement.[75] Taking the call for an underground railroad as more than a symbolic gesture means it may invoke a different way of doing politics. That would make the Underground Railroad more than a temporary, pragmatic, antebellum-era tactic.

The Underground Railroad would be a persistent resource for radical action, working both inside and outside of conventional institutional forms and the identities they privilege.

Following this proposal means taking seriously the types of resistance springing from the sort of "tense talk and whispers" Wright ascribes to the "black faces" that watch Brother Mann go to his death. Perhaps the tense talk proves more potent because it operates at a subterranean level, perhaps too minimalist to be considered routine dialogue. This is not to say that this talk is diametrically opposed to dialogue but that it is in surplus of the "I-you" relation structuring conventional speech. Because of its place outside so-called proper positions in communication, "tense talk and whispers" may appear meaningless. But this appearance provides greater cover to share information, feelings, plans, expectations, and more in multiple directions at multiple paces.

The optimistic underside of the spectral character of black connectivity is its existence outside conventional channels of desire, especially Freud's oedipal triangle, "which cages the production of desire, neutralizing it, inside figural forms of persons with a mythological character." The "partial objects"—those fragments of desire, threadbare but enduring kinship relations, protected escape routes, seemingly useless items and human beings—that insist on existing in the face of erasure and constraint can be reintroduced to "the multiplicity of impersonal flows,"—that is, those channels of movement that, in a political register, may open up new spaces of freedom.[76] The power of the underground railroad is that it never loses its spectral character, even when its shadowy passengers operate in orthodox institutions. It remains a spectral aspect of democracy.[77] We lose power only when we give up tapping into this underground resource, which provides a surplus for those of us with limited access to the protections of legal personhood, citizenship, class status, gender normativity, or racial privilege. The underground railroad *is* the plane in which that impersonal flow manifests itself in African American literature and culture.

In a final example from the archives of the 1927 flood, I find evidence of how such tense talk, whispers, and related underground languages function in a real situation in the Vicksburg, Mississippi, camp where a police officer murders a black flood survivor who refused to join the overworked men unloading cargo boats for free. Camp director William Percy attempts to calm a black mass he fears will revolt. He agrees to attend a church service to discuss the murder and notices the men singing an unknown hymn. He cringes at "verse after verse, from an almost inaudible mutter to a pounding barbaric chant of menace" and claims to "feel their excitement and hate mount to frenzy." Percy says, "I knew there was no chance here to appeal to reason. Retreat was out of the question. Attack was imperative." Making sure to note that he was "unapplauded" when he "mounted the pulpit," Percy's principal goal in the passage that follows is to alter the affective regime of the black congregation.[78] To do this, Percy fabricates a drastic role reversal:

> I look into your faces and see anger and hatred. You think I am the murderer. The murderer should be punished. I will tell you who he is. . . . I have struggled and worried and done without sleep in order to help you Negroes. Every white man in this town has done the same. . . . We served you with our money and our brains and our strength and, for all that we did, not one of us received one penny. . . . Instead we stayed with you and worked for you, day and night. During all this time you did nothing, nothing for yourselves or for us. . . . You were asked to do only one thing . . . to unload the food it was giving you . . . and you refused. Because of your sinful, shameful laziness, because you refused to work in your own behalf unless you were paid, one of your race has been killed. . . . I am not the murderer. . . . That foolish young policeman is not the murderer. The murderer is you! Look into each other's faces and see the shame and fear God has set on them. Down on your knees, murders, and beg your God not to punish you as you deserve.[79]

This scene encapsulates all that is wrong with the racist operation of the camps. It marks the deepest motivations of a full-fledged plan to imprison and create a new labor force; reinstitute overwhelming debts for survivors forced into artificial nuclear family units; and most of all, produce a sense of guilt that means that even innocent victims of murder are already guilty, the murders themselves are innocent, and those who demand justice are actually the murderers.

However, the inner dynamics of the passage suggest a short-circuiting of Percy's plan and that the underground is operating right under Percy's nose. Percy's condemnatory hate speech characterizes all black flood survivors as broadly as possible. Of course his generalities are patently untrue. No, all the white flood survivors have not given all their time and energy to the black flood survivors. The protests from the NAACP and *Chicago*

Defender, even Hoover's own agreement to improve conditions in several of the camps, suggests that some white flood survivors acted fairly and a host of others acted selfishly, assuming their segregated privileges as they would in pre-flood conditions. No, it is simply not believable that Percy would give so much on behalf of the very people who are the target of his bitterness. No, Percy and other whites in the delta did not spend all of their hard-earned money on black folk. Only pages before his racist diatribe, Percy admits to stealing local resources for the camp leadership. Most importantly on this score, for their own selfish profit-motive, the planters misused millions of dollars donated by black and white alike. No, it is not reasonable to claim that people are lazy after they worked for free for weeks, keeping the camps running at the most fundamental levels; indeed, the Red Cross report partially legitimates its efforts by saying the camp work of black laborers foreshadows their preparedness for greater productivity on the farms. No, it is not the role of the black laborers to be lied to on all these fronts simply to assuage Percy's guilt that one of the officers in *his* camp did such an awful thing.

The last observation leads me to the greatest affront in Percy's speech, which most directly links this material to the critical edge of *Thinking Through Crisis*. Percy clearly identifies himself with God in the passage. Walter Benjamin, in his essay on the topic, discusses the inequality that results from mythic violence, a form of guilt that does not stem from breaking law, since laws do not exist yet or have been suspended. This guilt results from physical, emotional, and mental violence that, once fully internalized, compels people to accept the laws that follow. In other words, racial oppression is based on unfair distributions of resources, physical violence, intellectual assaults, *and* an affective regime dominated by guilt. Benjamin identifies this with turning into stone, with petrification. Brother Mann battled this same feeling when he found out Lulu had died. Even if the other progressive changes occur in a political space, racist hegemony will return if the guilt remains. The guilty will fight to restore their oppression as if it is their liberation, because they still believe they deserve their mistreatment. Benjamin uses the Niobe legend in Ovid's *Metamorphosis*, in which gods attack the mortals who refused pay homage, as an example of someone undergoing mythic violence's horrid process. As I read it, in mythic violence the inequality between the mortals and the gods is synonymous with the inequality between the guilty and ruling class. The relentless critique and development of an alternative to this guilt makes up a substantial component of the black radical tradition, going as far back as Phillis Wheatley's poetry, as I have argued elsewhere.[80] Percy's speech, then, is a last-ditch effort to restore that guilt holding this oppressive situation intact.

When the black congregation kneels to pray, Percy believes he has succeeded in convincing them to accept their mistreatment entirely. He has received the privileges of mythic violence for some time, which means instead of living with guilt, he feels a general blamelessness. In those terms, losing blamelessness to another group means receiving guilt and being their new blameworthy target. Percy's slight guilt about the death of an innocent black man indicates his loss of blamelessness and, in his view, means whites will suffer retaliation. Sadly, Percy remains stuck in a Manichaean perspective; he cannot imagine another form of power that does not need mythic violence. This pushes him into a position of either wielding that violence against black people or defending against its viciousness from black people, and nothing more. Hence his illogical claim that the black congregation killed the young man, as if he can redirect their rage so they will kill themselves instead of killing him. The garb of a judging god has fallen, and all we have left is another human hoping the majority will put down their swords and shields by the riverside.

The truth is that they both have and have not put down their swords and shields. Explaining what I mean will clarify how Percy misunderstands the "frenzy" mounting amid the black congregation, despite his supposedly liberal leanings. Percy thinks hate fuels the congregation's frenzy. No black mobs form to attack white people. The force of black collectives shows up in how they disrupt the operation of the camps and defy the expectations of camp personnel. We see this in the aftermath of Percy's prayer, where he admits: "But when I called for volunteers to unload the next boat only four stood up—a friend of mine, a one-armed man, and two preachers who had been slaves on the Percy place and were too old to lift a bucket."[81] While Percy perceives prayer to be a sign of subservience to him and his agenda, the congregation uses prayer to reassert its collective self-determination in the face of his racism, all the while knowing he is misreading the situation. Before, during, and after the murder, black flood survivors continue to strike, to disarm corrupt guardsmen, to sneak in and out of camps to see family and friends in other areas of the delta, and to escape the delta altogether for the North. They need not kill Percy, because this would only reinforce the camp's power.

This is not the scene of hatred and retaliation Percy feared it would be, based on his own guilt and hatred. When he recounts this scene, he unknowingly provides one of black life prioritizing love and care of the collective self over retaliation or soothing his guilt. The frenzy set the stage for devising strategies for surviving inside the camps, living with loved ones and allies in the surrounding area of the camps, and even escaping to the North. Eighty percent of the African American population in the delta left during the 1927 flood and never returned. Percy and other planters say that to "depopulate the delta of its labor" will be a "grave disservice" to their business agendas.[82] In the face of such powerful resistance, a great deal of their plans fall apart. In a way, these lines of flight turned out to be black folks' greatest weapon, the sword helping them cut new paths and the shield protecting the group from harm.

THE EVENT OF BLACK COMMUNITY

I have also turned to this murder of an actual flood survivor and its impact on other relief camp inhabitants as a way rethinking the death of Brother Mann, who runs from the camp guards, saying, "I'll die before they kill me" and gets shot in the leg and back. I veer from Cheryl Higashida's conclusion that "Mann articulates the will to die, but Wright's masculinist naturalism prevents him from capturing the will to live."[83] Abdul R. JanMohamed takes a different path, which I follow with a variation. JanMohamed argues that Brother Mann's decision to die before he gets killed undoes the bondage coming from the fear of death. "Social-death as a mode of 'life' is made possible only by the fact that it harbors at its center the threat of actual-death," he observes. "If, however, the slave can overcome the fear of actual-death, if he is willing to subjectify the possibility of actual-death . . . it can no longer be used as a mode of coercion."[84] Note that JanMohamed's comments focus on the place of actual death within the extremely limited form of life called "social-death." What if one characteristic of the Event, in the African diasporic critique of violence I am developing, is the renunciation of the fear of actual death that gives social-death its might? What if the renunciation of fear is "essential to the creation and proliferation of life and thought"?[85]

Perhaps the murder of the camp dweller in Vicksburg, Mississippi, and of Brother Mann in "Down by the Riverside" signals protest from a different form of life based on assertion rather than capitulation. That is to say, yes, they both died, but social-death says that they are already harboring decay, that they are already dead, that their death is of no consequence, and that it has no greater impact than their final exhalation joining the breeze. Beyond social-death's framework, their choices to die in defiance of their captors bespeaks a form of life that persists despite the death of particular individuals—this is one way of taking seriously the image of Brother's Mann's hand gliding in the Mississippi River's currents, endlessly flowing. Instead of death being a sovereign that controls them, death is a passage, an event that can intensify the power of those still living. The decision to "die" rather than "be killed" convinces others to relinquish the fear of actual death as well. Perhaps the unknown hymn in the church is the performative renunciation of fear. William Percy, with his mind fixed on making black life docile and disposable, can only misread the gathering's objection to the reign of social-death over their lives as the rise of barbarians. Instead, the frenzy conjures an unrest moving against and away from the camp's terms of belonging.

By ending with the event of Mann's death and him lying down by the riverside, Wright reminds his reader that such a backwater space can be the site of either revolution or continuing exploitation. The same point can be made for those who did not survive Hurricane Katrina. Any social change that does not include this region is unworthy of the name, insofar as the region anchors forms of exploitation spanning the globe. Finally, the 1927 flood was a rude awakening for black intellectuals to the challenges they would soon face with the onset of the "first" Great Depression hitting black labor harder and sooner than anyone else. I see Hurricane Katrina as presenting a similar challenge to black intellectuals today. How are we going to activate the "tense talk and whispers" of black labor in a "second Great Depression" that still afflicts black communities in a time of forestalled, one-sided relief? Ida B. Wells's letter to the *Chicago Defender* on July 30, 1927, opens a path for turning these muffled protests into ideas that manifest themselves in practical action. In this letter, Wells claims that African Americans congratulate her for exposing the problems with the relief camps but reports that when asked if they, too, made resolutions and protests, they "invariably say no." Thus, she concludes, "the only way to bring public opinion to action is for those whose race is suffering to *cry aloud*, and keep on *crying aloud* until something is done."[86] Wells joins Wright in mounting a critique of reactive forces that hopes to galvanize those who might see themselves as leaders and activists. Her mandate to "keep on crying aloud" echoes Wright's own call for "the pitiless glare of a criticism whose frame of reference is historical, political, and economic, as well as aesthetic" coupled with an affirmative concept of reconstruction: "Negro writers should never feel . . . their goal has been reached; always ahead should be the sense of . . . problems to be framed, pondered, and solved; always in them should reside the sense of becoming."[87]

NOTEBOOK 2

"CRUSADE FOR JUSTICE"

Ida B. Wells and the Power of the Multitude

Nothing is more definitely settled than he must act for himself. I have shown how he may employ the boycott, emigration, and the press, and I feel that by a combination of all these agencies can be effectually stamped out lynch law, that last relic of barbarism and slavery. "*The gods help those who help themselves.*"

—IDA B. WELLS, *SOUTHERN HORRORS: LYNCH-LAW IN ALL ITS PHASES*

If the multitude therefore do institute, the multitude may abrogate; and they themselves . . . can only be fit judges of the performance of the ends of the institution. Our author may perhaps say, the publick peace may be hereby disturbed; but he ought to know, *there can be no peace, where there is no justice*; nor any justice, if the government instituted for the good of a nation be turned to its ruin. . . . All *defense terminates in force*; and if a private man does not prepare to defend his estate with his own force, 'tis because he lives under the protection of the law, and expects the force of the magistrate should be a security to him. . . . *God helps those who helps themselves. . . . But such as neglect the means of their own preservation, are ever left to perish with shame.*

—ALGERNON SIDNEY, *DISCOURSES CONCERNING GOVERNMENT*

In *Thinking Through Crisis*'s Introduction, I locate the motifs for understanding the black dark proletariat's shift from actual being to historical being. In the first notebook, I examine a political reality based on movement working simultaneously on the level of individual and collective labor. This notebook begins an interrogation of what Cedric Robinson calls the "preservation of the ontological totality."[1] This effort will continue through the rest of *Thinking Through Crisis*. In this notebook, that interrogation starts with an examination of the concept of the multitude in relation to state power, followed by extensive remarks on the violence splitting the multitude racially between its major and minor expressions of temporality, which have quite different relationships to abolition. The notebook concludes with an exploration of the ontological totality, in which the multitude organizes its political might by claiming "blackness" as a sign of humanity in a "minor" key, which unsettles the majority/minority distinction in identity so those who are excluded from mainstream politics can foster alternative forms of power. The notebooks on W. E. B. Du Bois's *Black Reconstruction*; Zora Neale Hurston's *Moses, Man of the Mountain*; and Langston Hughes's 1930s poetry and journalism will elaborate on this notebook's initial effort.

Ida B. Wells's *Crusade for Justice: The Autobiography of Ida B. Wells* (1970) and her earlier speeches and pamphlets set the stage for this effort. Wells wrote *Crusade* from 1928 until her death in 1931 in order to record the black radical activity of black folk from the 1890s until the 1920s. She warned black civic organizations against adopting Booker T. Washington's conservatism as a method of surviving the Great Depression's devastation of black communities, especially in regard to increasing racial violence.[2] The turn to *Crusade* may surprise readers aware that since the 1980s, several scholars have characterized Wells as a "lonely warrior" and a "maverick whose beliefs and actions are hard to definitively link to those of very many people" seeing that she "ends up [at] odds with her collaborators."[3] But there are important insights in *Crusade* regarding the limits of black charismatic leadership, the history of skirmishes within black middle-class civic organizations, and the false boundaries set on women's activism through gender norms. At times Wells suffered under and also upheld these norms.

Nevertheless, the radicalism in Wells's writing and activism constantly upset black liberal and conservative organizations. Her writings hint at

collective subjectivities that the liberal position tends to ostracize, condescend toward, or suppress, as Joy James, Paula Giddings, Mia Bay, and other
Wells scholars so eloquently demonstrate. By calling on Wells's subtle
quotation of Algernon Sidney, by turning to her as a first step to think of
Cedric Robinson's formulation, and by using *Crusade* to identify a theme
traversing all her major writings, this notebook identifies that subterranean
intellectual project: a multigenre writing effort drawing on pamphleteering, editing, journalism, and oratory to comprehend the relationship between
blackness and the radical potential of the multitude.

A line from Wells's first pamphlet, *Southern Horrors*, inspires this uncommon path for exploring a minor theme: "The gods help those who help
themselves."[4] Wells quotes this phrase but provides no citation. Tracing
the phrase's history grants more weight to framing her intellectual project
in this manner. Some think it is a phrase from Benjamin Franklin. He is
merely the most famous American to utter it. It appears in Ovid's *Metamorphoses* but is more literally translated as "divinity loves the daring" in
the Latin original.[5] Ancient sources abound with similar phrases, including Aesop's fable "Hercules and the Waggoner," in which a wagoner prays
to Hercules for help to pull a wagon out of a ditch. Hercules replies, "Tut,
man . . . Get up and put your shoulder to the wheel. The gods help them
that help themselves."[6] This fable shares the exact phrasing of the line from
Southern Horrors but completely misses Wells's political occasion. The first
translation of this proverb into Anglophone political thought, Sidney's
posthumously published *Discourses on Government* (1698), serves as this
notebook's second epigraph and most effectively orients readers to Wells's
intellectual project.

Sidney made such a political impact that when the British monarchy
charged him with treason, they counted *Discourses* as a living witness
against him. When Sidney played coy, calling *Discourses* a modest consideration of various hypotheses, the prosecutors replied curtly, "To write is
to act!"[7] Sidney's execution made him a martyr for antityranny causes across
the Atlantic. His *Discourses* informed the American Revolution, with pam-
phleteers using his name as a pseudonym and several founders citing him
in their speeches and correspondence. Decades later, American abolitionists like Charles Sumner and William Lloyd Garrison cited Sidney in their
speeches as well. Therefore, Wells is not simply applying Sidney's thought
wholesale. This notebook's two epigraphs indicate that Wells ingeniously

adapts this North Atlantic debate over the multitude and state power for the post-Reconstruction context. In Wells's case, this debate has everything to do with two temporalities: one temporality suspends the revolutionary time of abolition in America; and another temporality aims to restore and sustain the time of abolition. In either case, the multitude's complexities are crucial to decisive action.

The concept achieved prominence among Roman historians blaming the empire's woes on the population's fickle nature. Most early modern philosophers—with several notable exceptions, like Sidney and Baruch Spinoza—took a similar position and argued that the state must cultivate "the people" out of the multitude to stabilize governmental power. The concept regained popularity in the 1990s as political philosophers like Antonio Negri returned to the early modern moment. They studied the multitude's radical potentialities, because the "working class," as concept and historical force, no longer served as a clear protagonist in modernity's radical struggles. Many thinkers have noted that the working class has become a great defender of the status quo because they will not relinquish the privileges that racial capitalism bestows on them. By returning to early modern considerations of the multitude, these thinkers stumbled on the period contemporaneous with black diasporic antiracist, anti-capitalist activity across the Atlantic basin that Robinson conceptualizes as the "ontological totality."

A fruitful engagement with the multitude and the ontological totality will keep in mind that both concepts grapple with the incompleteness inherent in the Western paradigm of the political. As Sidney himself says, "If the multitude therefore do institute, the multitude may abrogate," which means the multitude marks the political's basis and limit.[8] Robinson frames this as a dialectic between political and antipolitical modes of belonging, activity, and thought in modernity. The political mode finds its telos in the "positivity of the State." At best, in the European tradition this antipolitical approach has earned the name "anarchism." More often than not, however, this approach gets "translated" into "ethical theory, theology and philosophy, that is, into other forms of idealism."[9] However, the multitude and the ontological totality can never be completely translated into these forms of idealism, even for the benefit of radical projects. Nor will these concepts allow liberal commentators to simplify historical conflicts between "the individual and the state" or "the people and the state"—divisions so abstract that they obfuscate the conflicts, actors, and conditions repeatedly constituting the political. Robinson says "the people" is "a manipulative myth"; initially referring to "the rule of the mob and of the rabble," it then "suggests a sameness, boundedness, citizenry, continuity, territorial and proximal identifications, which are never fully empirical."[10]

To borrow from Warren Montag's considerations of the multitude, liberal interpretations are "haunted by figures of the inassimilable, the exceptions to the democracy without exceptions, and simultaneously by the impossibility of their exclusion." The multitude is "the abyss upon which every state is constructed," "an internal, insurmountable principle of negativity that condemns even the most stable and well-ordered government to eventual ruin."[11] Thus, the government and the multitude never coincide to form a general will. A gap between the state and the multitude always exists, and one can assess the character of a nation-state by how it characterizes, manipulates, or gets overtaken by this gap over time. In Wells's view, the state manipulates this gap to prolong its existence by turning the multitude against itself. By identifying an internal enemy within the nation, the state can wield some members of the multitude against others. In Wells's time, the state accomplishes this by leveraging racial resentment within state institutions and American civil society against Emancipation and the freedpersons who accomplished it, although Emancipation led to rights and protections the white majority and American corporations would enjoy for decades, if not more than a century.[12]

This pattern of compromises means black workers cannot depend on the state to protect their interests. They must depend on their own collective power to survive a politics of abandonment applied during ordinary and extraordinary circumstances, including economic depressions. Sidney makes a similar point by warning against "a private man," explaining that if he "does not prepare to defend his estate with his own force, 'tis because he lives under the protection of the law, and expects the force of the magistrate should be a security to him." As shown in the epigraph, Sidney asserts that "all *defense terminates in force*," saying that "God helps those who helps themselves" and those who fail to enact this principle and "neglect the means of their own preservation, are ever left to perish with shame."[13] Wells reasserts this principle from the publication of *Southern Horrors* to her final years writing *Crusade*. She turns "God" to "the gods" to signal the classical background of the reference and to reassert its emphasis on natural right, such that even the least privileged in a political circumstance can amass power to overthrow corrupt institutions. The relative prosperity of black entrepreneurs and townships from the 1890s to the 1920s and some limited government attempts to aid black people's economic distress in the 1930s do not overturn a powerful thesis. America's racialized distribution and withholding of resources supports Wells's sense that from the Long Depression of the 1870s–1890s, which led to the dismantling of the Freedmen's Bureau, up to the first wails of the Great Depression of the 1930s, which skipped another opportunity to strengthen a multiracial working class, the United States had imposed a politics of abandonment on several generations of black workers. Ignoring this is absurd, even embarrassing: "The more the Afro-American yields and cringes and begs, the more he has to do so, the more he is insulted, outraged and lynched." Therefore, when Wells says "every Afro-American" should remember that "a Winchester rifle should have a place of honor in every black home, and it should be used for that protection which the law refuses to give," she is asserting that black culture cannot sustain itself by bowing to the state as the final institutional expression of reason, redemption, or security.[14]

By the time Wells writes *Crusade*, she fears that this principle is forgotten. She stages this in the preface with the story of her encounter with a young woman who knew of Wells's reputation but not what she opposed or fought for. In *Crusade*, Wells goes beyond recounting her exciting life story with its many skirmishes between leaders and organizations. Regarding the theme of the multitude, readers find Wells at the vanishing point, where the spectacle of black leadership recedes in order to foreground subaltern activity, so those who look back will know that black life must organize itself, because the state will not consistently sustain black life and because the state does not deserve the validation it wants from those it fails to protect.[15]

This notebook begins by discussing how *parrhesia*—which can be translated as fearless speech, free speech, or truth-telling—allows Wells to shift perspectives from individual "exile" to collective "exodus." Reading *Crusade* and *Southern Horrors* together will reveal the significance of this perspectival shift, which begins her investigation of the multitude. The rest of the notebook holds onto Wells's performances of free speech amid national efforts to end abolition. To understand the main techniques that Wells saw forestalling abolition, this notebook turns to *The Reason Why the Colored American Is Not Part of the World's Columbian Exposition of 1893* (1893). *Crusade* critiques black Chicago politics in terms of the limits of black middle-class organizing, and *The Reason Why* can be read fruitfully within that frame because it tries to summarize the main forms of antiblack racial violence that Wells analyzes in her several other pamphlets. In addition to *Southern Horrors*, she wrote *A Red Record* (1895), *Mob Rule in New Orleans* (1900), *The Arkansas Race Riot* (1917), and *The East St. Louis Massacre* (1917). This notebook will reference all of these pamphlets within *The Reason Why*'s overview of racial violence. The most important character to this mode is "the beautiful soul" (a figure adapted from Hegel), whose resentment of Emancipation compels the formation of a cultural, political, and economic bloc called "the Solid South." That bloc enacts its resentment through "the twin infamies,"—namely, lynching and convict leasing—to forestall abolition's world-altering effects.

The notebook closes with a commentary on the second temporality that seeks to sustain the project of abolition with a discussion of the ontological totality, where the multitude operates under the sign of "blackness" to abolish oppressive political and economic structures. The first temporality stalls abolition for the sake of "progress" (a measure of success that validates state projects), and this second temporality is often pressured to do so. Wells herself uses this terminology in *The Reason Why*. But this notebook will call "progress" into question. The second temporality returns to the time of abolition for the sake of "becoming," which abides by different terms of change and wealth that are not so easily appropriated by the state. This process will receive brief attention by turning to an incident Wells mentions in *The Reason Why* but fails to discuss: the Coal Creek rebellion. As stated earlier, the rest of *Thinking Through Crisis* will elaborate on this final section's initial considerations.

Methodologically, because the multitude is a concept designating a population that, by definition, upsets conceptual parameters, this notebook must operate in several theoretical registers at once. Therefore, this notebook continues to focus on laborers outside the conventional working class. But this notebook, much more than the first, carries out a heterodox engagement with "race and psychoanalysis." Du Bois calls the Civil War's immediate aftermath "fatal" due to the "*attitude of men's minds rather than because of material loss and disorganization.*" He says that "*the human mind, its will and emotions, congealed to one set pattern,*" compounded the strife when reconciliation should have taken shape. That strife shows up in the *cruelty* enabled by mythic violence—gratuitous, irredeemable violence that cannot be reduced to individual instances of horror but is necessarily politicized because it is propped up by the very political order it puts at risk. Cruelty identifies the libidinal economy at the heart of mythic violence.[16] As Jacques Derrida says, "No other discourse" than psychoanalysis, "be it theological, metaphysical, genetic, physicalist, cognitivist, and so forth—could open itself up to" such excess violence without minimizing its complexities at the outset.[17] Wells and her compatriots did not have this luxury. This notebook hopes to learn from their life and death struggle after emancipation.

FROM EXILE TO EXODUS

Free speech turns isolated, individual pleas for recognition into a collective demand against the institutions that wound and kill in their mundane operation. With this shift from individual to collective declaration, a new perspective opens for future collaborative action that cannot be reduced to working class vanguardism. Wells's early journalism, speeches, and pamphleteering against lynching demonstrate this difference. But the difference becomes clearest when *Crusade* provides the frame. When Foucault discusses parrhesia, which he translates as "free speech" or "fearless speech," he discusses the relationship to truth implied in the activity. For Foucault, the truth-teller's most important relationship is to oneself: one speaks the truth so as not to betray one's principles. Who hears the truth-telling also matters. Parrhesia occurs only when one tells the truth at the risk of persecution by a powerful audience. In Foucault's lectures, the truth-teller puts their reputation as a Greek citizen on the line. The citizen always has the option to not take on the activity of truth-telling—to remain silent to protect their privileges. Foucault's lectures cannot account for a *parrhesiastes* (a truth-teller) who infuriates the audience simply by having citizenship, who commits a capital crime by exercising citizenship rights, who knows taking an individual stand will change nothing. In other words, Wells's work with the *Memphis Free Speech*, the newspaper she coedited and co-owned with Reverend Taylor Nightingale and J. L. Fleming, quite literally offers a more sophisticated conceptualization and performance of parrhesia than Foucault's by operating in a more complicated political environment, where one's political standing causes violent disavowals but a powerfully organized region of that multitude demands that these disavowals get acknowledged and their repercussions be redressed.

Readers of *Crusade* know that "The Lynching at the Curve" marks the geographical location where lynchers murdered Thomas Moss, Calvin McDowell, and Henry Stewart, the owners of the People's Grocery Company, for outperforming nearby white grocers. Hearing of this horrific murder of her three friends and then hearing the police call the People's Grocery a "resort of thieves and thugs," changed Wells's life. White storeowners sent vandals to damage the store and intimidate patrons; Moss, McDowell, and Stewart rebuffed them soundly, which gave police an excuse to arrest the store owners for attacking white residents; lynchers then kidnapped Moss, McDowell, and Stewart from the jail and murdered them. Wells's new pursuit of justice for her murdered friends leads to a detailed account of historical conditions. Precisely because they were lynched in "one of the leading cities of the South" and "committed no crime against white women," Wells found a new reason for lynching: "An excuse to get rid of Negroes who were acquiring wealth and property and thus keep the race terrorized and 'keep the nigger down.'"[18] Wells's recollections in *Crusade* add a more personal dimension to her doubts in *Southern Horrors* that any reconciliation is occurring after the Civil War:

> From this exposition of the race issue in lynch law, the whole matter is explained by the well-known opposition growing out of slavery to the progress of the race. This is crystallized in the oft-repeated slogan: "This is the white man's country and the white man must rule." The South resented giving the Afro-American his freedom, the ballot box and the Civil Rights law. The raids of the Ku-Klux and White liners to subvert reconstruction government, the Hamburg and Ellerton, S.C., the Copiah County, Miss., and the Lafayette Parish, La., massacres were excused as the natural resentment of intelligence against government by ignorance.[19]

Wells's straightforward prose may rush readers past important insights. Her comments from *Crusade* and *Southern Horrors*, when read together, express the move from personal trauma to general antagonism, revealing the site where the multitude turns against its own power.

Wells condemns the South entirely and takes free speech into a resentful environment that reads any African American political expression as tyrannous. The beautiful soul epitomizes resentment in Hegel's *Phenomenology*. Hegel originally used this figure to critique German intellectuals' condescension toward the French Revolution. Hegel lambasted them for placing themselves above the political fray, for suggesting that Germany's intellectual renaissance meant the nation did not need revolution, and ultimately, for using all that as a screen for being unable to imagine and lead the revolution that Germany needed.[20] Taking that figure out of its original context and placing it in the context of post–Civil War America brings the racial implications of the beautiful soul to the fore. This unusual turn to Hegel may break with the knee-jerk use of the master-slave dialectic, when the true issue is how white Americans grapple with a political change that undermines the very possibility of having "masters" and "slaves" in the first place.

By the beautiful soul's logic, the black must be completely subjugated and compliant with the intellectual, affective, economic, political, and sexual desires of the white forever; it is by nature an asymmetrical relationship, and "equality" exists only if this asymmetry continues. For the beautiful soul, the inability to oppress others *is* oppression, since it has convinced itself that it is destined to rule all mankind. As Etienne Balibar puts it, whiteness becomes a "collective fetish,"

> an identity (national, religious, or racial) that is at once completely idealized and absolutely reified.... If one may hazard a tautology ... it is an *identity identical to itself* that, the subject is convinced, exists in him in exclusive fashion, or that he "possesses" while simultaneously representing the human as such through it.... Hence, its presence rules out all otherness, commanding its own realization ... by way of elimination of every trace of otherness and thus all "internal multiplicity." ... An identity of that sort as well, and, of course, the subject subjected to it, are in precisely the sort of position in which one's own death is preferable to any mixing, intercourse, or hybridization, the threat of which is perceived at the fantasy level as worse than death.[21]

Wells's epiphany about the cause of lynching, first expressed in *Southern Horrors*, then further developed in her other pamphlets and *Crusade*, reveals an aporia regarding the US polity's treatment of its black population. Those who wished to quiet Wells—but did not necessarily care to stop lynching—called the violence isolated incidents in which a handful of uncultivated, poor rural white men killed a black person, usually for attempting or carrying out some criminal act against white women. Precisely because of the negrophobogenesis discussed in the first notebook, one must take seriously the lynching response, at one and the same time, to black activity and nonactivity. Being black counts as a crime in itself, worthy of violent punishment. The violence responds to the fear that blackness is maleficent *and* to the fear that it is not so, but something else entirely beyond forms of life delimited by the West. When subjects glued to such a fantasy witness Emancipation, no matter what material gains accompany it, they feel they have suffered an end of the world all the more devastating because the objective world continues. Their black other becoming increasingly closer to their social and political status only deepens their nightmare, their anger, their fury. This fantasy structure dictates to its subjects how to draw the line between public and private, which means it cannot be limited to the private realm and separated from political matters. This fantasy structure inculcates a sense of omnipotence and fear of reprisal. In the post-Reconstruction era, this leads to white-on-black violence because the black is both the object upon which this omnipotence expresses itself and the threat to be neutralized. But this fear speaks to a vulnerability that cannot be done away with, and so the black worker is killed for its proximity to the white in all things social, economic, cultural, and political, as Wells suggests by mentioning the massacres in Hamburg, Ellerton, Copiah County, and Lafayette during Reconstruction.

Consider the situation Wells confronts: being enslaved means acquiescing to a life that goes unlived, since one remains ever in the hands of another; seizing freedom means risking one's life to live, since the one who has held you suffers a loss in the process; and participating in the rights that come with said freedom counts as tyranny to the one who offers you only different ways of dying. One need not simply refute this situation. Rather, it provides another detail to Emancipation's power. Despite significant shortcomings to its legal formulation and implementation, Emancipation ulcerates the world-making process that requires the very identities of "master" and "slave." Emancipation signals the decadence unraveling the sovereign world of slavery from within. Emancipation also signals an alternative world-making process already underway. No wonder that Wells identifies resentment as the primary affect animating Jim Crow life. Hence this notebook's suggestion that the beautiful soul—the master bankrupted by Civil War, living off credit and old prestige; the Southern Belle who watched her inheritance walk off the plantation as she received her father's body in a coffin; or the poor white worker who can no longer depend on plantation owners paying his taxes through the revenue of slave labor—is a more appropriate analogue because it registers the nagging effort to stall black progress at every turn.

By narrating the function and fate of the *Memphis Free Speech* newspaper in *Southern Horrors* and *Crusade*, Wells offers more insight into her claim, echoing Sidney, that "the gods help those who help themselves." Rights gained through collective struggle cannot be maintained by individual accomplishment. They must be sustained with the same collective verve that enacts them. As a corollary, the less one can depend on one's rights, the more one must turn to concerted action. Thus, Wells's writings surpass Foucault's theorization, because she ponders the power attained from a group acknowledging, repeating, and acting on a truth that entails risk before a number of vicious foes. The *Memphis Free Speech* played an indispensable intellectual and political role for numerous African Americans in the Deep South. Wells was personally responsible for increasing the newspaper's subscribers. Solidarity grew so strong that, at one point, the *Free Speech* decided to use pink publishing paper so that illiterate African Americans could find and purchase it. This means the newspaper served as an institution and symbol for black culture that crossed class lines. In *Southern Horrors*, Wells speaks of the movement to which these lynching deaths contributed and the impact this has on the *Free Speech*:

> Although the race was wild over the outrage [the lynching], the mockery of law and justice which disarmed men and locked them up in jails where they could be easily and safely reached by the mob—the Afro-American ministers, newspapers and leaders counseled obedience to the law which did not protect them.
>
> Their counsel was heeded and not a hand was uplifted to resent the outrage; following the advice of the *Free Speech,* people left the city in great numbers.[22]

Crusade provides additional information on this episode. One newspaper report, most likely from a member of the lynch mob, says that before being killed, Moss gave a final statement: "Tell my people to go West—there is no justice for them here."[23]

Moss's message recalls the finale in "Down by the Riverside," where one person's bold confrontation with actual death helps unchain others from the fear of social-death. Unless this fear is overcome, group apathy will obstruct defenses against vigilantism and state violence. Moss's courage before his murderers emboldened black Memphis. Even entrepreneurial respectability would not assuage the mob's weekly hungers. But his message had such a powerful effect because the *Free Speech* amplified his charge: "There is nothing we can do about the lynching now, as we are out-numbered and without arms. . . . There is therefore only one thing left that we can do; save our money and leave a town which will neither protect our lives and property, nor give us a fair trial in the courts, but takes us out and murders us in cold blood."[24] Wells's narrative helps distinguish exile from exodus. With exile, isolation means each single voice can do little to change the conditions perpetuating injustice. Exodus, on the other hand, involves a deliberate abandonment of an unjust situation. Exile and exodus both involve risk. But an exodus of people and their resources more effectively destabilizes the unjust situation being left behind. "To Northern capital and Afro-American labor the South owes its rehabilitation [after the Civil War]. If labor is withdrawn capital will not remain," Wells says. "A thorough knowledge and judicious exercise of this power in lynching localities could many times *effect a bloodless revolution*."[25] Wells imagines that this strategy could shut down the New South if applied broadly to stop lynching and related forms of oppression.

The exodus transforms its participants as well. Speaking strictly of Wells's exile, which happens about ten weeks into the exodus from Memphis, leaves one with Foucault's rendering of an individual parrhesiastes from his exploratory lectures. But speaking in terms of exodus, Wells's newspaper, the *Free Speech*, surpasses and rewrites Foucault's insights on a larger scale. The *Free Speech* illustrates how a group of people would be true to themselves, at the risk of injury or death, rather than capitulate to a political order grounded in hatred. At one point, some of those leaving Memphis were "hemmed in" by the Arkansas River. So black churches in Memphis collected four hundred dollars "the following Sunday . . . They were instructed to use this money in paying railroad fare over the high-water zone, *so the people would have no excuse to come back to Memphis in case any were sighing for the fleshpots of Egypt*."[26] With the biblical reference to the "fleshpots of Egypt," Wells teaches that the exodus, to be worthy of the name, must embody a principled difference from Memphis's mainstream. Said differently, Wells does not imagine the participants using the exodus as another avenue into fitting current norms. Assimilation, integration, or other forms of reconciliation yield no progress, because they would wed the exodus to the very resentment that must be excised from the multitude.

The exodus's consistent opposition confounds the beautiful soul all the more. The beautiful soul of the New South not only expects to attack, exploit, or deprive the black at will; it expects the black to stay and endure this without being explicitly told to do so. Indeed, this expectation reflects the beautiful soul's need to reshape the entire world to affirm its view of things, no matter how mistaken its view may be. The beautiful soul could only consider the exodus as a final straw. By this logic, if those departing cannot be punished, then certainly those who led the departure can be. The newspaper's role in Memphis's black exodus explains why the mob destroyed it:

> The mob-spirit was not to be satisfied until the paper which was doing all it could to counteract this impression was silenced. . . . The mob would have lynched the manager of the *Free Speech* for exercising the right of free speech if they had found him as quickly as they would have hung a rapist, and glad of the excuse to do so. The owners were ordered not to return, the *Free Speech* was suspended with as little compunction as the business of the "People's Grocery" broken up and the proprietors murdered.[27]

More will be said about how destroying the *Free Speech* fits into the logic of lynching. For now, it is notable that this event indexes exile and exodus. Destroying the *Free Speech* deals a dreadful professional blow to Wells and the paper's other owners, who leave journalism altogether. Others have rightly argued that destroying the *Free Speech* inadvertently launched her international career as a journalist and anti-lynching activist. In keeping with this notebook's theme, it is more fitting to argue that the mob's destruction of the *Free Speech* convinced her of the significance of the multitude that speaks truth to itself and to the state, since no single class of black workers has the combination of social recognition, legal rights, and economic power that leftist narratives associate with the European working class. Wells's pamphleteering and other writings theorize black culture's persistence in the face of the beautiful soul's paroxysms. In *The Reason Why*, Wells employs the World's Columbian Exposition of 1893 as a test case for the logical, political, and cultural endpoint of a multitude whose power gets channeled through racist resentment, disavowals, and enjoyment. Precisely because this resentment takes such a complicated, contradictory, but still coordinated form throughout the South, Wells's call to black self-organization takes on greater significance in this notebook and in the rest of *Thinking Through Crisis*.

THE BLACK PRESENCE IN THE WHITE CITY;
OR, BANQUO'S GHOST AT THE BANQUET

> The race problem or the negro question ... has been omnipresent and all-pervading since long before the Afro American was raised from the degradation of the slave to the dignity of the citizen. It has never been settled because the right methods have not been employed. . . . *It is the Banquo's ghost of politics, religion, and sociology which will not down at the bidding of those who are tormented with its ubiquitous appearance on every occasion.*
>
> Ida B. Wells, "Lynch Law in All Its Phases"

> For mine own good,
> All causes shall give way: I am in blood
> Stepp'd in so far that, should I wade no more,
> Returning were as tedious as go o'er
>
> . . . .
>
> "Come, we'll to sleep. My strange and self-abuse
> Is the initiate fear that wants hard use:
> We are yet but young in deed.
>
> Shakespeare, *Macbeth*

The exodus does not simply differentiate between the moral principles of the black community and the rest of Memphis. It hints at different forms of collective organization. Precisely because the violence dominating Memphis in this period frames the situation as white versus black, it is tempting to think that the black participants in the exodus are equally as interested in racial exclusion as the citizens of Memphis. To the contrary, the exodus is worthy of the name because it primarily maintains a heterogeneity that Memphis government and civil society hopes to hide or consume in the interests of maintaining purity. To think through this issue in more detail, readers must shift from Memphis to Chicago at the World's Columbian Exposition of 1893. In *Crusade*, Wells makes sure to reiterate her claim that "the gods help those who help themselves" when she discusses Chicago politics. She does so by quoting British investigative journalist W. T. Snead's "talk" at Bethel A.M.E. Church during his three months in Chicago after he attended the 1893 World's Fair:

> I have been visited by several groups of your people—all of whom . . . appealed to me to denounce these outrages to the world. I have asked each delegation, "What are you doing to help yourselves." Each group gave the answer, namely, that they are so divided . . . that they have not united their forces to fight the common enemy. At last I got mad and said, "You people have not been lynched enough! . . . You say you are only ten millions in this country, with ten times that number against you—all of whom you say are solidly united by race prejudice against your progress. *All of you by your own confession stand as individual units striving against a united band to fight or hold your own.* A ten year old child knows that a dozen persons fighting as one can make better headway against ten times its number than if each were fighting singlehanded and alone.[28]

Wells felt that Snead's comments confirmed her approach to calling out the "outrages" of antiblack racism in *The Reason Why the Colored American Is Not in the World's Columbian Exposition*, a collaborative project Wells edited and passed out to fairgoers near the fair's Haitian Pavilion. The majority of this notebook will focus on the style of organizing that white supremacists took up; the violence inherent to it (as Snead's interlocutors mentioned); and how the 1893 World's Fair came to symbolize this vast regional, national, and imperial project. The closing of this notebook and subsequent notebooks of *Thinking Through Crisis* will examine the complexities of organizing in black culture that prize difference.

The 1893 World's Fair provides an occasion to understand how the white supremacists in Memphis, Chicago, and beyond organized to craft a world. Wells's analysis of American race relations presupposes that "the historical world is what humans make, and that capacity is absolutely universal in the species."[29] The multitude's world-making capacity takes different forms based on its relation to the practice of truth-telling. That relation is necessarily overdetermined by racial and class fantasies that collide in the subject's pursuit of power. That subject is individual and collective, as Lindon Barrett says: "No individual posture is ever entirely about fantasy and, equally, no fantasy is ever simply about an individual posture. Fantasy is never individual but always *at some* level group fantasy," such that individuation only occurs through "terms" that find "systematicity" in "group affiliation."[30] Since desire is often *productive*, parsing out how worlds are fashioned reveals the group fantasies permeating those productive processes. This approach counters psychologisms ignoring constructive activity and privileging intentions over effects. Thus, fantasy proves central to Wells's study of the multitude in ways that her journalistic rhetoric understates.

Wells could not have chosen a more compelling event than the 1893 World's Fair to understand how racialization, class conflict, fantasy, and political power interact to support white supremacy. Commentators gave the exposition fairgrounds the official nickname "the White City" for the white plaster composite used to erect grand buildings and monumental statues. For Wells, Frederick Douglass, Ferdinand Barnett, and her pamphlet's other contributors, this nickname inadvertently admits to the board of directors' racialized vision. The directors would have attendees believe that the 1893 World's Fair opened a bourgeois metropolitan space motored by efficient technology, a fairly compensated labor supply, and a harmonious civil society. The marvels produced would place the United States at the vanguard of modern countries; indeed, it would prophesy US imperial power in the new century, as the counterrevolution of property enabled US economic interests to link to Europe's imperial exploits across the world. But the beautiful soul's thumbprints left smudges all over the White City's plans. The design, implementation, and marketing of the event depended on Jim Crow's resentment. As Wells says, "The whole history of the exposition is a record of discrimination against the colored people," initiated by President Harrison, who selected "more than two hundred and eight national commissioners" but not a "single representative of seven and one half millions of colored people, more than one-eighth of the entire population of the United States."[31] Wells brilliantly links the idealized subjects of the 1893 World's Fair to "class legislation,"—that is, how a select arrangement of racial and class interests dominates US culture, economics, law, and politics. The White City, then, should be the beautiful soul's crowning symbolic achievement for imagining a Jim Crow space.

Wells and one of her collaborators on *The Reason Why*, Frederick Douglass, offer the most radical analysis of the violence that makes this achievement possible. Even before the White City opened its doors to the public,

Wells had already critiqued its triumphalism with a compelling allusion. In one of her speeches, she compares "the race problem" to Banquo's ghost disrupting Macbeth's celebration after attaining hegemony. In Wells's day, the 1893 World's Fair approximates this Shakespearean scene. Just as the beautiful soul raises its glass to toast the White City, so enters the race question. Like Macbeth hallucinating at the feast, the beautiful soul realizes the past bloodshed required to achieve this purity and knows more will be required in the future. Post-Reconstruction era reactionaries are "young in deed," Wells realizes, and the twin infamies of lynching and prisons are the primary way these bloody deeds will endure into the twentieth century, at least. They are hidden but essential pillars of the White City, as Wells and Douglass persuasively argue in *The Reason Why*. But first, I provide an analysis of how the White City's layout corresponds to Jim Crow dreams at home and imperial visions abroad.

A number of commentators identified the construction of the White City with group fantasy, even if they did not admit that fantasy's racist and classist overtones. In *Harper's Chicago and the World's Fair* (1893), Julian Ralph says, "One cannot be among them [the fair's buildings and sculptures] . . . without feeling that one is upon novel ground . . . and that the entire work is like a *materialized dream*."[32] He calls the 1893 World's Fair "a fascinating study during all the stages of the preparation for the great display; a scene so peculiar that no public exhibition except the completed Fair can exceed it in interest."[33] Ralph's comments fit comfortably in the nineteenth century's City Beautiful movement, whose proponents included aesthetic philosophers, sociologists, and urban planners at the University of Chicago. There, among other places, "aesthetics became institutionalized as an academic subject charged with the mission of creating and maintaining a democratic culture."[34] The American bourgeoisie emerging at the Long Depression's tail end stands at the center of this mission. Wells would have fairgoers reading *The Reason Why* consider what horrors accompany the beauty idealized by this urban planning movement. She would also emphasize the stakes of making aesthetic balance a stand-in for a just political, economic, and legal order.

The beautiful buildings and sculptures of the 1893 World's Fair get attributed to artisans carving civilization out of unruly nature, thereby associating beauty with labor harmonized to the overlapping rhythm of city life, national belonging, and the settling of unclaimed land. Ralph says: "It is custom of the persons concerned in the work to refer back to the time when not a spade had been thrust in the surface of the Fair Grounds . . . and truly it is wonderful, now, to see the finished avenues and lawns around the great palaces and the trim-sided lagoons and the orderly beach of Belgian blocks against which the lake's wavelets lick, and to know that here, a year ago, was part jungle, part marsh, and part sandy waste."[35] Considering that the exposition celebrated Christopher Columbus, this passage reenacts the colonial gaze on the "barren" lands of North America during European exploration over the previous four centuries. However, the reenactment improves on what the original colonial gaze fails to do—namely, to reflect social order through the fair's layout. "For the first time," one historian says, "hundreds of thousands of Americans saw a group of buildings harmoniously and powerfully arranged in a plan of great variety, perfect balance, and strong climax effect."[36] This "vision of harmonious power" is explicitly imperial, with "no parallel since the Rome of the emperors stood intact."[37]

The 1893 World's Fair grants an unusual significance to the architect-artisan relationship so as to frame labor's place in this materialized dream: "A tour of the exposition" "awaken[ed] a visitor to a consciousness of architecture's role as a fine art . . . [and] an obvious cooperation among the architects."[38] Thus, beauty combines the aesthetic, the political, and the economic, since the frescos, buildings, and statues covering the fairgrounds entailed labor cooperation between ten thousand craftspeople, the architects, and the nation-state.[39] Barely three decades earlier, Marx noted how mass labor gets romanticized as aesthetic harmony under capitalism: "All combined labor on a large scale requires, more or less, a directing authority, in order to secure the harmonious working of the individual activities. . . . A single violin player is his own conductor; an orchestra requires a separate one. The work of directing, superintending, and adjusting, becomes one of the functions of capital, from the moment that the labor under the control of capital, becomes cooperative."[40] Marx's words remain true in 1893 when fairgoers are expected to identify with this materialized dream. This romanticization ignores that "resistance to the domination of capital" will increase "as the number of the co-operating laborers increases" and that capitalism will reply with increasing "counter-pressure." The post-Reconstruction era's many strikes, strike-breakings, corrupt law officials, and congressional hearings confirm Marx's claim.[41] Eyewitness testimony uses the relationship between architect and artisan to elide the volatile relationship between capitalist and indebted-, slave-, prison-, and wage laborers.

The fairground layout creates a paradoxical effect of being cutting edge yet timeless. Each building contains examples of the nation's industrial and cultural progress. The White City's architecture, landmarks, and statues declare that the United States is the newest nation to achieve an imperial telos initially epitomized by Rome. The Ship of State was the largest fountain in the world at the time and was "heralded by Fame at the prow and guided by Father Time at the helm," then "propelled by eight maidens representing industry and the arts," with "Columbia enthroned on a central pedestal" surrounded by "sea horses with riders, mermaids and tritons" in the Great Basin.[42] Placing this structure in the Great Basin gives it an aura of infinite expansion and control. Taken together, industry and Father Time serve Columbia, the longtime Latinate name for the United States. The Ship of State imagines the nation as transcending the risks of fortune. A nation identifying as the vanguard of change as well as outside all change is nonsensical, especially considering that this imagery excludes seven million people who accomplished the leap from slave to citizen in a generation. But this only exposes the intensity of racial fantasy in the White City and how crucial "progress" is to this frame. The board of director's decision to destroy the fairgrounds (aside from a handful of buildings) after the event's end further protects the purity of the fantasy from admitting its vulnerability to fortune. As I will show, this paradoxical temporality enables (rather than overcomes) the antiblack violence Wells protested.

"ITS ASSERTED SPIRIT REMAINS . . ."

The architecture and statuary in the 1893 World's Fair announced but did not explain the US's vanguard position. The nation saw itself at the forefront of progress yet outside time. This circumstance requires explanation, along with an exploration of the differing ways that national subjects experience this temporality. *The Reason Why* explains this predicament in hopes of identifying the violent racial and class fetishisms subtending the fiction of the White City. Frederick Douglass begins this work in the introduction to *The Reason Why*. Although Wells considered Douglass a mentor, he always acknowledged that Wells's arguments on lynching surpassed his own. Their contributions provide the most radical stance in the pamphlet. Read together, they identify the racism of the White City.

Douglass begins with a passage reminiscent of his vexing speech "What to the Slave Is the Fourth of July?" In that famous speech from 1852, Douglass chides his listeners for claiming the cultural and political inheritance of the American Revolution while failing to continue that legacy by fighting chattel slavery as the current example of tyranny. They invite him to make arguments against slavery that they already know and "drag" "a man in fetters" "to join you in joyous anthems" of freedom.[43] Douglass's speech makes enjoyment a political factor. Forty-one years after that compelling oration, Douglass witnesses this enjoyment and its hypocrisies expand with the emergent American bourgeoisie in the White City:

> There are many good things concerning our country and countrymen of which we would be glad to tell . . . if we could do so, and at the same time tell the truth. We would like for instance to tell our visitors that the moral progress of the American people has kept even pace with their enterprise and their material civilization; . . . that two hundred and sixty years of progress and enlightenment have banished barbarism and race hate from the United States; that the old things of slavery have entirely passed away, and that all things pertaining to the colored people have become new; that American liberty is now the undisputed possession of all the American people; that American law is now the shield alike of black and white; that the spirit of slavery and class domination has no longer any lurking place in any part of this country; . . . that mobs are not allowed to supercede courts of law or usurp the place of government; that here Negroes are not tortured, shot, hanged or burned to death, merely on suspicion of crime and without ever seeing a judge, a jury or advocate; that the American Government is in reality a Government of the people, by the people and for the people, and for all the people; that the National Government is not a rope of sand, but has both the power and the disposition to protect the lives and liberties of American citizens of whatever color, at home, not less than abroad; that it will send its men-of-war to chastise the murder of its citizens in New Orleans or in any other part of the south, as readily as for the same purpose it will send them to Chili, Hayti or San Domingo; that our national sovereignty, in its rights to protect the lives of our American citizens is ample and su-

perior to any right or power possessed by the individual states; that the people of the United States are a nation in fact as well as in name; . . . that this World's Columbian Exposition, with its splendid display of wealth and power, its triumphs of art and its multitudinous architectural and other attractions, is a fair indication of the elevated and liberal sentiment of the American people, and that to the colored people of America, morally speaking, the World's Fair now in progress, is not a whited sepulcher.[44]

Douglass arranges his statement into a latticework of subordinate clauses following a main clause in the conditional verb tense. The passage achieves an impressive symmetry to mimic and indict the neoclassical design of the fair. This beauty only compels *if* the White City's morality outpaces its material gains, and that morality only succeeds *if* slavery has truly been ousted from America's shores:

But unhappily, nothing of all this can be said, without qualification and without flagrant disregard of the truth. The explanation is this: We have long had in this country, a system of iniquity which possessed the power of blinding the moral perception, stifling the voice of conscience, blunting all human sensibilities and perverting the plainest teaching of the religion we have here professed. . . . That system *was* American slavery. *Though it is now gone, its asserted spirit remains.*[45]

The Reason Why makes enjoyment a political factor once again but in a more complicated terrain. The United States has already gone part of the way to end slavery, then suspends that effort for the sake of industrial development and offers bourgeois enjoyment to an American majority that resents the obligation to complete abolition's tasks. In this way, the United States can stand at the forefront of change and outside it at once.

These are aftereffects of the counterrevolution of 1876 against Reconstruction, in which the political economic structure of slavery has collapsed, but slavery's spirit—the *desire* for complete subjugation, incorporation, or consumption of the other—haunts by regaining institutional legitimacy and setting the ethical standards for civil society. Hence Douglass speaks of slavery's "asserted spirit" reappearing, while Wells speaks of Banquo's ghost disrupting Macbeth's feast.[46] America achieved its imperial status by giving up on establishing and enforcing the freedperson's citizenship rights, not to mention political and economic power. This ensures that while the white worker majority cannot withstand monopoly capital's most violent exploitative habits, it can still enjoy privileges that other racial groups lack. As Douglass himself says, "Your high independence only reveals the immeasurable distance between us. The blessings which you, this day, rejoice, *are not enjoyed in common.*"[47] That observation from 1852 remains true in 1893, though the need for enjoyment has increased, since the white worker majority supports America's aims for global power in the upcoming century.

One can call this version of futurity *abolished time*. The White City's layout, architecture, and statuary proclaim the nation-empire subduing time, making time serve America's interests. In "What to the Slave Is the Fourth of July?," Douglass sees the American majority cutting the American revolutionary moment short to protect its ego from admitting its hypocrisy. Less than a decade later, Douglass witnesses another revolutionary temporality open with the Civil War and Reconstruction—some call it the Coming of the Lord; others call it Jubilee. By the 1893 World's Fair, abolished time has abruptly halted that second radical process to end slavery. In this odd logic, the process of ending slavery has ended. Fairgoers hold onto America's radical moments by selling trinkets—like copies of John Brown's writings—and concentrating on America's role as a vanguard nation and nascent empire. Abolished time synchronizes with the nation's imperial grabs, stultifies domestic protest for the sake of international dominance, and forsakes moral advancement for material abundance.

The 1893 World's Fair poses a problem for this strategy. The liberal approach, which *The Reason Why* turns to at times, argues for the value of black Americans as human beings who have made tremendous contributions to America as slaves and as freedpersons, with the hopes of persuading the beautiful soul, who will parse the logic and evidence coolly, to realize its error and join in creating space in the White City for black accomplishment. The liberal argument would simply add black accomplishments to the White City's many exhibits after gaining the American majority's recognition. This strategy follows from the well-known association of Douglass with a "redemptive critique," which inverts Hegel's master-slave dialectic so the enslaved overcome their self-alienation through life-or-death struggle with the master. After achieving victory against the master, the enslaved become a new subject who can escape their bedeviled position.[48] A number of thinkers in black studies and postcolonial studies have built on this theorization of the slave overcoming alienation. Reading Douglass and Wells differently can reveal the limits of the master-slave dialectic as an explanatory model for anti-racist revolt. The shortcoming with this does not arise with positing the humanity and spiritual potential of the once-enslaved but with the liberal approach's failure to gauge the former master's subjective and *political* reaction to defeat. Nor have the researchers considered that the dialectic is not written from a master's position but from a slave's, meaning that the dialectic is shot through with unacknowledged resentment in its orthodox form; this re-rendering does not excise that resentment.

Slavery's end further *de*valued black life to an American majority that resented any theoretical or practical expression of black freedom. This resentful attitude nullifies the terms informing the asserted spirit's movement beyond the master-slave dialectic to former master and slave, though in different ways. This model cannot account for the observation that "in the language of the law" any moral obligation to the slave came indirectly, only because no one had the right to damage another white person's property. Victory over chattel slavery fails to cultivate a new moral obligation toward the freedpersons. Douglass observes, "The abolition of slavery against the will of the enslavers did not render a slave's life more sacred."[49] Regarding labor, the slave's newfound sense of self-possession does not outweigh being seen as property from a capitalist perspective. Wells says the aftermath of the Civil War *"left us free, but it also left us homeless, penniless, ignorant, nameless and friendless."* While "Russia's liberated serf" received "three acres of land and agricultural implements with which to begin his career of liberty and independence," to the freedpersons "no foot of land nor implement was given. *We were turned loose to starvation, destitution and death."*[50] The enslaved have become *vogelfrei*, as Marx described it: birds free to fly without resources or protections.

Wells recognizes that, from a capitalist viewpoint, emancipation simply means the release of "things" that are susceptible to recapture in a new economic form. The freedpersons are recognized not simply as workers but as abandoned or stolen property waiting for reclamation. Objectifying the freedperson alters how the master views the dialectic's life-or-death struggle. Douglass concludes that "the mass of" Southerners *"are the same to-day that they were in the time of slavery,"* save for a "new advantage," that "if a Negro was killed, the owner sustained a loss of property. Now he is not restrained by any fear of such loss."[51] Newfound self-possession among freedpersons did not lead to liberal recognition. Although the nation promised to expand legal personhood to include African Americans excluded from the body politic, Douglass's contribution to *The Reason Why* suggests that inclusion has given way to incorporation—segregation functions like a false burial, disavowing the freedperson's activity and making the American bourgeoisie into the moral ideal. Hence Douglass renamed the White City a "whited sepulcher."[52]

Douglass sees no reason to correct this hypocrisy by explaining the freedperson's humanity, just as he refused to explain the slave's humanity in his speech decades earlier: "Must I undertake to prove that the slave is a man? That point is conceded already. Nobody doubts it."[53] The problem is that the beautiful soul disavows black humanity, triggering a deviation between affect and knowing. The deviation precedes and quietly shapes the debate, such that the beautiful soul may follow the antislavery argument's logic, condemn antiblack violence, and alleviate some of racism's sting with milder policies and sentimental speeches. Yet the beautiful soul will always stop short of altering the structures granting its resentment political legitimacy. Thus, the beautiful soul can hide in plain sight wearing centrist or progressive garb, claiming to help when it truly aims to exhaust radical energy with pointless proofs. Douglass proposes an alternative strategy with a clamorous phrase: "scorching irony."[54] He identifies a broad range of practices for enjoying resentment and disavowal, thereby disabusing black workers and their allies of the fantasy that liberal recognition ensures protection from racial violence. *The Reason Why* makes the White City and bourgeois refinement the locus of bloodshed, violation, lawlessness, and theft, not the exception to these decidedly modern injustices, especially in the case of the twin infamies of lynching and convict leasing.

THE TWIN INFAMIES

Lynching

In a nation that abruptly sacrificed Reconstruction for the spoils of monopoly capital; that failed to reinvent moral obligation because of its attachment to property relations as the ground for identity; that left the freedpersons surrounded by those who resent them as disposable, unclaimed, rogue property, violence was inevitable. In *The Reason Why* and her other pamphlets, Wells pushes her contemporary readers beyond the convenient outlook that uneducated poor white Southern men lynched blacks out of random violent urges or a warped version of chivalry. Quite the contrary, lynching "has left the out-of-the-way places where ignorance prevails, has thrown off the mask and with this new cry stalks in broad daylight in large cities, the centers of civilization, and is encouraged by the 'leading citizens' and the press."[55] Reading Wells effectively today also means abandoning the outlook that lynching stopped with World War II. Those who make this point are commending the work of Wells and other anti-lynching activists. They are right to do so. Still, a more accurate claim would be that Wells and her compatriots combatted lynching so forcefully that the beautiful soul had to alter lynching's form. Wells would have her attentive readers accept that the struggle for abolition continues and read *The Reason Why* to account for past violence and prepare for racial violence's new permutations. While *The Reason Why* provides the thesis and framework, surveying Wells's other writings offers broader evidence for understanding how the government turns toward the nation's ruin, organizes politics around a resentful majority, and then coordinates this effort in such a way that no single radical class alone can become a counterpower but requires another region of the multitude to organize itself to craft another world.

The beautiful soul's resentment harbors a "secret gratification." One may officially declare solidarity with the Lost Cause, but "fidelity to the dead can always be a fidelity to ourselves: it's all too often our own wounds we are deliriously enjoying."[56] The counterrevolution of 1876 provided the beautiful soul with a new opportunity to form a multiclass, multigender, multigenerational, bipartisan political bloc called "the Solid South." Discussing this social formation takes seriously a different facet of *The Reason Why*'s reproduction of lynching imagery from the murders of Lee Walker and C. J. Miller. Scholars have done the agonizing work of studying lynching images to join Wells in turning them into indictments against the New South, the United States, and modernity at large. Going farther in this direction means confronting the representation of whiteness in these images as well. Seen straightforwardly, these images are the crude showing of trophies announcing the social-death of black folks. Seen with second-sight, they are portraits of the Solid South that unveil the White City's most vicious proclivities.

The Reason Why's two lynching images contrast a detailed foreground centering the murder victims with a background filled with a ghostly white mass. Some in the mass stare up at the murder victim; others stare directly into the camera and even point to the life they stole; fathers stand proudly hugging their children. The lynch mob overpopulates the frame of both images, oversaturating the photograph in particular. The image unsettles liberal distinctions between perpetrator and witness, since that distinction typically attributes guilt to single individuals, not an entire populace that claims the murder as if they all participated. Lynching photography waivers between several hauntings, then. The lives of the innocent haunt the image as they are reduced to atomized bodies. The Solid South haunts the image as liberal moralism loses its momentum, unable to expand accountability and penalize an entire hegemonic order. Finally, within the pages of *The Reason Why*, the Solid South haunts the White City's fairgrounds, because the former provides the theoretic, historical, cultural, legal, and political conditions for the latter. The White City arises from the same structure of resentment as the lynching postcard.[57]

From the vantage of *The Reason Why*, the White City's sanitized image appears farcical, even delusional, for pretending that it does not convey the very image of whiteness that the Solid South esteems. The Solid South's founding principle is placing whiteness above the law when attacking non-white peoples of any age, race, class, gender, or ability. At the same time, the Solid South wishes to present itself as the epitome of ethical superiority. The proof comes from the lynchers' own mouths and from the selective way they lynched some people and not others for similar crimes, the only difference being who was white or black in the situation. In the section "Color Line Justice" from *A Red Record*, Wells shows that despite attempts to associate lynching with chivalry, white mobs would aggressively protect white sexual assailants. After a white man "outraged a colored girl in a drug store," rumors spread that "five hundred colored men had organized to lynch him." One might expect the mob to say that this sexual assailant would receive what he deserved. No, the mob sees white people as a law unto themselves; they consider below their station any principle that protects them in the same way as people of color. No wonder, on that rumor alone, "two hundred and fifty white citizens armed themselves with Winchesters and guarded him. A cannon was placed in front of his home, and the Buchanan Rifles (State Militia) ordered to the scene for his protection."[58] Scorching irony, indeed, that a white man caught raping a black child could rally so many people—comprised of everyday citizens, militiamen, and administrators coordinating the effort—to his protection, but a black girl could not receive a fifth of those resources to protect her against a sexual assailant or ensure that assailant's legal punishment. Undoubtedly, such assailants knew the Solid South would protect them. More precisely, such assailants counted on how effectively the Solid South would coordinate their efforts to enjoy their resentment.

That coordination deserves close scrutiny. Wells's pamphlets, especially *Lynch Law in Georgia* (1899), *The East St Louis Massacre* (1917), and *Arkansas Race Riot* (1920), demonstrate how the Solid South used lynching to enjoy its resentment from the 1870s to the Great Depression. As stated earlier, the Solid South had many members, playing multiple roles. It gathered white laborers, capitalists, and politicians into "a unit for white supremacy" that rallied against those they considered racially, economically, sexually, religiously, and regionally other.[59] In *Lynch Law in Georgia*, Wells narrates an investigation done by a hired detective in Palmetto, Georgia, of the lynching of Sam Hose for killing his boss (in self-defense) and the murder of nine black men by ad hoc firing squad for alleged arson. First, lynching had the greatest political, economic, legal, and social effect when carried out by a multiclass group. As the detective, Louis P. Le Vin, discovered, "It was not the irresponsible rabble that urged the burning [alive of Sam Hose], *for it was openly advocated by some of the leading men of Palmetto*."[60] These "leading men" were the president of the local bank; the *Atlanta Constitution*'s president and editor; the former superintendent of Palmetto's school system; the police officers who held Hose in custody and waited to hear the governor's decision on where he would be tried; several supervisors running the Central Georgia Railroad, which organized a special train to take Hose to the place where he would be lynched; and the mob of "six thousand," which included "the rabble," the petit-bourgeoisie, and the upper crusts of central Georgia and nearby areas. A second feature of the Solid South was its propaganda machine, which saw itself as an organizing force reiterating the region's ideological stance. As Le Vin's reference to leaders indicates, local newspapers and newly conglomerating mass media constantly incited mob violence with sensational headlines and provided specific information for the mob to carry out its deeds. Third, officials in the local judicial and executive branches of government disobeyed the governor's orders to take

Hose to Atlanta. They rerouted him to Newnan, Georgia, for his torture and execution, knowing that they would write the reports to justify their actions with at least six thousand people backing their position.

Several scholars have noted the aforementioned features, which are encapsulated in *Lynch Law in Georgia* and other early pamphlets. Scholars have spent less time theorizing about the roles of state and federal military personnel in what some call race riots, which are an outgrowth of lynching and the Solid South's transformation of legality into lawlessness. For this discussion, *The East St Louis Massacre: The Greatest Outrage of the Century* (1917) provides ample evidence. This "race riot" ignited when Illinois's governor commanded the National Guard to coordinate with local police to quell public disturbances incited by cross-racial labor competition and vigilante violence. One observer from the *Chicago Herald* says that in East St. Louis, "A black skin was a death warrant."[61] No spectators say the same about a white skin in the *Chicago Herald*, which leaves a serious strike against the idea of a race riot, which implies some mutual contest between armed racial groups using the cityscape as their battlefield. The *Chicago Herald* report indicates that readers were facing the dilemma identified in *The Reason Why*, that the post-Reconstruction moment did not lead to liberal recognition of black folk but to a Solid South committed to socially devaluing the black body.

Reporter Carlos F. Hurd's comments in the *St. Louis Dispatch* help clarify the Solid South in action, explaining why the military augmented rather than suppressed the Solid South's agenda. He finds the word "mob" insufficient for describing how white supremacists operated in East St Louis. His reconsideration of the term aligns with Wells's conceptualization of the Solid South: "A mob is passionate, a mob follows one man or a few blindly. . . . The East St Louis affair . . . was a man hunt, conducted on a sporting basis, though with anything but the fair play which is the principle of the sport. The East St Louis men took no chances. . . . They went in small groups, there was little leadership, and there was a horribly cool deliberateness and a spirit of fun about it."[62] Hurd's observations effectively dismantle *any* suggestion that black individuals could ensure their safety based on individual accomplishments and prestige. No single individual has the power to defend against this networked form of power. Hurd feels uneasy, since "mob" usually denotes a group of ignorant, misinformed people acting blindly in response to the charisma of a single, manipulative leader. In such a situation, one need only dissuade the followers of the leader's charisma and, from there, the group disbands and their project implodes. In the "East St Louis affair" the "small groups" do not blindly follow but mix "cool deliberateness" with "a spirit of fun."[63] Their shared will to enjoy their resentment facilitates their ability to strategize together for common goals. The Solid South functions so effectively because resentment and enjoyment are the affective glue working across differences in class status, gender, sexuality, and age to form a white supremacist unit. *The Chicago Herald* bemoaned the "indescribable barbarity" "perpetrated with malicious deliberation." The report places "boys of 13, 14, 15 and 16" at "the forefront of the felonious butchery" while "girls and women, wielding bloody knives and clawing at the eyes of dying victims, sprang from the ranks of the mad thousands." "Negro women" "pleading that they had harmed no one, were set upon by white women." One report "saw one of these furies fling herself at a militiaman who was trying to protect a Negress, and wrestle with him for his bayonetted gun, while other women attacked the refugee."[64]

In such a context, stopping the Solid South, whose members hunt unarmed human beings for "fun," would be paramount to restoring order. Nothing of the sort occurs in East St. Louis. After the counterrevolution of 1876, state and federal governmental structures grant privilege to all who can affirm being white, which makes military personnel into pawns of the Solid South's agendas. When state or federal military make the protection of property paramount, they hide a disturbing nuance in seemingly evenhanded rhetoric: really, military personnel aim to protect property holders' ability to control property. There is no secret here that the Solid South assumes black people are that property. Carl Schurz confirmed this presupposition with his research right after the Civil War, saying that "although the freedman is no longer considered the property of the individual master, he is considered the slave of society." The destruction of the "individual relations of masters and slaves" did not touch a social relation, the "ingrained feeling that the blacks at large belong to the whites at large." This creates an aporia in which no one and everyone owns the black, making this figure unclaimed but reclaimable and disposable at once. Now that Jim Crow laws incentivize violence against said property, the military will mildly discourage, encourage, or overtly collaborate in antiblack violence. As the *Chicago Herald* says, "Hundreds of episodes are jocundly detailed here by spectators to the slaughter and rioting of Monday evening *to evidence that the soldiers were toys in the hands of the determined and mobs when they were not actually co-operating with them.*"[65]

The military commits to the Solid South by upholding the latter's meaning of equality: equality means whatever places white Americans at a political, economic, legal, and cultural advantage over black Americans and other people of color. "Race riot" does not refer to an even contest between two races fighting each other; the military ensures "anything but" "fair play." Of the many "horrible stories" Wells heard firsthand or read about in the newspapers, she says "the saddest part of them" was that "in every instance," "the soldiers or the police help up the black men, searched them and even took their pocket knives, then left them at the mercy of the mob."[66] The military considers white-on-black violence a natural response of civilization to barbarism, making it a lesser violence or no violence at all. Meanwhile, the military reads black self-defense as rogue property attacking its rightful owners, as threats to the owners' inalienable right to property, and as threats to property ownership as the standard for social belonging. Tripling their trespasses in this manner justifies bloody fits and seizures. This rarely stated set of assumptions crystallize into a horrifying paradox: the Solid South can break all laws, and the military will read it as legal actions that protect the law; the black worker can use legally protected forms of self-defense, and it will be read as illegal; and when black self-defense has a chance to equal the violent force of whites, the military will intervene to place blacks at a disadvantage. No wonder that when members of a nearby majority black suburb mobilized to help black victims in East St. Louis, a Colonel Tripp sent a "commandeered truck full of guardsmen to the 'black' bridge to meet any attack that might be attempted."[67] The advantage is fully given over to the white masses. For this reason, Wells dislikes the term "race riots" and prefers the term "massacres."

Last, the Solid South consumes whatever they consider "black" in lynching/massacre scenes. Of the ghastly details that *The Reason Why* recounts from a lynching reported in the *Memphis Commercial*, one matters here. After a Detective Richardson cut down Walker's corpse—and the mob "laughed at the sound" of its fall—they denied Richardson the corpse and built a makeshift pyre. After they burned Walker's corpse,

> The rope that was used to hang the Negro, and also that which was used to lead him from the jail, were eagerly sought by relic hunters. They al-

most fought for a chance to cut off a piece of rope, and in an incredibly short time both ropes had disappeared and were scattered in sections of an inch to six inches long. Others of the relic hunters remained . . . to obtain such ghastly relics as the teeth, nails, and bits of charred skin. . . . The teeth were knocked out and the finger nails cut off as souvenirs.[68]

Attentive readers will connect this scene in *The Reason Why* with Wells's account of the destruction of the People's Grocery Store and the *Memphis Free Speech*. Wells does not say only that her friends were killed. She says, "The mob took possession of the People's Grocery Company, helping themselves to food and drink, and destroyed what they could not eat or steal." Then "creditors" sold what was left "at auction."[69] Consumption has a twofold purpose that differs from the incorporation/false burial identified by Douglass. Explaining this distinction adds a final explanation for lynching's importance to racist enjoyment as well as to upholding the Solid South's hegemony.

False burial masquerades as a landmark to progress and moral reconciliation. It corresponds to the beautiful soul's desire to stop emancipatory change without losing the moral high ground. Consumption does not adhere to the same moralism. Consumption operates differently in the same subject, because it signals the site where deliberative moral decision-making unravels in response to the "idealization of hatred," which sees another as "both potential victim and mimetic persecutor."[70] In this way, the decision to stage an encounter between the beautiful soul's moralism and Macbeth's bloodthirst is strategic. They are different expressions of the same violent process, although one cannot construct a linear relationship between the two. Their relationship functions by their disjunction. The white lynch mob member may blabber incessantly about being different from the inhuman black. But the lynch mob members pull the noose tighter or pose with corpses to kill something within themselves that betrays their fantasy of omnipotence. All this occurs "against the backdrop of a generalized destruction of symbols and monuments inherited from a multicultural past."[71] Wells hints at this logic with the title of her third pamphlet, *A Red Record* (1895). The title means a record of violence *and* the violence done to the record itself. Lynching mars histories of black self-governance and histories of racist violence. Across the South, it would appear that black people had not moved beyond being slaves, another bludgeoning of the record meant to hide all the businesses, professional offices, professional associations, hospitals, pharmacies, farms, art studios, schools, homes, and other sites deliberately destroyed by racist mobs.

The lynchers have a ghostly ability to enter and leave the situation, giving the impression that the mob's victims lied about what caused their grief. This is a material effect of the Solid South's actions, projections, and disavowals. Socially, even the boldest lynchers who publicly brag of their crimes can also achieve anonymity, since the South's majority approves of the violence and would never identify them as perpetrators whose crimes place them outside the community. The same people who approve socially also operate the legal apparatus. The combined social and legal disavowal that any assailants exist leaves the victims alone at the scene. It gives the impression that the victims suffered at their own hands, that black self-destructive tendencies are the true plague of African Americans, rather than antiblack resentment. Most importantly, this illusion of self-destruction relieves the state of accountability. The state does not have to resolve the conflict if one party exits the scene. But that exit never fully occurs because the state summons the very violence it claims to dispel.

Convict Leasing

The second of the twin infamies, convict leasing, works in tandem with the Solid South's lynchings and massacres. Again, one can pay homage to Wells by recognizing how she combatted lynching in her day. She deserves even greater respect for giving those who follow her the interpretive apparatus for understanding the future of American racial violence. The phrase "twin infamies" explains a dynamic relationship between lynching and convict leasing, which are the unacknowledged force behind the White City's splendor. From Reconstruction's end until the 1940s, racial violence played out primarily through lynchings and massacres. After that, the beautiful soul altered and broadened its strategy. From World War II's aftermath until the present, racial violence has sought to disrupt black activity through quadrupling the political, legal, and economic power of the nascent convict leasing system that Wells identifies in *The Reason Why*. If Wells makes lynching a shorthand for several iterations of racial violence, which includes what is now called the prison-industrial complex, then it is impossible to say that lynching stopped. Instead, lynching grew to proportions Wells could never

have imagined. Multiple generations of activists and politicians have challenged this development. Still, the fact that so many people take the prison-
industrial complex for granted indicates that praising Wells's image has
interfered with understanding her ideas. Lynching's expansion means the
Solid South has served as a useful model for increasing the militarization,
economic exploitation, and antidemocratic posture of the entire nation. By
twinning lynching and convict leasing, Wells offers today's readers another
warning: even moderate reform of the prison-industrial complex and policing will prompt the beautiful soul's shift back to vigilante violence and
massacres. This means that one must continue Wells's study of the multitude, its affects, and its relation to state power and that the "scorching irony"
in *The Reason Why* remains a useful method.

Examining convict leasing with this method highlights a discrepancy in
the White City's claim that the United States' marvels result from harmony
between architect and artisan. The White City is largely built from an exploitative relationship surpassed only by the chattel slavery grounding the
nation's founding. Wells cites George Washington Cable's comments on
the need for convict labor, which corresponds with the desire for spectacle among the White City's tourists:

> The Southern States have entered upon a new era of material develop-
> ment. Now, if with these conditions in force the public mind has been
> captivated by glowing pictures of the remunerative economy of the con-
> vict lease system, and by the seductive spectacle of mines and railways,
> turnpikes and levees, that everybody wants and nobody wants to pay for,
> growing apace by convict labor that seems to cost nothing, we may also
> assert beforehand that the popular mind will—not so maliciously as
> unreflectingly—yield to the tremendous temptation to hustle the misbe-
> having black man into State prison under extravagant sentence, and sell
> his labor to the highest bidder who will use him in the construction of
> public works.[72]

Wells cites Cable because he combines a critique of the state, the New South
economy, and bourgeois American spectacle. But she arrives at drastically
different conclusions than Cable. *The Reason Why*'s commitment to scorching irony cannot accept that convict leasing occurs without malice or reflection, either from the "popular mind" wanting industrial progress or from
government officials satisfying their electorate. That thought may assuage

an individual's guilt at bedtime, but it has never rescued a child from a chain gang.

The violence of convict leasing is nothing but malicious and deliberate, because it issues from the same resentment as lynching. Like lynching, convict leasing seeks to disrupt black activity and deny any progress, on any standard, for that population since Emancipation. Like lynching, convict leasing presupposes that whiteness means the control of property and black people who are socially the property of whites, owned by all and none of them at once. However, convict leasing aims to tap into that social property differently than lynching. Convict leasing contributes to enjoyment in the White City by exploiting the labor-power that lynching would simply extinguish through outright murder. In that way, convict leasing invokes slavery's asserted spirit. This does not deny the pointless torture and deaths occurring in the convict camp, chain gang, jail, or prison. Those deaths are tied to extracting the greatest labor-power possible from the black body in building the New South. Through convict leasing, the South enters modernity in a tangle of recaptured black bodies, feudal production, the demand for increased state infrastructure, and the life-or-death commitment to a racialized libidinal economy. To understand Wells's account of convict leasing, one must address these features, in that order.

The Reason Why adds nuances to the exploration in "Down by the Riverside" of the camp as a site of political and economic reorganization. Recall Wells explaining that, from a capitalist standpoint, Emancipation is merely the release of things from one political economic form and available for recapture in another. The camp provides the method for recapture. Though the premises for the flood relief camp and the convict camp seem different, both versions of the camp delineate the black's relationship to birth and labor. The camp does not represent a recent, late-nineteenth century decline in the stability of juridical logic. Western law's indeterminacy has always been apparent to racialized subjects without the political recognition linking birth to nationhood. The camp is no sharp fall after a centuries-long decline of the polis but the continuation of the West's misuse of the law toward nonwhite subjects on the plantation. Wells mentions "the details of vice, cruelty, and death thus fostered by the states whose treasuries are enriched" by convict camps, where "men, women, and children" are "herded together like cattle in the filthiest quarters and chained together while at work."[73] The convict camp is the beautiful soul's boldest attempt to funnel black workers back into a labor regime that revives plantation slavery following the counterrevolution of 1876. The White City is not threatened but made possible by the camp.

The Reason Why says the chief justification for convict leasing is in its "economy to the state."[74] By the 1893 World's Fair, that economic form involved a state that did not want the burden of paying for the inmates they jailed, so they leased them to private companies at prices that provided state revenue and offered a cheaper work force. By the Great Depression, a combination of calls for reform, revolts, and economic transformations altered convict leasing's form several times. At the turn of the twentieth century, convict leasing to private companies gave way to chain gangs, in which inmates directly build public works for the state. In yet other cases, after doing some combination of leasing or chain gang work, some workers, especially black women, finish their sentences in the camps and get leased again to white families for terms of domestic labor that could last years. *The Reason Why* rails against the 1893 World's Fair and its sycophants, who herald the architect's bond with the artisan but remain silent regarding the brutish relation between camp guard and convict, building tender and convict, or the hand-selected warden and political patron.

Quite literally, the most dazzling buildings of the fair—the Manufactures Building, the Agriculture Building, the Horticultural Building, and the Women's Building—boasted of accomplishments done by a free nation but were actually built by the hands of unjustly profiled, arrested, convicted, and sentenced captive workers. Historical scholarship teaches of the many contributions of captive workers to the nation. They served as shovelers, ditch diggers, brickmakers, street cleaners, street pavers, macadamizers, coal miners, cooks, cart drivers, plow hands, rock crackers, mechanics, and blacksmiths. They constructed state and regional railroad systems. They worked in broom factories, lumberyards, sawmills, lime quarries, turpentine farms, and iron ore mines. They cleaned white households and cared for the children of those households while being kept from their own. Over the years, the raw materials they extracted, the buildings they erected, and the locations they industrialized made fortunes for a new white elite rising after the economic destruction of the antebellum planter class; provided town halls and other spaces for democratic gatherings; and created spaces for leisure among the white masses while excluding black citizens. Unquestionably, the White City could not exist without the captive black worker.

Nevertheless, the White City's inhabitants are chasing a ghost. The argument has thus far explained how the White City's inhabitants stole black bodies and their creations. But, as Rizvana Bradley has persuasively argued, following the work of Angela Davis and W. E. B. Du Bois, white supremacy wants the products of black labor and the black laborer's very capacity to produce.[75] The White City hopes to overtake, grasp, and control this capacity in the enslaved to create a world despite the many deprivations they suffer. This capacity is virtual, decipherable only through embodied action, which means it can never be fully divorced from the black bodies manifesting its power. Nor can whiteness fully quell this capacity's ability to inspire noncompliance, if not outright rebellion. Furthermore, white bodies cannot fully immunize themselves against this capacity, since the claim is not premised on biological racial difference but on a way of being in which some forms of power are not transferrable to the state. This is a notable contrast to the White City's inhabitants, who transfer their power to the state in exchange for being the protagonist in the nation's imperial pursuits, although they must accept an exploited position in a capitalist economy and convince themselves that enjoying their resentment against black workers makes up for the economic and political power they have relinquished. The inhabitants of the White City turn against the multitude itself, punishing those who keep their fidelity to the multitude's greatest potentialities.

The beautiful soul witnesses this alternative power at work but does not turn back, since that would mean abandoning the gratification that comes from redressing the wounds of the Lost Cause in camps across the South. The convict camp reclaims and updates the plantation's modes of production *and consumption*. In *Black Reconstruction*, Du Bois calls the planters sexually lawless. The violence of the plantation always implies sexual violence. As Saidiya Hartman argues, the plantation became a haven for this violence because its legal, economic, political, and cultural conditions create an aporia in which the enslaved cannot consent and have already offered consent to sexual encounters. Meanwhile, the planter does not need consent yet has already received it.[76] Recently, Alexander Weheliye has made the bold claim that racism necessarily implies sadism.[77] One need not look for long to find evidence for these claims. In his famous narrative, Olaudah Equiano sees a black woman locked into metal contraptions as she cooks the plantation family's meals.[78] Harriet Jacobs, writing as Linda Brent, speaks of her own attempts to escape Dr. Flint when he tries to get her to consent to his sexual pursuit—a sadistic demand that she consent to not having consent; Brent also writes of a young plantation mistress who gets pregnant from the "meanest," most "brutalized" enslaved man on the plantation, as revenge against her father's infidelities to her mother.[79] Taken together, these and countless other examples indicate that the plantation serves as a feudal economy supplying capitalism's raw materials and serves *as a libidinal economy* where sexual violence seeks to distinguish the politically and economically powerful from the disempowered, the humans from things, the "white" from the "black."

This enjoyment returns in the convict camp and its later shapes as the chain gang, the jail, and the prison. Wells signals as much in *The Reason Why*, when she mentions captive women "forced to criminal intimacy with the guards and cook to get food to eat."[80] One should not mistake this for violence hidden from oversight. Historian Talitha LeFlouria says that in Georgia, "camp officials insisted that corporal abuse was the only way to enforce discipline among inmates," so they "appointed" "whipping bosses."[81] Grounding the justification for prison violence in the rhetoric of economic and moral development provides a compelling cover for enjoyment in the camps. Whipping bosses would undress the prisoners fully or partially and whip them before other camp captives. Whipping bosses recruited other prisoners to hold down the one being punished. On chain gangs, camp violence took another shape with the appointment by camp officials of "building tenders" to control a dormitory (sometimes called a "tank" or "cage") of prisoners. Officials sought candidates based on their intimidating reputation and violent tendencies. The building tenders, in turn, used violence to sustain order. Of course, like the other institutional tendencies emerging from the beautiful soul's resentment, order becomes lawlessness. The very violence—including sexual violence—that should be outlawed becomes the main pathway to monopolizing power, not to sustaining order. Meanwhile, officials had other punishments for captive workers besides whippings, including "stretching," chaining workers to spikes until they fainted in the Southern heat; hanging people from the ceiling by their thumbs and wrists; and other tortures—none of which had anything to do with economic productivity or moral rehabilitation. Whether corporations leased convicts for private gains or the state mandated chain gangs to build public infrastructure, the camp enabled these forms of recapture and their violent amusements, all to construct the White City and to obstruct the world-making process that black workers began envisioning after Emancipation.

No wonder Wells recalls Macbeth's encounter with Banquo's ghost to think about America's race problem. Like Macbeth, the Solid South can see a more upright path but refuses it, since it would require as much work to change as to stay the current course. More importantly, the Solid South refused to give up the sweet taste of melancholia, acknowledge political defeat and moral responsibility, or lose the material gains that came from inequality. As bloodshed built the White City, so bloodshed must maintain it. The twin infamies fed the White City's voracious appetite for death and surplus-labor. Between the Long Depression and the Great Depression, lynching in the broad sense of vigilantism outweighed the use of the prison-industrial complex. During the "second Great Depression," the rising visibility of vigilantism may indicate another shift in the beautiful soul's methods. Vigilantism may be increasing as mass imprisonment becomes less practicable or ideologically justifiable. The militarization of the police means that resources reserved for infrequent race riots becomes almost indistinguishable from daily policing, thanks to the war on terror initiated before the stock market crash of 2008. However, Wells's pamphlets seem to suggest that for the beautiful soul, in the Solid South and elsewhere, the militarization of the police is another update on the twin infamies obstructing the emancipatory projects.[82]

THE REASON WHY AND THE TIME OF ABOLITION

Second-sight enables one to invert the White City's temporality and see a different set of political, economic, and cultural possibilities. While the state suspends its work toward emancipation with the abolition of time and a significant portion of the multitude collaborates with this suspension, a remnant holds on to the time of abolition. The multitude now includes those who betray their own potential and those who believe freedom does not come on a single day or through a single amendment but through a lifelong, collective process. Cedric Robinson calls the second group the "ontological totality." The notebooks that follow will elaborate on this claim. For now, this notebook closes by arguing that Wells's concern with self-governance contributes to understanding what Robinson means by the ontological totality. The ontological totality exists within the multitude and never leaves it behind. However, the ontological totality claims blackness as a sign of humanity's ongoing abolition, emancipation, and invention. That effort persists alongside other temporalities, which makes the work complicated, incomplete, late, and on the edge of unraveling. That is the risk and the strength of this syncopated way of being.

A detail complicates this analysis. Despite Emancipation's radical impact, the US government briefly supported it with a liberal framework and implementation strategy. Recall Douglass's eloquent indictment of the 1893 World's Fair, in which he wished that he could claim "that two hundred and sixty years of *progress* and enlightenment have banished barbarism and race hate from the United States," but he cannot do so honestly.[83] This is not just a flaw of the US government but of modernity itself. Conservatism, liberalism, and socialism become the West's three primary political categories, but they all share a liberal premise: "they take the *idea* of irreversible historical *change* for granted."[84] Meanwhile, white supremacists conclude that *any* black activity outside slavery is too much change, but they, too, abide by a premise of irreversible change—only they restrict the participants to a purely white majority. Just as politicians buttressed a radical event with liberal supports, so *The Reason Why* and *Crusade* frame 1890s black activity with the liberal language of "progress," and today's scholarship tends to do the same.

Wells's attempt to call out liberalism's limits to liberals themselves in *The Reason Why* (and to write, self-publish, and disseminate this large pamphlet on short notice) compels her to use this language. Wells's writings chart the Solid South's path of destruction and, equally important, record examples of what the Solid South sought to destroy to make its ideology of black inferiority and slavery appear self-evident. *Southern Horrors* offers an early example with the People's Grocery Store. One can find in *The Reason Why* and her other pamphlets numerous examples of black landowners, entrepreneurs, and tradespersons. One can also find the establishment of a number of institutions, especially hospitals and schools. *The Reason Why* even includes a list of inventions from African Americans. In liberal terms, these examples indicate the rapid development of "Afro-Americans" beyond the condition of slavery.

But black self-determination exposes the limits of this liberal model of cultural achievement and political progress. Wells offers a much more interesting example in *The Arkansas Race Riot*. She opens the pamphlet with "Their Crime," in which she describes the putative cause of the titular riot.

As Ann V. Collins explains, Robert Hill decided to organize a labor union in Arkansas to protect sharecroppers from several abusive practices, including landowners allowing them to "purchase provisions only at specific stores" where they "paid more than the average retail prices" and where "they were not allowed to see an enumerated list of their debts, and they never knew the dollar value of their portion of the cotton sold."[85] Despite these hindrances, the sharecroppers knew the "cotton crops of 1919 would make them independent at last." Wells says, "The colored men who went to war for this democracy returned home determined to emancipate themselves from the slavery which took all a man and his family could earn, left him in debt, gave him no freedom of action, no protection for his life or property, no education for his children, but did give him Jim Crow cars, lynching, and disfranchisement."[86] The Progressive Farmers and Household Union of America hired legal counsel to ensure that this "emancipation" worked out as it should. To Wells, the race riot sought most of all to destroy this effort among black workers.

If the liberal model were sufficient, a riot would not have occurred. But the riot and its aftermath expose the limits of liberal reform. The liberal approach assumes that a minority group can comprise a majority that ensures their political recognition. If other examples were not enough to challenge this assumption, the union under discussion indicates not only how resistant the Solid South is to this possibility but also how quickly its anxiety transforms this possibility into the threat of annihilation. Rumors that the organization was really formed to murder white workers spread like wildfire among white Arkansas citizens. This rumor took off after police tried to infiltrate and attack a union meeting and were shot in self-defense. As with the lynch mob, those who would join the massacre ignored how white authorities escalated the situation and abused their power. By this logic, any involvement of black people in the death or near-death of a white officer necessarily means that black people are massacring white Americans (unless, of course, a reputable white voice dissuades the mob). After the riot, a number of black workers, especially leaders in the union, were arrested and charged with murder. Not a single white rioter was charged with a similar crime. Wells notes that "this union was first organized under act of Congress in 1865, fifty-five years ago; was revised and reorganized in 1897; and revised and applied by Robert L. Hill and others in 1918. It was ratified and incorporated under orders of the Supreme Court of Arkansas in 1918 at

Little Rock, Arkansas. *The men who are now awaiting the verdict of the Supreme Court on their sentence of electrocution were working under a charter permitting them to organize granted by that same Supreme Court!*"[87] This is a paramount example of the law's perversion after the counterrevolution of 1876 but also a paramount example of black visions of freedom surpassing the liberal willingness to act. The liberal viewpoint can imagine the formation of such a union and approve of its objective as standard labor practice. But that liberal viewpoint cannot fully acknowledge the backlash this will create. Nor can that viewpoint fully admit how the legal frameworks are designed to favor the backlash, to leave the white rioters unpunished, and to then supplement the backlash's efforts by legally punishing the riot's black survivors and union members. The fact that only a few black workers were convicted and that they then saw their sentences appealed does not make up for the fact that their trials should never have occurred.

The ontological totality's heterogeneity does not long abide the rhetoric of progress. The need for progress encourages the nation to prize economic expansion and reconciliation among whites over justice for the black worker. American progress falsely buries or consumes racial complexities, as Douglass and Wells each observed. Some unwieldy aspect of the present becomes the past or disappears from view so today's circumstances can count as progress. Consequently, progress at the 1893 World's Fair can include the products of convict labor but not black accomplishments in education. Lynching can be straightforwardly condemned, but the leaders of the lynch mobs, who often come from the leading business centers of the South, as Wells persuasively argues, would be the fair's main audience.

The language of becoming suits the ontological totality's complexities. The language of becoming may displace some of the intellectual constraints that come with making progress the starting point and telos of society. It also calls up a different array of thinkers from the black radical and European leftist traditions. Such an approach would remember that "human purposes grow slowly and in curious ways," as W. E. B. Du Bois once said, such that once they achieve "their full panoplied vigor and definite outline not even the thinker can tell the exact process of the growing, or say that here was the beginning or there the ending. Nor does this slow growth make the end less wonderful or the motive less praiseworthy."[88] While Du Bois speaks to the different epistemology that "becoming" implies, Marx translates this idea into a new standard of "wealth": "When the limited bourgeois form is stripped away, what is wealth other than the universality of individual needs, capacities, pleasures, productive forces, etc., created through universal exchange?" Marx continues with his rhetorical questioning by asking if "wealth" is anything else but "the absolute working-out of [humanity's] creative potentialities, . . . the development of all human powers as such the end in itself, not as measured on a *predetermined* yardstick? [Where humanity] strives not to remain something [it] has become, but is in the absolute movement of becoming?"[89]

This conceptualization of becoming not only relieves *The Reason Why* of the need to compete with the White City's account of progress, it reveals how narrowly the White City actually defines progress, such that mainstream progress is, in many ways, a pitiable impoverishment of humanity's potential. This conceptualization also allows for a seemingly "minority" perspective to have its full intellectual, cultural, and political reach. Wells's quotation of Antonin Dvorak discussing black culture in *The Reason Why* takes on a new significance here. Dvorak says that "there is nothing in the whole range of composition that cannot be supplied with themes from this source."[90] This means that the minor perspective is not simply a demographic descriptor or a position to abandon for assimilation in the majority. It means that the minor position encapsulates an intellectual outlook, an inalienable power, and a form of relation open to a range of identities, *if* it willingly dislodges from its conventional places in a liberal political schema. As Gilles Deleuze and Felix Guattari put it, "Becoming-minoritarian" involves "two simultaneous movements, one by which a term is withdrawn from the majority, and another by which a term rises up from the minority."[91]

In rushing to discuss examples of "Afro-American progress," Wells mentions an example of this radical form of becoming in *The Reason Why*: the Coal Creek rebellion of 1891 and 1892 in Anderson, Tennessee. Wells speaks of leased convicts enduring superexploitation in Coal Creek. However, she does not mention that in the Coal Creek rebellion, white and black workers organized to stop convict leasing even though this meant directly opposing Tennessee government and literally battling with the state military. Most importantly, the miners stopped convict leasing because they embraced the minor position, such that even white workers aligned themselves with an effort that continued the abolitionist efforts of black workers from previous generations. The mining community lived out the refrain for this notebook, taken from Wells: "the gods help those who help themselves."

In Coal Creek, the mining corporation tried to circumvent state-sanctioned checks and balances that ensured proper payment for miners. A general strike ensued. The corporation then demanded that the laborers sign labor agreements that would relinquish their voting power as workers. The corporation evicted all the miners who would not sign the agreement and then signed a five-year contract with the Tennessee Coal, Iron, and Railway Company to obtain convict labor. These convict laborers were placed in the mines to end the miners' strike and to "tear down the houses formerly inhabited by the evicted strikers." They used the lumber from the houses to add new stockades to house new convicts coming to work the mines.[92]

This conflict is fascinating because the coal miners did not lynch or terrorize the captive miners, who were vulnerable to death at any time in the camp, as Wells's account of convict leasing demonstrated. Had the miners taken this route, they would have joined that haunted, haunting mass in the lynching photograph, controlling individual black bodies to compensate for their inability to control the products of their own labor. Instead, the diverse group of miners understood that the corporation's decision threatened local labor, businesses that depended on miners to be consumers, and the larger community. Their decisions plunged them back into the time of abolition, pressing against the boundaries created by liberal progress or the retrogressive compromise of 1876. At a community meeting, "the miners, merchants, and other property owners" all agreed "to march on the stockade and demand the release of the convicts."[93] Three hundred armed miners disarmed the guards without physical force. They sent the guards and convicts on a train to Knoxville, Tennessee.

Unsurprisingly, Governor Buck Buchanan sent in the Tennessee National Guard and more convicts to replenish the convicts who had been sent away. This decision corresponds completely to the study of the military's role in the twin infamies earlier in this notebook. The military steps in to protect property or, more accurately, the Solid South's property holders who can use blacks as reclaimed property. In this case, those property holders were not individual people but corporate persons using captive black workers for nearly free labor. The military sought to suppress any force that would undermine this reclamation project. One reporter describes the reaction of the miners: "There is no division of sentiment. The entire district is as one over the main proposition, 'the convicts must go.' I counted 840 rifles on Monday as the miners passed, while the vast multitude following them carried revolvers. The captains of the different companies are all Grand Army men. *Whites and Negroes are standing shoulder to shoulder."*[94] Because the miners did not allow resentment to dictate their reaction, they constructed a strategy whose success did not depend on perpetuating the pain of the convicts. Without that resentment, the corporation or the state lacked a foothold for a compromise like the one devised at the national level. With their knowledge of the Rocky Mountains, the miners outflanked the Tennessee Guard, leading to the latter's surrender. The miners sent more convicts and prison guards on their way. Then they went to the Knoxville Iron Company to free 125 more convicts. Not only did their strategy lead to a relatively nonviolent defeat of the militia, they also won the support of a number of sympathetic national guardsmen.[95]

Because of the degradation of the working class in terms of exploitative labor relations, labor negotiations that ultimately stole the laborer's ability to negotiate, and eviction, the workers became more aware of their shared vulnerability. Rather than take out their anger on those who were more vulnerable, the workers focused on the community's shared condition, which galvanized them against those profiting from their dispossession. Furthermore, they did this fully aware of the retaliation they might receive, which in this case was sponsored by the Tennessee legislature. "The legislature refused to repeal the convict lease system . . . and passed laws which made the convict lease system even more obnoxious. Interference with the labor of a convict was made a felony punishable with five years' imprisonment."[96] At the same time, Governor Buchanan returned the convicts to their slave coal mining labor with a larger group of militiamen to "protect" them. The miners' committee disbanded because of these laws and released a statement lamenting their bare life: "As the state had willed it, and is prepared to enforce its will with bayonet and Gatling gun, that you peacefully give up your work, your homes, and your sweet memories that around them cling, and like Hagar did, find a protection in a Divine Providence, for surely you can find none elsewhere, with sorrow too deep to express, we ring down the curtain on the last act in the Briceville drama by tendering our resignation."[97]

In the wake of these developments, the miners literally and figuratively went underground. In October 1891, they met in mines, with "all lights" "extinguished so that no one could be recognized."[98] After constructing a plan, the miners, "1,500 strong," surrounded the convict stockade and demanded that the warden turn the convicts over to the miners." The miners gave the former convicts civilian clothes and set them free. Here, the underground was "composed of many subdivisions, chambers, conduits, and levels," where one entered a "mode of dissemblance" against the eyes aboveground.[99] While underground, one finds new togetherness that can have political effects aboveground. Among members of the underground, such dissemblance privileges *non*identity over identity. A shared problem united this diverse group. Decreasing labor exploitation by linking it to the abolition of captive workers brought former convicts into the underground fold, offering support to the former and rallying the latter. Consequently, this underground activity shifted the ground of civil society and the institutional sites securing its claims to universal legitimacy. Moreover, dissemblance may have helped protect the underground from impending retaliation from a state serving the wishes of corporations.

As suspected, Governor Buchanan sent in "trainloads of soldiers" with "field guns and Gatling guns" to go to war with the miners to either arrest or kill them. Despite local citizens hiding the miners in "cellars and attics," troops arrested hundreds of people, whether they were involved in the labor conflict or not, filling the prisons to the point that the local school and Methodist church were forced to house the newly arrested. Conservative newspapers began a smear campaign against the miners—for example, calling one of the labor leaders, African American Jake Witsen, a "desperado" after troops shot him twelve times for "resisting." However, the thousands who attended his funeral said he was murdered for his grassroots leadership role. The murder of Jake Witsen, along with the indictment and conviction of nearly three hundred miners for conspiracy, murder, and other unfounded crimes, precipitated a final battle. One hundred fifty disguised miners fought the soldiers once again. The miners were eventually outnumbered by troops and were "hidden and cared for by hundreds of friends and sympathizers who wanted to see the convict lease system abolished." In sum, a number of the leaders continued to organize labor in the South and beyond, even after some of them served shortened prison terms; of the 458 convicts freed during the conflict, two-thirds were hunted down but 165 made successful escapes; the conflict further strained the financial relationship between the state and the mining company; public support for the program fell so low that in Governor Buchanan's farewell address in 1893 he urged the ending of the lease system. The new governor, Peter Turney, in concert with the legislature, ended the program.[100]

The Coal Creek rebellion is but one instance of a multitude that treats blackness as a sign of shared vulnerability and empowerment. Had the miners accepted their predetermined place in the economy (of race and capital), then they would have been yet another set of performers feigning a perfect harmony and falling in line with the ideology backing the 1893 World's Fair. All the while, they would be resigning to the leadership of their exploiters, substituting that feigned harmony for the fruits of their labor that they deserve; they would also be allowing slavery's asserted spirit to return, unperturbed, thereby jeopardizing their own productive contributions and getting pulled into slavery's vortex. By freeing the convicts and making them indistinguishable from the miners themselves, the mining community refuses a "yardstick" that predetermines who lives a free life and grants that even the captive have a potential for "absolute becoming."

Privileging "becoming" over "progress" does not rule out futurity altogether. Of course, this alternate version of futurity would differ significantly from the Solid South's. The ontological totality reiterates the "rough draft" character of humanity. Ostracizing that feature of humanity as simply prehuman, subhuman, or inhuman locks the multitude into a narrow set of possibilities. It creates the illusion of transcending this rough draft dimension of humanity, which amounts to its violent suppression of oneself and others. But this is not simply a romantic claim. Being a rough draft means that the subject is always already written on, scratched out, partially erased. But that ontological condition also allows for reinscription. Said another way, the rough draft status can acknowledge the cruelty that the subject has undergone and still acknowledge that something other than that cruelty remains, and this otherness is beyond the state's reach. Reinscription will be tumultuous, even in circumstances that are relatively free of physical violence. It does not provide the sense of security offered to sovereignty's chosen people. Instead of security, such rewriting pulls one outside oneself.

IN CONCLUSION

In order to clarify Wells's thought on the multitude, this notebook has taken an unusual route. By the time Wells writes *Crusade for Justice*, she wants to steer readers away from thinking of her as a lone warrior and see her as part of a collective movement. The stakes are clear: radical narratives of a single revolutionary class are incapable of tangling with a resentful multitude that galvanizes to cross class, gender, sexual, religious, and regional distinctions to attack a minority group. Finding the conceptual backing for reading *Crusade* and the rest of her corpus in this manner took several complicated moves: elucidating the understudied intertextual relationship between Sidney and Wells, since she develops this interest from the American debates he influenced; engaging with multiple theoretical discourses, because the multitude constantly upsets conceptual boundaries; reading across her texts, with *Crusade* as primary guide, because all her writings abide by the principle that "the gods help those who help themselves"; and recovering the post-Reconstruction era's forgotten history of cruelty and resistance. Wells confronts a government turning toward the nation's ruin by institutionally legitimating antiblack racial resentment. She enters this life-and-death struggle because she believes in the multitude's potential for self-governance in the wake of the state. Reach beyond the liberal framework of progress to find the radical rhetoric of becoming, Wells seems to suggest. There, another region of the multitude, the dark proletariat, embraces the power of the minor position, where blackness counts as a new form of humanity, not just as Western humanity's antithesis. This alternate futurity embraces humanity's rough-draft character.

Crusade for Justice compels precisely because of its rough-draft character, which formally complements its attendance to the multitude's unpredictable inner power. One wonders how Wells might have revised the manuscript had she lived longer. Nevertheless, readers are indebted to Wells's daughter Alfreda Duster for making the wise decision to retain the autobiography's incompleteness. Perhaps Duster leaves these incompletions in order to thwart the violence threatening the record or legacy of Wells and other black intellectuals. This violence adds coherence artificially. It does not clarify the thinker's claims or theoretical conjuncture. It weakens the force of their insights, separates their insights from the conjuncture they influenced, and erases evidence of the intellectual process that connects ideas to concerted action. As John Hope Franklin says in his preface to *Crusade*, Duster deserves praise for "scrupulously avoiding the pitfalls of filial subjectivity."[101] One can add that Duster edits in "a materialist way," so readers can sense the "presence of conflicting forces within even the most apparently coherent text."[102] By placing the "text against itself," by holding on to *Crusade*'s heterogeneity, Duster keeps open the possibility for readers to understand Wells's theoretical conjuncture, to see how it both relates and differs from other moments, including one's own.[103] Most importantly, this move allows readers to join Wells at the vanishing point, as she deliberately foregrounds the life of black movements in the tumult immediately following the Civil War.

The most famous example of said incompleteness is the unfinished sentence of Wells's autobiography, with especial emphasis on the last word: "I also received some beautiful letters from members of the board of directors thanking us for calling attention to what was go . . ." Duster adds this footnote: "This is the last sentence in the autobiography, which the author never completed."[104] "Go" lingers in that last sentence from the momentum of the autobiography as a whole. Its motion takes off most dramatically "at the curve" when she was forced out of Memphis and continues until the autobiography's last word and beyond it, to begin yet another phase of activism. Even in her passing, Wells remains faithful to the vanishing point, because the book leaves readers with the sense that black movement will continue and must continue, since it is not tied to a single individual's life or death. Quite the contrary, the messiness of these movements offers a basis for new sociality and individuation. Understanding *Crusade* means that Wells's autobiographical writing is irreducible to the subject, neither objectified in homogenous collectivism nor in renegade individualism. "Go" implies a power embraced by the one and the many. For these reasons, *Crusade for Justice* may be the Depression-era autobiography par excellence.

NOTEBOOK 3

W. E. B. DU BOIS'S *BLACK RECONSTRUCTION*
Theorizing Divine Violence

Mine eyes have seen the glory of the coming of the Lord,
He is trampling out the vintage where the grapes of wrath are stored,
He hath loosed the fateful lightning of his terrible swift sword,
His truth is marching on!

—"THE BATTLE HYMN OF THE REPUBLIC,"
QUOTED IN *BLACK RECONSTRUCTION*

Freude, shöner, Götterfunken,
Tochter aus Elysium,
Wir betreten feuertrunken,
Himmlische, dein Heiligtum.
Deine Zauber binden wieder,
Was die Mode streng geteilt,
Alle Menschen werden Brüder,
Wo dein sanfter Flügel weilt.
     Seid umschlungen, Millionen!
Alle Menschen . . .
Alle Menschen . . .

—"ODE TO JOY," FRIEDRICH SCHILLER,
QUOTED IN *BLACK RECONSTRUCTION*

The previous notebook turned to Ida B. Wells's writing to elucidate the complexities of the multitude. This involved studying what happens when racial resentment dominates the affects of the multitude. The study on Wells ended by introducing a region in the multitude known as the dark proletariat, which claims blackness as a sign of humanity that stands in opposition to racial capitalism. This third notebook takes up the dark proletariat's forms of effective force. One term in leftist political thought for that force would be "divine violence." That term is derived from Walter Benjamin, who is himself responding to other European leftists.[1] The point here is not that W. E. B. Du Bois or any other black thinker derives their ideas from Benjamin but that bringing this term into the orbit of black thought renders it uncanny, so that readers can reconsider those thinkers and their theories in historical context. Du Bois's *Black Reconstruction in America, 1860–1880* addresses this theme in its fourth and fifth chapters, entitled "The General Strike" and "The Coming of the Lord," respectively. This debate grew urgent in the 1930s, as increased exploitation triggered strikes across the world, and especially in the United States, as corporations and governments turned to strikebreakers to suppress protest. In response, charismatic leadership and liberal organizations like the National Association for the Advancement of Colored People (NAACP) fumbled the opportunity to foster mass black economic movement to ensure their inclusion in the New Deal. That fumbling provided the final proof of the growing intellectual and political differences between Du Bois and the organization he helped found, which led to his resignation in June 1934. This freed Du Bois to return to Atlanta University and complete *Black Reconstruction*, a book that theorizes the radical force of the multitude with the truncated reach of liberal concepts of leadership and white supremacist backlash.

The stanzas in the epigraph close the fourth and fifth chapters of *Black Reconstruction* and highlight the revolutionary force of the multitude and its complicated relationship to national belonging and the law. Just like in his other works bordering on the social scientific and the literary, *how* Du Bois incorporates quotations into *Black Reconstruction* matters as much as their specific content. The sung verse concluding "The General Strike" comes from "The Battle Hymn of the Republic." It is no coincidence that instead of using that title, Du Bois describes it by saying that people "sang the noblest war-song of the ages to the tune of 'John Brown's Body.'"[2] Du Bois, a committed student of German culture, ignores Friedrich Schiller's broad influence on European poetry to concentrate solely on how "Ode to Joy" inspires "John Brown's Body," which, in turn, inspires "The Battle Hymn of the Republic." The movement from "Ode to Joy" to "The Battle Hymn of the Republic" would suggest that Schiller's ode, in which people find joy in paradisiacal "Elysium," comes to fruition with the victory of the Union Army. This teleology finds a thematic equivalence between "Ode to Joy" and "The Battle Hymn of the Republic." Du Bois offsets that apparent equivalence by emphasizing "John Brown's Body." Du Bois does not doubt that "The Battle Hymn of the Republic" speaks of a world-shattering violence, since "terrible swift sword" brings about the "Coming of the Lord" and with it, an unheard-of joy. However, American culture communicates this force through the decaying, executed body, burdened by a radicalism deemed treasonous by US law. Where one should find equivalence between "The Battle Hymn of the Republic" and "Ode to Joy," Du Bois highlights how "John Brown's Body" registers a mistranslation of the divine violence that ended slavery.

No recent work addresses the theme of divine violence in the United States more directly than theologian Ted Smith's remarkable *Weird John Brown: Divine Violence and the Limits of Ethics* (2015). Smith argues that the Raid at Harper's Ferry and its cultural-political legacy are crucial to theorizing divine violence in the American context. *Weird John Brown* does a great service to scholars interested in Walter Benjamin's conceptualization of "divine violence" as the revolutionary force that undoes "mythic violence," the force that uses guilt to bind the subject to the nation-state and positive law. Smith's conceptual effort will help elucidate subtle nuances in the chapters "The General Strike" and "The Coming of the Lord" in *Black Reconstruction*. However, returning to *Black Reconstruction* offers a step beyond *Weird John Brown*'s limit, which Smith himself acknowledged in a recent symposium. Smith said that if he could write the book again, he would "do more to locate Brown as part of a larger conversation in which African American people played key leadership roles and developed extraordinarily rich political theological reflections on the questions of the book."[3]

This notebook contributes to this "larger conversation" by offering an understanding of Brown's place in the dark proletariat. It is the only way to ensure that Brown's efforts count as more than a body sacrificed to redeem a nation-state. It is the only way that an even wider swath of the dark proletariat will receive attention for saving themselves rather than being rescued by Brown (or any other white abolitionist) as black people's salvation. In *Black Reconstruction*, the enslaved and those bound with them channel the theological imagination toward the overthrow of slavery. Yes, the question is how that divine violence plays out outside of Harper's Ferry. But the greater point is how Brown's raid fits into the context of the Underground Railroad and the general strike and how those methods of ending slavery were aided and complicated by black soldiery in the Civil War. Yet, even this argument depends on a bolder claim that divine violence never operates strictly under the terms of preservation or reserve but manifests itself as caesura and expenditure in its overwriting of social and political existence. The stanzas concluding *Black Reconstruction*'s fourth and fifth chapters provide a clue for this path of research. This notebook begins with an examination of Du Bois's intellectual evolution on the theme of black agency from *Souls of Black Folk* (1903) to his sole published biography, *John Brown* (1909). Then the notebook considers Brown as one co-laborer on the Underground Railroad, to understand the phenomenology of escape that preceded and helped create the conditions for the general strike and the Civil War. Finally, this notebook turns to *Black Reconstruction* to examine how the Underground Railroad transformed into the general strike and how this radical break splinters into several scenes that convey the parody, the romance, the tragedy, and the ecstasy of Emancipation.

AGENCY FROM *SOULS OF BLACK FOLK* TO *JOHN BROWN*

The radicalism that Du Bois demonstrates during the Great Depression finds only slight, muted expression in *Souls of Black Folk*. Even the best of Du Bois's insights, in *Souls of Black Folk* and beyond, have no use if black folk do not count as political agents in the first place. By including a line from "The Battle Hymn of the Republic" that says "the coming of the Lord," Du Bois signals that is he is building on and correcting some aspects of *Souls of Black Folk*. That corrective process leads readers to *John Brown* and, afterward, to *Black Reconstruction*. *Souls of Black Folk*'s eleventh chapter, "Of the Faiths of Our Fathers," examines conservative and radical tendencies within the black church. The conservative tendency sought joy in the next world. The radical tendency inhabits a different temporality, because "Freedom" becomes a "real thing and not a dream" for the Negro religious leader. "The

'Coming of the Lord' swept this side of Death, and came to be a thing hoped for in this day," Du Bois says.[4] Already in 1903, Du Bois gives readers the term that will become his variant of what, in today's critical theory parlance, would be called divine violence. In this way, Du Bois is *not* deriving his concept from Walter Benjamin, seeing that he offers the phrase two decades earlier than Benjamin's canonical expression. The majority of the key terms and events for chapters 4 and 5 in *Black Reconstruction* already show up in chapters 2 and 11 in *Souls of Black Folk*. How those terms get used will change tremendously over the next thirty years, which is why this notebook moves across three texts and considers *Black Reconstruction* Du Bois's most robust consideration of divine violence.

Souls of Black Folk does not decisively assert the slave's own striving for freedom just before and during the Civil War. Du Bois says that "when Emancipation came, it seemed to the freedmen a literal Coming of the Lord . . . [The freedperson] stood dumb and motionless before the whirlwind: what had he to do with it? . . . [The freedperson] stood awaiting new wonder till the inevitable Age of reaction swept over the nation and brought the crisis of to-day."[5] Then again, in *Souls of Black Folk*'s second chapter, "Of the Dawn of Freedom," which many consider the starting point for what will become *Black Reconstruction*, Du Bois also speaks of how the "fugitives" become "a steady stream, which flowed faster as the armies marched."[6] Later in the second chapter of *Souls of Black Folk*, Du Bois uses several terms that will receive more sophisticated usage in *Black Reconstruction*. Most importantly, in the following passage, Du Bois speaks of a collective power in blackness that can overcome their immediate condition as slaves:

> Some see all significance [of the Civil War] in the grim front of the destroyer, and some in the bitter sufferers of the Lost Cause. But to me neither soldier nor fugitive speaks with so deep a meaning as *that dark human cloud that clung like remorse on the rear of those swift columns, swelling at times to half their size, almost engulfing and choking them.* In vain they were ordered back, in vain were bridges hewn from beneath their feet; on they trudged and writhed and surged, until they rolled into Savannah, a starved and naked horde of tens of thousands.[7]

This passage separates the action from the actants. This is partly due to the idealism that informs much of *Souls of Black Folk*. But this also indicates the difficulty of the chosen topic. Du Bois is after the terms, the tropes, and a mode of exposition that can foreground agency among the enslaved, over and against the Western presupposition that this is an epistemological, historical, political, legal, and aesthetic impossibility, with the narrow exception that the black agent somehow gives up their blackness in the path toward liberation. With *John Brown* in 1909, Du Bois begins correcting and deepening his conceptualization of "The Coming of the Lord" in *Souls of Black Folk*. That renewed approach finds its full-throated expression in *Black Reconstruction* in 1935.

Du Bois composed *John Brown* for the American Crisis Biographies series after he initially hoped to write on Frederick Douglass. Booker T. Washington had already accepted an invitation from the series editor to write Douglass's story. Du Bois then proposed a biography of Nat Turner, and the series editor suggested John Brown as a compromise. These changes to the biographical subject do not sway Du Bois's overall goal to critique slavery's defenders and to affirm those who sought to overthrow it. Biography takes on a double function here. The critical component of *John Brown* fits under the following thesis: "The price of repression is greater than the cost of liberty. The degradation of men costs something to the degraded and those who degrade."[8] That cost for "the degraded and those who degrade" wrenches Brown's execution away from teleologies that make him a national hero when they are truly another instance of the false incorporation or burial identified by Douglass. The line "John Brown's body lies a mould'ring in the grave" fits into a redemptive narrative that betrays his principled stance: barely three decades after his death, in the same White City that *The Reason Why* critiques, tourists will purchase "souvenirs" that feature a facsimile of Brown's cursive writing, saying the "crimes of this guilty land . . . will never be purged away, but with blood."[9] Unsurprisingly, for an American civil society that, like Macbeth, has shed so much blood that stopping appears nonsensical and continuing the frolic and slaughter appears reasonable, this passage about blood and guilt is ripe for co-optation. Fairgoers can pretend the redemption Brown spoke of has already occurred, absolving the nation of crimes past, present, and future, all for the price of a trinket. The Du Bois of *Souls of Black Folk* would have little to do with this use of Brown's life and the defense of slavery motivating it. But his early idea of "The Coming of the Lord" offers no defense, since it makes black folk spectators to the conflagration.

Then again, the "Battle Hymn of the Republic" cannot do otherwise than focus on Brown's death. Detailing Brown's life would inevitably stumble into his connections with black communities, which speaks to the second function of *John Brown*. Du Bois uses a human life span to frame a biography of black liberation movements, an endeavor similar to Wells's efforts in *Crusade for Justice*. The biography explores "the little known but vastly important inner development of the Negro American" laboring for emancipation in the United States as part of a larger African diasporic project of liberation.[10] *John Brown* listens to and amplifies the internal dynamics of black radical collectivity, the relationship between that collective and its leadership, and the different forms of force that foster revolution out of social upheaval. *John Brown* uses the content of Brown's life to revise Du Bois's theory of leadership and the possibility of cross-racial alliances within the dark proletariat. With these narrative functions in mind, Brown serves as a biographical example that prioritizes collective liberation over individual accomplishment.

To do this work, Du Bois frames Brown's biography in such a way that the titular figure becomes minor, an aftereffect of the Haitian Revolution and other instances of revolt across the African diaspora in the New World. Throughout the biography, the theme of Brown touching the "little known" "inner development of the Negro American" persists, though Du Bois forces readers to rethink who Brown is by contextualizing his birth in an apposite age of revolution with Haiti at the forefront. Furthermore, Du Bois rethinks his own ideas by returning to the image of the "dark human cloud" from *Souls of Black Folk*. "John Brown was born" when "there was hell in Haiti." "In a flash," Du Bois says, "out of the dirt and sloth and slavery of the West Indies, *the black and inert and heavy cloud of African degradation* writhed to sudden life and lifted up the dark figure of Toussaint."[11] From *Souls of Black Folk* to *John Brown*, Du Bois expands the description of the radical subjectivity to which John Brown belongs. To that description he then adds another factor that influences that radical subjectivity's development and view of the world—namely, "degradation." Now an abstract metaphor from *Souls of Black Folk* becomes part of a thesis that speaks to the oppressor and the oppressed, such that the latter becomes an agent of world-historical change. For Du Bois, the Haitian Revolution fractures a fantasy of complete submission among the enslaved. The violence that should have guaranteed submission became a catalyst for overthrowing slavery. Moreover, with descriptors like "black," "inert," "heavy cloud" and "dark figure," Du Bois notes that black political action remains obscure to its witnesses and perhaps even its agents, past and present.

While the "flash" suggests revelation, light does not fully dispel the darkness. And it need not do so. Du Bois does not adhere strictly to an Enlightenment mode of knowledge here. *Weird John Brown* imagines John Brown "holding not just the Bible but also the Mayflower Compact, the Declaration of Independence, the Constitution . . . copies of the collected works of Jefferson and Shakespeare," to demonstrate Brown's broad reading and recontextualization of canonical texts in his radical outlook.[12] Du Bois goes even farther in the trajectory from *Souls of Black Folk* to *John Brown* to *Black Reconstruction*, to combine modernist prose style with Biblical references but also poetry and Greek tragedy, all for a "narration of thinking as generating complexities and complications in their density rather than resolving difference in its translucence."[13] In doing so, Du Bois continues what Richard Wright and Ida B. Wells accomplished in the 1930s, by calling up a Christian theological imagination and working within it to turn it outward toward other discourses and ways of thinking. When Brown embraces these "complexities and complications," he gains the opportunity to share the second-sight specific to the degraded, which Du Bois calls "the vision of the damned." Explaining that vision effectively depends on understanding how those degraded and damned by racism have an ethical basis to overthrow the current order of things. With this phase of the investigation, this notebook reveals the subjectivity that brings about Emancipation but gets disavowed in "John Brown's Body" and "The Battle Hymn of the Republic" and left out of the "joy" that comes with chattel slavery's demise. Rather than push Brown out of the narrative altogether, which would have been a weak argumentative strategy, Du Bois reveals that it is impossible to understand Brown's effort outside of the black radical tradition.

"THE DAMNED": A BRIEF GENEALOGY

The dark proletariat's struggle with and within degradation and damnation bespeaks a condition that pushes Benjamin and Smith to their conceptual limits. This brief conceptual genealogy crossing linguistic (Latin, Dutch,

French, Spanish, and English) and national boundaries can say nothing comprehensive about "the damned," which are "the peculiar outcome of a modernist and anticolonial condensation of extremely heterogeneous suggestions: literary, artistic, psychoanalytical, psychiatric, philosophical, anthropological, and autobiographical."[14] As David Marriott says, they are "the *between* . . . who are suspended between life and death, universal and particular, rabble and proletariat, heterogeneity and self-differentiation."[15] The damned refer to a group of people whose fundamental heterogeneity belies conventional sociological categorization. Nevertheless, the state always attributes to them a guilt preceding any trespass of the law. When Benjamin writes of the "guilt of mere life," he does not mean a feeling of accountability for specific wrongdoings, since specific moral standards do not have political force until they are wedded to legal and civil institutions.[16] Mythic violence produces the guilt that binds people to the law in the first place. This originary guilt compels people to respect their breaking of specific laws. But when Du Bois says the price of repression specific to slavery demands "surrender of body, mind, and soul," that reduces the enslaved to "unaspiring animal content" or when he says in *Black Reconstruction* that the slave "represented in a real sense the ultimate degradation of man," he agrees with and surpasses Benjamin's initial concerns with Weimar Germany and Western Europe in general.[17]

This has important consequences for Smith's wondering in *Weird John Brown* if Benjamin's category of the great criminal adequately accounts for Brown's rebellious activity. The great criminal's transgressions, however contemptible, are admired because they reveal the state's own misuse of violence. Smith argues that even this category cannot redeem Brown's actions: "The actions of a great criminal are not justified because they conform to some deeper sense of the virtuous, the right, or the good."[18] John Brown acted without legal and political justification that also tended to imply moral authority. This disjuncture is essential to divine violence's operation. But it also means, for Smith, that one can never confirm absolutely that John Brown or anyone else participated in the divine violence that overthrows slavery. Smith errs by saying "divine violence opens a space in which Brown can wrestle with the law in solitude, eventually taking on himself the responsibility for abstaining from it."[19] Acting single-mindedly differs from acting single-handedly. When Du Bois says Brown stands *with* and not just *for* black people, he has in mind a biblical reference from Brown's correspondence: "Remember them that are in bonds, as bound with them."[20] There are several implications to Du Bois pushing Benjamin's consideration of the great criminal to the limit through damnation, which radicalizes the link between John Brown's life and black social life, alters conventional understandings of his intellectual trajectory, and adds further richness to the dark proletariat's victories and losses in *Black Reconstruction*.

The great criminal centers on a charismatic figure pitting spectacular violence against the sovereign's violence. But the great criminal must commit a spectacular crime to gain the attention of the state and the people. The people cannot share in the great criminal's power or condemnation. They only prove themselves worthy to witness it. That figure cannot speak to the ontological complexities of the dark proletariat. The enslaved do not need to commit any crime, spectacular or otherwise, to be a criminal. Their very existence counts as criminal, and gratuitous violence toward them is already justifiable in mainstream civil society. Samira Kawash says that hegemonic power would have these people occupy a "static position" that counts as "dead, inert matter."[21] Similarly, in *John Brown*, Du Bois calls American slavery the greatest modern "school of brutality and human suffering," of "the darkening of reason" and "spiritual death."[22] Yet, *John Brown* does not try to solve this dilemma by making the impossible demand that every black person join the elite socio-economic class that Du Bois called the talented tenth in his early work. In contrast to the upward mobility of the talented tenth, the damned self-identify and organize by descending to that "utter naked declivity where an authentic upheaval can be born.'"[23] That upheaval would overpower and astonish the Western powers, as the Haitian Revolution demonstrates. John Brown's birth occurs "just as the shudder of Hayti was running through all the Americas, and from his earliest boyhood he saw and felt the price of repression—the fearful cost that the western world was paying for slavery."[24] Pointing to the intimate relationship between John Brown and "the damned" amounts to saying that he joined their number *before* being arrested, tried, and executed for the raid. Therefore, Brown's crime is not his individual trespass against the state or his failed raid with his small band. Brown commits his greatest crime by demanding that state sovereignty acknowledge the justice of a cause that calls into question the antiblackness that founds the state. Arguably, this crime is worse than criminal—completely damning—because it threatens legality itself.

The fact that Du Bois makes this argument in 1909, only six years after promoting the "talented tenth" theory of leadership, indicates how quickly he began rethinking the power of the masses. The relative silence of scholars on this move indicates how safe the talented tenth concept has been for disciplinary gatekeeping, not for remaining faithful to the evolution of Du Bois's thought about black concerted action. Nor is it concerned with remaining faithful to the power of black life or the obstacles it faces—namely, white supremacists that rally antiblack resentment across gender, class, sexual, religious, and partisan distinctions to achieve their political objectives. Ironically, Du Bois's appropriation of Brown's words implies that despite being condemned for their existence and told that they have no way of making a viable life for themselves, "the damned" rally together across internal distinctions through a shared ethics. Equally important, this move further confirms *John Brown*'s significance to Du Bois's radicalism in the 1930s. Furthermore, when Du Bois calls this agency "the damned," he joins an intellectual history that interrogates forms of collectivity that cannot and will not be fully situated among liberal-democratic identities or accept the guilt by which the nation-state operates. In this way, *Black Reconstruction* expands on what *John Brown* initiates. But by the 1930s, Du Bois joins several others in the black diaspora who are concerned with a different form of humanity that emerges out of degradation and damnation. Langston Hughes gives this group the voice of the "silent ones." Zora Neale Hurston's writes of "the multitude."[25] Jacques Roumain writes of "le sale nègres," the dirty niggers, and "les damnes de la terre." Beyond the 1930s, this theme—specifically Roumain's exploration of it—will directly inspire Frantz Fanon's most mature work on revolution in the early 1960s. Therefore, the trajectory from *Souls of Black Folk* to *John Brown* to *Black Reconstruction* not only identifies changes in Du Bois's philosophy of subjectivity but also marks the place where an agency from below initiates a new phase of overthrow and self-making.

Despite the dehumanization described above, the damned remain a force that nation-states and other state actors ignore at their peril. The damned create a "waking dream or nightmare [for the colonizer], one associated with deep existential ambiguities as the formerly dead begin to act out their aliveness."[26] Roumain's "Sales Nègres," and Langston Hughes's "Wait," both published in the 1930s, speak to this disruptive energy. First, to Roumain's poem:

que les nègres
n'accepent plus
d'etre vos niggers
vos sales nègres
trop tard
car nous auron surgi
Des caverns de voleurs des mines d'or du Congo
Et du Sud-Afrique
Trop tard il sera trop tard
Pour empecher dans les cotonneries de Louisiane
Dans les sucrieres des Antilles
La recolte de vengeances
Des nègres
Des niggers
Des sales nègres
Il sera trop tard je vous dis
car jusqu'aux tams-tams auront appris le langage
de l'internationale
car nous aurons choice notre jour
le jour des sales nègres
des sales indiens
des sales hindous
des sales indòchinois
des sales arabes
des sales malais
des sales juifs
des sales proletaires
Et nous voice debout
Tous les damnes de la terre[27]

The three-line refrain "des nègres / des niggers / des sales nègres" repeats several times in the poem, using blackness and its relation to pathology to bring to mind a range of populations crossing national and linguistic borders, political parties, and class positions—"des sales indiens," "hindous," "indòchinois," "arabes," "malais," juifs," "proletaires"—who, in the crescendo, become "tous les damnes de la terre." These are the populations who threaten to corrode the laws, politics, and economic forms that include their labor but deny them rights, who are objects for studies of exploitation but not protagonists in narratives of revolution.

In "Wait," Langston Hughes speaks paradoxically of the many who, like "les damnes" in Roumain's poem, threaten to strike a blow that will end all oppression. In "Wait," poetic stanzas are bordered on each side by names of locations, workers, cities, and events, including the labor leaders in Meerut who were arrested for the strikes they orchestrated, the conscription of Korean labor into Japan's military, Haiti's suffering under US imperialism, the boys of Scottsboro trapped in the United States' punitive paradigm, the newly urban populations facing the contradictions between industrialism and segregation in Johannesburg, the 35,000 unemployed workers attacked while protesting by police who became Henry Ford's private battalions in Dearborn, and the striking cherry pickers in Santa Clara. It is as if a voice—perhaps the "dark low whispering of some infinite disembodied voice" Du Bois mentions in *John Brown*—only reaches earshot in the nexus these groups may create.[28] Hughes concludes "Wait" with this paratactic arrangement:

HAITI UNEMPLOYED MILLIONS CALIFORNIA CHERRY PICKERS STRIKING MINERS ALABAMA SUGAR BEET WORKERS INDIAN MASSES SCOTTSBORO SHANGHAI COOLIES PATTERSON SUGAR BEET WORKERS COLONIAL ASIA FRICK'S MINERS CUBA POOR FARMERS JAPANESE CONSCRIPTS[29]

Roumain's and Hughes's poems depict a dark proletariat drawing a line of demarcation between working within state protocols and using them for revolutionary means. As Roumain says, "les sales nègres / nous n'acceptons plus / c'est simple / fini." In Hughes's and Roumain's poems *les damnes* refuse to fight each other as well. From Roumain's "Sales Nègres":

Finis vous verrez bien

. . . .

garde a vois, tirailleur
oui, mon commandant
quaund on nous donnera l'ordre
de mitrailler nos frère Arabes
en Syrie
en Tunisie

au Maroc
et nos camarades blacks grevises[30]

And from Hughes's "Wait":

And nobody knows my name
But someday,
I shall raise my hand
And break the heads of you
Who starve me.[31]

Roumain and Hughes agree that the damned rally their greatest strength by stressing a horizontal power structure. But their poetry leaves open the effective *articulation* between these different groups so this unified blow can land with full effect. Roumain, Hughes, and Du Bois think this in-betweenness makes this articulation difficult to arrange but formidable in its application. If Brown is no great criminal, but caught in the movement of a damned, dark proletariat, then he is less easily co-opted for narratives of national progress. In *John Brown* and *Black Reconstruction*, damnation bars one from progress, but not from becoming. In both works, Du Bois attempts to theorize how degradation and damnation promulgates a different form of political organization that is qualitatively different than "John Brown's Body" and "The Battle Hymn of the Republic." Instead of characterizing Brown as having special gifts of knowledge about world politics, Du Bois says that his engagement with life in black communities with a global outlook allows him to participate in second-sight as a general attribute of black culture, not as a property monopolized by charismatic leadership. Precisely what Brown sees alongside others in the dark proletariat requires investigation.

THE VISION OF THE DAMNED

Benjamin argues that one cannot even comprehend divine violence without a "gaze" that takes in more than "what is close at hand," the merely "dialectically rising and falling in the lawmaking and law-preserving formations of violence."[32] The damned have access to this "gaze" because it is another dimension of second-sight, a dimension that *Thinking Through Crisis* has touched on slightly by examining protests in the 1927 Mississippi

River Flood relief camps and even in the Coal Creek rebellion of 1891 and 1892. In *Souls of Black Folk*, second-sight pertains to culture workers in the talented tenth who are torn between leading the black masses and seeking the recognition of a white professional elite. In *John Brown*, second-sight takes a much bolder view of the stratum of black life doubly pathologized by the "price of repression" and by black adherents of uplift ideology. When the damned avail themselves of this gaze, they cut through the inter-subjective relationship and go beyond it, reconfiguring the terrain of inter-action in the process. David Marriott suggests one can grasp this ethics, this "new culture of judgment" among the damned "by opposing the historical diremption of civil society and the nation-state" and by cultivating the di-versity within the damned to get beyond racism's stultifying limits."[33] The point here is not just that "John Brown's Body" or "The Battle Hymn of the Republic" disavow the dark proletariat's agency, but that the dark proletar-iat's damned existence does not deny them an ethics, although that ethics is ultimately incompatible with the nationalism guiding both songs.

Du Bois may have something similar in mind in *John Brown*, when he describes abolitionist movements across the United States and even the Western Hemisphere:

> All men were thinking. A great unrest was on the land. *It was not merely moral leadership from above—it was the push of physical and mental pain from beneath.* . . . The vision of the damned was stirring the western world and stirring black men as well as white. Something was forcing the issue—call it what you will, the Spirit of God or the spell of Africa. It came like some great grinding ground swell,—vast, indefinite, immea-surable but mighty, like the dark low whispering of some infinite disem-bodied voice—a riddle of the Sphinx. It tore men's souls and wrecked their faith. Women cried out as cried once that tall black sibyl, Sojourner Truth:
>
> "Frederick, is God Dead?"
>
> "No," thundered the Douglass. . . . "No, and because God is not dead, slavery can only end in blood."[34]

Brown's intimacy with black culture shows in his sensitivity to this tension. For he, too, agrees with Frederick Douglass's and Sojourner Truth's apoc-ryphal dialogue that a force beyond immanent law and the sovereign state had caused the "unrest" that leads to "thinking." Could this be Hegel's Spirit?

Quite unlikely. According to Hegel's *Philosophy of History*, Spirit can begin its journey only by leaving Africa behind. In contrast, "the spell of Africa" prompts radical thought across the Americas. The more Du Bois contextualizes his biographical subject, the more effectively Brown belongs to the movement of African diasporic power, not because of phenotypical similarity or even complete cultural immersion, but because he shares their openness to a call working outside the terms of the social order to enact a divine violence that has "epochal or world-shattering effects."[35] Samira Kawash understands divine violence as something "never fully materialized [in the value systems of our present], that is always in excess of its apparent material effects and that is neither containable, specifiable, nor localizable."[36] Du Bois anticipates this by calling the Spirit of God/spell of Africa "vast, indefinite, immeasurable but mighty."[37]

The vision of the damned first sees that the current social order is increasingly losing its ability to control its excluded elements. The damned see increasing political suppression as greater reason to organize and revolt. For example, John Brown believes that incidents like the Fugitive Slave Law of 1850 and Bleeding Kansas inadvertently become "the means of making more Abolitionists than all the [antislavery] lectures we have had for years."[38] Far from giving up the slavery cause, the Southern planters see their new law and turning Kansas into a slave state by gun and intimidation as pivotal elements of their imperial plot to expand slavery across the Americas, indefinitely:

> The slavery of the new Cotton Kingdom in the nineteenth century must either die or conquer a nation. . . . The slaves must be curbed with an iron hand. A moment of relaxation and lo! They would be rising either in revenge or ambition. . . . Such a system could not compete with intelligence, nor with individual freedom, nor with miscellaneous and care-demanding crops. It could not divide territory with these things;—to do so meant economic death [for slavers] and the sudden perhaps revolutionary upheaval of a whole social system. This the South saw as it looked backward in the years from 1820 to 1840. Then its bolder vision pressed the gloom ahead, and dreamt a dazzling dream of empire. It saw the slave system triumphant in the great Southwest—in Mexico, in Central America and the islands of the sea. . . . Three steps they and their forerunners took . . . the first in 1820, when they set foot beyond the Mississippi into

Missouri; the second and bolder when they set their seal on the spoils of raped Mexico . . . and the third and boldest, on the soil of Kansas when they fought to enslave all territory of the Union.[39]

Years later in *Black Reconstruction*, Du Bois further explains why slavery's survival depends on its relentless expansion. Because the products of slave labor are more commonly on the raw material end of industrial capitalist production, the prices of the slaveholders' goods could rise only so far, keeping the planters at the whim of the industrial capitalists in the United States and abroad. The planters cannot stomach increasing education or rights for their workers, so raising profits comes "at the cost of raping the land and degrading the laborers."[40]

Black Reconstruction takes this point further by pitting two forms of economy against each other to identify slavery's internal contradictions. Slavery's material economy can never fully disassociate itself from slavery's racialized libidinal economy. The material economy involves the extraction of raw materials and their processing, sale, and consumption in other parts of national and international industry. The libidinal economy involves the mundane and spectacular ways in which the enslaved become the instruments and objects of desire for slave masters and anyone who can align with the latter's social, political, and economic power. Du Bois describes the planter's imperial vision in sexualized terms ("the spoils of raped Mexico") in the above passage from *John Brown*. But he goes much farther in *Black Reconstruction* to explain how this libidinal economy strengthened the resolve of slavery's proponents and withstood the attacks of slavery's mainstream opponents. *Black Reconstruction* states on several occasions that the most successful opposition based its argument "not so much from moral as from economic fear."[41] Abstract moral suasion snips at but cannot subvert the libidinal economy modeled by the plantation. The planters and their ilk would not relinquish the fantasies of omnipotence supported by the intimate instrumentation of the slave, no matter how that sacrifice might contribute economically or politically to the nation or even the planters themselves. Chattel slavery contributed unprecedented amounts of money to the Western world through the theft, possession, valuation, and physical consumption of black bodies. Yet Du Bois concluded that slavery's libidinal economy required limits that could not complement capitalism's demand for increasing productivity: "Slave labor in conjunction and competition with free labor tended to reduce all labor toward slavery."[42] This placed too much pressure on the nation's economy and the legal, media, and other apparatuses to persuade or intimidate the multitude into accepting the status quo.

After seeing that exclusionary structures cannot hold, the damned also see the limits of compromise. Justice does not work through a dialectical compromise. In his own context, Benjamin calls this "the decay of parliaments" across Europe who "lack the sense that a lawmaking violence is represented by themselves" and "cannot achieve decrees worthy of this violence, but cultivate in compromise a supposedly nonviolent manner of dealing with political affairs." Consequently, such apathetic legislation has "alienated as many minds from the ideal of a nonviolent resolution of political conflicts as were attracted to it by the war."[43] Compromises under such circumstances merely disavow the hidden "compulsory" power guiding the decision-making. In *John Brown* and *Black Reconstruction*, Du Bois sees a similar political situation. The planters considered a "free," property-holding, and/or educated black worker "a contradiction and a menace." The planters believed that figure "must not be" and sought every means of suppressing its existence, more or less violently, since that figure's sheer existence betrayed slavery's cultural justifications.[44] Ironically, legislators from the North tell themselves that their compromise will somehow resolve the uncompromising racism of the South's planters and political elite. Northern lawmakers thought they could decrease hostilities by giving into the political bloc that most readily used legislation to justify, protect, and incentivize unlimited violence; this indicates how little those lawmakers understood their identification with the planters and their inability to see exploited black workers as such.

The Fugitive Slave Law and Bleeding Kansas confirm that legislative process alone cannot end slavery, seeing how willingly the US government accommodates this mutual decomposition. The Fugitive Slave Law exemplifies such decomposition by demanding under penalty of law that law enforcement in the North assist in hunting, kidnapping, and returning freedpersons to the plantations they escaped. Furthermore, others have to sit idly by as bounty hunters and others enter their townships and drag people out of their homes into the night screaming, among other horrors. This restores a depleting labor force and perhaps increases it, as people who never were slaves or who purchased their freedom are kidnapped and taken to the South as well. Making Kansas a slave state by hiring border ruffians to terrorize and oust Free Soilers increases the territory of slavery. In the process, the violent destruction of families, the legal sanction and economic support of a new class of bounty hunters, the repurposing of the law to penalize any officials who do not help slave trafficking, the increasing visibility of slavery's remorselessness in the heart of Northern urban spaces, the overnight exoduses of black folk from major US cities for Canada—all this advances the reach of the slave cause while damaging confidence that the country can progress as half-slave and half-free.

Perhaps the greatest evidence for the impossibility of compromise came not from national legislation and the schemes of planters but from Brown hearing the plight of the enslaved and the free black workers themselves. Brown "remember[s] those that are bound, as bound with them." He makes an ethical guideline out of the double entendre "vision of the damned"— namely, to see the suffering of those condemned under the current system and to see that system as those who suffer the most see it. Bearing witness to trauma, in this case, entails listening to the third person, the one who cannot inhabit the "I-you" structure between citizens, in order to eradicate the system causing such suffering as a direct, necessary result of its operation. Incidents like the following are evidence that John Brown worked not only *for* black people but *with* them: "It was in 1839, when a Negro preacher named Fayette was visiting Brown, and bringing his story of persecution and injustice that this great promise was made. Solemnly John Brown arose . . . John Brown told [Fayette and his family] of his purpose to make active war on slavery, and bound his family in solemn and secrete compact to *labor for emancipation*. And then, instead of standing to pray, as was his wont, he fell upon his knees and implored God's blessing on his enterprise."[45] Brown saw the absurdity of thinking legislative compromise with the South would decrease hostilities. But only after hearing Fayette's "story of persecution and injustice" does Brown promise to "make active war on slavery." Slavery is necessarily "a state of war and the slave had a right to anything necessary to win his freedom."[46] Scholars have tended to understate the significance of war to justifying enslavement in the US context. In comparative sociological and humanities research into slavery, scholars have noticed that from the early modern moment up through the nineteenth century, the more compelling argument for slavery was that slaves were prisoners of war—the price paid for lacking the dignity to die defending one's home in battle. Then again, the reason for this inattention is obvious:

if slavery is already war, then the enslaved black and anyone who sympathizes with their plight has the natural right to wage war in return.

Whereas the "Battle Hymn of the Republic" has its titular character joining "the army of the Lord" after his execution, Du Bois urges readers to look at the abolitionist army Brown joined in life. Du Bois calls John Brown's vision of this effort "the black phalanx." Brown traveled throughout the United States, Canada, and even Europe to establish new connections and to strengthen old linkages between abolitionist organizations. He arrives at this position through analyzing current events and researching the causes of past revolts; he "studied the census returns and the distribution of the Negroes and made maps of fugitive slave routes with roads, plantations, and supplies. He learned of Isaac, Denmark Vesey, Nat Turner and the Cumberland region insurrections in South Carolina, Virginia, and Tennessee . . . of the organized resistance to slave-catchers in Pennsylvania, and the history of Haiti and Jamaica."[47] With this set of observations, Du Bois offers persuasive evidence that Brown believed deeply in the self-sufficiency of black communities. However, shifting his focus to the black phalanx also places Brown at the vanishing point where the spectacle of individual leadership recedes to foreground subaltern activity.

When Du Bois turns the "vision of the damned" into an ethical heading under which the excluded unite to overthrow oppression, he takes an insight from Brown's correspondence before his execution. Placing the phrase at a different place from Brown's original chronology has great significance for understanding the limits of *Weird John Brown*. That book's conclusion misreads Du Bois by saying he "anchored his story in descriptions of Brown's love for African American people," only to follow by saying, "above all" Brown demonstrated his love through his "willingness to kill and die for African American people. . . . Sacrifice established the boundaries of community—and respect."[48] Du Bois's use of "vision of the damned" steers readers away from the martyrology that so often surrounds Brown's execution and makes it a general claim of ethical belonging among the politically excluded. Doing so recalls a subtle but significant theme in Du Bois that goes all the way back to "Of the Coming of John" in *Souls of Black Folk*. There, Du Bois began imagining a form of black togetherness exiting the economy of sacrifice so central to Western Christianity, the sovereignty of whiteness, and their links to capitalist production and consumption. Indeed, Du Bois once said that "somewhere in this world, *and not beyond it*, there is Trust, and somehow Trust leads to Joy."[49] Du Bois says this without falling into the "immanent" ethics of mere "cause and effect." One can agree with Smith that this immanent "cause and effect" ethics leave no space for the divine violence that undoes oppressive orders. But one can also disagree and assert that this understanding of immanence proves too narrow for Du Bois's account of John Brown or divine violence. To understand this other kind of immanence, one must return to the chapter on the black phalanx in *John Brown*. Du Bois quotes someone saying that black Americans "could not afford to spare white men of [Brown's] stamp, ready to sacrifice their lives for the salvation of black men." To this, Brown exclaimed, "Did not my Master Jesus Christ come down from Heaven and sacrifice Himself upon the alter for the salvation of the race, and should I, a worm, not worthy to crawl under His feet, refuse to sacrifice myself?"[50] Du Bois hopes to pull Brown away from this economy of sacrifice toward a different theory of community when he deals with the lead-up to Brown's death and to his legacy in the biography's final chapters, "The Riddle of the Sphinx" and "The Legacy of John Brown."

Although Smith places greater weight on Brown's death than Du Bois and partly misses why Du Bois does this, Smith still dodges several intellectual missteps. He rightly agrees that Du Bois "refused to locate [Brown's liberatory visions] in a narrative of sacramental redemption."[51] Smith also says, correctly, that "Brown's violence created no enduring earthly community. It launched no great tide of history. It redeemed nothing . . . as a memory without a legacy."[52] Du Bois's argument for Brown's legacy actually considers it forever out of step with the movement of nineteenth-century history. Brown gets executed the same year that Darwin's writings on evolution reach the public. Brown does not herald a new phase of progress and reconciliation. He marks the closing of a particular window of Western radicalism as Darwin's writings get manipulated to revitalize a racism that was waning in the age of revolution. Out of step with mainstream world-historical movements, unable to redeem or be redeemed by America, Brown's death no longer has the transcendent meaning that songs like the "Battle Hymn of the Republic" attribute to it. While Smith will call it a "sign," this too misses why Du Bois tends so carefully to Brown's trial; his final writings; and a legacy that, from one angle, is not a legacy at all.

Granted, Brown can serve as a "sign" since his death warns of future violence resulting from the nation's compromises with slavery. However, Du Bois's characterization of Brown's death in the biography attends to how

Brown confronted his death as a complete expenditure. Said differently, in death Brown did not give up something of value to himself. Instead, he expended himself completely by sticking to the ethical principles that animated his life: "You may *dispose* of me very easily—I am nearly *disposed of now*," he says at a pivotal point in his testimony.[53] Du Bois quotes portions of Brown's trial testimony where he reasserts that living ethically requires opposing slavery as intently as possible and refuses to accept the law as the final word on the ethical. A law that supports slavery loses its ethical force, even if the penalties for breaking it remain in effect. As stated earlier, Brown differs from the great criminal in joining a population damned before they take any action, ethical or otherwise. The sacrifice Smith associates with Brown does not clear the damned for having the criminal audacity to exist and to become more than slaves. Like Brown, they should be a "sign." But this signification collapses because they are already damned. Their warning to others gets misread as a curse on themselves. In other words, Smith challenges how the nation would redeem Brown but does not fully acknowledge that the transcendence accorded to Brown will not be offered to the enslaved or the freedperson. Nor can the immanence in Smith's framework, which hearkens back to Kant's categorical imperative, account for the immanence motivating the enslaved and free black workers to fight for justice. Immanence and transcendence must be rethought to address these complexities for the multitude that Brown joined through his abolitionist work. This requires a turn to the Underground Railroad, which will eventually become the general strike in *Black Reconstruction*.

THE UNDERGROUND RAILROAD; OR, POLITICS WITH AN IMPROPER LOCUS

Weird John Brown makes no reference to the general strike despite its prominence in Benjamin's theorization of divine violence. This is no absurd oversight. Smith emphasizes the irredeemable event of the raid at Harper's Ferry. The general strike appears too palatable to mainstream legality. In Benjamin's essay, he acknowledges the general strike because it is one of the few legally recognized instances of collective power from below in a liberal-democratic society. Perhaps that legal recognition places the general strike too comfortably in the "immanent" order that Smith needs divine violence to disrupt. Nor does Smith follow Benjamin's several leads in "Critique of

Violence" on who influenced the general strike's role. On the theoretical and practical significance of the general strike to European Marxism, this much is true: no consensus existed in the early twentieth century. Georges Sorel, Rosa Luxembourg, and Walter Benjamin, among others, sought to revitalize the concept after Friedrich Engels dismissed it in the late nineteenth century. Engels assumes that a well-organized party would not need to strike. Those who need to strike lack the organization to sustain the strike's gains anyway. Du Bois knew these theoretical quandaries. He breaks this theoretical gridlock in Marxist thought and politics by writing of a successful general strike accomplished by a population with no party, no consistent claim to citizenship, and absolutely no legal right to strike.

For Du Bois, the general strike is always and already a fugitive maneuver, because it draws in workers who are not legal subjects but disposable objects intended for consumption. As Thomas Wentworth Higginson puts it, John Brown believes God "had established the Allegheny mountains from the foundation of the world that they might one day be a refuge for fugitive slaves."[54] And Du Bois writes in *Black Reconstruction* that before the Civil War, the planter "saw ignorant and sullen labor deliberately reducing his profits. *In fact, he always faced the negative attitude of the general strike.*" During the Civil War, "as it became clear that the Union armies would not or could not return fugitive slaves, and that the masters with all their fume and fury were uncertain of victory, the slave entered upon a general strike against slavery *by the same methods that he used during the period of the fugitive slave.*"[55] In other words, Du Bois saw what Benjamin could not see in regard to the general strike. Brown could see it because he opened himself up to the second-sight that others had already been using for generations to undo slavery's hold. In short, divine violence in the American context cannot be discussed without analyzing the general strike, and the general strike cannot be discussed without analyzing the Underground Railroad, placing its phenomenology of escape alongside its political and economic impact during slavery and the Civil War. Doing this work deepens the understanding of what gets disavowed in the sonic trajectory from "John Brown's Body" to "The Battle Hymn of the Republic"; reinterprets Benjamin's view of the strike through a new world-historical example; rethinks Brown's role in abolition; and reveals the sophistication of Du Bois's thought. It also requires a new assemblage of thinkers across black studies, Marxism, phenomenology, and political philosophy.

Black studies scholars have already begun reevaluating the complexities of subjection and black performance, especially after Saidiya Hartman's *Scenes of Subjection* (1997). Hartman defines stealing away as "the vehicle for the redemptive figuration of dispossessed individual and community, reconstituting kin relations, contravening the object status of chattel, transforming pleasure, and investing in the body as a site of sensual activity, sociality, and possibility, and, last, redressing the pained body."[56] Hartman wants to understand the everyday practices of stealing away and its "short-lived" success without "underestimat[ing] the magnitude of these acts, for they are fraught with utopian and transformative impulses that are unrealizable within the terms of the current order precisely because of the scope of these implicit, understated, and allegorical claims for emancipation, redress, and restitution."[57] Nevertheless, stealing away remains a "politics without a proper locus."[58]

If one forgets that Hartman restricts her analysis to studying everyday scenes of subjection, then one can conclude that these transformative impulses are forever unrealizable, because they never go beyond random free elements and have no greater articulation. But this scene does not tell the entire story (and Hartman never suggests that it does). These scattered sabotages amounted to something much greater. While "open revolt of slaves," overt "refusal to work" and "running away" could be discovered and spectacularly crushed, "nothing could stop the dogged slave from doing just as little and as poor work as possible."[59] Observers like F. L. Olmsted condescended toward slaves for "wast[ing] material and malinger[ing] at their work."[60] Du Bois's answer sounds almost comical for stating the obvious: "Of course, they did. . . . It was the answer of any group of laborers forced down to the last ditch. They might be made to work continuously but no power could make them work well."[61] The breaking of handheld equipment; the purposeful misplacing of supplies; the deliberate rotting of supplies; the construction of faulty edifices and instruments so they would break down sooner than intended; and of course, stealing oneself and others away—these activities are not expressions of laziness. They are reprisals against the conditions of labor based on the planter working slaves to death to compensate for stagnant profits; a limited ability enter new markets; and equally important, a libidinal economy that no financial profits could satiate. The planter's diminution of the slave to the lowest rung of society gives the slave nothing more to lose for sabotaging the planter's enterprise and much more to gain by rebelling individually and collectively, even when this appeared impossible with no promise of positive results.

Keeping in mind the perspectival shift from exile from exodus, one sees that these mundane rebellions across the South, often enough in collaboration with Northerners, gained unanticipated force at the collective level. To reiterate a passage quoted earlier from Du Bois: The planter "saw ignorant and sullen labor deliberately reducing his profits. *In fact, he always faced the negative attitude of the general strike.*"[62] "Negative attitude" understates the meaning. The general strike is "negative" for sabotaging the plantation machine and dislodging the conceptual and practical relationship between productive and unproductive expenditure that ensnares the captive worker. "Negative attitude" complicates the terms of effective, even if improper, political engagement. Nevertheless, Du Bois does not reduce the general strike to voluntarism accomplished on a whim. A more complicated route enables the strike's development out of fugitive practices along the Underground Railroad.

One can theoretically and practically posit the general strike through a prior concept of worklessness (*desouvrement*). Although I draw this term from Jean-Luc Nancy's famous *Inoperative Community*, there is ample theoretical and evidentiary precedent for thinking about this concept in the context of black radicalism.[63] As Cedric Robinson puts it, the ontological totality abides by a "metaphysical system that had never allowed for property in either the physical, philosophical, temporal, legal, social, or psychic senses."[64] When the Western concept of property becomes contingent to one's existence, then community need not boil down to labor productivity and profitability. Worklessness disrupts the rhythm of labor. That pause allows for a revaluation of labor practices and the presuppositions justifying them. A community is worthy of the name only if it can pause and question its labor practices and conditions. Worklessness helps explain why the labor for emancipation has such a syncopated character. Emancipation requires pauses to assess one's overdetermined positions. If divine violence alters the relationship between caesura, preservation, and expenditure, that is partly because a change to labor practices has to include breaks to reinvent communal making. In this way, *Black Reconstruction* affirms an anarchist tendency in the dark proletariat by loosening unproductive expenditure's links to Western models of ever-increasing productive togetherness.[65]

The negative attitude and the worklessness of the general strike remove the trappings of the plantation. The enslaved-turned-fugitive enters a new phase of becoming through escape, even if liberal-democratic and capitalist forms of progress are out of reach. Looking back from Du Bois's moment in the 1930s and from today's "second Great Depression," the general strike and its intellectual legacy are crucial to "to break[ing] up the somnolence of our bourgeois existence."[66] Such "escape is the quest for the marvelous," where freedom dreams meet reality in an explosive manner, where one "need[s] to get out of oneself, that is, *to break that most radical and unalterably binding of chains*."[67] The freedperson's breaking such chains goes unnoticed for proponents of Western theology, since that theological imagination links transcendence to an eschatology that leaves no place for black life. Blackness has the gift of being free from the West's eschatologies and their attendant conceptualizations of transcendence and immanence. In the triad of Du Boisian texts studied in this notebook, but especially in *Black Reconstruction*, immanence produces a surplus. Rethinking transcendence as surplus enables a consideration of change for those who have been conceptually and historically excluded from narratives of transcendence. That surplus immanence calls for a turn inward by stepping out. Said more completely, the rebellious workers are not just subjected but tragic artists who embody "the state *without* fear in the face of the fearful," a "courage and freedom of feeling before a powerful enemy, before a sublime calamity, before a problem that arouses dread."[68] William Still's *Underground Railroad* underscores this point. The document compiles correspondence from Philadelphia's Underground Railroad office. *Underground Railroad* serves as an archival tribute to the damned and the losses they suffer in their departures from the plantation. It provides a basis for the phenomenology of escape that informs the general strike's political momentum. Still's memorial finds joy for and among the tragic artists escaping by the railroad. In doing so, they change the world around them and the misunderstood world within them: by willingly risking disconnection, pain, and death for the sake of freedom, the freedpersons collectively achieve ecstatic experience, even though they are using the Christian rhetoric of transcendence.

Escaping the plantation home, the field, or the city where one gets hired out initiates this process of becoming. Some escape within days of being sold; others do not want to be "inherited" after their current master passes away; others avoid a routine punishment or execution; some escape jail;

others consider it their reward for years of free labor; of course, others have no horrific personal story to share and may have been relatively privileged on the plantation but refuse the general condition of being owned.[69] Some slaves literally perform being cargo by escaping in "boxes and chests" through the mail in "steamers and vessels," or "journey[ing] hundreds of miles in skiffs"; "men disguised in female attire and women dressed in the garb of men" steal away; some blacks, "whose fair complexions have rendered them indistinguishable from their Anglo-Saxon brethren" pass as whites traveling beside "slaveholders" and "slave-catchers" to escape the South; yet others "escape in confinement" by holing up for weeks, months, or years in floors, attics, walls, caves, and even tree trunks.[70] In these varied performances of escape, particular identities give way to nonidentity as people plunging deeper into a form of life that neither "subjecthood" nor "objecthood" can effectively describe, even if they are the terms most familiar to such a discussion.

Underground Railroad also enables a characterization of the forms of discourse that come with stealing away. The Underground Railroad is, paradoxically, a space without discourse, of communication based on "tense talk and whispers," as the first notebook mentions, thereby upsetting the terms of conventional dialogue. In this conversation occurring within the "hazardous space" outside the "I-you" structure legitimating citizenship and segregation, one finds the "faint stirrings of new forms of life."[71] This theoretical observation takes on practical significance when freedperson John Henry Hill gives fugitive slaves advice on a successful escape in a letter: "'Change your name.' 'Never tell any one how you escaped.' 'Never let anyone know where you came from.' 'Never think of writing back, not even to your wife; you can do your kin no good, but may do them harm by writing.'"[72] John Henry Hill's thirteen letters in *Underground Railroad* show that he does not always follow this advice to the letter. Nevertheless, his instructions illustrate how the normal terms of dialogue are overturned in such underground encounters where a double dissymmetry both unites and repels railroad passengers.

If the Underground Railroad serves as low-intensity predecessor to the high-intensity general strike, if a "negative attitude" and disruptive worklessness inform the railroad and the strike, and if all this works outside the conventional terms of intersubjectivity to expose discourse to a third-person position—then becoming strays from being simply negative or positive. The distinction falls short of the situation. It would be better to describe becoming as a combination of unmaking and remaking. Even then, nonidentity plays the close companion of any new coherence taking shape. The shifts in racial, class, sexual, and gender identification discussed here repeat the "cultural 'unmaking'" that made blackness legible to the West in the Middle Passage.[73] This unmaking recurs because the fugitive slave's escape means leaving behind the domestic space that secures national belonging and exclusion. Despite the fact that for the slave the domestic space primarily means labor exploitation, obliteration of family ties, and punishment (complicated by forms of enjoyment eliding the brutality), in the national imagination the domestic still registers safety, honorable filiation, sexual appropriateness, and socioeconomic integration. The fugitive slave's escape forms a counternarrative of remaking occurring outside of and impinging on the domestic sphere, raising questions about that sphere's legitimacy. Because of the dynamic relationship between unmaking and remaking, the *preservation* of the ontological totality comes into question, even as blackness signifies a shared radical commitment to a new form of life.

However horrible their reasons for stealing away, however utopian the rhetoric of reaching the North may sound, escape does not guarantee a fortuitous, utopian experience for the fugitive. Mainstream ways of reading and teaching the Underground Railroad implicitly require the fugitive-turned-freedperson to escape the South and immediately walk the path of liberal progress: earning property, voting for the first time, marrying and having children in a single-family home, and so on. Of course, these factors deserve evaluation. They are the most straightforward ways of asserting the freedperson's humanity to mainstream naysayers. Certainly, black folk in the North who obtained middle-class or even upper-class wealth often made significant contributions in time, money, and influence to ending slavery. Yet this standard asks both too little and too much of the (self-)emancipated: Too little, in that this standard is too impoverished to assess the psychical, filial, intellectual, and cultural transformations that traveling the Underground Railroad entails. Too much, in that middle- to upper-class mobility in the antebellum North remains wedded to the financial and libidinal economy of the South, and therefore still depends on slavery. It is yet another form of perverse enjoyment to expect the freedperson to prove their freedom with a standard demanding their enslavement.

The question is whether there are other terms for studying life during and after the Underground Railroad "when the limited bourgeois form is stripped away," even in part, to convey the struggles and achievement of escape. William Still offers such a term when he writes of Underground Railroad passengers enduring "the fight of affliction."[74] The phrase comes from Hebrews 10:32, "But call to remembrance the former days, in which, after ye were illuminated, ye endured a great fight of afflictions." Much of the passage that follows accords to the themes discussed in this notebook: "For ye had compassion of me [the writer of Hebrews, who some consider the apostle Paul] in my bonds, and took joyfully the spoiling of your goods, knowing in yourselves that ye have in heaven a better and an enduring substance."[75] Still's approach sustains the logic of this passage, although the reading offered here does not stress "a better and an enduring substance" elsewhere but seeks the joy that alters expenditure and endurance into a new relation in this world.

Travail accompanies illumination, in Still's estimation. The fight of affliction entails the severance of the ties one hopes to keep through escape. "Children left to the cruel mercy of slave-holders, could never be forgotten. Brothers and sisters could not refrain from weeping over the remembrance of their separation on the auction block. . . . Not to remember those thus bruised and mangled, it would seem alike unnatural, and impossible."[76] Romulus Hall, for instance, escapes slavery after being framed for murdering an overseer. He walks north for nine days straight, including three days without food, until he succumbs to frostbite from his waist down. A stranger runs into Hall and takes him to the Underground Railroad office in Philadelphia. Hall at first begins to recover but suddenly takes a turn toward death. Now suffering worse infection, including lockjaw; barely able to speak; and out of touch with his wife and children, he receives Still and another railroad operative for a routine interview. When Still's colleague asks Hall, now on his deathbed, "Do you regret having attempted to escape slavery?" the two decide to leave him, thinking that this question insults someone in such great pain. Hall stops them and, to the best of his ability, exclaims, "I am glad I escaped slavery!" He dies soon after.[77]

The fight of affliction indicates that stealing away does not always relieve the pained body of physical ailment or death. Still's *Underground Railroad* memorializes those who suffered unto death in this fight of affliction. And yet, little to nothing in *Underground Railroad* suggests that Romulus Hall and others like him escape in vain. Despite his Victorian moralizing, Still does not limit *Underground Railroad* to mainstream terms of progress to count Hall among the free. Hall's experience testifies to the complexities of investing in the body as a site of sensual activity in stealing away. This may involve physical healing, impairment, even mortification—but it does not demand petrification. It may involve painful living or even untimely dying, but it does not restrict people to a living death. If escaping slavery were strictly pleasurable, then freedom would not be free. If it were strictly misery, then it would merely confirm the ranting of paranoid masters. Hall's mix of suffering and gladness, like that of so many others on the railroad, makes his life the bearer of a freedom that vacates the political, legal, economic, and *psychic* site of the master. Hall's gladness—exclaimed through the pain of lockjaw and frostbite from his waist to his toes—charges readers with affirming his escape in the face of his short-lived freedom rather than revert to liberal conclusions over his escape's "success" or "failure."[78]

When Smith argues that John Brown "can wrestle with the law in solitude," it would be more appropriate to refer to him as joining others in enduring the fight of affliction. The Christological readings of Brown fall short here: one cannot endure the fight of affliction for someone else. One can only model for another the courage necessary to face it. Those models are indispensable for "stripp[ing] away" a bourgeois form of freedom that erases the raid's black participants and reduces Brown to an assuager of guilt for old and new forms of antiblack violence. Brown modeled this and *followed* the model of others in expending all he had for the antislavery cause. Because Brown joined with the damned, he could also join in their process of becoming. This context proves more suitable to Smith's proposal that Brown's life be studied in light of that of another participant in the raid, Shields Green. Though he was executed like Brown, barely anyone even knows of Green's participation in the raid. Historians and others did not make him a martyr for the cause as they did Brown. No national monuments or historic sites acknowledge his sacrifice, and in fact, a university took his body for medical examination afterward. Brown and Green are among the tragic artists who brave the unpredictability of becoming because they detest the path of progress, with its impoverished claim to success and a tendency to compromise with oppression to enjoy the objectification, consumption, and false burial of the other.

To defend the claim that Brown modeled and followed models of tragic artistry, one must supply evidence of who Brown and others admired as leaders on the Underground Railroad, how their leadership related to the masses, and how the relationship between the leadership and the masses contributed to the general strike's broader political impact. Returning to John Henry Hill's correspondence in *Underground Railroad*, one reads his urgency for collective action to overthrow slavery altogether, an urgency that others escaping the plantation share:

> I heard some good Prayers put up for the suffers on last Sunday evening in the Baptist Church. Now friend still I believe that Prayers affects great good, but I believe that the fire and sword would affect more good in this case. Perhaps this is not your thoughts, but I must acknowledge this to be my Polacy. *The world are being turned upside down, and I think we might as well take an active part in it.* . . . I hope this moment among the Slaves are the beginning. I wants to see something go on while I live.[79]

Saidiya Hartman says stealing away commonly involves "unlicensed movement, collective assembly, and an abrogation of the terms of subjection in acts as simple as sneaking off to laugh and talk with friends or making nocturnal visits to loved ones."[80] John Henry Hill's comments also suggest that stealing away involves turning the world upside down because the current order will never meaningfully include those it currently excludes. Ironically, Hill calls for the revolutionary activity he has already joined, though it reaches its crescendo several years later. *Underground Railroad* prompts us to see this world-historical effort and to see a collective exodus where others see only minor escapes.

Interrogating the organization of this effort entails an understanding of the leadership of a strike. Benjamin offers no suggestions on this issue, since he concerns himself strictly with the general strike's place in law. Considering a strike that remains unseen by the law, carried out by legally unrecognizable participants, means returning to the archive. To understand the Underground Railroad as the prelude to an effective strike, one must look to its "Moses"—namely, Harriet Tubman. A passage from *John Brown*, another from *Underground Railroad*, and another from *Black Reconstruction* can clarify Tubman's form of leadership. From *John Brown*:

> Back and forth she traveled like some dark ghost until she had personally led over three hundred blacks to freedom. . . . A reward of $10,000 for her, alive or dead, was offered, but she was never taken. . . . In this woman John Brown placed the utmost confidence. Wendell Phillips says:

"The last time I ever saw John Brown was under my own roof, as he brought Harriet Tubman to me, saying: 'Mr Phillips, I bring you one of the best and bravest persons on this continent—General Tubman, as we call her.' He then went on to recount her labors and sacrifices in behalf of her race."[81]

From *Underground Railroad*:

Harriet Tubman had been their "Moses," but not in the sense that Andrew Johnson was the "Moses of the colored people." She had faithfully gone down into Egypt, and had delivered these six bondmen by her own heroism. Harriet was a woman of no pretensions, indeed, a more ordinary specimen of humanity could hardly be found among the most unfortunate-looking farm hands of the South. Yet, in point of courage, shrewdness and disinterested exertions to rescue her fellow-men . . . she was without her equal. Her success was wonderful. . . . Running daily risks while making preparations for herself and her passengers . . . she seemed wholly devoid of personal fear. . . . She was apparently proof against all adversaries. . . . Of course Harriet was supreme, and her followers generally had full faith in her, and would back up any word she might utter. . . . Therefore, none had to die as traitors on the "middle passage." . . . Her like it is probable was never known before or since.[82]

From *Black Reconstruction*:

Under the situation as it developed between 1830 and 1860 there were grave losses to the capital invested in black workers. . . . The daring of black revolutionists like Henson and Tubman; and the extra-legal efforts of abolitionists made this more and more easy. . . . It is certain from the bitter effort to increase the efficiency of the fugitive slave law that the losses from runaways were widespread and continuous; and the increase in the interstate slave trade from Border States to the deep South, together with the increase in the price of slaves, showed a growing pressure. At the beginning of the nineteenth century, one bought an average slave for $200; while in 1860 the price ranged from $1,400 to $2,000. Not only was the fugitive slave important because of the actual loss involved, but for potentialities in the future. These free Negroes were furnishing the leadership for the mass of the black workers, and especially they were furnishing a text for the abolition idealists.[83]

Tubman is one of several Underground Railroad conductors called "Moses." As one of the above quotations indicates, John Brown, often called "Captain Brown" by his closest comrades, refers to "*General* Tubman," urging all to follow her leadership. While the name General Tubman proclaims her militancy, the nickname Moses invites further consideration of the internal dynamics of the exodus as a political model for black culture. When placed in the context of Du Bois's and Still's writings, the exodus narrative undergoes a fascinating transmogrification.

Tubman impresses for her ordinariness, which points to a general vitality among the common who enact their critique of exploitation through escape. That ordinariness allows her to become anyone and everyone, exploiting her invisibility as a "dark ghost" traveling between worlds. Because such a shrewd, dedicated, ordinary woman overcomes the fear of actual death from infuriated plantation owners, overseers, and bounty hunters, other railroad travelers could overcome their fear. Moreover, Tubman fears not the unmaking and remaking one endures on the railroad. Dozens of times Tubman willfully experiences the ungendering and re-engendering of escape. Abolitionist correspondence referring to Tubman in masculine and feminine terms bears this out. As John Brown says at one point while in Canada, "Harriet Tubman hooked on his whole team at once. He (Harriet) is the most of a man, naturally, that I ever met with."[84] Even William Still espouses this when he deems Tubman the true Moses in comparison to President Andrew Johnson, the self-proclaimed "Moses of the colored people." At stake here is not so much Tubman's or any other railroad traveler's sexual orientation but the way that John Brown, William Still, and Du Bois see that American gender norms fall short of what Tubman and others accomplish on the Underground Railroad. By attributing a performance of Moses to her alongside other railroad conductors, by calling her General Tubman, it becomes clear that past and present masculine and feminine gender scripts are insufficient for assessing or guiding black liberation struggles.

Tubman strays from the messianic bent of the Eurocentric exodus narratives, which turn collective departure back into individualist pursuits of power. There, Moses's extraordinary character is inextricably tied to his heroic masculinity. In addition to guiding others by the North Star, Tubman uses her travels to reinvest in her "body as a site of sensual activity, sociality, and possibility" outside conventional gender confines.[85] Perhaps among the varied forms of escape that Tubman exemplifies, one finds modes of escaping so-called romantic relationships forced by the planters for profit. Tubman does not simply become an antihero to the heroic male Moses of the Western exodus narrative. She intensifies and surpasses the Western rendering of the masses by re-engendering the critical intelligence and sensual activity of escape and by forging the communal links that Brother Mann lacked and that Wells called for, as discussed in the first and second notebooks, respectively. Significantly, Brother Mann and Tubman (Moses) wade in the same waters of possibility, keeping in mind that this version of possibility objects to rebuilding the world to mirror precrisis conditions. The unmaking and remaking construct of the Underground Railroad insists on an ongoing path of creation that no promised land can conclude.

While the passages from William Still's compilation and Du Bois's *John Brown* elucidate the ontological ramifications of the Underground Railroad, the passage from *Black Reconstruction* quoted above sketches its consequences for America's political, legal, and economic machinery. If the West's sense of community depends on fusion, in which all members are valued by their contributions to a completely productive society, then Tubman/Moses leads her people to recognize unproductive expenditure's significance. Tubman is a far cry from celebrating laziness. The lazy would have no interest in enduring the fight of affliction along the Underground Railroad. Tubman and other railroad passengers rebel, full-bodied, against the forms of productivity violently imposed on plantations. When he discusses the general strike, Benjamin quotes Sorel, who says, "This general strike clearly announces its indifference toward material gain."[86] Du Bois stands in agreement with Georges Bataille's thoughts on expenditure, published in the same period as *Black Reconstruction*, in which Bataille says that "the rich man consumes the poor man's losses, creating for him a category of degradation and abjection that leads to slavery," a slavery "reserved" "for the proletariat."[87] Tubman and others like her recognize that one cannot simply work one's way out of the guilt and debt that results from mythic violence. Tubman and others along the railroad decide their lives will not be judged primarily in terms of utilitarian productivity and aim for a form of "wealth" discussed several times in *Thinking Through Crisis*, comprised of the "universality of individual needs, capacities, pleasures, productive forces."[88] Living labor includes and embraces a concept of worklessness, though the distinct interplay between productive and unproductive expenditure cannot be predetermined.

This notebook is not just acknowledging the dark proletariat's role in revolution or noting the dark proletariat's ethics, which emerge from the degradation wrought by racial capitalism. The notebook also notes that a process of transformation within this collective and "John Brown's Body" and "The Battle Hymn of the Republic" are incapable of registering this development occurring outside the terms of national progress. In what follows, the general strike deserves attention because it intensifies the Underground Railroad activities to a fever pitch that breaks the system of slavery altogether. The question then is, Can these two songs register this break and appropriate it for nationalist ends? Ample evidence suggests that this break is doing something much more difficult and abrasive, which is crucial to understanding divine violence and filling in a gap in Smith's account.

THE COMING OF THE LORD

The General Strike as Caesura

From this vantage, the slave is not simply the figure completely excluded from modern capitalist production. The slave is the ghostly figure inside the system because the slave, as speaking instrument, *is* the capital and collateral enabling the expansion of mercantile, industrial, and finance capitalism. The slave operates outside the system because the slave, as human being, gets ousted from the legal personhood providing access to capitalism's profits. Being the substance on which the system feeds, the machinery by which the system operates, and the outside through which the system identifies its privileged subjects, the slave becomes the most needed and the most threatening aspect of capitalism's operation. Increase in profit for the planter depends almost exclusively on slaves. So too does the planter's political power. The three-fifths compromise makes the vote of one planter from the top percentage of the population equivalent to hundreds of thousands of votes from Northern workers. Despite the steady increase in prices for slaves, the economics of hunting and returning slaves, as well as the steady sabotage of equipment and work conditions, takes a persistent toll on the planter. The bolder legal and extralegal measures taken by planters to suppress the fugitive slave raises the level of conflict between those for slavery, against slavery, or indifferent to slavery's functioning. Planters incite a general distrust of federal lawmakers while instigating old and new factions in the conflict to defend their sides through physical force, and this proves to be a key factor contributing to the onset of the Civil War.

The North and the South move steadily toward civil conflagration and are almost completely blind to the dark proletariat's political interests in it. Du Bois says, "The North shrank at the very thought of encouraging servile insurrection against the whites" of the South, since insurrection against Southern whites threatened all whites, in the Unionist's view.[89] Therefore, the white majority's movement toward Civil War was not against slavery but for which form of slavery whites could have. Du Bois quotes Frederick Douglass on this point: "The Civil War was begun in the interest of slavery on both sides. The South was fighting to take slavery out of the Union, and the North fighting to keep it in the Union; the South fighting to get it beyond the limits of the US constitution, and the North fighting for the old guarantees;—both despising the Negro, both insulting the Negro."[90] Thus, the North and the South try to delay open conflict but inadvertently set the stage for war and create the conditions for the Underground Railroad to become the general strike.

When the Civil War begins, the political hopes of slaves, fugitive slaves, and freedpersons are almost entirely ignored by the Union and the Confederacy. Paradoxically a war that had to be about slavery—due to historical conditions and to overt statements in each Confederate state's articles of secession—became a war about anything but this issue, because it provided the only means for ignoring the agency of the enslaved and the injustices they were experiencing. Admitting this would send the entire ontology of the West crashing down on its adherents. Du Bois sees the same assumption persist decades later in the field of history, which leads to two divergent interpretations of black involvement in the Civil War. In one view, black folk run blindly into the Union camps the moment shots are fired, a thesis that suggests they are forever passive, but now to the Union's whims and not the Confederacy's. Another view says black folk are utterly oblivious to the Civil War and leave only after the Confederacy's unconditional surrender. Both views misname the dark proletariat's political objectives and strategic response to this sudden turn of events.

The Underground Railroad's irrupting into the general strike goes beyond revolutionary myth-making in the Sorelian sense at issue in Benjamin's "Critique of Violence."[91] The general strike "was not merely the desire to stop work," Du Bois says. "It was a strike on a wide basis against the conditions of work. It was a general strike that involved directly in the end perhaps half a million people. They wanted to stop the economy of the plantation system, and to do that they left the plantations."[92] Similarly, Benjamin says that the general strike "takes place not in readiness to resume work following external concessions and this or that modification to working conditions, but in the determination to resume only a wholly transformed work . . . an upheaval that this kind of strike not so much causes as consummates."[93] Du Bois and Benjamin agree on the strike's aim to transform work. But Benjamin responds to vibrant discourse on the strike's potential among Europe's urban workers. Du Bois stands alone in finding a historical instance for theorizing this political and economic act among the enslaved. More than that, Du Bois stands alone in arguing that this group's successful strike occurred without a party or a party leader. Thus, Du Bois offers a detailed account of how this collective effort materialized.

To ensure that current circumstances would further the abolitionist effort, "the black mass began not to move but to heave with nervous tension and watchful waiting," and then "crouched consciously and moved silently, listening, hoping and hesitating."[94] This makes sense, considering "the redoubled" surveillance of the Confederates remaining on the plantations; the propaganda being spread about the evils done to slaves by the Union army; and the difficulties in communication, seeing that "nine-tenths of the four million black slaves could neither read nor write, and that the overwhelming majority of them were isolated on country plantations."[95] Nevertheless, "the Negroes of the cities, the Negroes who were being hired out, the Negroes of intelligence [that is, formal training] who could read and write, all began carefully to watch the situation" and spread word wherever old routes of escape were advantageous for small and larger groups of people. Du Bois associates this "swarming" with the "quiet and unswerving determination of increasing numbers no longer to work on confederate plantations" and to "seek the freedom of the Northern armies" who do not even understand their role in aiding abolition.[96] No matter the "obstacle," including racist "attitudes of the commanders," the general strikers came. Attempting to curb the flow was "like thrusting a walking stick into an anthill."[97]

While this notebook has diverged from Smith in making the Underground Railroad and general strike central to divine violence, it leads back to several important claims from Smith. He persuasively argues that "divine violence" "produces nothing" and "operates not by the destruction of bodies but by the destruction of the systems of law or ethics that declare an action to be right or wrong."[98] Elsewhere, Smith says that even if a historic event signals that divine violence is at play (because a structure of dominance collapses along with its ethico-juridical justifications), divine violence should not be reduced to that discrete instance. Smith claims that this violence is more dispersed and persistent than that. This leads him back to another theoretical fragment of Benjamin's, which allows Smith to associate divine violence with the passing of human history such that the history of the Kingdom of God will arise. Divine violence is the negative presence of this messianic power that will have its full expression at the end of human time. Ironically, Smith makes these points in the chapter that is least concerned with John Brown and the raid at Harper's Ferry. Smith could not do otherwise, seeing that the most relevant illustrations come not from Brown's armed assaults on slavery but from black workers radically disrupting the time of slave labor over generations.[99]

The Du Bois of *John Brown* and *Black Reconstruction* would veer from Smith's language of the Kingdom and his eschatological timeline. Influencing these two texts is a lesser-known theoretical work, "Sociology Hesitant," in which Du Bois speaks of temporality as "a primary and secondary rhythm," also called "Law" and "Chance," respectively: "a primary rhythm depending, as we have indicated, on physical forces and physical law" and "a secondary rhythm which, while presenting nearly the same uniformity of the first, differs from it in its more or less sudden rise at a given tune, in accordance with prearranged plan and prediction and in being liable to stoppage and change according to similar plan."[100] The first sentence of *John Brown's* first chapter grants this secondary rhythm a name: "the mystic spell of Africa is and ever was over all America," and by "America," he means the entire Western hemisphere.[101] By chapter 5, Du Bois waivers between two names for this secondary rhythm in a passage quoted in a previous note. Recall the passage in which Du Bois says, "All men were thinking. A great unrest was on the land" in regard to the perpetuation and abolition of slavery. He says that "something was forcing the issue—*call it what you will, the Spirit of God or the spell of Africa*." He described this spirit or spell as "vast, indefinite, immeasurable but mighty, like the dark low whispering of some infinite disembodied voice—a riddle of the Sphinx. It tore men's souls and wrecked their faith."[102] Although mystical experience often gets associated with irrationality or arationality, here that Spirit or spell incites critical thinking as full-bodied, affected, and vulnerable to disruption and wreckage, but also remaking.

The general strike emerged as much from the primary and secondary rhythms of labor as it did from the rhythms of law and physical violence. When the enslaved combined a persistent "negative attitude" and worklessness on the Underground Railroad, they used that secondary rhythm to erode the power of slavery over generations. When the North and the South arrogantly turned their legislative bickering into outright conflagration, they inadvertently provided the conditions for such a "sudden rise," because they could not imagine the enslaved as more than passive spectators. But that sudden rise does not translate into a crescendo. The rise amounts to a "stoppage," a jarring break that steals the breath from the primary rhythm. When the general strike begins, with dozens, hundreds, and even thousands of black workers escaping plantations for the Union camps across the South, it creates such a break. By stealing themselves, the enslaved withdrew the Confederacy's living infrastructure, collateral, property, and greatest investment. The Confederacy simply could not compensate for this loss of economic power, labor power, and morale (since Confederates had to leave the battlefield to do the labor of slaves).

When divine violence disrupts a social order's political, juridical, and economic functioning, Smith says that it "unmasks the collusion of fate and violence within the law, thus undoing the binding power of law." There are several effects from this break. Divine violence "shatters the economy of sacrifice" indispensable to drawing the boundary for "community" in the West. After shattering this economy, divine violence "forces free action. It demands responsibility." Smith makes an important philological distinction by saying that divine violence is not the "suspension" of law, but the "relief" of law. Divine violence does not "revoke" or "issue a new commandment. It simply opens a space for deliberation between commandment and action. . . . Divine violence offers not legitimation but renewed occasions for responsibility."[103] Because the link between law and punishment has been broken, one must claim one's action and offer an ethical reasoning for it that goes beyond the constraints of the law. No one can deem an act ethical simply because it is legal. Nor can one deem an act unethical because it is legal. Furthermore, the political order and its proponents must come to terms with allowing a wholly unethical practice—slavery—to become not simply legal but a driving force determining legislative decision-making. I would add that divine violence reveals one's investments in the libidinal economy established by mythic violence and offers a choice to disinvest or reinvest. The form such disinvestment and reinvestment takes will shape the practical effort of building another social order that draws on and distances itself from the previous order in various ways. The next portion of this notebook examines the national response to the massive disruption produced by the general strike. Doing so shows how Du Bois reaches beyond what he had already asserted in *John Brown*, even as he continues with that book's themes, key terms, and tropes. While this examination goes beyond the historical material pertaining to *Weird John Brown*, what follows will directly comment on issues in Smith's understanding of divine violence.

Emancipation and Montage

African diasporic thinkers often describe divine violence as a radical disorganizing of the political, though they differ on its effects. In the most well-known and controversial formulation, Frantz Fanon's *Wretched of the Earth* (1961), this divine violence remains "radically unwritten," "enigmatic, and outside of teleology or eschatology."[104] Fanon proposes a blank slate without guarantees of redemption, a messianism without a messiah.[105] Du Bois's argument is on its way in Fanon's direction, despite several differences based on Du Bois's theorizing from an 1860s and 1870s revolution in the United States and Fanon writing on a North African revolution in the 1950s. Nevertheless, Du Bois anticipates that divine violence disrupts society and is followed by an overwriting of society. He searches for inventive narrative and argumentative forms to articulate this overwriting without ignoring the urgency, risk, sophistication, and incompleteness of what the dark proletariat accomplishes. As Michelle Stephens argues, *Black Reconstruction* examines black workers propelling themselves *into* the state to overwrite it.[106]

Black Reconstruction proves challenging to read here. Although Du Bois sets the chronological narrative between 1860 and 1880, one can cluster different chapters together based on how they deal with events happening simultaneously, though some events happen on the battlefields and others in Congress, on the plantations, in the Union camps, or even across Europe. Du Bois would not overstate the general cohesiveness of the process or the result of Emancipation, nor would he understate the problems that emerge in different portions of the South, since some states are struggling in the

1930s with issues left unresolved from the 1870s. That is one reason his discussion of different states is in clusters in several chapters of *Black Reconstruction*. Another is the theoretical claim that divine violence is, in itself, unrepresentable and untranslatable, seeing that it has no obligation to any narratives, tropes, or their sedimentation in specific power relations and historical teleologies. These historical facts and theoretical quandaries provide the substantive reasons for Du Bois's constant search for something more than orthodox academic prose.

Blackness—the nonidentity performed by the third person, confounding the subject/object distinction and its first- and second-person dialogic structure—designates the literary, audio, and visual experimentation that founds, enacts, and redeploys genres. No single genre can delimit it. Montage offers one way of understanding the overwriting following the divine violence of the general strike. Although montage plays out as an audio-visual historiography in several different scenes, it remains more honest about its strained relation to movements it cannot adequately represent—namely, the Coming of the Lord and the prerogatives of a nation-state attempting to reconstitute its authority in response to this divine violence. Montage both enables and troubles because it "disavows unity through the disparateness of the parts at the same time that, as a principle of form, it reaffirms unity." Montage does not accommodate an "organic unity" that "synthesiz[es]" all the disparate parts "gaplessly into the dynamic continuum" while "subordinating" all else to the "authority of the whole." No. Montage espouses a form of unity that "wants to make the facts eloquent by letting them speak for themselves," challenging the "blunt primacy of a planned whole over the details and their interconnection in the microstructure," since the idea of the whole itself "compels the failing coherence of the parts."[107] In other words, the aftermath of the general strike can be considered through montage because that aesthetic mode attends to the uniqueness of specific scenes of emancipation in complex relation to the changes the entire nation undergoes; at the same time, montage notes that the nation's subordinating tendencies threaten the synthesis it desires; finally, montage remains open to whatever new forms inscription may take.[108]

Upon investigating *Black Reconstruction* for signs of this new form of inscription this notebook can only respond modestly and schematically to the freedperson's overwriting the nation in several generic modes that contaminate each other and proliferate into yet other genres: the parodic, romantic, tragic, and ecstatic. Their soundtrack is blues, an "exuberantly melancholy" sound expression that "though replete with a sense of defeat and downheartedness" carries "an almost exultant affirmation of life, of love, of sex, of movement, of hope."[109] The parodic, romantic, tragic, and ecstatic forms of this overwriting within the camps bespeaks the contingencies the dark proletariat confronts in its attempts to recompose the polity, its institutions, and legitimating documents around a common humanity. The response of others outside the camps reveals the libidinal economy of racism and how it shapes the (re)founding of nation-states. This reconstructive effort did not involve black folk completely transitioning from enslaved object to free subject. A degradation or decomposition persists, not because of something pathological about black life, but because the black pursuit of emancipation will destabilize the familiar grammar of the nation-state.

This montage-style destabilization of America's political grammar adds greater layers to the Union camps as historical sites and to the "camp" as theoretical object in contemporary humanities scholarship. Giorgio Agamben says that "the state of exception constitutes a point of imbalance between public law and political fact that is situated—like civil war, insurrection and resistance—in an 'ambiguous, uncertain, borderline fringe, at the intersection of the legal and the political.'"[110] As the first and second notebooks argued, the freedpersons were merely movable cogs waiting for recapture in capitalism's atrophied view of emancipation. The introductory notebook to *Thinking Through Crisis* notes that Agamben brackets "insurrection and resistance" from his study of the state of exception. In his effort to offer a more focused history of the state of exception, to consider when "fact" gets "converted into law," he ends up offering only a partial theorization of the camp. This partial theorization leads Agamben to the worrisome conclusion, mentioned in the introductory notebook, that Abraham Lincoln freed the enslaved through dictatorial mandate, a claim that inadvertently complements Confederate ideology, paves the way to proclaiming "No Negro Domination," and yields the atrocities that the first and second notebooks have examined. It is now time to consider what the introductory notebook proclaimed, that *Black Reconstruction* reveals the "inverse movement" where "the law is suspended in"—or, to use Ted Smith's language, "relieved by"—"fact," in which the camp is a site of repression *and* revolution, when being turns to unrest and objectivity turns to motion, producing parody, romance, tragedy, and ecstasy in the Coming of the Lord.[111]

The stubborn influx of freedpersons into the camps compelled military leaders to demand guidance from Washington, D.C., since the Union did not expect the general strike or its effects. This first scene parodies the government and the triumphalist narratives of reconciliation embodied by songs like "John's Brown's Body" or "The Battle Hymn of the Republic." The freedperson's occupation of Union camps exacerbated the legislators' search for a legal framework justifying the state of exception and its end. Du Bois links this gridlock to "legal metaphysics" involving "grown, sensible men arguing about a written form of government adopted ninety years before, when men did not believe that slavery could outlive their generation . . . when no man foresaw the Industrial Revolution or the rise of the Cotton Kingdom." Du Bois jokingly says that "with incantation and abracadabra," after probing the "magic crystal," Congress finds in "that bit of paper called the Constitution" the "eternal and immutable law laid down for their guidance forever and ever, Amen!"[112] Du Bois lampoons legislators and members of the Dunning School of Reconstruction who question the legality of Emancipation and Reconstruction era policies. As Allison Powers has recently argued, the Dunning School endorsed a legal metaphysics in which black people were necessarily barbaric and could never achieve the civilized humanity of whites, so Emancipation amounts to barbarians taking over civilization.[113] Therefore, the legislature is unmoored from the political authority granted to it by the American Revolution, since that radical force was too weak to stop slavery or forestall civil war but also unwilling to overwrite the law based on the black radical force granting it authority in the present.

Du Bois rereads this "maelstrom of logic" to find the cardinal questions, which persisted no matter "how far afield" the legislators "strayed" into legal metaphysics.[114] First, Will the South be rewarded for its betrayal of the nation with increased political power? Second, Can the newly free be properly integrated into American democracy? Third, and most significantly, Can the dark proletariat serve as the constituent power reestablishing the United States? Du Bois parodies the argumentative acrobatics of legislators who tried to avoid these questions and the Constitution's inability to provide an "omniscient law" immediately rectifying the matter. The logic goes:

These states are dead; but states can never die. These states have gone out of the Union; but states can never go out of the Union, and to prevent this we fought and won a war; but while we were fighting, these states were certainly not in the Union, else why did we fight? And how now may they come back? They are already back because they were never really out. Then what were we fighting for? For Union. But we had union and we have got union. . . .

Where was the Constitution during the war? But the war is ended; and now the Constitution prevails; unless the Constitution prevails, this is no nation, there is no President; we have no real Congress, since it does not represent the nation. But who represented the nation during the war? . . . [And] who saved the nation and killed slavery? Shall the nation that saved the nation now surrender its power to rebels who fought to preserve slavery? There are no rebels! The South is loyal and slavery is dead. How can the loyalty of the South be guaranteed, and has the black slave been made really free? Freedom is a matter of state right. So was secession. . . . Gentlemen, and fellow Americans, let us have peace! But what is peace? Is it slavery of all poor men, and increased political power for the slaveholders? Do you want to wreak vengeance on the conquered and the unfortunate? Do you want to reward rebellion by increased power to rebels?[115]

Du Bois's mocking characterization reminds readers that no immutable force sustains a law deprived of the force inaugurating it. Then again, no law retaining that originary force is easily undone. The dark proletariat behind the general strike can provide the basis for rewriting the founding documents and stop generations of doublespeak and compromise. This is yet another brilliant reason for the phrase "the Coming of the Lord," which ponders the limits of Western legislation's ability to translate revolutionary force immanent to this world into the transcendental terms for law. The Coming of the Lord challenges the nation-state to accept the dark proletariat as the constituting force of a new political structure.

Congress winces at embracing a force that the legal framework assumes will have no (positive) impact on the political. Ignoring the force does not do away with that force's effects, however, which must be flatly denied or attributed to other sources. The legislators try denial, which would be amusing if they were not the only path for (reinventing) nationwide legislative authority following slavery's collapse. The freedpersons knew all too well the feeling of unmitigated economic violence with no state protections. The freedpersons recognize the need to overwrite the state's operation, despite the opposition indicated by this parodic performance of a Congress with several bold abolitionist politicians far outnumbered by legislators who create antiblack laws, whether deliberately or with good but mistaken intentions.

All of this clarifies Du Bois's intellectual differences with the NAACP, which led to his resignation in June 1934. Du Bois's personal correspondence, editorials in the *Crisis*, and other materials from the 1930s show a dispute over the NAACP's function based on its history and contemporary circumstances. Several NAACP leaders thought the organization aimed at all times to combat legal segregation, on the assumption that racism, if not racial identity itself, would have no institutional power in upcoming decades. They either forgot or, based on their age, were too young to remember when they could not desegregate hospitals and other institutions and instead focused on strengthening those institutions so much that they eventually competed with the quality of their "all-white" institutional counterparts. Over time, Du Bois saw these as more than tangential successes. They bespoke a different model, *especially if racism was not fading* but remaining steadfast or intensifying. It made no sense to dismantle institutions focusing on and run by people of color, only to have those same people leave to find jobs and support in institutions that despise their existence. It would be better, in the face of continuous racism, to build or support institutions led and frequented by the dark proletariat so they could multiply their intellectual, economic, political, and affective power in the face of open and secret hostility.

Yet *Black Reconstruction* goes even farther with its parodic retelling: Du Bois remembers the NAACP responding ineffectively to segregationists setting the legal terms. By the 1930s, Du Bois believed that by following a concept of the dark proletariat, the NAACP could have joined with other progressive legal minds and black economic movements. Black workers, among others, should not just seek recognition by the New Deal. They should help set the very terms of the law and its attendant policies. In other words, the parody does not simply mock overt and well-meaning racist legislators. The parody implicitly targets liberal political and civic organizations who would wait to fight until *after* the legal terms are set against them and the populations they serve. The NAACP failed to see the strikes of its day as a disruptive force that required something new of their organization and missed its chance for direct influence on the literal legislative and economic overwriting of the twentieth century, thereby leaving black workers even more vulnerable to the predations of capitalism. This parody makes it clear that one *must* return to the camp, and not just to federal buildings and state capitols, as ground zero for what the rewriting of America will and will not become.

The second and third scenes of this montage play out a romance defined "by its capacity to depict and resolve social, historical, and political conflict through resolution of narrative tensions." At the same time, romance testifies to "black insurgency."[116] This romance plays out through the self-sufficient black townships emerging during the Civil War and through the record of the Negro soldier. The second and third scenes most accommodate the progress that "John Brown's Body" and "The Battle Hymn of the Republic" celebrate. Brown's executed body marks the country's overcoming of the single contradiction corrupting its democracy. Thus, the white worker and planter can be redeemed of their guilt, since they are no longer accountable for the horrors of slavery, while the black workers can be redeemed from the guilt of being enslaved and prove their moral and economic value to the country. But that familiar narrative is divorced from the inner development of the Negro. The second and third scenes focus on that inner development and its noncoincidence with the mainstream romantic narrative. In this phase of the rewriting of the nation, Du Bois draws evidence from John Eaton's *Grant, Lincoln, and the Freedmen* (1907). Eaton serves as chaplain for General Grant's army of forty-five thousand soldiers, which is traveling south to Mississippi for the "great Vicksburg campaign" after the battle of Corinth. There, Eaton sees black folk abandoning the plantations and coming to the Union armies. His misrecognition of the dark proletariat on general strike epitomizes the obstacles to this group recovering after their exhausting efforts:

> Imagine . . . a slave population, springing from antecedent barbarism, rising up and leaving its ancient bondage . . . coming garbed in rags or in silks, with feet shod or bleeding, individually or in families and larger groups—an army of slaves and fugitives, pushing its way irresistibly toward an army of fighting men, perpetually on the defensive and per-

petually ready to attack. The arrival among us of these hordes was like the oncoming of cities. There was no plan in this exodus, no Moses to lead it. Unlettered reason or the mere inarticulate decision of instinct brought them to us. Often the slaves met prejudices against their color more bitter than any they had left behind. But their own interests were identical, they felt, with the objects of our armies: a blind terror stung them, an equally blind hope allured them, and to us they came. Their condition was appalling. There were men, women, and children in every stage of disease or decrepitude, often nearly naked, with flesh torn by the terrible experiences of their escapes. Sometimes they were intelligent and eager to help themselves; often they were bewildered or stupid or possessed by the wildest notions of what liberty might mean—expecting to exchange labor, and obedience to the will of another, for idleness and freedom from restraint. Such ignorance and perverted notions produced a veritable moral chaos. . . . A few had profited by the misfortunes of the master and were jubilant in their unwonted ease and luxury, but they stood in lurid contrast to the grimmer aspects of the tragedy—the women in travail, the helplessness of childhood and of old age, the horrors of sickness and of frequent death. Small wonder that men paused in bewilderment and panic, foreseeing the demoralization and infection of the Union soldier and the downfall of the Union cause.[117]

The entire passage unfolds from the directive "Imagine," evoking the fictions held by Union soldiers, officials, reporters, and others toward black folk. This particular directive guards against several truths. Without that single word, "imagine," the author would have readers thinking his narrative takes a realist, eyewitness look at black people when the entire passage serves as a *look away* from their situation in order to keep stereotypical projections alive. Eaton means to call the freedpersons intellectually deficient by speaking of their inarticulacy. He also means to vacate any possibility of political agency in their decision to enter the camps. Otherwise, Eaton must consider the group-centered leadership of the strike. He must accept that they accomplished a strike without a party or more precisely, without a party leader. For Eaton holds tightly to the idea that only a single charismatic leader could guide this lost group of people: "There was no plan in this exodus, no Moses to lead it. Unlettered reason or the mere inarticulate decision of instinct brought them to us." Exploring this mess of projections and defenses in Eaton's imagining of the general strike will reveal a romance in black life, irrespective of the Union camp's equivocation between cross-racial reconciliation and hostility toward Emancipation.

Oddly enough, in the passage, "an army of fighting men" fears "an army of slaves and fugitives." It is difficult to envision the Union fighting the Confederacy if it dreads "helpless" people "garbed in rags or in silks, with feet shod or bleeding," with "flesh torn" from their escapes, suffering from "horrors of sickness and frequent death." Eaton overtly admits that many in the Union army said black camp occupiers led to the "demoralization and infection of the Union soldier and the downfall of the Union cause." Eaton admits to Union racism but not to its consequences. Making the freedpersons the cause of sickness also recasts Grant's camps as a once-healthy space—a miracle indeed, after Grant's army had just finished the slaughter at Corinth and walked across a field of seven thousand corpses. The freedpersons did not bring demoralization and infection to an otherwise clean camp. The camp's Union soldiers allowed sicknesses to combine and spread, because of their own fantasies about what could go wrong by actually helping black people: "The white [Union] soldiers, for the most part, were opposed to serving Negroes in any manner, and were even unwilling to guard the camps where they were segregated or protect them against violence," Du Bois says.[118]

Beyond this warped medical discourse, "demoralization and infection" associates the freedpersons with destroying the Union cause. This should give pause to any casual acquaintance with conventional narratives of the Civil War. What could the Union cause be, if the Union considered it a distraction to attend to freedpersons who were risking life and limb to find freedom? Certainly it undermines the idea that, from the outset, the Union fought to end slavery. But even for those who wanted only to preserve the nation, the Union army proved shortsighted if it did not see the strategic advantage of the Confederacy's living infrastructure abandoning that position to join the Union cause. Thus, Eaton wrongly attributes blindness to the terror and hope of the freedpersons, who know full well the terror they escape. The Union, not the freedpersons, remains blind to how Emancipation morally justifies defeating the Confederacy, how strategically invaluable the freedpersons would be in defeating the Confederacy, and how the freedpersons had their own objectives despite the Union's lack of awareness.

Eaton makes his most troubling comments when he distinguishes each group's relationship to labor. The concept of worklessness practiced by the freedpersons troubles Eaton the most. Eaton worries that the freedpersons' rejection of slave labor conditions means a refusal of all labor conditions, so the freedpersons will work only under external controls. To him, only a "perverted notion" of "liberty," being "stupid" or "possessed" could lead the dark proletariat to "expect to exchange labor, and obedience to the will of another, for idleness and freedom from restraint." Bitterness breaks through the seemingly objective prose when Eaton says the freedpersons "profited by the misfortunes of the master and were jubilant in their unwonted ease and luxury." The well-worn yarn about the black worker's immediate shift from slavery to freedom with an exultant Union fighting *in the slave's place, on the slave's behalf* unravels with Eaton's doubts about black political agency, his fears over "infection" of the Union cause, and his worry over black "idleness." Still's conflict of the fight of affliction continues to yield insights, because after the extraordinary accomplishments of the Underground Railroad and then the general strike, the dark proletariat must brave the Union camps, troubled as they are by confused notions, hatreds, fears, and projections. Only by following the dark proletariat's lead do some in the Union army learn to counterbalance these debilitating affects with affirmative ideas, affects, and actions that recognize black agency.

This means challenging Eaton's confused notions precisely because he mistakes his ignorance for expertise and charity toward black life. Although the freedpersons do not expect to exchange "labor" for "idleness," they do aim to exchange subservience for "freedom from restraint." The problem is these objectives run counter to a context that believes laborers must work under varying degrees of restraint. Even the most dedicated Northern abolitionists remain committed to the idea that a free black laborer would only mean a free *non*laborer. It is this conceptual limit that inspires many of the projections in Eaton's account. Without a concept of worklessness, which allows workers to pause, question, and transform the conditions of their labor, the freedpersons would still be slaves. Were Eaton to admit this, he would betray the need for conventional labor disciplines and the enjoyment that comes from applying them. Hence Eaton's absurd statement that the same ragged, bleeding, infectious horde also lives sumptuously off the planter's misfortune as well. Never mind that the slaveowner actually enjoyed "unwonted ease and luxury" off the poor black and white workers' miseries.

Eaton never pauses to consider that after escaping one site of slave labor, they are apprehensive about the potential for slave labor in the camps, especially, as Eaton himself admits, since Grant's army had not yet made Emancipation a primary objective. In other words, if the camps are so racist that the freedpersons were "segregated" for their own protection, then it is the freedpersons, not Union soldiers, who have won the right to feel "panicked."

In contradistinction to Eaton's initial prejudicial reactions, many of the freedpersons continued with their own plans of occupation by organizing townships outside the camp that would become almost fully self-supporting. "The experiment at Davis Bend, Mississippi, was of especial interest," Du Bois says:

> The place was occupied in November and December, 1864, and private interests were displaced and an interesting socialistic effort made with all the property under the control of the government. The Bend was divided into districts with Negro sheriffs and judges who were allowed to exercise authority under the general control of the military officers. Petty theft and idleness were soon reduced to a minimum and "the community distinctly demonstrated the capacity of the Negro to take care of himself and exercise under honest and competent direction the functions of self-government."[119]

Although other instances of black life during the Civil War are not equally as "socialistic," the Davis Bend experiment is paradigmatic of black productivity and self-governance spreading across the South with the collapse of chattel slavery. Du Bois notes this tendency in Louisiana, Virginia, North Carolina, South Carolina, Florida, and Georgia.[120] From raising crops to working in trades to paying taxes to aiding the poor, the freedpersons acted with the passion of "a new labor group, who, for the first time in their lives, were receiving money in payment for their work."[121] "New" here must be qualified. They are "new" based on the different role they are playing in the circuits of production and self-governance, because they have helped tear down one economic structure to design a new one to better their conditions.

Giorgio Agamben claims that the camp and its horrors arise in modernity with the undoing of the link between birth and nation. One finds more affirming results in these select cases for several reasons. In antebellum

America, the plantation harbors biological life stripped of political protections and powers. The general strike momentarily breaks the link between birth and labor as well as birth and nation. In other words, with the abandonment of the plantations and the occupation of the Union camps, the freedpersons have the opportunity to rewrite the nation's self-conception *and* develop a more egalitarian economy. In this romantic scene, the state does not necessarily become a lethal machine, because it "assume[s] directly the care of the nation's biological life as one of its proper tasks."[122] The breakdown of state power and a crucial economic system enables the camp to be used for different means. The government uses it as a site to control biological life. At the same time, in these instances, that control is also disrupted by an account of life's self-sufficiency on its own terms. However, this self-sufficiency and aspect of the romance hinges on forms of the black worker's place in the circuit of production. More must be said about those outside of the circuits of production—the young, the elderly, the ill, the frostbitten, those with differing abilities unable to work in agriculture, those too devastated by losing loved ones during the strike to function, etc.

Even within a production-centered romance, black self-sufficiency remains veiled to the hubris of Union officials. Some officials think they taught black folk to want to work. Others are surprised that black folk willingly contribute to the nation without the threat of the whip. Although Du Bois lists John Eaton among historians "sympathetic to the Negro," Eaton still calls Davis Bend the "'Negro paradise *that General Grant had urged us to make of it*,"—that "us" consists of Eaton and his white colleagues.[123] Eaton even says Davis Bend is "originally occupied at the suggestion of General Grant," though the general strike precedes Grant's or any other Union officer's plans.[124] The antagonisms between black life and whiteness do not evaporate even in Grant's would-be paradise. Black folks' hard work in a context fetishizing labor activity may provide a path for asserting their humanity and even persuading some (or many) that they deserve citizenship. Such genuine hard work fails to circumscribe Eaton and his colleagues' self-aggrandizement. They abandon stereotypes of black laziness but believe they have fashioned a paradise for black life, suggesting that they continue to desire (rather than relinquish the desire for) a frontier dividing the empowered and disempowered based on race.

An unresolved tension remains in Eaton's surety that he carves out a paradise for black folk and black folks' own effort at caring for themselves. To ignore this unresolved element would be to simplify the scene. For Eaton, black self-governance signals the freedperson's capitulation to a protestant work ethic and the rights and protections that promises. Eaton's wish to align the entire project with Grant's foresight depends upon erasing the general strike that facilitated the encounter between the freedpersons and the Union armies in the first place. The formal subsumption of black labor in the townships at the beginnings of post–Civil War capitalism hopes to create a completely harmonious refrain. A low rumbling of unrest among the freedpersons remains unassimilable to Eaton's account. The tension between Union policy and black planning remains, like a dissonant sustained note plucked between sweet-sounding chords. In this way, resolution is romance's putative object; black insurgency is its underground aim.

The third scene continues the romance, this time turning to the record of the Union soldier to think about the misrecognition of black agency as well as the physical violence enabling and undoing the conditions for Emancipation. Whereas the song the "Battle Hymn of the Republic" boasts of the "terrible swift sword" that leads unwaveringly to freedom, Du Bois takes a critical posture toward the role of mass physical violence in the project of liberation. Without doubt, Du Bois takes pride in the fugitive's willingness to fight for freedom. Yet, his argument implies that with greater support the general strike could have ended slavery sooner with much less bloodshed. In chapter 4 of *Black Reconstruction*, Du Bois says that the majority of slaves "did not wreak vengeance" on "unprotected" white women, children, or seniors. He says the enslaved "found an easier, more effective and more decent way to freedom. Men go wild and fight for freedom with bestial ferocity when they must—when there is no other way," Du Bois adds. "But human nature does not deliberately choose blood—at least not black human nature."[125] Here Du Bois is not saying that people with a particular physical phenotype or complexion are necessarily less violent. He is saying that a humanity operating under the sign of blackness does not resign itself to the forms of force that become inevitable under Western imperialism. Du Bois opposes liberalism's belief that emancipation must be obtained through murder: "How extraordinary, and what a tribute to ignorance and religious hypocrisy, is the fact that in the minds of most people, even those of liberals, only murder makes men." Du Bois continues, "The slave pleaded; he was humble; he protected the women of the South, and the world ignored him. The slave killed white men; and behold, he was a man!"[126] Finally, he speaks in *a priori* terms about liberalism: "the ability and willingness to take human life has always been, even in the minds of liberal men, a proof of manhood." Therefore, when Du Bois says that "nothing else made emancipation possible in the United States. Nothing else made Negro citizenship conceivable, but the record of the Negro soldiers as a fighter," he acknowledges historical fact and exposes the limits of liberalism.[127] This also means that the movement from "John Brown's Body" to "The Battle Hymn of the Republic" does not place violence in its final, appropriate confines. Executing Brown cannot amount to exorcising lawlessness from the polity, so long as murder makes one fit for liberty. At the same time, Brown's body cannot count as a final sacrifice for freedom. It marks a new interval of bloodshed.

While the scenes at Davis Bend capture a romance achieved through a new integration of black life into economic production and self-governance, the scenes on the battlefield reiterate Du Bois's earlier writings on the record of black soldiers. Recall Du Bois's description of romance in "Criteria for Negro Art." There, Du Bois discusses "the story of the conquest of German East Africa." In this "untold tale," "thousands of black men from East, West, and South Africa, from Nigeria and the Valley of the Nile, and from the West Indies still struggled, fought and died," "fought and won and lost German East Africa; and all you hear about is that England and Belgium conquered German Africa for the allies!" He continues by calling this the "true and stirring stuff of which Romance is born and from this stuff come the stirrings of men who are beginning to remember that this kind of material is theirs; and this vital life of their own kind is beckoning them on."[128] That essay's categorization of romance anticipates Du Bois's attention to the black soldier in *Black Reconstruction*. Instead of considering colonial conquest, as the story of German East Africa does, this scene in *Black Reconstruction* narrates a nation's battle with itself and the revivification of materials from this history in a liberal masculine imaginary. This masculine imaginary, formed through Emancipation and war, signals an international solidarity unsure of its relation to the black soldier.

While the freedperson's transformation to soldier opened greater space for involvement in the American polity and a new internationalism, the status of fugitive property did not disappear. When the North finally decided to strip the South of its work force, it did so not by announcing the slaves free, but by "declar[ing] them 'contraband of war.'"[129] In this view, the

North's advantage was to take away the South's materials, which included its slaves. Written in all capitals, and quoted in *Black Reconstruction* as such, one memo to Union military leaders states:

> THE ADMINSITRATION HAS DETERMINED TO TAKE FROM THE REBELS THIS SOURCE OF SUPPLY—TO TAKE THEIR NEGROES AND COMPEL THEM TO SEND BACK A PORTION OF THEIR WHITES TO CULTIVATE THEIR DESERTED PLANTATIONS—AND VERY POOR PERSONS THEY WOULD BE TO FILL THE PLACE OF THE DARK-HUED LABORER. THEY MUST DO THIS, OR THEIR ARMIES WILL STARVE.[130]

The language here is utilitarian, a matter of reducing enemy "supply" and increasing one's own. The clause ending the first sentence shows that the federal government is aware of the psychological toll poor whites will suffer in taking the place "of the dark-hued laborer." The Union memo mocks the Confederate's descent from the battlefield's glory to the slave's drudgeries. Utility haunts the freedpersons because the war is framed primarily in terms of productive expenditure; it is merely a question of who occupies which utilitarian functions, whether for the Union or the Confederates. Nevertheless, the Negro soldier, simply by taking up this role, punctures a hole in a framework premised on the utter vulnerability of black life without any protections from the state and repercussions for the killers.

The Negro soldier's efforts foster "international solidarities," but Du Bois finds that solidarity wanting, even in more radical circles. Du Bois turns to a resolution drafted by Karl Marx from meetings in London and Manchester, England. Marx's rhetoric stages a language of international fraternity against industrial capitalism's emasculating tendencies. Despite suffering due to the cotton crisis brought on by US Civil War, the European "men of labor" understand that the "counter-revolution" of slavery must be stopped. The Workingmen's Association believes that just as "the American War of Independence initiated a new era of ascendancy for the Middle Class, so the American Anti-Slavery war will do for the working classes." The complete "uprooting of slavery" is crucial to understanding the future of labor. More precisely, it will condition the potential for masculine solidarity: "the context for territories which opened the epoch [that is, industrial capitalism], was it not to decide whether the virgin soil of immense tracts of land should be wedded to the labor of the immigrant or be prostituted by the tramp of the slave driver?" Marx effeminizes the "root," which the economic husbandman can cultivate or prostitute. While slavery has limited this masculine development of international labor, the resolution claims that "this barrier to progress has been swept off by the red sea of Civil War." Lincoln agrees to the resolution's masculine terms in his reply to the resolutions, praising the English workingmen for their "sublime Christian heroism."[131] Combining masculine husbandry of feminine soil with the red sea's destruction of Egyptian enslavement in the exodus, the Workingmen's Association's image of liberation *limits* the implications of the Underground Railroad, general strike, and Negro soldier. This employment of the exodus narrative makes Lincoln into Moses and the international workers into faithful Hebrews enduring the overseers' lashes on Moses' behalf. Darker members of the proletariat, the true constituting force behind slavery's collapse and the Union's victories, function as catalysts without their own agenda.

Du Bois looks to Douglass to voice the freedperson's decision to fight. Douglass recalls "when McClellan shamelessly gave out that in a war between loyal slaves and disloyal masters, he takes the side of the masters"; when Union officers "threatened to throw down their arms" if "men of color" were "invested with the dignity of soldiers"; and when our "loyal camps were made slave-hunting grounds" in which Union officers "performed the disgusting duty of slave dogs to hunt down slaves for rebel masters."[132] The moment whiteness cannot be mapped completely onto the nation, racial loyalties compromise national loyalties in the Union military. When Douglass says that "the opportunity is given to us [black men] to be men," he is not endowing Lincoln or the Union army with the power to grant or deny freedom, though he plays into their masculinist rhetoric. He is commenting on the critical conjuncture that black folk are seizing on their own accord. Moreover, he is commenting on black soldiery transforming the archive of black life for the future: "With one courageous resolution we may blot out the *handwriting of ages against us.* Once let the black man get upon his person the brass letters U.S. . . . a musket, and bullets in his pocket, and there is no power on earth or under the earth which can deny that he has earned the right of citizenship in the United States."[133]

It is precisely this future-oriented element that the Confederates attack the most fiercely. To be killed by one's former slaves was an unsurpassable insult against white manhood and the law. With regard to the "raising of a black regiment" by the Union cause, the Confederacy offered an "order" that "said general [Hunter, who proposed the plan], his staff, and all officers under his command who had directly or indirectly participated in the unclean thing, should hereafter be outlaws not covered by the laws of war; but to be executed as felons for the crime of inciting Negro insurrection wherever caught."[134] If the Confederacy is to maintain its authority, under this logic, it must place the black soldier and those who aided this figure's emergence outside the law—that is, outside legitimate existence and ethical responsibility. The irony is that Southerners who caused the greatest insurrection in the nation attempt to label others insurrectionists.

Hidden within the Confederacy's language to suspend the "laws of war" for black soldiers and white soldiers who fight alongside them, one finds the Confederacy's desire to erase the very record of black revolt and participation in their own emancipation. Attempts to erase the black soldier's involvement revert inevitably to the claim that their existence is improper, unnatural, unclean, and therefore undeserving of memory. To capture this conflict between black assertion of freedom and citizenship and the Confederate nullification of this assertion, Du Bois incorporates a series of battlefield accounts to imply that the present *and future* histories of these events were being fought over right alongside the most immediate political agendas. Du Bois guides readers to the record of Colonel Bassett who, with his troop,

> went on, from morning until 3:30 P.M., under the most hideous carnage that men ever had to withstand, and that very few white ones would have had never to encounter, even if ordered to. . . . They rallied . . . losing thirty-seven killed, and one hundred and fifty-five wounded, and one hundred and sixteen missing—the majority, if not all . . . now lying dead on the gory field, and without the rites of sepulture; for when . . . our forces in other directions were permitted to reclaim their dead, the benefit, through some neglect, was not extended to these black regiments![135]

In another passage, Du Bois tells of a Colonel Shaw, who "with scores of his black fighters, went down struggling desperately. Resistance was vain . . . the rebels drilled their recovered canons anew on the remaining [Union] survivors. When a request was made for Colonel Shaw's body, a Confederate Major said: 'We have buried him with his niggers.'"[136] Du Bois's decision to include such large quotations in *Black Reconstruction* rather than minimize quotation to short references in narrative commentary can best be explained in this context.

Recent scholarship has also noted the many freedwomen who joined the fight against the Confederacy. Their many difficulties raise other issues for this romance, even as it lays bare the sheer courage of black freedom fighters across gender differences. Historian Thavolia Glymph says before and especially after Lincoln's executive order, the congressional measures that followed—like the Confiscation Acts of 1861 and the Militia Act of 1862—offered clear paths for recruiting black men into the army and making military service an administratively supported path to freedom.[137] However, the Union government did not open these administrative paths to women soldiers. This means the Union codes that condemned the Confederacy's decision to treat black soldiers as outlaws made no mention of black women fighters. In theory and in practice, any black women fighters remained insurrectionists, to be treated no different than highway robbers or pirates. Thus, a number of black women, some who led nonmilitary rebel groups against the Confederacy, were taken prisoner and executed for their stand for freedom. This provides another angle on the aporias that opened up because the general strike was followed by a freedom achieved through war.

An eyewitness account from the battle of Milliken's Bend offers another image of this aporia for its visceral nature and theoretical difficulty. In this battle, "three Negro regiments were ambushed by Confederates." In the aftermath, one witness saw "two men, one white and the other black . . . found dead, side by side, each having the other's bayonet through his body. If facts prove to be what they are now represented," the witness continues, "this engagement of Sunday morning will be recorded as the most desperate of the war." In their death, the two soldiers exhibit the "madness" that comes with thinking war will lead to progress, that it will move otherwise self-interested individuals toward a national unity.[138] Though one can speculate on the heroism of the ambushed soldiers, no notion of progress can be deduced from this image. The witness, unsure if the "facts" will actually capture what is "represented," senses this aporia. The concluding sentences in this account contain something worse than the aporia: "Broken limbs, broken heads, the mangling of bodies, all prove that it was a contest between enraged men, on the one side from hatred to a race; and on the other, desire for self-preservation, revenge for past grievances and the inhuman murder of their comrades."[139] The "mangling" of these soldiers does not even suggest an aporia from which a new path might be created. Instead, one finds total fragmentation of peoples whose final moments perform what happens when the ex-slave burns with revenge.

Despite his apprehensions, Du Bois reconstructs this record to combat the idea that black folk sat idle during the Civil War. In *Souls of Black Folk*, he describes the slaves as being "dumb and motionless" before the "blood and dust of battle."[140] To challenge decades of propaganda that blacks were passive recipients (and mismanagers) of rewards from the nation's ultimate conflict, Du Bois highlights a record of black activity for their own freedom and for the future of the nation. He uses the words of a Union general to capture the need for this record: "History has not yet done justice to the share borne by colored soldiers in the war for the Union. Their conduct during that eventful period, has been a silent, but most potent factor in influencing public sentiment, shaping legislation, and fixing the status of colored people in America. *If the records of their achievements could be put into shape that they could be accessible to the thousands of colored youth in the South, they would kindle in their young minds an enthusiastic devotion to manhood and liberty.*"[141]

Tragic elements show up in the romantic scenes of this montage. However, subsuming the tragic into romance yields the mistaken view that all things can be salvaged, that losses are never truly losses. This becomes yet another reason not to mourn with or for the black worker and to ignore how others gain at that worker's expense. Too often, the state justifies this refusal to mourn, based on how it caters to majoritarian claims of who and what count as worth mourning. In this regard, beyond the Hegelian thesis that the state embodies reason, the state also comes to embody redemption. The body of John Brown comes to symbolize this possibility for redemption, fulfilled in "The Battle Hymn of the Republic." And yet, this path to redemption confesses its own inadequacies. The raid at Harper's Ferry forewarns of this danger of being a nonevent at the heart of every radical Event. *Weird John Brown* attends to how the black participants in the raid were almost completely forgotten. Several black participants suffered conviction and execution, like John Brown. While Brown's executed body gets moved to West Virginia, no one can locate the bodies of the black participants. Rumor suggests that some of those bodies went to universities for research. Some say that the family of raid participant Shields Green requested his body and a university refused them. It is simply impossible to imagine a majority of Americans during or since the Civil War finding unity under the song of "Shield Green's Body." The record of the Negro soldier, while immensely productive during the war and inspiring to the "thousands of colored youth in the South," has served as a limited inspiration to the American majority overall. The state identifies as the source of redemption and, in the same breath, finds the convicted white treasonous body redeemable, memorable, and worthy of mourning before the black Union soldier, let alone the black participants in the raid. This is no attack on John Brown but an attempt to lay out the logic that will allow Brown to become a vehicle for redemption while his closest compatriots *have* to be forgotten on behalf of national unity. Redemption, in this form, dictates that some *must* be mourned while others must go ignored. And those dictates openly follow racial lines, beginning with this impoverished appropriation of the raid.

Mourning this nonevent means returning to the Union camps with different theoretical tools, knowing that this is a cursory look at what requires further attention and, frankly, endless mourning. Two passages from the "Looking Backward" chapter in *Black Reconstruction* remind readers that this flaw of being a nonevent partly flows from the libidinal economy shaping a whiteness fallen victim to "servile insurrection." Taken together, these two passages suggest how old and new historical forces could complicate Emancipation's occurrence. Near the beginning of "Looking Backward," Du Bois describes the antagonism prompting tragedy:

> It was said that even if free Negro labor miraculously proved profitable, Negroes themselves were impossible as freemen, neighbors and citizens. They could not be educated and really civilized. *And beyond that if a free, educated black citizen and voter could be brought upon the stage this would in itself be the worst conceivable thing on earth; worse than shiftless, unprofitable labor; worse than ignorance, worse than crime.* It would lead inevitably to a mulatto South and the eventual ruin of all civilization.[142]

On the one hand, the white culture on all class levels staggers backward at two horrible possibilities. The first is that people would waste time integrating the black worker into the nation as a rights-holding citizen, since the inherent inadequacies of black people meant this would never succeed. But the gravest possibility, which would cast down civilization, is that the black worker was equally capable as the white worker, that this integration could succeed, that it was succeeding, and that it will continue succeeding unless it is violently halted. In other words, the greatest horror among these white workers is that humans are actually equal, that there never was any natural inferiority or superiority, and that any gains based on this model are ultimately unjust.

The second passage comes from the same chapter but discusses the relationship between the white worker and the decimated planter class. Du Bois quotes a report from 1866, with comments from General Hatch and others, to capture the self-destructive results for whites who refused to detach from that old order:

> The poorer classes of the white people have an intense dislike toward Negroes. . . . Five sixths of the soldiers in the Confederate Army were not slave-owners, and had fought against the competition of Negroes, and for their continued slavery.
>
> *The most discouraging feature was the utter helplessness of the white community* in the face of the terrible problem. Almost any traveler could see that the majority of the whites were parasites, idlers, and semi-vagabonds. According to Sidney Andrews, "The Negro, bad as his condition is," said he, "seems to me, on the whole, to accommodate himself more easily than the whites to the changed situation. . . . The question at issue in the South is not "What shall be done with the Negro?" but "What shall be done with the whites?" . . . The whites, accustomed to having all their affairs managed by an aristocracy which was then ruined, seemed powerless. . . . It was hoped that aid for the whites would come from the North, for fearful distress from hunger was inevitable.[143]

There is strong possibility here that General Hatch and Sidney Andrews understate the difficulties the freedpersons faced. Nevertheless, the report acknowledges that black folk could adapt because of their own cultural prerogatives. At the same time, the passage indicates how subservient the poor whites are to the image of the planter—an image that no longer has a physical representative. At the end of *Black Reconstruction*'s third chapter, "The Planter," Du Bois points out that "with the Civil War, the planters died as a class. We still talk as though the dominant social class in the South persisted after the war. But it did not. It disappeared." Briefly connecting this claim about the "submergence" of a dominant class will help explain why this contributes to the noneventful aspects of Emancipation.

Du Bois makes it abundantly clear in *Black Reconstruction* that a "psychological wage" shapes the relationship between the white worker and the planter. Whiteness takes shape partly through financial economy and partly through libidinal economy. With the destruction of the plantation economy during the Civil War, the South could not return to the slavery it once knew anyway. A change in financial economy became inevitable. But this shift in financial economy did—and could not—guarantee a wholesale transformation of the libidinal economy for the white worker. For the white worker who remained faithful to the planter's cause, who sacrificed life and limb for the planter's Confederacy, who endured the planter's abuses and expected in return to find a place in a victorious Confederate South—for that worker, losing the planter meant losing oneself. One could counter that with this loss, the white worker could gain so many other cultural connections and enter other political coalitions. This is true. But to the white worker still attached to the plantation and the social structure it produced, these options count as a loss as well. In this structure, increased equality counts as a loss, not a gain. Shamed by unconditional surrender, bewildered by planter's submergence, and intimidated by the black citizen's emergence, a white worker could count himself among the privileged only by suppressing the black worker at every turn. The objective will always be to curb political power. But even if political equality occurs, the white worker will still refuse the black worker socially. Du Bois says it best: "Many knew perfectly well that at least some Negroes were capable of education and even of culture, [but] these stood like a rock wall against anything further: against Negro citizens, against Negro voters, against any social recognition in politics, religion or culture."[144]

Consider this attitude's implications within the Union camps. Recent scholarship has attended to the understudied but widespread deaths in the camps due to illness and exposure. Recall John Eaton's comments about the masses of black folk on general strike entering the Union camps, along with this notebook's reading of the "fight of affliction" from William Still's *Underground Railroad*. Taken together, one can grant greater significance to observers from the era who noted that in 1863, freedpersons entered "Union camp[s] with swellings, open sores, and eaten up with vermin."[145] The general strike from the plantations separated some families and, as a result, separated some freedpersons from the loved ones who would have nursed them to health back on the plantation. In escaping the plantations, freedpersons left behind their own personal gardens; access to regionally specific natural remedies; and the tools needed to raise, grow, or hunt for their food. Besides, even if they kept their tools, how could one raise food on land battered by canons? How could one raise food among the rivers of blood? With bodies weakened from days, weeks, or even months of travel, the freedpersons could not withstand the sicknesses already running through the camps. In some cases, the same soldiers praised in the third sequence of this montage have wives and children dying from sickness and neglect in or outside Union camps. This leads to the decision not to subsume the tragic under romance here, since the soldier's valor does not guarantee protection for his loved ones.

Perhaps this tragic element captures a romantic spore, considering that treatment of the freedpersons marks the first instance when the federal government accepted any responsibility for taking care of its (potential) citizens. Nevertheless, this governmental effort reacts to the initiative taken by the freedpersons, since the nation had never claimed responsibility for the health of its citizens—let alone for the freedpersons—who entered the camps with no rights to protect them or to ensure medical care. Even after it belatedly embraced the banner of emancipation, the US government did not understand the physical risks involved in the general strike. The centralization of medicine struggled with accepting the freedpersons as subjects of medical examination; the Union military minimized the hardships borne by freedpersons since it fueled Confederate propaganda. Long-held prejudices about bodily differences between black and white stalled much-needed treatment for the newly free; the Union desire to reconstitute the freedpersons as a labor force focused their discourse and energies on able-bodied men. The Union needed images of a reconstituted black family for political legitimacy. It is difficult to see the risks black folk took to become free when their freedom, in itself, gets read as a threat. Finally, after years of belittling, attacking, or simply not knowing about the Underground Railroad, government officials cannot fathom the fight of affliction that the freedpersons endured to reach the Union camps. That transformative, grueling experience remains invisible, inaudible, or irrelevant for a nation-state concerned with national progress, rather than the more complex evolution happening in the dark proletariat. The very marker "Emancipation" inadvertently erases an unnerving neglect of the (self-)Emancipated.

The Union's military objectives and administrative and cultural blind spots, the Confederacy's self-destructive stubbornness, the white worker's helplessness before an increasingly equal world, and the general ignorance among all these groups regarding the inner development of black folk complicate any ability to mourn effectively for or with the freedperson. One scholar, relating the story of a freedwoman being transported along the Underground Railroad by suffragist Laura Haviland, says about the death of the freedwoman's child:

> The freedwoman's troubles did not end with the tragic and sudden death of her son. . . . Without having time to mourn her son, the freedwoman was ordered to pack her belongings and board the boat. She approached Laura Haviland a second time for help. . . . "Oh, Missus, it 'pears like I can't leave so; they leave him here tonight, an' dess wharf-rats are awfu. Da eat one dead chile's face all one side off. . . . I don't want to leave my chile on di bare groun. . . ."
>
> Fearing that the government would not properly bury the dead child, Haviland went back to the captain. "What is the difference," resounded the Captain, "if that child shouldn't be buried . . . or whether the wharf-rats eat it or not?"[146]

It is hard to imagine a more telling episode. "John Brown's Body" makes audible and visible the pain of the enslaved who wish for freedom and wait for a hero. The song can even make more attentive listeners aware of the black man as brave Union soldier. But the song has no place for the (self-) Emancipated mother whose child dies unexpectedly of illness. The captain's insensitivity betrays the image of the valorous soldier putting the state's redemptive power into action. Episodes like this help explain why the dark proletariat constantly "enshrine[s] the political importance of ancestry, mourning and commemoration" in the fight against "social alienation."[147] The issue here is whether this same practice can be extended to the nation-state. On that score, one must answer, no.

Thinking Through Crisis has focused intently on the links between politics and the libidinal economy. Ample evidence indicates that the state's redemptive tendencies would ultimately subsume and get rid of this mourning process, without holding others accountable for their unwillingness to mourn. In that regard, this notebook stands in agreement with Smith's argument near the end of *Weird John Brown*—namely, that Brown should *not* be thought of as a hero in the state's pantheon. He should be thought of alongside Shields Green and other black raid participants. He should be thought of alongside the many who died in their escape from slavery. He should be thought of alongside the mother being pushed past properly mourning her child's death (as he was hindered from mourning his own children's deaths in the raid). Brown's body should be thought of alongside the children's corpses left to decay, available for the rodent's feast, irredeemable, because the state has never articulated or embodied an ethics worthy of the role.

When the state can give up this redemptive role, guilt will no longer be needed to bind citizens to the law. New forms of justice can be pursued, with the intent of opening up to the fragility of human life, rather than attempting to reinforce the potency of the state. But until the deceased black child's commemoration can be distinguished from the rat's hunger, then Emancipation remains, in part, a nonevent.

The final sequence of this montage explores the ecstatic. It can address several concerns regarding the relationship between the stanzas from the "Battle Hymn of the Republic" and "Ode to Joy" in *Black Reconstruction* and leads to a final response to *Weird John Brown*. These questions can only be answered by first clarifying how the ecstasy in Emancipation goes beyond the limits of Western sovereignty. For Agamben, the sovereign singlehandedly wields the decision. This decision-making capacity grants an "ecstasy-belonging" to "the sovereign [who] stands outside of the normally valid juridical order, and yet belongs to it."[148] With this description of sovereignty as ecstasy, Agamben may go too far in critically appropriating Carl Schmitt's outlook here. Agamben's theory, with Lincoln as the only sovereign force, would make the movement from the "Battle Hymn of the Republic" to "Ode to Joy" a nationalist telos. This is the first step of assuming an *equivalence* between "Ode to Joy" and the "Battle Hymn of the Republic," such that the former becomes the sonic, thematic, and philosophical basis for the latter.

Applying Agamben's theory here means there is only one form of ecstasy at play, such that the violence of Civil War is the only way of leading the joyous, "fire drunk" ones into Elysium. The stanza from the "Battle Hymn of the Republic" certainly complements an ecstasy that fuses the freedperson with the nation. Several passages in *Black Reconstruction* could support this approach. An "unlettered leader of the fugitive slaves pictured" Emancipation this way: "And then we saw the lightning—that was the guns! And then we heard the thunder—that was the big guns; and the we heard the rain falling, and that was the drops of blood falling; and when we came to get in the crops it was dead men that we reaped."[149] This version of the ecstatic affirms the agency and bravery of the black soldier, something Du Bois himself has already affirmed. But this version makes murder the conduit to national belonging, with the execution of John Brown being the titular case.

This notebook has put great effort into countering the claim that only the sovereign, especially in the case of Lincoln, holds the decision in states of exception. *Black Reconstruction*'s account of Emancipation suggests that the history contrasts so sharply with Agamben's conclusions about the Civil War that his theory must be rethought. Within the terms of his own argument, Agamben can effectively say that modern sovereignty, from a topological perspective, fits inside and outside the juridical order it controls. At every turn of this notebook, and especially in the montage currently under discussion, the dark proletariat's efforts have worked outside the forms of fusion that link ecstasy and nationalism. This failure renders the movement from the "Battle Hymn of the Republic" to "Ode to Joy" theoretically untenable, despite the popular link that keeps the songs together. Actually, these poetic fragments draw on two distinct theological imaginaries, despite their frequent encounters over the centuries. The antebellum South imagined itself as the revivification of classical culture. As early as *Souls of Black Folk*, Du Bois turned to the Greek imaginary to counter Jim Crow at home and abroad. Translation across imaginaries always yields divergences, however slight, which mark thought's movement. The "Battle Hymn of the Republic," draws sonically and thematically on "Ode to Joy" and changes the meaning of the ecstatic in the process. Specifically, the "Battle Hymn of the Republic" conflates the mythic violence that binds people to the law through guilt with the divine violence that expiates, allowing for the creation of a different social order. *Thinking Through Crisis* has concentrated on distinguishing between mythic and divine violence conceptually, aesthetically, and historically. Keeping that difference in mind, perhaps this teleological movement is so untenable that Du Bois uses "Ode to Joy" to signpost a confusion of means and ends: one can conclude that the law-preserving violence that protected slavery and then redeemed the slaveowners, but not the enslaved, cannot lead to the Elysian fields in Schiller's poem. Another form of ecstasy manifests itself in the dark proletariat.

As Gerald Bruns says in *On the Anarchy of Poetry and Philosophy: A Guide for the Unruly*, "Ecstasy means that (starting with myself) I am outside of and uncontainable within any order of things, an exile or nomad. However, this does not mean no one shares my condition." Ecstasy "is always a movement from one to another that produces a gathering," a "sharing or division of voices in which the divine voice or 'voice itself' is multiplied by being passed from one singularity to another."[150] Ecstasy involves "fascination." Maurice Blanchot's discussion of ecstasy in terms of flight and stealing away partly inspires Bruns's comments and is worth quoting here as well: "Flight now makes each thing rise up as though it were all things and the whole of things—not like a secure order in which one might take shelter, nor even like a hostile order against which one must struggle, but as the movement that *steals* and *steals away*. Thus flight not only reveals reality as being this whole . . . that one must flee: flight is this very whole that steals away, and to which it draws us even while repelling us."[151] Bruns will go on to say that flight precedes any form of "the settlement, the village, the realm, the social contract, civil society, liberal democracy, the total or merely procedural state."[152] Blanchot's and Bruns's arguments converge with Du Bois's account in *Black Reconstruction*. Ecstasy depends on a sharing of differences that combats sovereignty's effort to subsume all differences. Ecstasy inspires the fugitivity that will never submit to the sovereign ban. This other version of ecstasy, with its emphasis on those who steal away, necessarily brings attention to the figures who have received closest attention in this notebook: the fugitive slave, the freedperson in Union Camps, the dark proletariat in its myriad expressions. In other words, for Du Bois, ecstasy is not another property of the sovereign. It manifests the transformations internal to the proletariat that no social order can own or abstract from its performance.

Du Bois finds an analogy between the dark proletariat's ecstasy and the ancient Greek. As far back as *Souls of Black Folk*, Du Bois considers the "frenzy" of the black church analogous to the spiritual cults "as old as religion, as Delphi and Endor."[153] Du Bois is *not* suggesting that black life derived its ecstasy from Delphi and Endor. These religious sites stand out to him because they are within continental Europe's geography but unclaimed by the Enlightenment. In other words, if the West cannot even claim this tragic-ecstatic way of being within its geographical and cultural borders, then blackness's frenzy will appear not simply foreign but dangerous. *Souls of Black Folk* also associates the ecstatic with a range of performances, from the "silent rapt countenance or the low murmur and moan to the mad abandon of physical fervor—the stamping, shrieking, and shouting, the rushing to and fro and wild waving of arms, the weeping and laughing, the vision and the trance."[154] Du Bois says "many generations" of black folk "firmly believed that without this visible manifestation of the God there could be no true communion with the Invisible."[155]

More than thirty years later, Du Bois reshapes this ethnographical observation into a way of describing the revolutionary meaning of Emancipation within the dark proletariat. He asks his readers, "Suppose on some gray day, as you plod down Wall Street, you should see God sitting on the Treasury steps, in His Glory, with the thunders curved about him?" He assumes his readers will reply that this is "foolish talk." Yet, for the "four million black folk emancipated by civil war, God was real. They knew Him. They had met Him personally in many a wild orgy of religious frenzy, or in the black stillness of night." God planned that "they were to suffer and be degraded, and then afterwards by Divine edict, raised to manhood and power; and so on January 1, 1863, He made them free."[156] Institutional religious devotion matters little here. Besides, as early as *Souls of Black Folk*, Du Bois identifies but does not try to explain the "dimly understood theology" within black culture, whose "real poetry" operates "beneath conventional theology."[157] Du Bois invites his readers to see the political implications of a subjectivity whose divinity infuses lines of flight and whose singular escapes convey a different totality still in realization, not subsumable by sovereignty's powers.

Therefore, the freedperson wanders onto an Elysian landscape quite different than national sovereignty would expect. The freedperson's path does not begin with an Elysian dream culminating in a reborn republic. "The General Strike" and "The Coming of the Lord" chapters chart the path of a misrecognized humanity taking an underground path that undoes its shackles by fugitive means, mounting a revolution that reverberates around the world. And yet, a world so unwilling to change for them could not negate the change in them. The freedperson's joy involves "the trembling of a deliverance beyond all freedom."[158] The complicated arc of this notebook, which has centered on an unrelenting fugitivity that never finds a home despite its victories against slavery's menace, means something other than freedom being the pursuit of happiness. Without doubt, the slaves accomplish a centuries-long dream: "The mass of slaves . . . were in religious and hysterical fervor. This was the Coming of the Lord. This was the fulfillment of prophecy and legend. It was the Golden Dawn, after chains of a thousand years. It was everything miraculous and perfect and promising." Yet, the joy they feel cannot be reduced to "appeasement" or satisfaction. This is partly because racism remained a formidable threat to their well-being. But this is also because they experience a joy so overflowing that it goes beyond appropriation and accumulation. No single being or community could feel the determination, diligence, excitement, and suffering that wrenches the subject in multiple directions toward unity, parody, fulfillment, and nonevent simultaneously and honestly claim to possess it. Ecstatic experience involves freedom liberated from the need to accumulate.

Under these conditions, the "glory" of the Coming of the Lord changes drastically. *Black Reconstruction*'s first uses of the word indicate that different traditions give "glory" quite different definitions. At one point, Du Bois lays out the planter's logic for slavery, saying, "They said: slavery was wrong but not all wrong. . . . God made black men; God made slavery; the will of God be done; slavery to *the glory of God* and black men as his servants and ours; slavery as a way to freedom—the freedom of blacks, the freedom of whites."[159] It is impossible for Emancipation, accomplished by black folk and for black folk, to count as glorious on those terms. Du Bois could have restricted his new definition to battlefield heroism and related military spectacles. He could have limited glory to the new entrepreneurial opportunities of a black petty-bourgeoisie. Instead, he leads with examples that locate glory in its most "brilliant form" in depictions of the everyday:[160]

> They prayed; they worked; they danced and sang; they studied to learn; they wanted to wander. Some for the first time in their lives saw Town; some left the plantation and walked out into the world. . . .
>
> It was everything miraculous and perfect and promising. For the first time in their life, they could travel; they could see; they could change the dead level of their labor; they could talk to friends and sit at sundown and in moonlight, listening and imparting wonder-tales. They could hunt in the swamps and fish in the rivers. And, above all, they could stand up and assert themselves.[161]

It seems nonsensical for Du Bois to identify dancing, singing, hunting, and fishing with the miraculous. Their exuberance shows in the participant's relation to the activity, the participant's relation with themselves, and the participant's relation with other participants—relationships that operate beyond appropriation, expropriation, or accumulation. With the Coming of the Lord, these activities index relations outside the sovereign ban. As the first and second notebooks reveal, Jim Crow must restore the sovereign ban by stigmatizing these instances of free common use and self-making as sinful idleness. For the new freedperson's process of becoming, though, these activities indicate a temporary break from the sovereign ban that produces bare life. From this other vantage, nothing could be more "promising" to those who just overturned the slave system, who smote the hands that cracked the overseer's lash and want a style of life that is virtual to its form.[162]

Du Bois repeats in *Black Reconstruction* what he says of the Coming of the Lord in *Souls of Black Folk*—with a crucial difference. In *Souls of Black Folk*, the Civil War fascinates for what white soldiers and politics did for enslaved spectators detached from the action. In *Black Reconstruction*, the dark proletariat frees itself, the nation, and the world. In other words, the miracle is not the dictator's decision. The miracle is the surplus of the dark proletariat's shared labor for emancipation. That surplus is not exhibited primarily through increasingly efficient productive forces for the economy, the military, or state bureaucracy but through an unproductive social expenditure that allows for the making of new ethical relations.

It is difficult to hold on to these disparate characteristics of revolution. On the one hand, Du Bois says that "the emancipation of the laboring class in half the nation" is "comparable to the upheavals in France in the past, and in Russia, Spain, India, and China today." And yet, the most important examples of freedom are not linked to the operation of the state, the economy, or electoral politics but to the mundane interactions discussed a moment ago. The tentative answer points back to the ecstasy at play in black life. It carried a transcendence—in this case, an upheaval of world history accomplished by those who were not even considered historical beings. But that transcendence turns back toward the everyday, toward immanence. Ecstasy is an internal labor of self, community, and world, an immanent transcendence that affirms life even in its risks and many afflictions. And so, Smith critiques immanentist ethical philosophies but fails to consider how the immanent and transcendent inform each other in Du Bois's account of a divine violence.

With one final twist, Du Bois goes farther than Schiller by saying that with Emancipation the dark proletariat sang a new song:

A great song arose, the loveliest thing born this side the seas. It was a new song. It did not come Africa, though the dark throb and beat of that Ancient of Days was in it and through it. It did not come from white America. . . . It was a new song and its deep and plaintive beauty, its great cadences and wild appeal wailed, throbbed and thundered on the world's ears with a message seldom voiced by man. It swelled and blossomed like incense, improvised and born anew out of an age long past, and weaving into its texture the old and new melodies in word and in thought.[163]

Between "John Brown's Body" and the foreign language representation of "*An Die Freude*" ("Ode to Joy") at the end of chapters 4 and 5 of *Black Reconstruction*, Du Bois seems to suggest that if we heard the song of Emancipation with our own ears, it would be like hearing a foreign language. Pro-Confederate Southerners "heard it and never understood" while "white Northerners" "*listened without ears.*" Their inability and unwillingness to hear comes from an inheritance of willful ignorance. But the song does not stop there: "Yet it lived and grew; always it grew and swelled and lived." Notably, Du Bois does not say it ever died, even in the 1930s. And how could it? Du Bois characterizes the song by its impact on the world's ears, by its break with historical frameworks, and by its internal dynamics: "improvised and born anew out of an age long past, and weaving into its texture the old and new melodies in word and in thought."[164] Just as this song arises and lives on unnamed but deeply felt, the emancipatory effort among black Americans sustains its force outside conventional intellectual categories. It endures without outside justification. Du Bois would have his readers sit with a provocation—namely, that blackness is its own adequate cause. Learning the movement, the feeling, the relation, and the force of this joyous, earth-shattering song and becoming its cocreators as we create ourselves—this is the challenge *Black Reconstruction* poses for the present.

ZORA NEALE HURSTON'S *MOSES, MAN OF THE MOUNTAIN*

An Anthropology of Power

If slavery only laid its weight of chains
Upon the weary, aching limbs, e'en then
It were a curse; but when it frets through nerve
And flesh and eats into the weary soul,
Oh then it is a thing for every human
Heart to loathe, and this was Israel's fate,
For when the chains were shaken from their limbs
They failed to strike the impress from their souls.

. . . .

. . . but the saddest trial was
To see the light and joy fade from their faces
When the faithless spies spread through their camp
Their ill report; and when the people wept
In hopeless unbelief . . .
. . . and asked a captain from their bands
To lead them back where they might bind anew
Their broken chains

—FRANCES E. W. HARPER, *MOSES: A STORY OF THE NILE*

The first, second, and third notebooks grapple with the theological imaginary—Wright's use of "down by the riverside," Wells's "exodus" of black Memphians, Du Bois's expansion on the trope of exodus with the Underground Railroad and "the Coming of the Lord"—because of its centrality to modern politics. The first notebook takes seriously that at the "riverside" one can find an embodied, critical potential in the masses; the second notebook pushes a conventional Christian notion of passivity for a classically inflected demand for agency; and the third notebook registers the divine violence that takes up the multitude in its world-overturning movement. This fourth notebook ponders how the theological imaginary enables or represses liberatory political visions during social breakdown. *Black Reconstruction* searches out and dismantles the racist "propaganda of history" distorting the truth about black agency, including the claim that black workers did nothing to liberate themselves. *Black Reconstruction* takes great effort to demonstrate how white abolitionists, Union army soldiers, and Abraham Lincoln failed to understand the world-historical significance of Emancipation, let alone foresee it, which undermines the messianic narratives misrepresenting the dark proletariat. *Black Reconstruction* says much less about when the dark proletariat internalizes the need for a charismatic individual who will single-handedly overthrow oppression and walk the masses into a more just society.

At stake here is the issue of transference, when "the subject who is supposed to know"—be it a psychoanalyst, a teacher, or in this case, a political leader—becomes the locus of another subject's desires. Of course, the same subject may resist their own transference and accept that this leader will never have the answers to the subject's questions. Fred Moten's *In the Break* follows the lead of Felix Guattari on this topic by accentuating the resistance to interpretation within the concept of transference. Moten, like Guattari before him, considers that resistance generative of an open-ended ensemble performance based on new connections, interactions, ideas, and affects that work against the operations of the state. But that "graft" of transference must contend with the collective guilt induced by mythic violence. Fantasies within the leader(ship) and the multitude can confuse the collective powers discussed in these notebooks with something emanating solely from the leader. In the worst cases, that transference looks beyond the radical elements of the multitude and puts its faith in those who would curtail, or even suffocate, the multitude's movement. Therefore, this fourth notebook devotes itself to understanding how this guilty relationship between ensemble and leadership can exist alongside the achievement of radical accomplishments; when this transference undermines the momentum of radical movement in its spiritual strivings, its *conatus*; and how the black American theological imaginary does not simply push people into this conundrum but also warns of its development.

Zora Neale Hurston's *Moses, Man of the Mountain* (1939) is the most important and least discussed literary work from the 1930s on this crucial topic. *Moses* offers a retelling of the Biblical Exodus and its aftermath in novel form. The novel contends with the guilt curbing the dark proletariat's resistance and convincing that collective that it can integrate into the liberal-democratic nation-state by complete dedication to a messiah figure. With such hope, the dark proletariat reinterprets its own self-determination and collective accomplishments into chosenness for the messiah's miracles. Hurston fictionalizes the Exodus to critique chosenness and the collective desire for miracles as residual guilt. Such guilt is the byproduct of being targeted for mythic violence by those who attempt to control the "sphere of fate," the self-styled gods ruling the mortals, killing them at will.[1]

On the one hand, Hurston launches this critique in her novel to challenge the "nation within a nation" thesis, which assumes black culture's telos is or should be nationhood. That is to say, Hurston has no qualms with black folk making the most of current institutions to foster democracy for their betterment. As she will say, with some irony, a few years later in a famous essay, "I am crazy about the idea of this democracy. . . . I am all for trying it out. I want to see how it feels. Therefore I am all for the repeal of every Jim Crow law in the nation here and now."[2] On the other hand, Hurston does not believe the liberal-democratic nation-state form most fully exemplifies democracy and thinks it will eventually be left behind for a more just organization of social life. Hurston writes *Moses* to understand how the "drama" that "permeates" black life grapples with the illusions of a political messiah who will single-handedly rescue it from Western racism, class and gender exploitation, or—most importantly—from itself.[3] In what follows, the fourth notebook in *Thinking Through Crisis* will investigate Hurston's novel, its contemporary relevance during the "second Great Depression," its place in Hurston's intellectual-aesthetic project, and the Spinozist and Nietzschean philosophies informing Hurston's take on several key themes regarding the multitude and messianism.

LOCATING HURSTON'S RADICALISM AMONG
THE POLITICAL PHILOSOPHERS

Despite the central place Hurston has occupied in the instantiation of black literary studies, her most ambitious intellectual and creative project remains unacknowledged. This has everything to do with the institutional development of black literary studies and its obfuscating effect on Hurston's writing in the late 1930s, when she makes her strongest contributions to the black radical tradition. Placing *Their Eyes Were Watching God* (1937) in the Harlem Renaissance, a period much more amenable to late-twentieth century multiculturalism, allowed literary critics to retain a classic literary work and author without grappling with the fierce politics of the 1930s. This is the only way to explain the politics behind why *Their Eyes Were Watching God* is assimilable into the previous decade of black writing while *Moses, Man of the Mountain*, published only two years later, is relatively unknown to the average reader. To be clear, mainstream academic readings of *Their Eyes Were Watching God* lose sight of its concerns with 1930s politics. It is no coincidence that Hurston, trained in anthropology, memorializes African American, poor white, and even Native American folk cultures based on projections about their coming disappearance due to modernization. Nor is it coincidental that Janie and Tea Cake try to escape modernization's violence only to become "permanent transient" laborers made more vulnerable to rural economic exploitation and economic disaster, as evidenced by the hurricane at the novel's end. The hurricane was based on the Great Hurricane of 1928 that killed so many migrant laborers in southern Florida, where first responders buried victims of color in segregated mass graves. Even this cursory reading of *Their Eyes Were Watching God* reveals the discrepancy between the novel and the Harlem Renaissance's New Negro trope. If Hurston's most celebrated work remains so misunderstood, then it provides greater justification for recontextualizing her obscured and more violently misread depiction of Moses.

This misreading began with early reviews that belittled *Moses, Man of the Mountain*, the work that Hurston thought would be considered her magnum opus. But fellow black writers denounced the book in early reviews.

Ralph Ellison offers the harshest assessment, saying that "for Negro fiction" Hurston's *Moses* "did nothing." He says it lacks the class consciousness of Hughes's and Wright's works and carries "the blight of calculated burlesque," without considering how such calculation might repurpose the genre.[4] Not only did reviews like Ellison's insult Hurston's writing skills, they also regionalized Hurston as if she wrote of the folk to avoid tackling world events. Sadly, these reviews crafted a consensus that would last for the rest of the century.

Only in the 1980s do editors Blyden Jackson and Deborah McDowell introduce new editions of *Moses* that open new interpretive directions for later scholarship. Together, Jackson and McDowell make it clear that, despite the dismissals from Alain Locke, Ralph Ellison, Benjamin Brawley, and others, Hurston embraced the "pleasure of philosophizing" on "the international scheme of things," especially in *Moses*. McDowell emphasizes that one can only understand *Moses* in a "global context of cultural production" in the 1930s, based on Hurston's world-encompassing interests.[5] While McDowell goes further in clarifying the immediate geopolitical issues relevant to *Moses*, Jackson speaks to the intellectual history behind this Bible retelling. In his 1984 edition, Jackson says, "Hardly less than Machiavelli in *The Prince*, [Hurston] discusses power—the kind of power, political in its nature, which is the prime object of concern for the Florentine in his famous treatise on statesmanship."[6] Understanding what Jackson means when he compares Hurston's novel to Machiavelli's philosophical treatises will explain why this notebook stages an encounter between Hurston and several philosophers. It will also show how some recent scholarship overlooked this aspect of Jackson's and McDowell's efforts to reframe *Moses* as a creative and critical engagement with power.

Machiavelli deserves mention for how he challenged "the West's conceptual horizons" and became the first in that tradition to approach "the *political* field as such."[7] What "Machiavelli aim[s] at is a *new object*, namely, the autonomy and irreducibility of the political vis-à-vis cosmology and theology."[8] Machiavelli sought to make the political a site of earthly powers unburdened by the divine right. It is no coincidence that in this ambitious effort Machiavelli associates his titular figure with the exodus narrative: "And if, as I said, it was necessary for the people of Israel to be enslaved in Egypt to make known the virtue of Moses . . . then at present, to make known the virtue of an Italian spirit, it was necessary for Italy to be reduced to her present conditions, and that she may be more enslaved than the Hebrews."[9] Just as Machiavelli realized the exodus narrative allows one to rethink the political as such, so Hurston's *Moses, Man of the Mountain* enters a global conversation about the theoretical and practical refashioning of the political. It is mistaken, then, to shift Hurston's argument from a "Machiavellian" to a "Hitlerian" basis, as Mark Christian Thompson would have it. Arguing that Hurston's *Moses* translates a far-right "fascist" politics into the black diaspora ignores how the left, center, and right of Western politics find their themes in messianic myths inspired by the exodus narrative.[10]

Still, Machiavelli's interest in Moses may appear far removed from Hurston's treatment. Finding these connections means placing Hurston among black writers appropriating the exodus narrative and, from there, understanding the philosophical influences that distinguish her intervention. Michael Lackey provides a detailed account of the black literary tradition's equivocations regarding Moses. One line harkens back to the spiritual "Let My People Go," which renders Moses a liberator. That line summarizes Frances Harper's *Moses: A Story of the Nile* (1869), Paul Laurence Dunbar's "An Ante-Bellum Sermon" (1895), and Martin Luther King Jr.'s "I Have Been to the Mountaintop" speech (1968). But a second line warns against the dangers of Moses and his exodus, encapsulated in Rudyard Kipling's *Recessional* and "White Man's Burden," respectively:

"If, drunk with sight of power, we loose
    Wild tongues that have not Thee in awe,
Such boastings as the Gentiles use,
    Or lesser breeds without the Law—
Lord God of Hosts, be with us yet,
Lest we forget—lest we forget![11]

Take up the White Man's Burden—
    and reap his old reward:
The blame of those ye better,
    the hate of those ye guard—
The cry of hosts ye humour
    (Ah, slowly!) toward the light:—
"Why brought he us from bondage,
    Our loved Egyptian night?"[12]

Both stanzas situate "the white man in the position of Moses" to legitimate their political domination, a relationship that does not relent because of the chosenness of the colonized.[13] Richard Wright, James Baldwin, and Zora Neale Hurston quote these exact passages from Kipling as proof of their worries about Moses being "an empty signifier that can be used to construct an epistemologically inaccessible God, one that could be used to set the captives free, but also one that could be used to re-enslave the 'lesser breeds' in an Egyptian night."[14] Several of Hurston's writings, including correspondence, *Moses*, and the unfinished novel *Herod the Great*, offer some of the most thoroughgoing challenges to the colonizing projects justified by the exodus narrative.

The challenge is so difficult because Hurston offers nothing short of a critique of the theological-political foundations that justified Western colonization and racism in the first place. Situating Hurston in a global context of cultural production and an intellectual history concerned with studying modern power, as McDowell and Jackson invite readers to do, wrenches Hurston from her familiar role as regional folklorist or novelist. To best understand this project, consider Hurston's letter to Carl Van Vechten in June 1945, in which she mentions her idea for a story on Herod the Great. Scholars have dismissed the project based on Hurston's notes, but they did not consider in their evaluation *Moses*, the project's single completed major work. Hurston's letter makes *Moses* part of "the biggest story in the world." The many epochs Hurston planned to write about illustrate the breadth of her vision. In one portion of the project, she consistently places Jewish culture at the center of the story, stretching from the Exodus to the nation of Israel to the Roman Empire, where she imagined a story on Herod Agrippa's life as a window into seeing Jewish culture under a later form of imperial rule, based on researching the "entire Bible, through Flavius Josephus . . . the Maccabees, Spinoza, and the contemporary Roman and Egyptian histories."[15] She also planned to expand the story to discuss "the long struggle in England from the time that the nobles stopped King John at Runnymede and wrung the Magna Carta from him, to the first labor government in England. Same in France, Germany, Russia, etc, and the Emancipation of the slaves in the Americas."[16]

The historical trajectory in Hurston's letter makes several intellectual and political interventions that shape *Moses* and her other writings on this topic. As Lackey recently argues, Hurston has to reach back to the Roman Empire because she is trying to find the historical conditions for Western Christianity. Hurston hypothesizes that the Bible's erasure of these conditions creates the pattern of racism that will inform the entire development of the West until Hurston's present and beyond. In other words, according to Hurston, the Bible flattens out Jewish culture to make Jesus appear as a *sui generis* emergence and not a complicated product of several Jewish contemporary cultural movements. That same stripping of complexity becomes the model for stereotyping the Jews and any other so-called minority cultures that the West will encounter. While the West's racial others become static entities too subhuman to evolve historically, the West envisions itself as so superhuman it can transcend history. Lackey goes to great pains to show that this understanding of the Christian subject provides the basis for modern racism. In Lackey's account, Immanuel Kant's "Christian idealism," both in the philosopher's original argument and in popularized accounts, depends on this same distinction between the white Christian, who is fully human with a moral agency that supersedes natural forces, and the ritualistic, materialistic Jew who is subhuman and lacks moral agency. Nazis like Adolf Hitler will take up this religious ethos as the basis for the modern state, which means excluding Jews by definition.[17]

Lackey's argument confirms Hurston's commitment to "philosophizing" about "the international scheme of things," despite what Hurston's earliest critics say to dismiss her. Still, he does not exhaust Hurston's philosophical interventions. Of the several convergences between Hurston and others in this rich intellectual context, the most fascinating are Baruch Spinoza and Friedrich Nietzsche, because they directly inform Hurston's writing of *Moses*. Few notice that in *Dust Tracks on a Road* (1942), Hurston's autobiography, she hoped to "re-read Spinoza with love and care" when she retired.[18] Only Deborah Plant's *Every Tub Must Sit on Its Own Bottom: The Philosophy and Politics of Zora Neale Hurston* (1996) brings this influence to bear on her fiction and nonfiction writings. Lackey links several of Hurston's major critiques to her anthropology, when it is more precisely a Spinozist anthropology. Pointing out this Spinozist influence reveals two different philosophical lines that her work *anticipates* and once again unsettles her relationships in black American writing.

By extrapolating Hurston's argument about the racism inherent to Western Christianity and its centrality to Nazism, Lackey puts Hurston two generations *ahead* of the scholarly acknowledgment that Nazism was not strictly secular but inherited a Christian idealist thesis that justified, if not mandated, the persecution of Jews and other nonwhite groups. By claiming that Spinoza and Nietzsche also influence Hurston, Plant places Hurston one generation ahead of philosophers in the 1960s who sought to wrench Nietzsche away from far-right thinkers and make him relevant again to leftist intellectuals and activists. Already in the 1930s, Hurston read Spinoza with Nietzsche, because she "perceived in the masses a character flaw that figures in Nietzsche's concept of 'slave morality,'" which Nietzsche deemed the "antithesis of the master morality . . . wherein the oppressed, downtrodden, and enslaved create a system of values designed 'to make easier the existence of their suffering'"[19] French philosophers will come to this same conclusion but decades later. Yet academic categorizations of Hurston made it so difficult to analyze her work that it wasn't until the 1980s and 1990s that scholars like Jackson, McDowell, and Plant could find the starting points to describe the scope of Hurston's project and the intellectual resources it requires. From there, only in the 2000s have scholars begun to read *Moses* for the complexity that its first reviewers dismissed. Even this short mapping of Hurston's routes and returns upsets Plant's thesis that Hurston found Booker T. Washington's philosophy complementary to Spinoza's.[20] Hurston had great admiration for Washington's institution-building accomplishments, admiration that he deserved. Nevertheless, the Hurston who writes *Moses* and constructs this Spinozist-Nietzschean critique of political theology comes to conclusions that are ultimately incompatible with the canonical representation of Washington's thought and work.

While Plant recovers this project to get at Hurston's general philosophical reference points and theses and Lackey redirects these claims to look at Hurston's critique of the racism integral to Western Christianity, *Thinking Through Crisis* reads *Moses* for its critique of the multitude's reactive passions. Hurston makes Moses the utmost figure (for universality in the West as well as in the black diaspora), as she says in her preface to *Moses*: "Some students have come to doubt if the Moses of the Christian concept is real. . . . Some even maintain that the stories of the miracles of Jesus are but Mosaic legends told again."[21] Yet, Moses's centrality serves to highlight the multitude's recalcitrance, equivocation, and power that cannot be fully transferred to any form of government. Based on the timeline Hurston has assembled, Egypt's attempt to preempt these features of the multitude bespeaks the fear all governments have of those who inhabit their borders. She will continue this strain in her correspondence when she laments that no documents remain from the "rebels" who opposed Moses's reign (contrary to Sigmund Freud's *Moses and Monotheism*, the opposition does not emerge from oedipal rivalry but from Moses's attempt to impose monotheism on a population who did not want or *need* it). Farther along this timeline, Rome will fear the enslaved no less than the Egyptians or Moses. Roman senators and historians will deem *bellum servile,* the slave revolt, to be the greatest internal threat to the republic's and the empire's stability.[22] Therefore, Hurston does not err when she ends the trajectory with the "Emancipation of the slaves in the Americas." The endpoint entangles Europe into a geography of struggle that must attend to the dark proletariat's efforts across the Western Hemisphere.

Yet, *Moses, Man of the Mountain*'s universal reach does not lose sight of the American folk. This line of inquiry deepens Hurston's anthropological interests. Hurston's anthropology draws on disciplinary shifts in the early twentieth century, with its "transition" from "'amateur' to 'professional' identities and practices, from artifact collection to participant-observer fieldwork."[23] Sonnet Retman agrees with Fatimah Tobing Rony's conclusion that "instead of participant observation, Hurston's methods may be characterized as observing participation."[24] Anthropology links Hurston's exploration of the West's theological-political roots to contemporary political events. The dark proletariat's political accomplishments and internal dynamics can receive greater attention as a result. These disciplinary moves radicalize the examination of "the inside state" of things, as Hurston's narrator says in *Their Eyes Were Watching God*.[25] In an interview in *Small Axe*, historian and archivist Robert Hill says that in the past, he "would also have discounted the role of intrapsychic life as well as the symbolic in the generation of meaning." He says this discounting "stems from our cultural and intellectual upbringing which has largely deprived us of the tools to investigate" such complexities. Hill has compassion for those "inside and outside the radical movement" who suffer "anxiety or fear about what the unconscious might disclose." Yet he underscores that "*this avoidance . . . has caused no end of personal and political havoc in the social movement for change.*[26] Hurston deserves celebration for standing among the "sisters," as Hills says, who took on the duty of blasting "pretensions" in the radical movements of the nineteenth and twentieth centuries. Hill adds another dimension to the stake for this chapter: without questioning the affective regimes within social movements, it is easy to fall back into the charismatic leadership structures that the movement's very own successes disqualify, because that single-leader approach is the most amenable way for the West to misread, contain, and sabotage black movement. The inside state of political movement deserves consideration when political goals have been accomplished, so the multitude can protect or even extend its gains while continuing to break with the epistemologies and affective confines of the past.

TRANSLATION AND DISPLACEMENT

Hurston's primary narrative strategy in *Moses* is "translation and displacement," which she uses to expose and critique the hold that the priestly class has on black movement. Hurston's narrative strategy has two sources. The first comes from Hurston's engagement with the black diaspora in the 1920s and 1930s. Her anthropological work and international travels acquainted her with the complexities of translation. The second source, which requires more elaboration here, comes from her study of Spinoza's approach to interpreting scripture. Spinoza challenges the presupposition that the Bible's "textual existence is merely ... the outward dress of what [scholars] claim is a 'deeper,' 'hidden' truth but which is in fact their own invention."[27] Spinoza's contemporaries attributed a uniformity and evenness to scripture that simply does not exist. Perhaps this appealed to Hurston's frustration with people trying to make Negro expression into something uniform when its practices, ideas, and affects bespeak an overdetermined existence and expression. As Hurston says, "asymmetry is a definite feature of Negro art" that she finds in "both prose and verse," characterized by "abrupt and unexpected changes."[28] In the "frenzy of creation," Hurston says, the Negro recreates and reinterprets the biblical text: "The beauty of the Old Testament does not exceed that of a Negro prayer." When black communities engage with scripture in this asymmetrical way, it frees them to work with the gaps, the inconsistencies, and the nuances that give each biblical work its complex character. This collective impulse prepared Hurston to take seriously Spinoza's claim that the books of the Bible are historically contingent.

Hurston's attendance to contingency allows her to inhabit her opponent's arguments and displace them from within. Subtle shifts of the language, selection of examples, or redefinitions of well-known terms can expose unexpected features of an opponent's claims. Spinoza developed this technique to address audiences directly hostile to his conclusions. The tendency to read Spinoza as on the right, the center, or the left has much to do with detecting the assertions and feints of this writing strategy and the reader's ability to notice the displacements when they occur. One needs only to recall his excommunication from his Jewish community, which happened before publishing his most radical statements, to understand why he hid his radicalism in traditionalist guise. For that matter, one need only to look at the deprecatory remarks of Hurston's peers to see why she hid her most radical claims in a recasting of the most canonical narrative of nation-formation in the West. Translation and displacement accentuate the arbitrariness of interpretations thought to be the single divine answer.

Had Hurston's reviewers understood this strategy, they may have attended to her materialist mode of reading, which would have altered their take on her vernacular writing. Following Spinoza's lead, Hurston allows no ideal meaning outside the Pentateuch or the other texts in her political and theological archive to erase or diminish the textual idiosyncrasies, contradictions, and multiple meanings. Hurston is especially interested in how much balances of power can shift by transvaluating the symbols of power. In taking this approach, Hurston responds to her intellectual and political environment in a way similar to Spinoza, who said that "nearly all men parade their own ideas as God's word, their chief aim being to compel others to think as they do."[29] This is to some extent unavoidable, since scripture is an irreducible site of commonality *and* dissensus. But this dialectic cannot be overcome if humans are to be social beings. Spinoza worries the most over forms of compulsion that threaten the very common status of scripture, which allows the multitude to join in political deliberation and self-reflection. Spinoza asserts that "the chief concern of theologians . . . has been to extort from Holy Scripture their own arbitrarily invented ideas, for which they claim divine authority," in order to amass followers who cannot question the leadership without risking divine retribution.[30] For Hurston and Spinoza, then, the multitude "emerges negatively, in the contest between civil and priestly authority."[31]

Hurston's research led her to Nietzsche's critique of the priestly class, as her letter to Carl Van Vechten attests. There, Hurston turns to the theme of leadership in Jewish history and then shifts that theme to the black diaspora. Hurston agreed with Wright, who felt compelled to rise "not only against the exploiting whites, but against all of that within his own race that retards decisive action and obscures clarity of vision."[32] Hurston sees two hallmarks of this in the priestly class, which complement Nietzsche's objections several decades earlier. The first feature has to do with their wholly reactive form of power. Hurston says the priests "slander" others and "justify" "present-day prejudices,"[33] and she traces this to the priestly civic leadership role in disciplining the multitude during and after their exodus from Egypt:

> Beginning with Sinai, and on to the final destruction of Jerusalem by the Roman emperor Titus . . . there was one long and continuous struggle of the people against the arbitrary rule of the priesthood. And from Exodus on to the fall of the Capitol City, *the priests have nothing but denunciation for the people.* They are "stiff-necked" "generation of evil people" "generation of vipers" all sorts of curses and maledictions are hurled at them for not adhering to the Laws. But nobody seems to consider that the Hebrews did not value those laws, nor did they ask for that new religion that Moses forced on them by terror and death.[34]

Hurston's comments resemble two remarks from Nietzsche:

> To the sort of men who reach out for power under Judaism and Christianity,—that is to say, to the priestly class—decadence is no more than a means to an end. Men of this sort have a vital interest in making mankind sick, and in confusing the values of "good" and "bad," "true" and "false," in a manner that is not only dangerous to life, but also slanders it.[35]
>
> Under the hands of the Jewish priesthood the *great* age of Israel became an age of decline; the Exile, with its long series of misfortunes, was transformed into a *punishment* for that great age—during which priests had not yet come into existence. Out of the powerful and *wholly free* heroes of Israel's history they fashioned, according to their changing needs, either wretched bigots and hypocrites or men entirely "godless." . . . They went a step further: the "will of God" (in other words some means necessary for preserving the power of the priests) had to be *determined*—and to this end they had to have a "revelation." In plain English, a gigantic literary fraud had to be perpetrated, and "holy scriptures" had to be concocted—and so, with the utmost hierarchical pomp,

and days of penance and much lamentation over the long days of "sin" now ended, they were duly published.[36]

These intertexts from Hurston and Nietzsche blast the priestly class for denouncing the masses. Denunciation produces sad passions in the multitude. But the sad passions cover a broad range of affects with varying degrees of impact on one's sense of agency. In this case, the priestly class incites the saddest of passions within the multitude: self-renunciation, a passion in which the multitude hates itself because it feels plagued by some pathology curable only through self-destruction. Destruction of self then gets reformulated as sacrifice. Arguably, Pauline theology, among other lesser-known Christian sources, will augment this logic of sacrifice in the West. Even Paul's call to accept the thorn in one's flesh becomes an echo of Moses's priestly class in light of *Moses*'s preface.

Three themes arise from Hurston's letter to Van Vechten, themes that also show up in *Moses*'s critique of self-renunciation: chosenness, which the novel translates and displaces as unnecessary submission to persecution; a style of leadership in which self-sacrifice of oneself locks the multitude into a similar denial of self; and the power of miracle, in which the supernatural ability of a single person comes to mean more than the collective labor for emancipation. But before these themes can receive attention, the setting of *Moses* deserves attention. That setting turns "New Egypt" into a zone that refracts the New South after Reconstruction in the United States and, at a farther remove, the fascism surging across Western Europe.

NEW EGYPT / NEW SOUTH

The project outlined above raises the stakes for vernacular writing in *Moses*. The novel's vernacular retelling reflects more than America's multicultural patchwork. If the multitude is in a contest between civil authorities and the priests, then vernacular writing gauges the vexed relationship between Goshen's Hebrews and New Egypt's apartheid-like regime in *Moses*'s first nine chapters. *Moses* spotlights "the children of Africa [who] have been scattered by slavery," especially those in the New South from the end of the Civil War into the 1930s.[37] Considering the scope of Hurston's project, the New South's Jim Crow government and culture would be the most familiar instance of institutionalized racist oppression for Hurston. One cannot read this early section of *Moses* without considering the other camps, ghettos, and exceptional zones strewn across the world in the 1930s, all designated for racial, religious, and ethnic others. For this very reason, Hurston does not tarry with the beautiful pastoralism hiding the New South's horrors. She pushes this nostalgic rendering to one side at the novel's outset, with Hebrew women wailing from labor pangs and the fear of birthing a son when Egyptian soldiers have been commanded to kill Hebrew boys on sight. Hurston, like Wright in the first notebook, turns to black women in labor to signify the struggle against the conditions oppressing the dark proletariat. While Wright associates darkness with nonhierarchical possibility and light with interpellating violence, Hurston depicts a Pharaoh vying to expand his reach into the underground. As the narrator says, "The shadow of Pharaoh squatted in the dark corners of every birthing place in Goshen" while "the sign of the new order . . . shadowed over [Hebrew] work" and Hebrew expectant mothers and midwives went to "out-of-the-way places" and "caves" to dodge Egypt's surveillance and labor exploitation.[38]

Black women in the pains of human reproductive labor expose mythic violence's policing of black (re)productive potential in all forms of labor. In *Moses*'s first chapter, Hurston follows scenes of birth with the segregationist rules regarding Hebrew construction work in the "brickyards," "roadcamps," and other labor sites in New Egypt.[39] These forms of labor are closely associated, yes, but not clearly articulated. The lack of a transition between forms of labor heightens awareness that the narrative is out of joint. The link between birth and labor proves to be the "shadow" of Pharoah, as he "squatted" in birthing places, "entered the bedrooms of Israel," and "towered over" camp labor, which grants him a sense of omnipresence and omniscience, recording and punishing all Hebrew acts not contributing to building New Egypt. Even a hint of Hebrew transgression increases their already backbreaking work: The police, the secret police . . . they were nowhere, but from the effects they were everywhere. . . . How did Pharaoh find out so much? Hebrew began to suspect Hebrew. . . . Everything was treason and subject to labor fines and lashings. . . . Every crime not punishable by death could be worked out in the brickyards, the stone quarries, or on buildings."[40] Pharoah's spectrality in *Moses*'s early chapters—being everywhere and yet nowhere—is the effect of his regime's surveillance, torture, and threats on any aspect of Hebrew life that hinders maximum extraction of labor-power. In these camps, just like the fictional camps in "Down by the

Riverside," bare life results from how birth relates to labor. Guilt once again legitimizes the labor practices and physical violence subjugating Hebrews in the camps. There, legal process becomes the servant of surveillance, not the other way around. Hurston thereby exposes a most pernicious feature of the camp, which tries to throw a wrench in the development of a collective critical consciousness among the laborers. Just as Wright sought to expose the dreadful consequences of passivity among the flood survivors in his novella, so Hurston reveals how a disunited multitude reacts passively to labor exploitation by a surveillance regime shrouding itself in mystery.

Extracting the maximum amount of labor-power from the workers is only one portion of Pharoah's grand scheme, which is to craft an impenetrable form of sovereignty, at the same time that he hopes to render the Hebrews endlessly vulnerable to invasion of all kinds. Pharaoh's power, however masculinist it may be, does not sit comfortably in an oedipal structure. Mark Christian Thompson observes that Pharaoh's "actions, mandates of the state, are reflections of his sovereign power," "figuring himself instead as a serial rapist/killer, a ruler beyond the law because he has the authority to create not simply the law, but its legitimating originary moment."[41] Racism overdetermines the figure of the father as well as patrilineage's integrative movement. For the Hebrews in *Moses*, the name of the father fails to ensure a proper relation to the law and to their individual and collective affects, since they are the object of society's racial hatred. Hurston's scenario anticipates and critiques claims that the father symbolizes the child's socialization into wider society, proper relationship to the law, and relationship to personal desire. Despite the absurdity of this sovereign figuring as a father when he makes sexual violence essential to his surveillance and labor regime, as the reference to Pharaoh entering bedrooms indicates, he remains central to socialization in that political order. Rather than enabling psychical and communal development, Pharoah's control over social organization leads to individual and collective unraveling, for the Hebrews as well as those in New Egypt, though the latter's identification with their victimizer will make the violence invisible. Any individual or collective opting out of this path to socialization will be read as threatening the entire order, and even if this rebellion succeeds, the question remains as to how much the rebels have already internalized such a familiar way of relating to others.

The following passage from *Moses, Man of the Mountain* illustrates the Hebrews' agony under this structure of socialization, which adds new dimensions to "the cry" that Wells called for in the first notebook. *Moses* says that "women in the pains of labor" "must cry, but they could not cry out loud. They pressed their teeth together" and "shuddered with terror at the indifference of their wombs to the Egyptian law." Meanwhile, "men learned to beat upon their breasts with clenched fists and breathe out agony without sound." Altogether, "a great force of suffering accumulated between the basement of heaven and the roof of hell."[42] Pharaoh attempts to align himself with language such that any speech in his empire speaks his word, so that dissent remains unstated and unheard. He essentially vies to nullify any primal scene that ushers the newborn into life's complexity, to make it as if no birth has occurred, with all its sonic dissonance and turmoil. Pharaoh only recognizes newborn sons through a rivalry with expecting Hebrew fathers. He carries castration to its most destructive ends, by ordering the instant murder of sons. The newborns are not the only ones enervated by Pharoah's iron hand. Hurston composes the passage so that black bodies nearly convulse in reaction to silencing their physical and mental anguish.

Controlling language alone does not satisfy Pharaoh. His sovereignty seeks to discipline bodies down to and against their involuntary processes. The cry marks either a tragic hubris or an extraordinary triumph for New Egypt, that it could force bodies to submit against their own functioning. Such rigidity would demonstrate that mythic violence needs guilt for what it does to the guilt-filled body, rigidifying it, foreclosing its chances for extension, turning it inward while obstructing its sense of interiority. But this attack on the body yields equivocal results, since the "pressed teeth," "beaten breasts," and "clenched fists" can count as transgressing or abiding Pharoah's laws, leaving the Hebrews awash not simply in the sweat of fear and desperation in muggy caves during labor but also in the myriad feelings that these juridical, filial, and communal pressures create: "A night might force upon them a thousand years of feelings."[43]

With this sentence, Hurston warns against fitting the suffering of the Hebrews into a stagism, in which mistreatment automatically fades when the Hebrews leave New Egypt. Such stagism depends on a mind/body dichotomy in which the body falls in line with a transcendent historical consciousness. This fundamentally misunderstands how consciousness itself emerges at the encounter between affect and corporeality: "When men say that this or that physical action has its origin in the mind, which latter has dominion over the body, they are using words without meaning," Spinoza says.[44] This misunderstanding treats one's dream of freedom as its complete realization although one's environment and place in it remain unchanged. Spinoza asserts that the mind cannot change without a bodily change. Nor can a single body change if the bodies around it remain tethered to the same daily patterns. Goshen's Hebrew inhabitants may want change, but what they truly mean by change depends on the affective, material, and intellectual conditions shaping this specific want.

Hurston uses dialogue, among other features of the early portions of *Moses*, to indicate that the Hebrews have internalized a fear of life, even a denunciation of living, and this limits the extent of the change they have in mind. Though some intuit that Pharaoh's death or a departure from New Egypt could mean a way out, they primarily desire relief rather than social reconstruction. Without an extensive discourse of self-examination coupled with a new stylization of survival, they are bound to perpetuate the feelings of hatred Pharaoh has toward them wherever they go. Consider this conversation between Caleb and Amram. Amram and his wife, Jochebed, are expecting their third child within days (unaware that they will birth Hurston's titular character, Moses). Amram laments that "we" Hebrews are outlawed from worshipping Egyptian gods. Caleb replies, "That don't leave me no way out at all." Amram agrees, "*I don't see no way out but death and, Caleb, you are up against a hard game when you got to die to beat it.*"[45] Later, Caleb says, "I hate myself for not trying [to kill Pharaoh] even if they all kill me for it." Amram has already come to the same conclusion: "That's what I hate em for too, making me scared to die. It's a funny thing, the less people have to live for, the less nerve they have to risk losing—nothing." Caleb compliments his friend, asking, "Where'd you get that good word, Amram? It sure is the truth. I know it by myself." The relevant dialogue concludes with Amram saying, "I hope I don't have another boy, Caleb. Even if the soldiers don't find him and kill him, I don't want him feeling like I feel. I want him to be a man."[46] Both men know the veracity of this "good word" does not bring them closer to taking action for their loved ones in Goshen.

Indeed, their sense of fear and guilt paves the way for them to perpetuate the very feelings that leave them disempowered and disillusioned. There is no greater proof of this repetition than when Amram and Jochebed bear a son days later, and Amram immediately says, "It must not live to cry again.

Give it to me."[47] Amram temporarily feels overtaken by the fear that the man he hates most has already taken his life and impregnated his wife (recall Pharaoh entering the bedrooms of Goshen). In this nightmare, the death of Amram's son is merely a matter of time and should be carried out in a "loving" manner. Notice that Amram feels compelled to silence a "cry," following Pharaoh's instructions to the letter. Jochebed, minutes after giving birth, stands up to his dreadful plans: "No! My son is going to live. If the Egyptians come to kill it, then they got to kill me before they do him. If Pharaoh done scared all the love out of its papa, then let all Egypt come against me. I can't die but one time nohow, and it might as well be now. Puah, hand me my son!"[48] Amram thinks he is reasoning with Jochebed. Even his attempt at rationalizing finds its wellspring in the feelings of fear, self-hatred, and death that Pharaoh hoped to instill: "Jochebed, there are different kinds of courage. Sometimes ordinary love and courage ain't enough for the occasion. But a woman wouldn't recognize a time like that when it come." Jochebed only wakes Amram from this self-abhorrence when she actually points out his identification with their oppressor: "Is my son got a Hebrew for a father or a Pharaoh?"[49]

Spinoza calls this the imitation of affects. To be sure, Spinoza's term references more than (self-)destructive tendencies or "sad" affects. Joyous affects can be imitated as well. In Spinoza's lexicon, joy involves an increasing ability to act, think, and organize with others. Joy in Spinoza's lexicon requires a critical perspective that sad affects do not. Thus, sad affects spread much farther and easier than joyous affects. Pharaoh's laws for the camps have spread sad affects across Goshen. The above passages demonstrate how self-renunciation troubles the desire for liberation. As stated earlier, self-renunciation is not synonymous with the death drive. The Event, as the previous three notebooks have shown, entails confronting, going through, and coming out on the hither side of the fear of actual death, triggering an internal transformation that grants one and many the courage to risk changing society. The Event interrupts one way of life so living can take another form. But Amram's self-renunciation does not allow transformation because that affect suggests that he does not deserve to exist. By this logic, Amram would be foolish to oppose his current circumstances, since they are already more than he deserves. Amram's fear of masculine incapacity produces what he dreads. His attempt to outman Pharaoh on the latter's terms blinds Amram to acting outside Pharaoh's limits.

Fortunately, Jochebed abides by a second-sight that does not identify her or her husband with Pharaoh's condemnation of families in the camps. That disidentification allows a different affective regime to take shape. An affective regime only lasts based on a set of perspectives, physical practices, interactions, and infrastructures. Remove them, and the affective regime in place (which is usually a combination of sad and joyous affects) will falter. In contexts where sad affects reign, Spinoza urges us to refrain from imitating others' emotions, though he admits this takes a singular strength of mind.[50] Jochebed possesses this "singular power," which calls Amram to take up a different viewpoint, and he responds affirmatively. Only after Amram disidentifies with Pharaoh's racism and chauvinism, thanks to Jochebed's insight and assertiveness, does Amram stop following Pharaoh's model and consider how his family can work together to save their newest member:

> Well, if we must fool the crocodiles, let us begin and do it right. Aaron, go and watch up and down the road while I dig out a cave under the inside wall of the house [for the newborn]. . . . As soon as I have finished I will come and stand guard myself. . . . The sound of my battle with the soldiers will warn you all to hide the child [in case we are found out]." Jochebed, clutching her new son to her breast, threw her husband a look so full of love and happiness that Amram felt for the moment that the sacrifice of his own body as a little thing.[51]

Here Hurston brilliantly marks and interrupts a primal scene that cuts two ways, informing readers that Goshen carries the potential to denounce or affirm life. Since Pharaoh's violence and surveillance disrupts the black family's affect forming solely on its own terms, the direction of this primal scene depends on whether the family disidentifies with Pharaoh's hatred. The passage tells readers what the result will be for Hebrews who completely identify with Pharaoh: denunciation of life by murdering newborns based on a twisted sense of mercy. The affirmation of life takes a very different tack in this passage. "Fooling the crocodiles" demands that every family member take action to protect their ensemble relationship. There is romance here—Jochebed's "look of love" toward her husband—but this is not a romanticized scene. The children are afraid of being caught. A newborn son was murdered hours earlier several homes away. The scene touches the reader, however, because it does not demand a single-handed messiah but invites all to act according to their abilities to protect the entire ensemble. This is the affirmation of life in the face of the most vicious violence.

New Egypt's camps provide the primal scene for establishing and opposing sovereignty and for renouncing and affirming life. This notebook stays close to the major thread of *Moses*—namely, the way that self-renunciation can fester and sicken the subject, such that the change the subject wants amounts to the destructive violence the subject internalized. That internalization partially involves chosenness. At first glance, chosenness seems to promise a viable, peaceful future. Chosenness should also ensure an inheritance with the same sense of security for one's descendants. Keeping in mind that "translation and displacement" as well as Spinoza's own thoughts on chosenness from the *Theological-Political Treatise* inform Hurston's writing, I consider in the next section how chosenness harbors a willful surrender to persecution.

CHOSENNESS AND PERSECUTION

A number of great thinkers in the 1930s considered the theme of chosenness, including Freud in *Moses and Monotheism*. Indeed, Freud's thought on chosenness also informs Cathy Caruth's theorization of trauma and her primary route for examining "the structure of Jewish historical experience." In Caruth's estimation, chosenness measures a culture's response to a "determining force" that "makes [the passing on of monotheism] not fully a history they have *chosen*, but precisely the sense of *being chosen by* an Other, which, in Freud's hypothesis, is what has enabled the Jews 'to survive until our day.'" Caruth deems chosenness absolutely unknowable, an "*unconscious force*" passed down over centuries up until the present.[52] Caruth then follows Freud's controversial hypothesis that Moses's followers killed him and only after the murder did his monotheistic teaching take hold. Interestingly, Caruth does not consider the daily practices this murdered Moses instituted so his religion would endure and instead focuses on an unconscious force that controls this culture from the outside. Caruth stresses the murder and not the practices of the movement Moses founded. In effect, any sense of political movement—which must have some modicum of conscious decision-making—disintegrates in the face of a chosenness so strong that it amounts to predestining the subject for suffering; said differently, political movement becomes nothing more than the collective effort to bear that suffering, rather than to end it by radically altering one's conditions.

Spinoza's and Nietzsche's critiques of Judeo-Christian institutional religion support Hurston's translation and displacement of chosenness. All three thinkers are concerned with the form of power this institutional religious structure produces, and their critiques anticipate the limits of Caruth's notion of chosenness. When Spinoza discusses chosenness in *Theologico-Political Treatise*, he disabuses his readers of a population supernaturally separated to carry out a special mission. He says that, concerning "intellect," the Hebrews "held very ordinary ideas about God and nature." They "were on an equality with other nations" with regard to "virtue." "Therefore," concludes Spinoza, "their election and vocation consisted only in the material success and prosperity of their state."[53] Chosenness loses its supernatural quality and becomes nothing more than the Hebrew state's specific historical conditions, with the fortunes and misfortunes that follow those conditions, just like any other state. Spinoza upsets the providential history his readers project onto the Hebrew state. The blessedness of the Hebrews amounts to the effects of the power relations, affective regime, and ways of thinking that characterize the state's functioning—nothing more, nothing less.

Nietzsche will attend to how the guilt of chosenness "destroys man's sense of causality" and solidifies an economy of power.[54] Making this claim ties affect to epistemology. In this eschewed viewpoint, the victim becomes guilty and the wrongdoer becomes the proper instrument of fair punishment. Counterarguments that fail to identify this causal reversal will fail. The past will remain unknowable while guilt with no apparent origin (which means it also has no prior point of guiltlessness) dictates the subject's future, giving the mistaken conclusion that the subject was chosen for this disempowerment even before being born. Again, the birth scene in *Moses* demonstrates how lethal this sense of guilt can become. Caruth fails to consider that allocating guilt is an operation of power, of determining *who* can declare another guilty, and *who* can declare themselves blameless with the same verdict. Chosenness becomes a most useful supplement for mythic violence, because its guilt triggers a logical and affective confusion that encourages victims of mythic violence to applaud their mistreatment and to endure it until another outside force deems them worthy of better treatment.

Hurston's *Moses* worries that this guilt underpins much civil rights activism.

Chosenness misses how the "great accumulation of suffering" works to the benefit of one's torturers. Against those who champion "the primacy of sacrifice" in nation-building, Hurston's *Moses* shows how much Pharaoh enjoys punishing the Hebrews.[55] Hurston provides an indispensable example of Pharaoh's perverse enjoyment when he builds New Egypt with calloused Hebrew hands. Consider an early incident when some Hebrews in Goshen feel optimistic about protesting Pharaoh's draconian law. Amram, Moses's father, aims to sabotage this perverse relationship between the people and their leader. Amram warns his community members that Pharaoh "ain't sending for us to better our condition. . . . He wants to destroy us and enjoy seeing it gripe us."[56] Amram finds nothing "accident[al]" about their predicament, since Pharaoh "hunted around in his heart for something to measure one's feelings by and the things that would hurt us the most." "When he found them," says Amram, "he has done those things with calculated spite."[57] Amram proved to be correct. Pharaoh had no plan to relent, only to torture the Hebrews more.

Most importantly, his justification depends on a narrative of chosenness bearing the same affective and epistemological structure that shows up uncritically in Caruth's formulation and becomes the target of Nietzsche's writing. When Pharaoh replies to the protests, he manipulates their guilt to explain why they deserve his abuse and, beyond that, why his abuse is not truly abusive but merely the logical response of a victim (Egypt) to victimizers (the Hebrews). In Pharaoh's revisionist history, the Hebrews entered Egypt as "allies" of Egypt's "oppressors," and essentially "trampled on the proud breast of Egyptian liberty for more than three hundred years." Pharaoh "might have killed them all." Instead, in his mercy he spared their lives and demanded only that they work and build him a few cities in return. Pharaoh considered this the only way to return "the wealth they had so ruthlessly raped from the helpless body of Egypt when she was in no position to defend herself."[58] Protesting Pharaoh's actions strictly on his terms makes for no protest at all. Amram's comments warn us not to confuse protest with identification with one's oppressor, a clarity that requires self-reflection instead of looking to oppressors for the answers. If chosenness links current persecution to multigenerational guilt, then it cannot save

Goshen's inhabitants from Pharoah's wrath. It would likely make them willing victims. Chosenness cedes the underground to those who would use it to buttress the power of repressive aboveground institutions. Under these conditions, no protest can even occur, since a protest requires some knowledge that the government has obtained or used power improperly and must be held accountable.

This study of chosenness highlights the limits of aligning Hurston with Washington's doctrine. Hurston's *Moses* is incompatible with Booker T. Washington's accommodationism. In all fairness, Washington's momentous founding and leading of the Tuskegee Institute places him among other world-historical men modeled on Moses.[59] Industry baron Andrew Carnegie employs this model when he calls Washington "the combined Moses and Joshua of his people. Not only has he led them to the promised land, but still lives to teach them by example and precept how properly to enjoy it. He is one of these extraordinary men who rise at rare intervals and work miracles."[60] No one should ignore the millions of dollars Washington raised single-handedly every year as Alabama legislators vowed to close the Tuskegee Institute's doors for good; no one should ignore his working under constant death threats to his person or bomb threats to his institution. Finally, no one should ignore the many people whose livelihood depended on his patronage, in addition to the educations they received at Tuskegee. But the characteristics that position Washington among the world-historical men also make him vulnerable to Hurston's critique in her novel.

These characteristics indicate Washington's commitment to improving the black worker's productivity for the market, on the theory that their economic indispensability would ensure political empowerment. But this approach, for all its accomplishments, falls short of wrenching the dark proletariat away from the chosenness or the whims of Pharaoh and New Egypt. Contrary to Plant's view, Hurston's use of "Spinoza's doctrine of self-preservation and self-perfection," can be leveraged against Washington's accommodationism. The popularized version of Washington's model calls for the short-term sacrifice of certain political possibilities for long-term economic and political stability. But that model does not effectively distinguish sacrifice from self-renunciation. More pointedly, in Washington's "Atlanta Compromise" speech from 1895, he uses a theological imaginary to tie black workers to slavery's affective regime:

In the future, as in the past . . . you and your families will be surrounded by the most patient, faithful, law-abiding, and unresentful [Negro] people that the world has seen. As we have proved our loyalty to you in the past, in nursing your children, watching by the sick-bed of your mothers and fathers, and often following them with tear-dimmed eyes to their graves, so in the future . . . we shall stand by you with a devotion that no foreigner can approach, ready to lay down our lives, if need be, in defense of yours.[61]

As the second notebook on Ida B. Wells suggests, Washington mischaracterizes the problem by urging black workers to rid themselves of resentment toward white Southerners, when white Southerners longing for the Confederacy are the true bearers of resentment. By 1895 Confederates were effectively redesigning the political machinery to legitimate any post–Civil War violence they committed based on that resentment. In effect, this speech asks black workers to abandon anger at injustices they suffered and to mimic Confederate nostalgia for race relations in the South that never fully existed. And when those race relations did exist, they were for the comfort of whites, not the justice of blacks. This imitation of affects makes the sacrifice for black uplift and self-renunciation for the benefit of white Southerners virtually indistinguishable: "As we have proved our loyalty to you in the past . . . so in the future . . . we shall stand by you with a devotion that no foreigner can approach, ready to lay down our lives, if need be, in defense of yours."

As this notebook's reading of Spinoza and Nietzsche suggests, such an affective structure reverses causality, and Washington's speech follows this pattern. Despite what Washington experienced and witnessed firsthand, when he accepts the logic of chosenness for black people, he adopts a logic in which they become the authors of the crimes carried out against them. One need only recall Washington's difference from Wells. She traveled to Europe to cry out against lynching, while Washington traveled to Europe to say that despite lynching, black people have nothing to cry about. But the point here, like Wells's cry, is not to seek mercy from the merciless but to assert alternative theses that shift the terms of the debate: black workers need not prove their value to the market after centuries of working for free to build the nation, nor do they need to prove their loyalty after suffering every insult and physical violation imaginable. The white workers intoxicated by Confederate nostalgia must prove *their* willingness to view black people as more than (dis)owned objects, especially if both sides would stand up to the increased economic exploitation they would experience in an industrializing nation.

Perhaps Washington aims to beat the Confederates at their own game—accommodate this balance of power momentarily through a calculated masquerade, *as if* he shares these emotional investments, in order to turn the tables, win the game, and leave it behind. There are grounds for this claim in Spinoza's argument that social contract matters only so long as the forces at play require the contract be respected; when those forces weaken, the contract is irrelevant, even if it stays in effect. By this logic, black workers make the compromise until it becomes irrelevant based on the immediate economic and eventual political power they have amassed. Precisely when that economic power transitions into political force remains unclear, since Washington's famous speech says that certain political and legal rights can wait until a future date. The popular model minimizes how violently Confederates, already shamed by their unconditional surrender a few generations earlier and infuriated by any sign of material increase among black workers, would react to seeing the compromise lose its power.

In the meantime, black workers in this compromise agree to do the affective labor that Confederates need not do in return (and if the Confederates do join in this affective labor, they would consider it maintaining intimate bonds with no impact on the political situation). These circumstances make it difficult to forecast when this strategic masquerade would end and raise the question as to how long one can pretend to renounce oneself before one believes it. One might counter, with some strain, that one can perform accommodation with the body without accepting it mentally or emotionally. Even if this were true for short periods of time, the intellectual lineage that Hurston claims for *Moses* would charge this counterargument with reversing causality yet again. Beliefs are not produced in another plane safeguarded from bodily practices. Bodily practices produce beliefs. It is impossible to square the determination required by Washington's economic program with the self-renunciation that Jim Crow's adherents would require of any "compromise." Either increased determination will undermine the compromise, or increased support of the compromise will undermine determination.

Washington's speech leans toward the latter, in spite of his motivations: "There is no escape through law of man or God from the inevitable: the laws of changeless justice bind oppressor with oppressed; and close as sin and suffering joined we march to fate abreast."[62] This bond is soaked in resentment—"suffering" and "sin" marching toward "fate." Depictions of Washington the realist or pragmatist tend to skip over this passage, which fails to explain the terms upon which the suffering is shared and whether any racial inequalities are overcome through the sharing. Then again, Washington promising that "if need be," black workers will die for white workers, without requiring white workers to make the same promise to their black counterparts, already suggests the suffering will be one-sided. Beyond that, there is never a time when it is practical to identify with another's hatred of oneself. Such a claim only compels, because it corresponds to the way Confederates intend to reorganize the social environment for their gain, so the dark proletariat will remain vulnerable to mass violence and economically destitute despite the wealth they have earned for the nation.

Washington's compromise in the South presages a national unity for imperial gains. Deborah McDowell has already pointed out how Hurston used scenes like these to critique a US imperialism that censored dissent at home to present itself as the model nation meant to subjugate all other nations during World War I and World War II. With the help of Roderick Ferguson, one can trace Hurston's critique farther back to the US imperial exploits in the 1890s, which illustrates the distance between Washington and the Hurston who wrote *Moses*. Washington states that black workers find their role in the United States and the world through their labor in the capitalist market, since "no race that has anything to contribute to the markets of the world is long in any degree ostracized."[63] Ferguson has already pointed out the problems with Washington's understanding of black workers' moral and economic place in the New South. Washington, like several other prominent black intellectuals, considered the college or university the moral compass for the black masses. They needed this moral training so they could play a proper role in the US's imperial expansion. The "simultaneity of emancipation and moralization" for Ferguson suggests that the "the history of morality may very well be the history of empire."[64]

Hurston's *Moses* raises the specter of American imperialism at the turn of the twentieth century when Moses grows up to become general of the Egyptian army. The prince Ta-Phar, who would become Pharaoh, hates hearing of Moses's new appointment, but Ta-Phar sets aside his "personal feelings" based on "the enthusiasm of the military bloc and the intensified nationalism which had been whipped up for a generation by [Ta-Phar's] father." The narrator continues: "Egypt was spreading by conquest and alliances based on force. If they didn't keep on getting more they would begin to look weak. . . . The might of Egypt was stretching across the world. Ethiopia was conquered; Assyria kept in fear, Babylonia was terrorized. All tributes flowed towards Rameses and Memphis."[65] At one point, military campaigns make Moses's soldiers so weary that he requests Pharoah to give Hebrews full citizenship so they may join the military and ease the plight of Egyptian soldiers. As an added bonus, Moses told Ta-Phar, this would relieve tensions within Egypt. "Egypt has no home problems that I can see," Pharaoh says to Moses. "What internal problems we had, got settled before you were born."[66] Pharaoh plays ignorant so as not to upset his primary backers, the "military bloc" that attained its populist support through scapegoating the Hebrews. Pharaoh knows that rights for the Hebrews would break his coalition, which would require an entirely new coalition and a new leader.

Therefore, the novel keeps Spinoza's theory of power and contract in mind but in a way that reveals the limits of Washington's compromise. *Moses* suggests that such a compromise leads to the false idea that the nation resolved its internal racial strife generations earlier. Black workers must prove their allegiance by keeping this open secret for the ascendant US empire. Several black educational leaders see their role in cultivating the black worker for this mission; Washington says, "The wisest among my race understand that the agitation of questions of social equality is the extremest folly." But if one is forced by another to keep the former's secret, the latter has the power to break the promise without accountability. The empire promises black people the reward of eventual increased political rights by keeping this secret, when keeping this secret already means the empire can forget its promise to grant increased rights in the future.

The chosen enter a "new heaven and new earth" largely on another's terms, as Washington's compromise admits openly: "I pledge that in *your* effort to work out the great and intricate problem which God has laid at the doors of the South, *you* shall have at all times the patient, sympathetic help of my race."[67] Perhaps here Washington overstates his deference. Washington also admits, "Progress in the enjoyment of all the privileges that will come to us [black workers] must be the result of severe and constant struggle rather than of artificial forcing."[68] After speaking so clearly about deference that binds "oppressor" and "oppressed," Washington's remarks make it difficult to distinguish "severe and constant struggle" from "artificial forcing." Filtering Washington's speech through Andrew Carnegie's frame makes the former a Moses who wants the Hebrews to stay in Egypt to prove their indispensability to an emergent empire. Translating this compromise into his own Coming of the Lord requires black people to accept their place in the imperial design, when Jim Crow allowed the United States to substitute conquests abroad for Reconstruction at home. The peace proffered in this unity leads the chosen into a debilitating relationship. The logical endpoint of chosenness proves antithetical to the project of "self-preservation and self-perfection" that Spinoza elaborated, and the Hurston who sought to "re-read" Spinoza "with love and care" had already taken this thesis seriously for black culture and writes of its importance in *Moses*.

ON LEADERSHIP

Critiquing chosenness has led inexorably to a consideration of leadership in *Moses*. The interrogation of Washington's speech demonstrates that even though the multitude always has the possibility of veering into chosenness, this affect most effectively takes place through leaders. *Thinking Through Crisis* has consistently attacked the "degenerate aristocrat," borrowing from Charles Chesnutt's phrase, to note political leadership who secure their own class gains at the political and economic expense of the masses in times of upheaval, all the while pretending that they usher the masses into abundance.[69] Richard Wright critiques the planters who profited from sabotaged reconstruction efforts after the 1927 Mississippi River Flood in "Down by the Riverside." Ida B. Wells critiques the lynchers, politicians, and corrupt entrepreneurs who steal power in the counterrevolutions of the 1890s South. Du Bois critiques the planter class in *Black Reconstruction*. Hurston identifies the "priests" as the degenerate aristocracy threatening to sabotage radical collectivity after it has made significant political gains: "The Jewish people have suffered and still suffer from the slander of their own Priests. *I do not mean that the present Rabbis do it*. I mean that Gentiles have formed their opinion of the Jews through what is taught in Sunday Schools, and the slanders of their oppressors is taken for granted, and justifies our present-day prejudices."[70] The priests are whoever use their institutional legitimacy to cultivate prejudices that stultify the multitude's evolution. This tendency motivates Hurston to offer her most painstaking analysis of this leadership class and its impact on radicalism, nation-formation, and notions of power in *Moses*.

Although the theme of leadership runs through the entire novel, chapters 9–20 of *Moses, Man of the Mountain* chart the titular character's transformation into the leader of the Hebrews. Tracing this thread in *Moses* makes legible the sophistication of Hurston's thought on intellectuals. While Plant rightly explores Hurston's resistance to the "herd instinct" as proof of Hurston's direct reading of Nietzsche, one must add that Hurston derives her critique of the priests from the same source. Because of their privileged relationship to writing, archiving, and interpreting texts, the priests aim to revise past history to limit the multitude's vision of the future, so they will settle for narrowly defined progress and ignore broader possibilities of becoming. Hurston writes:

> In all the long history of the nation how few Levites ever distinguished themselves. King Saul was of Benjamin. David of Judah. Joshua of Ephraim. Herod the Great was an Idumean. . . . No one but the Levites were allowed to read and write. . . . And in all of them [the books of the Pentateuch] the Levites are reviling the people for not being obedient to them. We have no written side of the people other than the direct testimony of their behavior recorded by their oppressors. . . . It is indeed a great loss to the world . . . comparable to the loss to the world in the Middle Ages when the Christian Church had gotten a stranglehold on Europe.[71]

Nietzsche states:

> The whole history of Israel ceased to be of any value . . . [after the] priests accomplished that great miracle of falsification of which a great part of the Bible is the documentary evidence. . . . In the face of all tradition and all historical reality, they translated the past of their people into *religious terms*, which is to say, they converted it into an idiotic mechanism of salvation, whereby all offenses against Jahveh were punished and all devotion to him was rewarded. We would regard this act of historical falsification as something far more shameful if familiarity with the *ecclesiastical* interpretation of history for thousands of years had not blunted our inclinations for uprightness.[72]

Hurston and Nietzsche's comments link a long history of struggle to the form of its documentation. The struggle's power in the present is supplemented, hindered, or rerouted based on its framing in the archive. For Hurston, the priest's primary method of disarticulating thought from action stems from narrow reinterpretations of the greatest actors in Hebrew cultural history. The illiteracy of the masses made it severely difficult to upend this interpretation and establish a new one that could shape the critical consciousness of future generations.

By concluding this section of her letter with a jump from ancient Israel to the Middle Ages, Hurston joins Nietzsche's lament over the centuries-long ascendance of the "ecclesiastical" historical approach, which judges the masses purely in terms of obedience or disobedience to "God." Once again, Hurston and Nietzsche extend Spinoza's analysis of "a novel form of ecclesiastical authority" that leaves the "common people" uninformed so that the latter must depend on "the authority and testimony of philosophers for their understanding of Scripture."[73] The matrix of punishment/reward accompanying the ecclesiastical approach is necessarily heteronomous—one's "punishment" is based on supposedly innate guilt, while one's reward or salvation depends solely on the beneficence of absolutely external forces. In short, all incapacity comes from within while any creativity, critical thinking, or action comes from without. Mythic violence could find no greater complement then this way of thinking and feeling, which tempts the multitude to give up its greatest gains.

After comparing Hurston's analysis of the priestly class with Nietzsche's, one can now consider the complex relationship between Pharaoh and Moses. Erica Edwards notes the straightforward doubling of Pharaoh in Moses's actions after the exodus, which reveals the gothic underside to charismatic leadership.[74] However, this thesis may forget that Moses did not plan to become Pharaoh in Hurston's novel, and the process of *how* Moses becomes Pharaoh matters. Explaining this process recalls second-sight's surreal, anamorphic character once again. Like an anamorphic image, one angle reveals a great Moses while another angle reveals Pharaoh in new dress. Complete correspondence would get rid of the anamorphosis and the need for second-sight. Only the nonidentity between political leader, popular support across a number of coalitions, and political institutions makes this question urgent.

In *Black Reconstruction*, Du Bois emphasizes that this issue has less to do with individual personality and more with the complex forces shaping and reshaping political roles. To describe it, Du Bois employs a theological vocabulary and calls it "transubstantiation." Du Bois supports his point with a quotation of Charles Sumner lamenting the failure of Andrew Johnson's presidency: "The suffering at the South is great, through the misconduct of the President. His course has kept the rebel spirit alive, and depressed the loyal, white and black. It makes me very sad to see this. Considering the difficulties of their position, the black have done wonderfully well. They should have had a Moses as a President; but they had found a Pharaoh."[75] Du Bois and Hurston are of like minds on this matter. Neither writer reduces the matter to personality or temperament. Combine Hurston's comments on the priestly class in her correspondence with those in her novel and it becomes clear that even under the best circumstances, the very structure of the presidential office indicates that *Moses always has the potential to become Pharaoh*; that active forces can never be maintained based on Moses's goodwill; and that wherever a movement allows Moses to decide the future of its cause, there one finds the effective limit of that movement's active force. If one keeps Du Bois's idea of transubstantiation in mind, however, the question remains as to the concrete forces at play that place the elect and their leadership into such a contradictory position. With this frame, one can read *Moses* for its critique of leadership.

Hurston's most intimate portrait of Moses comes in his interactions with his mentor, Mentu. There, Moses is more fascinated with the search for knowledge than with political positions, although he soon becomes "Suten-Rech," commander-in-chief of Pharaoh's army. Even then, Moses asks several times to leave Egypt's military campaigns to pursue his real interest, the search for the "Book of Thoth," located in Koptos. Early on, Moses says:

"The man who interprets Nature is always held in great honor. I am going to live and talk with Nature. . . . Then I will be powerful, no matter where I may be. And now that I am free from wars and warfare, I shall go to Koptos." . . . He realized now how Mentu had aroused his thought, and that once you wake up thought in a man, you can never put it to sleep again. He saw that he had merely been suppressing himself during his military period. . . . Everybody has some special road of thought along which they travel when they are alone. . . . And his road of thought is what makes every man what he is.[76]

Moses's pursuit of knowledge is highly reminiscent of Spinoza's thought in *Treatise on the Emendation of the Intellect* and *Ethics*. Hurston capitalizes "Nature" throughout *Moses* like Spinoza does in *Ethics*, designating the oneness of all things in a single, self-proliferating substance, which is the ultimate object of the highest level of wisdom. "It is self-evident that the more the mind understands of Nature, the better the mind understands itself," Spinoza says.[77] Even if Moses does not go so far as to achieve the *amor intellectus dei*, the intellectual love of God, as Spinoza calls it, a part of Moses remains incommensurable with Pharaoh, who is at worst a racist, heterosexist, and elitist mass murderer or at best an opportunist who "played the instrument" most readily available to him, the instrument being the New Egypt's racism.[78] These complications beg for explanation. Fortunately, Hurston has already pointed the way. One must travel Moses's singular way of thinking, without forgetting that "thought" includes one's practices in their specific conditions. Doing so will help explain Moses's development as a leader who oscillates between deliverer and Pharaoh.

Significantly, Moses's path to leadership of the Hebrews always involved a relationship with priests. Mentu first taught Moses the fundamentals of military battle and introduced him to the Book of Thoth. Although Mentu only worked in Pharaoh's horse stables, Mentu asked to be buried as a priest, a wish that Moses fulfills. Moses also spent significant time with the priests in Egypt's royal palace. "By his own inclination," the novel says, "he was better educated than any scribe in Egypt. He read all of the books and the library, and all the priests knew that he had read them." Surely, the priests saw this as a boon, since "it gave new prestige to the priesthood, which had declined considerably under the war party now in power."[79] Beyond the priests' interests, splitting Moses's education between the prophets and the military foreshadows his becoming an "armed prophet," the figure Machiavelli considered the most successful of the leaders who combine religion with politics. Only armed prophets could proselytize, win over a population, and develop and sustain a state.[80] But this is far from Moses's mind at the moment. For now, it is only another phase of his self-education in understanding different forms of power.

As Pharaoh Rameses grows older, he spreads rumors that Moses is actually one of the Hebrews. Others in the monarchy believe this rumor to be true, because it explains why Moses has continued to demand rights for the Hebrews even after the previous Pharaoh refused to budge on the issue. For all of Moses's interest in the Hebrews, he has not developed a strong alliance with them. The scene in which Moses kills the Egyptian foreman demonstrates this. Although one can see that Moses sympathizes with and likely saves the life of the Hebrew worker being brutalized by the Egyptian foreman, this has not convinced other Hebrews that he cares about their plight. When Moses runs into another conflict in the work camps, this time between a Hebrew worker and a Hebrew foreman, he thinks he can reason with the two. Moses tries to convince the worker that this is a sign of progress and that they should strategize so that one man's promotion helps the group advance. Instead, Moses runs into even greater resistance. The Hebrew worker is insulted that he should work for one of his own "kind," so to speak. The text offers no sign that the foreman has mistreated his supervisee. One could say this is a scene of transference, in the sense that Fred Moten gives it, in which an ensemble forms that refuses to be interpreted, and therefore mastered, by its oppressor. But the dialogue, which implies that if the Hebrew worked for an Egyptian foreman he would be even less resistant, complicates this approach. It is as if he is resistant only because of role confusion. He can be controlled, just not by a fellow Hebrew. Moses does not fare better. The Hebrew basically threatens to tell the world that Moses killed the foreman and sees this reckless spewing of information as proof that he got the best of Moses—"I showed him," he says.[81]

In these two scenes, Moses never developed what Antonio Gramsci would call an "organic" relationship between himself and the Hebrew masses. The murder he committed and the personal sacrifice it entailed—the body of the Egyptian foreman was soon found by Pharaoh—meant little to a population that could not imagine the power of a strong leader, especially an Egyptian general, augmenting their collective force. And this says nothing of that population's inability to see that its own power goes beyond impudence to supervisors. Hurston marks this emphatically in the novel by using free indirect discourse to meld Moses's thoughts with a philosophical statement from the narrator:

If you want that good feeling that comes from doing things for other folks then you have to pay for it in abuse and misunderstanding. It seems like the first law of Nature is that everybody likes to receive things, but nobody like to feel grateful. And the very next law is that people talk about tenderness and mercy, but they love force. If you feed a thousand people you are a nice man with suspicious motives. If you kill a thousand you are a hero. Continue to get them killed by the things and you are a great conqueror, than which nothing on earth is greater. Oppress them and you are a great ruler. Rob them by law and they are proud and happy if you let them glimpse you occasionally surrounded by the riches that you have trampled out of their hides. . . . The only time you run a great risk is when you serve them. Men give up property, freedom, and even life before they will have the obligation laid on them.[82]

It seems perfectly logical for workers in the brickyards to want Moses, the commander-in-chief of Egypt's imperial army, on their side. Yet several of Spinoza's propositions at the beginning of *Ethics*, Part IV, which focuses on the power of the affects over reason, inform this passage from Hurston's novel. Spinoza's third proposition says, "The force whereby a man persists in existing is limited, and infinitely surpassed by the power of external causes"; the sixth proposition says, "The force of any passive emotion can surpass the rest of man's activities so that the emotion stays firmly fixed in him"; and finally, the seventh proposition says, "An emotion cannot be checked or destroyed except by a contrary emotion which is stronger than the emotion which is to be checked."[83]

Taken together, these propositions explain how a "single body," whether it be a person or a population, can be tossed to and fro by emotions produced from much stronger external forces. This is especially true of any "single body" that is not also reasoning about its situation, for reason is essential to developing one's own internal power in order to face external forces. In the passage mentioned above from *Moses, Man of the Mountain*, these external forces are mass murder, imperial conquest, and mass theft of property. One can associate these forces with a long list of fascist dictatorships and imperial projects reaching a fever pitch while Hurston composed this novel. But the mass theft mentioned in the passage points directly to the daily operation of capitalism and once again distances Hurston from Washington's doctrine. To "rob them by law" reiterates Marx's thesis that capitalism seeks to render its thievery invisible—invisible, because legislation designed to protect capitalism will not outlaw the crime inherent to the system. After reading of the Hebrews suffering so much abuse, one might wish that killing the oppressive foreman would count as the "gift" needed to advance a radical underground movement among the Hebrews. A closer look at Hurston's passage explains why this does not occur: "It seems like the first law of Nature is that everybody likes to receive things, but nobody likes to feel grateful. . . . Men give up property, freedom, and even life before they will have the obligation laid on them."[84] Obligation in itself does not upset them. But the obligation to abandon their acquiescence, as Moses demonstrates when he kills the foreman, cannot help but remind the Hebrews of a series of instances of indecision, inaction, and acceptance of the unacceptable. When Spinoza speaks of emotions "firmly fixed," he refers to longstanding emotional effects from external forces, which can be countered only by an affective shift. *A new idea, alone, will not challenge the affective regime in place.* As Spinoza notes, an emotion can be checked only by an equal or stronger emotion. Moses mistakenly assumes that reasoning with the Hebrew worker and foreman would suffice, when both men feel unable to combine their forces for some collective goal. They must combine a new logic with a new feeling. It remains to be seen whether Moses ever fosters this in the Hebrews or if they cultivate it themselves. For now, suffice it to note this gulf between Moses and the Hebrews. To understand how this gulf gets filled requires a turn to Moses's time in the wilderness, his being called, and his return to Egypt as deliverer of the Hebrews. This time in the wilderness shapes Moses's conceptualization of leadership and the affects he seeks to develop in his followers.

Only when Moses escapes New Egypt and enters the wilderness does he begin "seeing visions of a nation he had never heard of where there would be more equality of opportunity and less difference between top and bottom," visions that stray from his long-held belief that he will live peacefully and study nature without involving himself in "missionary work."[85] Jethro, on the other hand, considers it "selfish" that he and Moses know "about the one true God" while "others been grabbing hold of little parts of Him and calling them parts a god by itself," like "calling each limb of a person a man." Jethro tells Moses, "I *feel* the command to bring other people besides the Kenites to know this god and worship him. . . . I feel that the call was never meant for me. I know that the God of the mountain has been waiting for you."[86] When Moses responds apprehensively and wonders who else needs to learn about "Jehovah," since all the Midianites and related groups are aware, Jethro says, "How about them Israelites? They're down there in Egypt without no god of their own and no more protection than a bareheaded mule. How come you can't go down there and lead them out?"[87] Despite Jethro's "feather touch" in his language, he rhetorically "crowded Moses farther and farther into a corner."[88] Moses becomes a prophet *only with the call in the wilderness*, when Jethro urges Moses to combine his military acumen with a priestly worldview. As the narrator says, Jethro "was making of Moses what he himself had wanted to be—a great priest."[89] In Jethro's view, Moses's only flaw was that "he had no mission in life except to study," when Moses could become "King over all the local [Midianite] chiefs," but "had no wish to govern his fellow men." Moses admires Jethro too much to see how much Jethro desires power more than knowledge.

In chapters 14–18, Moses receives, flees from, and then finally accepts the call to deliver the Hebrews:

> "Moses, I want you to go down into Egypt. . . . I want you to go down and tell that Pharaoh I say to let my people go." . . .
>
> "Well, Lord, if I go, tell me what to say; they won't believe in me," Moses said with hopeless resignation. "I don't even know your name. Who must I tell them sent me?"
>
> "Tell them I AM WHAT I AM."[90]

A little-read essay from Hurston called "Conversions and Visions" can clarify the inflection of this passage. The terminology in Hurston's novel does not completely match that in the essay. Nevertheless, Moses's experience in the novel fits the essay's special category of "the call to preach."[91] Hurston explains that whereas "in conversion, we have the cultural pattern of the person seeking the vision and inducing it by isolation and fasting, in the call to preach we have the involuntary vision—the call seeking the man."[92] The essay associates "the call" with a "cultural pattern," adapted from a particular strand of Christianity, that has had important political consequences for generations of African Americans in the US South after slavery and beyond. At first glance, the essay's style seems neutral, even detached in its account of conversion and the call. But Hurston invests in a philosophy of self-perfection that links thought, affect, and action, so this essay's reference to the "involuntary vision" should give pause. Nowhere in this study does the involuntary count toward self-empowerment, individually or collectively.

It turns out that this is another instance of translation and displacement that can be identified by how the essay's matter-of-fact propositions stand alongside its well-chosen examples.

In "Conversions and Visions," Hurston critiques a cultural pattern based on guilt, passivity, and punishment: "The man flees from the call [to preach], but is finally brought to accept it. God punishes him by every kind of misfortune until he finally acknowledges himself beaten," she says. For Hurston, this anthropomorphic view of God as a person who chases after and punishes those who ignore him is fundamentally flawed. It is humans projecting their own attitudes and habits onto Being. Hurston adds, "Some preachers say the spirit whipped them from their heads to their heels."[93] She then includes testimony from several who fled from and eventually accepted the call. Here is Deacon Ernest Huffman's testimonial about his call on June 9, 1886:

> I accepted Jesus when I was a lad of a boy. . . . All my friends was getting religion . . . but I never paid it no mind. But I don't keer how hard you is, God kin reach you when he gits ready for you. When I was walkin in my sins, wallerin in my sins, dat He touched me wid de tip of His finger and I fell right where I was. . . . And [in my vision] I walked over hell on a narrer foot log . . . and the hell hounds was barkin on my tracks and just before dey rushed me into hell and judgment I cried: "Lawd, have mercy." . . . Then I found myself on solid ground and a tall white man beckoned for me to come to him and I went, wrapped in my guilt, and he 'nointed me wide de oil of salvation and healed all my wounds. . . . Then Christ spoke peace to my soul.[94]

Although this essay has been read in several ways, none so far make the point that the essay offers another way of discussing *interpellation*—that is, the way one is "called" and internalizes being subjugated by another. On this score, Hurston anticipates another close reader of Spinoza, Louis Althusser. Indeed, Althusser also associates interpellation with being halted and seized, as Hurston describes in this vision. More than that, Althusser also turns to the quote "I am that I am" from Exodus as Hurston does.[95] While the call is typically understood in terms of a higher moral vocation, Hurston and Althusser remind us to analyze forces at play in a specific situation, in which the call is quite often associated with unfair guilt and physical punishment. The one calling and the one being called obtain new identities in the process, with new power dynamics specific to the encounter. Whoever occupies the position of "I am what I am" now subjects others to his will, but in a curious way, since "the individual is interpellated as a (free) subject in order . . . that he shall (freely) accept his subjection."[96] Moses's oath to heed the "command" from Jethro's deity counts as such a "free" decision.

A quick reference to Althusser helps one hear a different ring to Deacon Ernest Huffman's testimony. Sadly, his testimony reads just like a call to be lynched, "hell hounds" and all, when lynching was reaching its dystopian heights in the New South, that "new heaven and earth" premised on resentment and mass violence. Nor can attentive readers ignore Huffman's reference to the "tall white man" who "beckons," with the power to save or condemn the black lad "wrapped in guilt," although he has committed no crime. The "peace" concluding the passage bespeaks acquiescence to an entity that saves only by condemning first, that chases Huffman down to heal him, and that walks him across hell's planks to place him on solid ground. Huffman's paradise exemplifies a most troubling notion of possibility, as options made in the likeness of what has already been considered "real."[97]

Moses's acceptance of the call is much less dramatic than the testimonial documents Hurston includes in her earlier work. Nevertheless, the testimonials inform her depiction of Moses's call in her novel. The point here is that Moses decides to lead the Hebrews out of bondage only after seeking Jethro's guidance. Jethro minimizes the effort necessary to fulfill the call. "It stands to reason that anybody in slavery would be glad to be free. . . . A nation of folks with no particular god would naturally be glad for a god to choose them for his own and then pick out a land to give them."[98] Moses does not see Jethro's own schemes at work, since he has already met with Hebrew leaders who might want to take the Hebrews out of New Egypt.[99] The source of Jethro's efforts can be traced back to a single comment, when he first met Moses:

> Well, I tell you, Moses, my house has always been powerful. . . . But for the last few years a weak King has been on the throne and the robbers and things are just about to take us. . . . Nobody can have any more than he has the might to protect. It all started with the downfall of the Hyksos in Egypt many years ago. Bands of them retreating before the Egyptians'

army overran this country and got things so upset we just haven't been able to get straight since. No real unity any more.[100]

Jethro desires to restore lost power. However, he fails to accomplish this himself as a mere prophet alone. He needs an armed prophet, a warrior-priest, to do this and believes Moses is the perfect instrument for restoring the prestige of his lineage. While Jethro cares deeply for Moses and vice versa, one must not ignore the manipulation functioning in the background. Jethro actually has the chance to encourage Moses to follow his best insights. Instead, Jethro accepts the premise that the call is a "command" from "I am what I am," which then turns Moses's "promise" to go into an indictment against him for doubting the mission. Of course, this is a slight of hand, considering that Moses agreed to go but immediately said that "it won't do any good."[101] In other words, Jethro ignores that Moses feels forced to do an impossible task and instead urges him to keep the promise while downplaying the effort it will require. In the temporality of Hurston's story, there have been many before Moses who felt "chosen" in the sense described here. Theoretically, though, one could say that Moses is the first of the chosen because of his role in spreading, systematizing, and later on, codifying a sense of chosenness among an entire population for the foreseeable future.

Hurston has designed this part of the text as another example of priestly power taking hold in a time of decadence. Remember, for the priest, "decadence is no more than a means to an end"—that end being political domination. "Men of this sort have a vital interest in making mankind sick, and in confusing the values of 'good' and 'bad,' 'true' and 'false,' in a manner that is not only dangerous to life, but also slanders it."[102] Jethro is shrewd for seeing monotheism's ability to accomplish his task, specifically for a group like the Hebrews, who are suffering and passively awaiting their savior. Even if Jethro's conception of the divine is problematic for its anthropomorphism, it still grants a total worldview to the Hebrews, who have been segregated so tightly as to have no gods of their own to worship. The "I am what I am" "takes in the whole world and the firmaments of heaven," Moses says, appealing to the Hebrew's search for universality.[103] But this grand scheme does not alter the passivity of the people. The first moment of dialogue in chapter 20 between two unnamed Hebrews supports this analysis:

"They say he owns a god. . . . The point I'm coming out on is, this god wants to work on our behalf. He aims to put us in power with the Egyptians."

"Hush your mouth! You don't mean to tell me that! . . ."

"They say he can really do what he says."

"What you say his name is?"

"The new god or the man—which one you talking about?"

"The man, fool."[104]

This humorous exchange illustrates how this necessarily collective project, even before it begins, is already being turned into a single person's magical feats. At the beginning of the dialogue, Moses "owns" the god. By the end of the passage, Moses and the god become interchangeable. Moses's/the god's goal aims not to deliver them from suffering but to place them alongside their oppressors, the Egyptians, in the same decadent milieu. Moses/the god becomes a new way of identifying with their oppressors rather than breaking away. This poses problems before and after the exodus. If Moses's first meeting with Goshen's leaders already involves coupling Moses with a god who works for him, then they will be hard-pressed to understand how much intellectual, affective, and physical labor it will take (of themselves) to leave Egypt and thrive. As Moses's power increases, so does the tendency to confuse him with the "I am what I am."

So the Hebrews think that Moses, the newly armed prophet, promises them power with the Egyptians, based on a god that contains the entire world and the heavens. However mind-boggling all this is for them, they learn to believe even as they question. "That was a great mouthful for the people and they went off muttering to themselves in their unlettered tongues 'I am what I am' over and over and blowing in the ashes of their hopelessness to kindle hope."[105] Hope stems not from material shifts but from the promise of a fullness based on personal wishes divorced from action. The chance to fulfill those hopes remains some ways off, so the encounter between the Hebrews and Moses's monotheistic worldview needs something to encourage belief in the meantime. What truly endears the people to the "I am what I am," the novel suggests, is Moses "institut[ing] the ceremonies to the god of the mountain and establishing alters and more and more the people came to them and began the new practices."[106] Readers of Spinoza will be aware that here Hurston alludes to chapter 5, "Ceremonial Law," of *Theological-Political Treatise*. Once again, Hurston follows Spinoza in translating and displacing common notions. Spinoza grants his readers that ceremonial law was crucial to ancient Israelite culture but refrains from making the ceremony necessary for blessedness. Hurston thinks this belief among the Hebrews is symptomatic of feeling preordained for suffering and salvation, all based on external forces and their own inaction. At best, then, these customs created a basis for mutual respect in the Israelite common-wealth. What was once a practice working toward eternal salvation becomes a historically contingent set of customs and legal rules for a political state with no bearing on eternity.

The use of "hope" in this portion of the novel deserves further exploration before concluding this section of the notebook. The term is a charged one in Spinoza's lexicon, especially when linked to contingency. For Spinoza, we humans are prone to believe what we hope for and apprehensive of believing what we fear. Over- and under-estimating in this way provide the origins for superstition. In Spinoza's psychology, all humans are vulnerable to superstition's influence.[107] The fact that the hopeful/fearful can be "prey," even to their own inadequate view of themselves, means that hope can induce passivity as effectively as fear.[108] Moses institutes rituals so the object of hope, which once seemed to be a matter of luck, is now inextricably linked to dedication to the state.[109] Ritual, in itself, is ethically neutral. In Spinoza's psychology and Hurston's anthropology, ritual is essential to human activity. Judging a particular ritual depends on how it orients participants temporally. The ritual learned by the Hebrews hints at a future beyond their current hardships. Having accepted that this future must come to pass, the Hebrews need an agent who can bring this future about, no matter the contingency. Through newly instituted ritual sacrifice, Moses's anthropomorphic conception of God combines with the Hebrew desire for an absolute force working within Nature but outside Nature's laws. For Spinoza, this is where "superstition" finds its prey and Moses sets the trap. Hence his followers say, "You can see further with your eyes closed than we can with ours wide open. . . . You're our rod of salvation, Moses. Lie down and sleep and dream for us."[110] The confusion between Moses and God finds new consistency through new rituals and nearly deifies Moses, mistakenly placing him above ritual, community, and perhaps even Nature.

The sovereignty Moses achieves depends on the multitude confusing a fallible human leader with a deity restricted to Eurocentric expressions of masculinity. *Thinking Through Crisis* has primarily attended to how racial and class exploitation impact gender and has tried along the way to evaluate the potentials and perils of life that betray the Western gender scripts imposed on it. In "Down by the Riverside," when Brother Mann makes Lulu the ethical center of his action despite her near incapacitation in the dangers brought on by flooding and relief camps; in Wells's writings, when she calls for every black American to keep a Winchester rifle in their possession and she speaks of being armed while traveling; when Harriet Tubman serves as "Moses" and "General Tubman," even in the eyes of John Brown; when John Brown's daughter speaks of him as a valiant fighter who cared for her like a "tender mother"; when *Black Reconstruction* applauds Robert Smalls, who embarrassed the Confederates by stealing their Confederate naval ship, loading it with loved ones, and taking it to the Union side—in all these cases, blackness surpasses the expectations of Western gender scripts. Hurston realizes that the call to Western sovereignty places intolerable limits on the multitude's varied performances of gender, all under the fantastical image of the impenetrable, ever-conquering, miracle-working armed prophet who disciplines his followers into their chosenness and future prosperity. *Moses* makes "the rod of power" the metaphor for this political move. Gathering the multitude under this figure abruptly halts the transformative potential of divine violence; perpetuates the superstitions induced by hope as much as fear; and links them to a form of sacrifice that, when read honestly, amounts to self-renunciation rather than strategy in struggle.

The rod of power signals to the reader that the nation the Hebrews agree to build mirrors the Egypt they just abandoned. The rod of power is indispensable to evaluating how a Moses can become a Pharaoh. Despite the importance of Moses's contest with Pharaoh in the exodus narrative, which conventionally aims to distinguish the chosen Hebrews from the oppressive Egyptians, there is a deeper stake in this portion of Hurston's novel. One cannot use the contest to delineate Moses's followers from Pharaoh's, since the dialogue shows that some Hebrews side with Moses to be in power *with* the Egyptians. Equating the protagonist and antagonist in this manner urges readers to think in more complicated ways about political affiliation. In this portion of the novel, readers find two different conceptions of power at play, based on two different conceptions of the whole, of totality.

The rod of power proffers a "closed and systemic totality governed by the Law" based on an "exception that is beyond the law," and that the exceptional figure or system fairly distributes rewards and punishments based on individual effort and allegiance. The other conception allows no exception, which means it admits no all-seeing, all-knowing earthly sovereign (or the multitude). But it also means that the multitude cannot hide from its (mis) conceptions of itself. Either it faces its (mis)conceptions directly, or it will wrangle with them indirectly through a leader who is more likely to oppress than deliver, aided by a parasitic priestly class whose existence depends on misguiding the multitude to doubt its power. Jacques Lacan called the former the hypermasculine logic of the "all," while he called the latter the feminine logic of the "non-all." The "non-all" is no mere perverse deviation from the "all." These are two divergent approaches to nature and power. Furthermore, the "non-all" does not amount to an emasculating logic but registers a masculinity freeing itself from the fantasies of absolutist control, which allows it to engage with the feminine and other sexualities in more sophisticated ways.[111] Hurston uses the rod of power to illustrate how alluring and detrimental the hypermasculine logic of the "all" can be for political movements and for leaders and followers. Miriam's suffering testifies to the toll this sovereign logic takes on followers and leaders. Through an analysis of Miriam's predicament, readers can also see Moses and Aaron differently, because they, too, get consumed by the sovereign call to belonging.

The fact that Hurston contends with this sovereign logic from the beginning of the exodus in chapter 20 until Miriam's death in chapter 39 indicates that leaving Egypt, in itself, does not offer a final word. Yet to associate sovereignty with a hypermasculine logic does not mean that only women suffer its deleterious effects. The plot of and sexual innuendos in *Moses* depict the shift in authority from Jethro to Moses as if the impotent old man makes the young man an instrument for reasserting his sexual prowess. The novel suggests as much, considering that Jethro initiates Moses's calling and that Moses accepts that authority by holding the rod of power—a great "snake" writhing before the "burning bush"—all to serve Jethro's purposes. In chapter 21, Moses first confronts the new Pharaoh Ta-Phar to demand Hebrew liberation. Moses takes "his rod in his hand," and Ta-Phar's priests grab their rods. Moses "stood" next to the priests "with his rod in his hand and measured them." Hurston parodies one of the most canonical confrontations in the black theological imagination as a scene of penis measuring and even a masturbatory exercise in which Moses's "right hand" proves more powerful than Pharaoh's:

> So [Pharoah's] priests manipulated their rods and danced and finally threw them down on the floor before Pharaoh and they began to writhe and crawl. Pharaoh looked triumphantly at Moses. But Moses was looking all around the throne room in unconcern. . . . Moses merely handed his rod to Aaron and said . . . "Throw it down and get back out of the way." Aaron dropped the rod of Moses to the floor. . . . The rod of Moses came alive. Its head darted out and seized the snake nearest it and swallowed it. The next one and the next one was run down and disappeared head first down the throat of Moses's living rod.
> "Is that all you got to show me?" Moses asked casually."[112]

Moses enjoys this contest, although "his heart" never leaves Midian while "his thoughts" take him back to where "his father and friend," his wife, and his "sons that were young men" are located.[113] This detail reiterates that Moses never developed a relationship with the Hebrews. For these reasons, Moses's enjoyment in the passage comes from sacrificing his own desires for the command of the "I am what I am," for his allegiance to Jethro, and for his ongoing rivalry with Ta-Phar, as well as for his distant hopes of the Goshen peoples.

Hurston goes farther than most in noting that the so-called deliverer has already put himself through the gauntlet of privileges, losses, and enjoyments, such that the suffering of others in the departure becomes a necessary sacrifice. This differs from the fight of affliction in *The Underground Railroad* because those railroad passengers endure pain to disinvest from the affective regime that is indispensable to slaveholding society. Moses's competition indicates a different scenario in which the chosen consider the exodus another avenue for identifying with Egypt's conceptions of power. Hurston prompts her readers to consider *for whom* and *for what* one suffers as well as who gains from it. The plot's structure, which moves from Moses's and Pharaoh's contest to a bigger plan concerning "all Egypt," then changes location from New Egypt's palace to Goshen, which keeps Moses dislocated from his family in Midian, intimates that answering these questions with slogans like "the community" or "the people" are insufficient and may even be attempts to avoid the complexities.[114] Such slogans betray the heterogeneity of desires in any community or any person. Moreover, Hurston pushes us to consider when such sacrifices devolve from transformative opportunity to a denunciation of life—that is, when it devolves from an attempt at altering one's existence to a denial of one's existence.

Miriam is acutely aware that leadership entails this life-or-death decision. Erica Edwards makes several observations that add greater justification to the concern that the dark proletariat may forsake its group-centered leadership style for praise of the individual(ist) charismatic leader. As a corollary, Edwards warns against the dark proletariat attacking those rebelling against charismatic leadership and uplift ideology. Miriam's experience reveals the decadence within the exodus. Edwards has already offered a persuasive reading of Miriam's plight. I repeat several passages from her reading to show where they jell with my own and where I take my reading elsewhere. From her reading, it becomes clear that Miriam had the relationship with the masses that Moses did not. "Miriam's story is heteroglossic; it is a dynamic, moving narrative that merges her fantasy, the people's knowledge, and the community's desire for an insider in the palace," Edwards tells us.[115] Miriam goes from being the "protagonist" who expresses the Hebrews' collective fantasies to being victim of a "textual burial": "the novel makes a space for Miriam to dream before burying her underneath Moses's story." Miriam gets buried because her leadership abilities disrupt "the patriarchal line of charismatic authority. The authority is passed down vertically from one generation to the next . . . rather than diffused horizontally among Moses, Miriam, and Aaron."[116]

So Miriam goes, so this fantasy goes. Miriam's life becomes so intimately linked to the Hebrew people's collective fantasy of freedom that the two share the same fate. Edwards calls "Miriam's story" the "story of a martyr" who gets "punished" with "death" for exposing the charismatic model of leadership's failures.[117] But what Edwards means by "martyr" requires further elaboration, because she does not want to turn the Miriam subplot into a story of eventual redemption for the Hebrews, for Miriam, or for other leaders. When Miriam befuddles Moses by asking for his permission to die, the novel upsets any sense that Miriam's death fits a triumphalist narrative or that Moses creates this narrative or has special access to it:

"What makes you think you got to get *my* consent to die?"

"'Cause I know I can't die without it. That right hand of yours—its got light in front of it and darkness behind. I come in the humblest way I know how to let you know I done quit straining against you."

"But, Miss Miriam, you ain't had time to enjoy your freedom yet. You ought to want to live to enjoy it and see Israel a nation."

"This freedom is more than a notion, Moses. It's a good thing. It's bound to be a good thing 'cause everybody wans it. But maybe I didn't know what to do with it, cause I ain't been so happy."[118]

The dialogue continues, and Moses asks a question critical to the notion of transference discussed in this notebook:

"Do you think I am God, Miriam?"

"Indeed, I don't know, Moses. That's what I been trying to figure out for years. . . . Sometimes I thought God's voice in the tabernacle sounds mighty much like yours. But ever since you punished me with leprosy, I knew you had power uncommon to man. . . . When I found out I couldn't do no more in Israel than you let me, I made up my mind to go on off and die, but I found out I couldn't even do that unless you let me. I saw all them people dead in the wilderness and I looked at their bones and wished it was me. I waited and I waited, but death always avoided me."[119]

Earlier in the novel, Miriam shares Aaron's view that they all are "on an equal balance" as leaders of the exodus.[120] By the time of this dialogue, however, Miriam now accepts the patriarchal line, her place outside it, and her punishment for trying to join it. As this dialogue demonstrates, she is totally enrapt in guilt for not accepting the so-called order of things earlier. One could say she is the most unfortunate victim of mythic violence in the novel, because she was deeply invested in the fantasy of freedom that provided the unifying basis for the exodus. Worst of all, Miriam has accepted the denunciation of life that has haunted the Hebrews since Moses's birth.

The erection of Miriam's monument can be interpreted in two different ways. First, it can be interpreted as the nation-state's attempt to acknowledge Miriam's suffering. The text suggests Moses's sincere sadness for Miriam. But his sincerity never leads him to question what produced her memory. The title of martyr offers little compensation for the years of life Miriam relinquished. Still, critiquing this in terms of compensation falls short, because that standard implies an attempt to look back and balance the scales after years of ignoring Miriam's competence and skills before and during the exodus. That final balancing act cannot occur, certainly not in the conditions produced under the current political regime. The second way of reading Miriam's monument amounts to national mythmaking, in which Miriam's stand against the Egyptians counts toward her inclusion in a pantheon of Hebrew freedom fighters. Whether the monument acknowledges Miriam's misery or her heroics, the fact remains that the nation-state does not give up its techniques of persecution.

The state's power hinges not on monuments to freedom fighters but to Miriam's irreparable downturn after she contracts leprosy. This incident mirrors the plagues that come against the Egyptians for not letting the Hebrews go. Hurston reveals the underside to Carl Schmitt's complaint that the "modern constitutional state" "banished the miracle from the world" and his attempt to imbue the dictator with justifications for intervening, like a deity enacting a miracle, in the political world.[121] Hurston sees no proof that the modern state has banished the miracle. By matching Moses's brutality with Pharaoh's, Hurston does not find "affinity" with fascism but laments the violence essential to the nation-state.[122] Furthermore, the leprosy episode makes Moses's miracles interchangeable with Pharaoh's magic, because both focus on inducing fear and, from there, cultivating superstition. Hurston shows her attentive readers that the miracle linked to mythic violence and the totalizing logic of the exception always undercuts the process of self-perfection it promises.

Hurston would disagree with Schmitt for a second reason that diverges from the sovereign violence that he considers essential to proper government. The logic of the "non-all" offers another conceptualization of the miracle. Again, Spinoza serves as a touchstone. In his *Theologico-Political Treatise*, Nature's, and therefore God's, laws are "sufficiently wide to extend to everything that is conceived even by the divine intellect." Any other view would suggest that "God created Nature so ineffective and prescribed for her laws and rules so barren that he is often constrained to come once more to her rescue if he wants her to be preserved."[123] Since this is impossible in Spinoza's intellectual perspective, the sovereign miracle indicates an error in humanity's interpretation of Nature rather than a breakdown in Nature's laws. Spinoza is quite clear that, in his reading of the Old Testament, those who receive the benefits of a miracle never increase their agency:

"But although these miracles succeeded in carrying conviction with the Egyptians and the Jews on the basis of their prior assumptions," Spinoza says in one example, the miracles "could not impart the true idea and knowledge of God." While miracles increase a particular group's devotion to a particular order of power, that group does not "excel others in true human perfection."[124]

Hurston, like Spinoza before her, is interested in the shortcomings of political miracles in regard to a population's preservation and perfection. While Spinoza considers the logical inadequacies of the political miracle, Hurston considers the affects it produces. She begins her exploration with Moses's education as a general in Egypt's army. When Moses is still part of the Egyptian monarchy serving as a military leader, he often spent time with the priests: "He learned all of [the priests'] tricks . . . but only to sift them through his mind to see if any of them led towards real knowledge." After trying these magical spells, he found no "real knowledge," "but he learned many things to distract the minds of unthinking people from their real troubles, and to taint men with the fear of life. In this he saw a certain mastery over people if one cared to use it."[125] From that moment forward in *Moses*, miracles do the impossible, but always "taint men with fear of life" in the process. By comparing these passages from Hurston to passages I quoted earlier from Spinoza, one sees that they both agree that miracles do not lead to real knowledge. But for Hurston, even more than for Spinoza, miracles lead to the fear of life, which is the greatest threat to "self-preservation and self-perfection."

Miracles, in their Western political valence, depend on an uncritical perspective swaying us purely by feeling. Miracles teach passivity to a greater Other who always saves us. In Hurston's novel, Moses never understands this. He could never understand why the miracle of manna falling from the sky didn't encourage the Hebrews to grow their own foods in the wilderness. Instead, they demand more miracles from Moses:

"Here I am struggling to make a great nation out of you and you are worrying about fried fish and cucumbers! Do you see me eating anything like that?"

"Oh, you got that right hand of yours and that rod, ain't you? You got quails and this manna and water and a whole heap of other things with it. You could give us anything we wanted if you would."[126]

Perhaps Moses was so surprised at these discussions because he believed, more than anyone else, that miracles would convince the Hebrews to pursue their freedom more aggressively. But actually, Hebrew inaction was the logical outcome of using his "right hand" and "rod" to resolve all problems. Sooner or later, the rod of power will reach its own limits, like Moses "struggling" with his followers, and there will be no one to pick up the slack, because their intervention would compromise the exceptional space the rod of power inhabits. Instead, Hurston's multitude oscillates between hatred of and nostalgia for the Egypt that hates them, between absolute faith and doubt in those who lead them. But this never transforms into faith in their own collective ability to take action.

From Hurston's perspective, then, Schmitt's understanding of the political miracle denies the possibility that the sovereign's force can weaken over time. Schmitt's argument depends on a fantasy of ever-increasing potency. Sovereign impotence is beyond contemplation, although powerlessness is the most direct and widespread result of this conception of power. Put bluntly, this conception of power, which requires that the many transfer their power to the few, turns leadership into dead labor. Although the first notebook explored dead labor primarily to discuss the reduction of life's complexities to exchange-value, I expand its application here to spotlight the overexertion leaders suffer under this paradigm, with constantly diminishing results over time. In my analysis of "Down by the Riverside," I analyzed the scene in which Brother Mann was sent to work on a levee, where he saw men moving "like dim shadows." The scene illustrates the inanity of recreating the sharecropping system after the flood had washed it away. While Wright wanted that scene to illustrate the plight of the black rural agrarian worker, I suggest that we think of the political leaders of *Moses* in a similar way. The analogy is not exact, of course. Nevertheless, it highlights the irony that in both cases, the sole virtue of such labor is getting worked to death. Miriam may come to mind immediately here. But it would be problematic to think she is the only one who suffers. There's Aaron, the political opportunist in the exodus, who becomes such a hindrance to the movement that Moses murders him. But even Moses, the so-called sovereign in this exceptional space, has fallen prey to the fear of life. When Aaron begs to be spared, Moses replies, "I haven't spared myself, Aaron. *I had to quit being a person a long time ago, and I had to become a thing, a tool, an instrument for a cause.* I wasn't spared, Aaron. No."[127] This is the conclusion Moses reaches, with the wilderness as his levee. Transference, in which mass movements turn leaders to miracle workers, also turns leadership into dead labor.

In conclusion, this fourth notebook finds several radical insights in Hurston's neglected novel. An affective regime premised on inadequacy, inevitable suffering, and metaphysical guilt will not sustain the labor for emancipation. "Miracle" marks the mechanism by which sovereignty feeds parasitically off the surplus produced by the labor for emancipation. Only the dark proletariat itself can cast off this frequent misnaming, misinterpretation, and misappropriation of its world-altering efforts. But doing so requires an examination of the inside state of things. Any leadership worthy of the name must accept this need or risk guiding the masses down a path of superstition and self-renunciation.

NOTEBOOK 5

THE NEW DAY

Notes on Education and the Dark Proletariat

I am the life that's trodden by the dance of joy
My flesh, my death, my re-birth is the song
That rises from men's lips, they know not how.

. . . .

I melt as wax the willful barriers of human mind
Gently even in this, except to the tyrant mind
That thinks to damn the flood-tide from the Hills.

—WOLE SOYINKA, *THE BACCHAE OF EURIPIDES*

Listening to the fading drums,
Because the undead were loose,
To do as they pleased.

—BARBARA CHASE-RIBOUD, "EVERYTIME A KNOT IS UNDONE,
A GOD IS RELEASED"

POETRY, PEDAGOGY, ECSTASY

The fourth notebook of *Thinking Through Crisis* questions the dark prole-tariat's attachment to the sad passions promulgated by the Judeo-Christian understanding of sovereignty. This fifth notebook now seeks to examine the joyous passions of the multitude by displacing self-renunciation with a fren-zied ecstasy. Details from the second and fourth notebooks illustrate that black writers have intensified their aesthetic, intellectual, and political pursuits by leveraging underground traditions apposite to Western thought. When Du Bois says that "words and music [in Negro Spirituals] have lost each other and new and cant phrases of a dimly understood theology have displaced the older sentiment," or when Hurston writes of "Negroised white hymns" "converted" into a "chant that is not a chant," but a "liquefying of words," they assert that blackness produces meanings and nonmeanings such that Western theological markers lose their hold on their intended objects.[1] Similarly, while the language of exodus ushers a broad academic and popular audience into a discourse on politics, emancipation, and revolution, the Coming of the Lord bespeaks a divine violence that is only divine to the extent that it betrays Western origins or destinations. Just where the Western models would predict the onset of metaphysical guilt, the dark proletariat indulges ecstasy as a condition of possibility for communal survival.

Education is inseparable from this ecstatic way of being. But knowing *how* this occurs requires a recalibration of concepts, literary examples, and historical narratives. That recalibration can begin by turning to *On the Anarchy of Poetry and Philosophy: A Guide for the Unruly* (2007), where Gerald Bruns links poetry to ecstasy to separate them from conventional forms of pedagogy:

> Poetry itself is not a kind of learning but a species of ecstasy. No one studies to be a poet. No one asks to be such a thing. One is, for no reason, summoned out of one's house and exposed to a kind of transcendence. Exactly what kind of transcendence is not always clear. . . . Like biblical prophecy, poetry is a kind of election and a mode of responsibility, as much a curse as a calling since one is now hostage to a "divine voice." . . . In ecstasy I am turned inside out, exposed to others, still myself perhaps but no longer an "I," that is, no longer a spontaneous agent but only a "who" or a "me": a passive, responsive, obsessive repercussion of the Muses.[2]

In Bruns's estimation, mainstream education has limited poetry "to institutions not of its own making," thereby reducing poetry's "divine frenzy" to a mere "rhetorical topos." This reduction hearkens back to Aristotle's conceptualization of the *polis*, which makes poetry a spectacle for "spectators upon whom it has a therapeutic or calming effect. Instead of fascination it produces or enhances an essentially philosophical subjectivity. . . . A principle of *disengagement* has been introduced into the theory of poetic experience."[3] Bruns then offers brief vignettes on the College of Sociology, *La Bohéme*, Black Mountain College, the L-A-N-G-U-A-G-E Poets, and others to consider different poetic communities—institutions of poetry's own making, so to speak.

Bruns's account of poetic communities warns against conventional educational curricula distorting poetry's function to produce disengaged spectators. Most certainly this warning complements the introduction to this project, which took issue with Shoshana Felman's accounts of trauma and pedagogy. By returning the students to normalcy while providing no evidence that the students aimed to alter their institutional conditions, Felman exemplifies the principle of disengagement in full operation. This notebook can go a step further than the introductory critique. Felman justifies her pedagogy by claiming that after all the upheaval, the youth return to normal. Her account seems unaware that for a wide array of students, the most violent, traumatizing decision possible would be returning them to the university's or the college's normal operation. Bruns's work indirectly acknowledges this point but then cedes the ground for debate by not addressing the tensions between his poetic communities and more mainstream liberal educational projects. This means that Bruns leaves open the question as to what forms of agency inhabit educational institutions not of their own making—or at least, institutions of a conflicted making. Said differently, this notebook ponders the agency that endures in a university or college structure that traumatizes academic laborers in its normal functioning; how the professoriate, as one group of academic laborers, can inhabit this agency; and what kind of poetry gets produced through this agency's endurance.

Material from the previous notebooks can supply a tentative answer to these questions: Poetry exposes the existentially homeless and the political-theologically hailed to an immanent transcendence. Poetry calls the receptive beyond chosenness to accept responsibility for and alongside those who have never (and perhaps can never) become an "I" in the liberal sense. Black life *is* lived in ecstasy, turned inside out, exposed to others, and to all creation. That shared vulnerability is lived *only in part* due to myriad instances of institutional violence. So long as this part does not get mistaken for the whole, a greater claim emerges—namely, that this shared vulnerability offers a different way of being human rather than an inadequate way of being Western. Sustaining this momentum against frequent hostilities does not occur automatically or randomly but through fully immersive interrogation of the self and of the world. Poetry, therefore, is a species of ecstasy sustaining itself through study. From this vantage, the dark proletariat manifests itself as a poetic community.

Elaborating on this reformulation requires a turn to several black intellectuals, including W. E. B. Du Bois, Langston Hughes, Katherine Dunham, and Carter G. Woodson. Few will be shocked that Woodson's classic *Mis-Education of the Negro* (1933) plays a role here, but this reformulation puts that book in proper perspective. The knee-jerk return to "mis-education" from Woodson's broad corpus yields the mistaken view that opposing one form of education can substitute for envisioning and implementing other models. Knowing what one opposes cannot substitute for knowing what one stands for. This notebook takes up the concept of "the New Day" from chapter 14, "Founding the Public School," in *Black Reconstruction*. Du Bois offers the concept as an affirmative instance in the history of black education that makes this ecstatic communal orientation a condition of possibility for the dark proletariat's intervention in American education. This notebook does not promise a new model of education but tries to understand ecstasy's significance to black study and the institutions issuing from that critical practice. In the process, the work of Langston Hughes and Katherine Dunham will nuance Woodson's critique of mis-education and Du Bois's account of the New Day.

This notebook stakes a challenge to the resentment permeating many critiques of American education. Oftentimes, the critiques themselves are warranted. Just as often, these critiques stem from nostalgia for an earlier industrial-era educational model that privileged the humanities. This nostalgia works rhetorically *as if* that model can be split off from Jim Crow governance and civic culture, which is conceptually, historically, and even geographically impossible. The current turn toward privatization, (re)segregation, and adjunctification are direct outgrowths of Jim Crow, not aberrations from it. While turning away from "neoliberal" educational models back to industrial-era ones may offer some respite, this still amounts to turning from one version of Jim Crow back to another.

1930S MIS-EDUCATION; OR, "THE DEFEAT OF THE FLESH AND THE TRIUMPH OF THE SPIRIT"

Hughes has much to teach about radical education, because his poems from the 1930s prefigure the increasing precarity of all academic laborers, even the privileged position of the professoriate. Surely, a wide range of exploited academic laborers are challenging exploitative education conditions. However, an increasingly proletarianized professoriate testifies to the drastic restructuring of US academic institutions and viewpoints on labor. No other position in US educational systems can play so equally and directly into shaping reaction or revolution among students over brief periods or even over decades.[4] Hughes is well aware of the professoriate's reputation for job stability, influence in the public sphere, and access to power brokers around the nation, if not the world. In fact, in the first two stanzas of "Letter to the Academy," Hughes writes sarcastically to

> The gentlemen who have got to be classics and are now old with beards (or dead and in their graves) will kindly come forward and speak upon the subject

> Of the Revolution. I mean the gentlemen who wrote lovely books about the defeat of the flesh and the triumph of the spirit that sold in the hundreds of thousands and are studied in the high schools and read by the best people.[5]

Hughes takes up the epistolary form in "Letter to the Academy" to speak forthrightly to a professoriate operating comfortably, either because it cannot see its exploitative role or, worse, because it hopes to occupy this position to enjoy such exploitation. Hughes appears to be of the same mind as Antonin Artaud, who published "Letter to the Chancellors of European Universities" in *La Revolution Surréaliste* around the same time Hughes wrote "Letter to the Academy." Artaud also greets the "gentlemen" scholars with a mix of anger and determination: "The fault lies with you, Chancellors, caught in the net of syllogisms . . . the false scholars blind in the other world, philosophers who pretend to reconstruct the mind." Artaud asks, "By what right do you claim to canalize human intelligence and award spiritual certificates of merit?" Artaud concludes his final verse with greater confidence than Hughes in the inability of academics to join a radical movement: "Through the sieve of your diplomas is passing a whole generation of gaunt and bewildered youth. You are the plague of a world, and so much the better for that world, but let it consider itself a little less at the head of humanity."[6] Later, this notebook ponders whether Hughes's "Letter to the Academy" rejects the professoriate's contributions to revolution as thoroughly as Artaud's poem. The "gentlemen" academics in "Letter to the Academy" could never be in league with the damned in a poem like "Wait," which received attention in the third notebook. Nor could these academics identify with the "hungry ones" in "Advertisement for the Waldorf-Astoria," who are invited to rent a suite in the luxury hotel "when the last flop-house has turned you down this winter." With this absurd invitation made to "roomers," "evicted families," "negroes," and then to "everybody," the hotel epitomizes capitalism's decadence and confirms that the most vulnerable are governed by a politics of abandonment. Hughes would also have those with "Dr. in front of their names" come to terms with the violence inherent to their humanistic enterprise.[7]

That self-interrogation hinges on questioning their commitment to the "defeat of the flesh and the triumph of the spirit." With this Pauline reference, Hughes's poem makes the college/university a privileged site for contesting a certain form of theological imagination and its disciplinary techniques. Warren Montag analyzes the place of disciplinary regimes in Pauline scripture, noting that something more lurks behind the commonplace assumption that this aspect of Christian tradition stresses abandoning the body for spiritual fulfillment. Behind this ascension from body to spirit (which corresponds well to the sense of beauty Hughes associates with the professoriate), Montag finds the descent from spirit to body. The proof of transcendence only comes through one's submission to discipline, even torture, worked out on the physical body.[8] Spiritual transcendence, in other words, is measured by one's willingness to give one's body over to the dominant powers. In Hughes's genealogy, Aristotle's principle of disengagement in education reaches today's faculty, students, and administrators through Paul's valorization of submitting to discipline. In turn, the Pauline trajectory treats the disempowerment that ensues as beautiful transcendence.

With this language, Hughes signals to his readers to think of professors in relation not just to the content they disseminate but to the disciplinary techniques that shape expertise and to the disorientation, terror, and enjoyment that stem from occupying this role, whose relationship to political economy and civil society keeps changing. The sonnet "Ph.D." speaks of the well-disciplined student-turned-academic abiding by the protocols of thought and of power. Reading it in today's context amplifies its facetiousness and the loss of the triumphalist narrative attached to academic labor in the industrial era:

> He never was a silly little boy
> Who whispered in the class or threw spit balls,
> Or pulled the hair of silly little girls
> Or disobeyed in any way the laws
> That made the school a place of decent order
> Where books were read and sums were proven true
> And paper maps that showed the land and the water
> Were held up as the real world to you.
> Always, he kept his eyes upon his books:
> And now he has grown to be a man
> He is surprised that everywhere he looks
> Life rolls in waves he cannot understand,
> And all the human world is vast and strange—
> And quite beyond his Ph.D.'s small range.[9]

The sonnet's octet and sestet recount the Ph.D.'s entire educational history as one dedicated to "decent order." Long ago, the subject of the poem successfully unlearned any "disobedient" urges. In Bruns's view, this exemplifies the subjectivity proposed in an Aristotelian tradition of education and disengaged spectatorship. Indeed, Hughes chooses the sonnet form because it recalls the fundamentals of mainstream arts education.

The sonnet itself becomes an instrument through which the student is trained to obey the forces enveloping him and the force he himself possesses. The naturalist language preceding the final couplet—"life rolls in waves"—identifies the forces that the student has been trained to misunderstand. That misunderstanding comes from teaching strictly in terms of identity, in which "paper maps" are "held up as the real world to you," at the expense of the nonidentity making possible and complicating any representation. Still, Hughes does not scapegoat the Ph.D. The poem makes its critique of education toward "you,"—that is, any potential reader, not just the highest certified. In this way, the Ph.D. is but the peak of a general trend of wrongheaded teaching. The standard grammar and regularity of the poem, quite unusual compared to Hughes's corpus full of bent blues lines, chants, and monologues, indicates how easily the Ph.D. passes this way of thinking and tameness on to others who enter American civil society, join the labor force, and more precisely, become new educators.

The class dynamics of "Ph.D." demand attention. Hughes equates the subject's desire for academic work with a desire for "decent order." Academic training cultivates both desires. Academic workers internalize narratives about who sustains this decent order and, conversely, those against whom the order is sustained. Whoever fails to obey this regularity will lose the rewards that come with decent order, the latter being the way it has won its long-term validity across diverse teaching institutions and through the generations. Among academic laborers, scholars might ignore or downplay capitalist expropriation because of the lucrative entrepreneurial, administrative, and public intellectual opportunities promised by submitting to decent order. The Ph.D. flounders partially because this social role should remain safe against the disordering forces of capitalist expropriation. Now the Ph.D. is a primary target of expropriation as a result of working *with* the order.

The world appears "vast and strange" when one sees oneself, against one's want, inhabiting the space between one's desired economic success and the material privation resulting from capitalism's shift away from the Great Society model. Now many more academics who anticipated middle-class comfort find themselves inhabiting the caesura between two stanzas of Hughes's "Good Morning Revolution," between the boss and the dispossessed speaker of the poem:

The boss's got all he needs, certainly
    Eats swell,
    Owns a lotta houses
    Goes vacationin'
    Breaks strikes
    Rubs politics, bribes police,
    Pays off congress
    And struts all over the earth—

But me, I ain't never had enough to eat
Me, I ain't never been warm in winter
Me, *I ain't never known security.*[10]

A range of scholars have constructed the specific histories of how these forms of insecurity took shape for the professoriate, college students, graduate students, colleges, and universities in recent years. I do not have the space to rehearse these intricate histories here, though they all relate to the neoliberal attempts to privatize higher education, make higher education more dependent on and answerable to financialization, depoliticize education, and disempower faculty and students alike. The proletarianization of the professoriate has increased disparities in pay, departmental support, and labor contingency, which means the same group of laborers can occupy the position of the bosses and the poor in Hughes's poem, though most will be closer to the latter than the former. This split sense of identity pinches the nerves so sharply because scholars still expect the rewards of decent order.

The insecurity directly acknowledged in these verses could be read as Hughes predicting the decline narratives dominating academic media today. But this betrayal does not guarantee that the Ph.D. has given up loyalty to this order and the rewards it promises. Even if the startled Ph.D. has a change of heart about the university, this does not immediately mean the internalized principles of disengagement will suddenly dissipate. There is no solace in Pauline rhetoric for the Hughes of the 1930s, who wrote poems like "Goodbye Christ," who abandons Christianity for it being used by "too many / Kings, generals, robbers, and killers."[11] In Hughes's view, Pauline rhetoric stands opposed to revolution. Revolution is premised on the force of ideas, affects, and practices based on full engagement. The Pauline rhetoric for Hughes prides itself on sacrificing one's material force to strengthen the regularizing tendencies of institutions. Hughes touches on the knot of desire in which one enjoys one's loss of power in exchange for professional accomplishment. Perhaps the conscious awareness of proletarianization emerges when revelation—in this case, the separation of the spirit from its material force—no longer earns the same enjoyment and rewards; that possibility will get closer attention later in this notebook. The other insight is that this knot of desire remains despite the diminished returns.

The conversation on the crisis of education and the humanities has understated how an array of punishments, rewards, privileges, and sacrifices

teaches students to accept "defeat of the flesh" and "triumph of the soul,"—
that is, give their bodies over to these processes while believing that somehow they will still maintain a sense of political agency. Such a conclusion
understates how intellectual engagement is performative, based on individual and shared bodily comportments. While on a nine-month lecture tour
in the mid-1930s, Hughes witnesses this discipline firsthand. More precisely,
Hughes focuses on the professoriate's centrality to teaching students to enjoy spirit's "triumph" over their flesh. He publishes his views on it in "Cowards from the Colleges" in the *Crisis* in 1934. Hughes asserts that "many of
our institutions apparently are not trying to make men and women of their
students at all—they are doing their best to produce spineless Uncle Toms,
uninformed, and full of mental and moral evasions."[12] He says, "At a number of schools, dancing on the campus for either faculty or students is absolutely forbidden. . . . At some schools marching in couples is allowed
instead of dancing." Hughes realizes this "absurd ban" on dance is intended
"to keep the sexes separated," rules he likens to "monasteries and nunneries in their strictness."[13]

This issue may appear minor compared to the political inactivity Hughes
mentions later. But Hughes believes that shaming links both events, based
on a more general disciplinary principle, which teaches students to relate
to their own bodies, sexually and otherwise, through a mediating structure
of domination. This structure operates via moral judgments that consider
black bodies pathological at the outset, hence Hughes's references to medi-
eval "monasteries and nunneries" that represent an asceticism severing the
relations between oneself, one's body, other bodies, and the world. Contrary
to the hyper-individualist mysticism in the West, the black intellectual tradition doubts that such conditions can cultivate ecstasy.[14] By attending to
the moralism of the Negro colleges in his day, Hughes adds another reference to a broader genealogy of the "principle of disengagement" that Bruns
noted at the start of this chapter.

Hughes then reports on "two double tragedies of color in one day" that
he heard of while visiting colleges in Virginia—"one a distinguished and
widely travelled young woman" who died in a car accident because local hospitals refused to treat her; the other an athletic coach who "was beaten to
death by a mob in Birmingham on his way to see his own team play." Hughes
finds these tragedies telling because through this loss the college students
learn how spirit triumphs over the flesh. The faculty, unfortunately, are

instrumental in spreading this message of docility. Several seniors invite Hughes to join in planning protests for these tragedies. Then Major Brown, a faculty representative, intercepts the students, claiming that his institution does not "like the word 'protest'" and prefers that the students "move slowly and quietly, and with dignity." Brown uses that dignity to barely cloak threats that these students would "face expulsion and loss of credits" if they carried on. Hughes laments that "the brave and manly spirit of Hampton students who wanted to organize the protest was crushed by the official voice" of the institution.[15] Hughes places these rules on dancing and double tragedies in the same report, because he is saying that, in these mundane and extraordinary cases, the students conduct themselves based on the same regime of regulations, rewards, and punishments. The double tragedies are real-life examples of the "human world" becoming "vast and strange" in the sonnet "Ph.D." However, the report goes further than the poem by discussing the soul-crushing results of living fully by such moral regulation and the faculty's centrality to doing this work. In Hughes's report, this is not about the faculty representative's personal attitude but about the structural role he plays in suppressing the college student's agency in pursuing social justice.

Hughes would have his readers consider how many "moral evasions" occur in disciplinary regimes that exist only because of their intellectual legitimacy. These double tragedies and the official response in Hughes's report complicate the popular distinctions between "the real world" and the college/university. Rhetorically, the phrase "the real world" separates the university from other institutions such that real exploitation and struggle happens elsewhere. Yet, any academic laborer knows this distinction does not hold.[16] Too often, painfully often, the college or university functions as a state of exception whose laws produce lawlessness. Hughes's report only hints at the many ways students are "crushed by the official voice" of the institution. That violence can include structural exclusions depending on a student's racial identification, family income levels, gender, sexual orientation, or religious identity. But much more aggressive factors count here too: racist assaults, rapes, intimidation, and bullying all make campuses uninhabitable for some students, who would have to share dormitories, classrooms, library study rooms, and other spaces with their assailants. Needless to say, the selective application of accountability makes some educational institutions into refuges for abusers and assailants with patterns of misconduct. Students switch classes, change majors, and sacrifice research time to avoid an assailant or group of assailants who move where they please; lose intellectual community and friendships when others side with an attacker because the latter has a so-called future; consider dropping out of college or university because the likelihood of repeat attacks is too high and the opportunity for protection and support is too low; and endure the subsequent physical ticks, anxiety, and disorders that come from initial assaults or the aftermath that revictimizes.

What "docile dignity" have students gained by accepting this mortification? This revelation founds and preserves a reactive way of life in which students also claim a moral victory against injustices they have not actually combated.[17] Increasing debts, decreasing job prospects, and crushed possibilities of assertion reveal the knot of desire animating college students who find enjoyment suffering under such regulations. Therefore, the college student as well as the Ph.D. share this perverse enjoyment, claiming their anguish is for a greater good embodied by institutions of higher learning. Without taking seriously what the educational disciplinary regimes do to bodies, critical thinking about education will amount to little more than "moral evasions," which institutions use to save their ethical legitimacy while dodging their greatest ethical problems.

At this point in "Cowards from the Colleges," Hughes completes the circuit described in "Ph.D." Faculty and students experience the vast strangeness of a world noncoincident with mainstream academic representations of life or of educational institutions. In pondering who will break this circuit, Hughes admits that he has "no hope for a new spirit" in most colleges, "unless the *students themselves put it there*." Despite the "distinct cleavage between the younger and older members of the faculties," on most campuses, "almost everywhere the younger teachers, knowing well the existing evils, are as yet too afraid of their jobs to speak out, or to dare attempt to reform campus conditions." Instead they "whisper to sympathetic visitors from a distance how they hate teaching under such conditions." To Hughes, "brave and progressive students" who combat "the suppression of free thought and action" are the "antidote to the docile dignity of the meek professors and well-paid presidents who now run our institutions." Otherwise, one must "look to the unlettered for their leaders and expect cowards from the colleges."[18]

In this section of the notebook, Hughes's 1930s writings nuance the meaning of mis-education by bringing race and libidinal economy into the discussion in ways that Bruns's critique invites but does not investigate. However, Hughes's project would not deserve such a close reading if it applied only to the 1930s. In the following section, this notebook extends Hughes's critique to the 1950s, when desegregation threatens the principle of disengagement at the heart of Jim Crow education. Extending Hughes's analysis to the 1950s will further clarify this notebook's critique of nostalgia for industrial-era education. Hughes's insights will have to adapt to the new strategies being sought out to discourage student agency as well as the professoriate's potential role in political change.

ON 1950S MIS-EDUCATION

Among the black students who were pressured to accept docile dignity, many objected and sought to transform educational institutions from within. Educational institutions pursued ways to punish these empowered students. At the same time, more forward-looking segregationists recognized that so long as the debate was political, they held an untenable position. Depoliticizing the institution provided a new avenue for opposing the demands of desegregation. The position proved to be equally untenable, but it reinforced the Aristotelian principle of disengagement by pretending to separate education from political considerations altogether. This move can make political activism among people of color appear wrongheaded or, worse, appear as a threat to democracy that justifies segregation indirectly. In "Crisis in Education" (1954), Hannah Arendt makes a claim that forges a fugitive connection with the dark proletariat's educational project. There she says that "education, too, is where we decide whether we love our children enough not to expel them from our world and leave them to their own devices, nor to strike from their hands their chance of undertaking something new, something unforeseen by us, but to prepare them in advance for the task of renewing a common world."[19] Unfortunately, Arendt abandons this idea four years later with "Reflections on Little Rock," an essay that epitomizes the effort to depoliticize education as the counterintuitive way of sustaining Jim Crow's political dominance and reactionary worldview, when disciplinary measures fail to produce the docility that Hughes identifies in his writings. In "Reflections on Little Rock," one sees Arendt repositioning American education so that, even when Jim Crow mis-education is most under siege, the Aristotelian principle of disengagement could endure. For this reason, "Reflections on Little Rock" serves not simply as an example of how the principle of disengagement persisted from the late nineteenth into the mid-twentieth century (and to our present day), the essay models the arguments that many will marshal to suppress the dark proletariat's presence in American education, even today.

This notebook lacks the space to consider how Arendt slides from urging adults to help children "renew a common world" to "Reflections on Little Rock," which erects numerous arguments against the common world and against youth as agents building it across racial differences. Only an active orientation to possibility, one that accentuates difference, multiplicity, and becoming, could place children at the center of renewing the world, as Arendt initially proposed. This notebook focuses on how her earlier proposal gets counteracted by the latter essay's concepts, claims, presuppositions, and omissions. Arendt's "Reflections on Little Rock" underscores homogeneity, teleology, and stasis and promotes a reactive orientation. Arendt's ruminations press on the common world from all sides to make it a privatized, exclusive, ultimately anti-common space. This has everything to do with the categories Arendt constructs, which are byproducts of her racialized identifications that sustain Jim Crow. The discussion that follows shows how her tripartite categorical structure paves the way for new generations to learn "the defeat of the flesh and triumph of the spirit" that has characterized the long history of US mis-education.

"Reflections on Little Rock" features three categories, each with its own operating principle. The political sphere functions through the principle of equality; the social sphere operates by the principle of discrimination; and the private sphere functions through the principle of exclusivity. Arendt creates the space for these categories by erasing a wide array of historical conditions. One could defend her by saying that, as a philosopher, she need not concern herself with such details. And that defense would fail, because the essay was written to respond to urgent circumstances, which means her essay denies the very conditions of its emergence. Following up her disavowal of the conditions of her philosophizing with yet *another* disavowal would mean being taken up uncritically into the forces shaping her essay and the forces that her essay creates. For example, Arendt says that "the color problem in world politics grew out of the colonialism and imperialism of European nations—that is, the one great crime in which America was never involved. . . . The unsolved color problem within the United States may cost her the advantages she otherwise would rightly enjoy as a world power."[20] This is not just factually incorrect but also wrong in ways that do ideological work on behalf of oppression. A barbed irony it is, that Arendt is so close to referencing Du Bois's famous phrase, "the problem of the color line," and even agrees with the concept's global scope, only to then wrench that concept from the one nation that Du Bois *always* had in mind when mobilizing the phrase.[21] Far from a mere conceptual misstep, this move thickens the veil covering myriad abuses done in the name of nationalism in the United States and imperialism abroad, as the second notebook of this project has already noted.

Another erasure denies the dark proletariat's active role in expanding education across the United States after the Civil War and denies its refusal to settle for Jim Crow's lackluster variant of learning: "The dividing line in the South was never between those who favored and those who opposed segregation—*practically speaking, no such opposition existed*—but the proportion of people who prefer mob rule to law-abiding citizenship."[22] This passage makes several moves at once. By denying practical opposition to segregation, Arendt will not even acknowledge the liberal or conservative aspects of the civil rights movement, let alone the radicalism that receives attention in this notebook. Consequently, black life, which conceptually and historically embodies the dissonant character of nonidentity, only appears in her analysis in terms of misplaced efforts, bad strategies, guilty black mothers, and black and white children getting forced into politics when they should have no inkling of the political tensions in their environment. This passage changes the terms of the discussion. So long as the Little Rock Nine raised concerns about the proper political structuring of American society, the dark proletariat's protests are legitimate though discomfiting attempts to challenge injustice. By refocusing the conflict on law-abiding citizens versus the mob, Arendt is saying that one side of what could have been a legitimate political debate is actually illegitimate and therefore a threat to the political *as such*. Arendt hearkens back to the same legal metaphysics that showed up in the second and third notebooks, in which blackness counts only as barbarism while whiteness counts as legality and civility, and any attempt to include black people in political life amounts to barbarian conquest. Refusing to acknowledge this interpretive choice while implementing its objectives means the racists can have their way *and* hide their hand in one stroke by claiming they are simply following the racially neutral letter of the law. Arendt intends to protect American education from segregationist excesses, but her intellectual presuppositions place her in league with the segregationists and at odds with the most fervent antisegregationist forces. The questions, then, are whether the white majority and the dark proletariat obey the principles that Arendt sets forth and whether Arendt's framework can retain coherence when the historical forces she disavows return to the fore.

Making these observations leads to a preliminary point about the political sphere and its principle of equality. The political sphere needs this ahistoricism to function so that Arendt does not have to address an equivocation in that very category. That is, Arendt never clarifies whether the principle of equality refers to a logical assumption or a historically achieved fact. Consequently, she cannot address the ways her theory will impact students who live with markedly different cultural histories and relationships to American political institutions. Arendt's doublespeak allows her to overstate past successes regarding educational equity, since equality is now here; understate the political efforts needed to sustain those positive results, since equality has always been here; and to confound today's political movements, since the prevailing equality will logically solve current problems and movements are threats to this process. Arendt seems to decide, in the end, that equality has been established but remains vulnerable to impending threats by segregationist laws. For this reason, she makes legally supported segregation in the South "a matter of constitutional principle which by definition is beyond majority decisions and practicality."[23] However, the legal metaphysics that Arendt evokes have always functioned based on an ontological divine between a racialized majority and the minority. The second notebook investigates how white supremacists used their majority status to turn their resentment into law, to distort the principles of the Constitution, to carry out endless cruelties, and then to represent themselves as the models of law-abiding citizenship. Arendt imagines herself among a white majority that prioritizes law over mob rule, when the second notebook indicates that the mob's brutality became the very basis for Jim Crow's law and order. As the second notebook explored, the civic authorities called on to investigate and judge criminality are committing the crimes. The judges, lawyers, and city councilpersons Arendt would associate with law-abiding citizenship are complicit in the most violent acts. Add to this the fact that lynchers sabotaged and destroyed every instance of black self-governance and black institutions that they could, and one can only stand befuddled at Arendt claiming that "the arrival" of federal troops *in the 1950s* "did little more than change passive into massive resistance."[24] No such passivity existed among Confederate sympathizers embittered by unconditional surrender.

Belying history so a Confederate fantasy of the past can triumph, ignoring the most vicious racism and its more tempered accomplices, and then calling this state of affairs "equality"—in such a context Arendt finds it "startling" that the federal government decided "to start integration in, of all places, the public schools," because with a little "imagination," one could see "this was to burden children, black and white, with the working out of a problem which adults for generations have confessed themselves unable to solve."[25] How far Arendt has come from "Crisis in Education" with these words. And how far she is from understanding the "burden" that children carry under segregation's juridical and cultural imperatives. No family arrangement could completely shelter children from racialization's violence. But Arendt would have to learn this from the very history she disavows. The problems do not stop at historical conditions, however. Arendt's own categories hinder her fantasy from coming to life. Shelter could come only from the social and private spheres, which are linked in ways that Arendt cannot fully admit. Even if this shelter could be provided, Arendt asserts that the social sphere's principle of discrimination *cannot* operate based on equality.[26] In effect, Arendt's argumentative moves position her to ignore black political activity: "Arendt seems unable, *or unwilling*, to connect her own upbringing and preparation to survive in anti-Semitic schools with the techniques used by black parents and community leaders in allowing black children to integrate legally racist and hostile traditionally white schools."[27]

When Arendt explains the social realm, she says that "each time *we* leave the protective four walls of *our* private homes and cross over the threshold into the public world, *we* enter first, not the political realm of equality, but the social sphere."[28] Arendt makes inequality unavoidable and productive for people making healthy affiliations. What sounds like a universal "we" actually amounts to a small, privileged group who must have "private homes" that effectively protect the inhabitants from outside forces. Arendt's Aristotelianism allows her to make the logical leap that the private American household is apolitical, which is an absolute impossibility in a nation built through settler colonialism. Homes become the primary instrument of establishing political superiors and inferiors. The many home invasions, torchings, bombings, and vandalisms of the homes of people of color, without any accountability for the wrongdoers, indicates that Jim Crow withholds this promise (or fantasy) of safety based on race, class, and gender dynamics. Arendt puts no effort into thinking about what education means for those whose homes are always at risk and that risk targets them in the social and political spheres as well. Nor does she mourn the losses this group has experienced in pursuing any form of institutionally supported education. Thus, Arendt's formulation comes at the expense of people of color whose homes are terrorized to sustain political, social, and private privileges for a select group. None of this violence degrades the condition of the South, in Arendt's view. However, the possibility that the federal government will properly enforce its old and new amendments, laws, and policies around equity leads Arendt to sound alarms. As she says unequivocally, "The general situation in the South has deteriorated" since "the Supreme Court decision to enforce desegregation in public schools."[29] This amounts to mourning the loss of Jim Crow, to mourning the dismantling of its principle of discrimination, and to mourning the inequalities that will go away.

Arendt's problematic linking of the social and private spheres continues with her discussion of children in the home. In her argument, children "are, or should be, brought up in that atmosphere of idiosyncratic exclusiveness which alone makes a home a home, strong and secure enough to shield its young against the demands of the social and the responsibilities of the political." Arendt worries over the "conflict between home and school, between [children's] private and their social life."[30] Unfortunately, her examples in "Reflections on Little Rock" do not model a concern for the plight of black and white children alike. Arendt fears white students will feel guilty when they see themselves in photographs threatening the black youth integrating Central High School. Shielding black children from racism matters to Arendt, but she blames black parents, especially black mothers, who make their children front-line soldiers in the conflict over segregation. She admits the shortcomings of white parents, since "a rise of mob and gang rule" means that white children were not properly sheltered.[31] Nevertheless, Arendt places the shame for this problem more on the federal government than on white parents. She alleges that federal intervention turned white people's passive distaste for desegregated social and private spaces into outright rebellion. No such passivity ever existed among white supremacists.

The problem is that white children often learned to hate their black peers in the very social and private locations that she hopes will shelter children from racism. Nearly the entire second notebook grapples with this question and features examples of children who join in the horrific festivities of lynching and massacres and then pose proudly with their older relatives in photographs taken in the aftermath. The rhetoric of chivalry falls flattest when one considers the black women and children killed in front of or in earshot of white children. But Jim Crow does not want its children to remain bystanders. Participating in these activities became rites of passage to identify children with different racial destinies, and this is completely absent from Arendt's consideration. Its absence warps her argument's evidence in favor of white households to such a degree that it could not be coincidence. Nor can it be unintentional, since "Reflections on Little Rock" as a whole directly contradicts the position Arendt takes in her earlier work. That is to say, Jim Crow's adherents have used all three spheres to assert their superiority violently. The question is not why the federal government grants students the responsibility of ending Jim Crow, the question is why Jim Crow needs students to imbibe its bile so they can feel that they belong, whether as racial superiors or inferiors.

Attentive readers will recognize that omitting this evidence does not effectively protect the tripartite structure of "Reflections of Little Rock" after all. The essay hopes to serve as a call to order to protect the Constitution, the political sphere, and its principle of equality. Arendt directs her call to order to black people, who risk rending the sociopolitical fabric with their political tactics and objectives and therefore threaten the orderly democracy she finds among white Americans. Consider how the photograph immediately preceding Arendt's "Reflections on Little Rock" raises doubts about such an orderly majority in Little Rock. The photograph features a mob of white high schoolers threatening the sole black student in the image, Elizabeth Eckford. The image portrays the very opposite of what Arendt claims. Eckford looks determined and vigilant, while the white students look out of control, irrational, unmannered, and violent. Unable to deny the hate on the white faces in the photograph, Arendt instead critiques the orderly black children for being hated, though she understates the situation by saying they are unwanted:

The situation of being unwanted . . . is more difficult to bear than outright persecution because personal pride is involved. By pride, I do not
mean anything like "being proud of being a Negro" or a Jew, or a white
Anglo-Saxon Protestant, etc., but that untaught and natural feeling of
identity with whatever we happen to be by the accident of birth. Pride
which does not compare and knows neither inferiority nor superiority
complexes, is indispensable for personal integrity, and it is lost not so
much by persecution as by pushing, or by being pushed into pushing,
one's way out of one group and into another.[32]

Arendt correctly states that being unwanted causes greater harm than persecution, since the former means facing rejection in a more intimate, vulnerable state. Arendt supports black people having a personal pride that
precedes racial identity. But shifting her call to social order to a question of
personal affect leads to several missteps. Left unexplained is how that personal pride can withstand a majority organized politically, socially, and privately to extinguish it.[33]

Arendt falters when she thinks that this intimacy can remain in the private
realm, *when Jim Crow racism exists only through the cross-racial intimacy it
outlaws.* Little Rock's white residents admit in newspapers their greatest
fear of desegregation: that black students will have sex with white students
and produce multiracial children, which will destroy the white race. This
fear animates segregationists more than concerns over state spending, de-
creased quality of education, or future career opportunities for their children.
The white supremacists feared they would become too intimate with their
so-called inferiors, which means the distinction between superior and inferior would fade. No matter that one cannot consistently measure this excess
of intimacy, which has already occurred, as Jim Crow laws indicate. The
need for superiority prompts segregationists to hold on even tighter to the
fantasy of superiority because it is so elusive. More importantly, even if
integration raises the quality of the school—if scholastics, if athletic teams,
if the social interactions in the school and the surrounding community
improve—then this counts as a loss, because there would be no inferiors to
look down on and abuse, and this means there are not and never were any
racial superiors in the first place. Segregationists are making a matter for
the private sphere into a priority for the social sphere, such that the social
sphere's native concerns fall to the wayside.

The political sphere is just as vulnerable to outside forces as the social sphere. Arendt strives to protect the Constitution, its political sphere, and its principle of equality. Yet her own argument offers no evidence that the American majority will join in that work if it means sharing that equality with nonwhite groups. Without this deliberate effort, matters in the private sphere will impact the political as well, which means that the principle of exclusivity can dominate precisely where equality should reign. In other words, the desire for a lesser, inferior subject obeys no categorical restrictions and *precedes* the principle of equality in Jim Crow America. The politics at play here hearken back to an Aristotelian ontology in which some are naturally free and others are naturally slaves. In practice, despite the defenses set up in Arendt's theory, the private and the social subtend the political, which means that a principle of inequality provides the limited basis for the principle of equality, such that the former can always overtake, suspend, or further limit the operation of the latter. Arendt's "Reflections on Little Rock" inadvertently replicates, rather than repels, the racialized sovereignty of the US South. Rather than salvage democracy, she ushers it into Jim Crow's wormwood embrace.

All of this leads to the most puzzling dimension of "Reflections on Little Rock," which has important theoretical and political complications for this notebook. Arendt takes for granted that Arkansas's segregationists have a right to discriminate against letting outsiders into the educational structure they created. Arendt imagines herself mediating between the rightful claimants to Central Rock High, who are assumedly white, versus the well-meaning but unwanted interlopers in the dark proletariat. This investigation leads to a very different claim: With the principle of exclusivity dominating the private, social, and political spheres of white American society, and doing so in a way that colonizes racialized and sexualized relations at once, it is impossible to say that Jim Crow envisioned a democratized educational project after the Civil War. The very idea of this educational project antagonizes Jim Crow's organizing principle. In what follows, this notebook considers the hypothesis that both logically and historically, the segregationists are the interlopers and could not be otherwise. Their "no" is their greatest innovation. As educational advances became crucial to keeping up with industrialism's developments, Jim Crow's adherents merely tolerated public education enough to sustain privileges among white working class, middle class, and upper-middle class enclaves and to discipline students of color so they, too, could learn to defeat their flesh so their spirit could triumph. When desegregation could no longer be avoided, the white majority almost immediately began shuttering down, attacking, and restructuring public schools and opening private schools, so they could unabashedly run their institutions on their preferred principles.

American education has obeyed this principle of discrimination and exclusivity to this day, precisely because of the increasing research that shows how culturally informed, properly resourced educational institutions could benefit students intellectually and ensure social equality politically. And yet, Arendt and so many other well-intentioned thinkers would have us believe that a worldview fundamentally organized against equality would produce the one institution, in a nation of (forced and willing) transports, that could cultivate the political as a site of equality. For this reason, Arendt is ahead of her time, foreshadowing the missteps of more recent thinkers who believe diversity is merely an addition to an American education that was originally white property. This explains the haphazard and half-hearted way that many students, faculty, administrators, and staff make demands regarding diversity in educational institutions, because they sincerely believe that the nonwhite students they stand up for are interlopers or, in a different psychological parlance, imposters, who do not have a historical claim on the spaces they inhabit. A frustrating case of confused notions, this is, with fighters for social justice still operating under the defeat of the flesh.

Having analyzed changes in strategy in 1950s mis-education, this notebook finds little reason for today's nostalgia for that period. Instead of a golden age for the humanities at midcentury, this notebook finds a shift in Jim Crow's strategy to sustain disengagement. Arendt's "Reflections on Little Rock" acknowledges that change is occurring and is indeed inevitable to some degree but misrecognizes the cloud of her own intellectual (and affective) investments in raced notions of social order, of who can claim public educational institutions as their own, of who can alter this order, and of who counts as demanding too much change. But precisely because Arendt's essay responds in such a reactionary manner, it indicates that there are other forces at play that do not operate by the principle of disengagement and do not expect students to accept docile dignity as their reward for learning to acquiesce. The remainder of this notebook considers a different force animating the dark proletariat's rebellion against the defeat of the flesh produced by Jim Crow in its industrial-era and neoliberal expressions.

Fortunately, several black writers from the 1930s have already begun describing this force in ways that link education to a poetic, ecstatic form of life.

"THE NEW DAY": FOUNDING THE PUBLIC SCHOOL

The "gentleman" professor, the segregationist students harassing and threatening the Little Rock Nine, the philosopher who seeks to restore democracy by privileging its suppressors, and many others belong to a long history of backlash against "the New Day," the originary scene when the dark proletariat establishes common, public institutions of study. The discipline, privatization, deficit mentality, and other techniques of mis-education are all directed toward counteracting this event. Readers cannot overstate the significance of Du Bois commenting on education in "The Coming of the Lord," but the most gripping description of this event is the "Founding the Public School" chapter of *Black Reconstruction*. In *Black Reconstruction*, Du Bois highlights the pursuit of land ownership and entrepreneurship after Emancipation. Yet he finds something even more significant than those practical aims when he says the freedpersons "wanted to know; they wanted to be able to interpret the cabalistic letter and figures which were the key to more. They were consumed with curiosity at the meaning of the world. First and foremost, just what was this that had recently happened about them—this upturning of the universe and revolution of the whole fabric?"[34] Education becomes the primary avenue for the dark proletariat to understand and sustain its own revolutionary impact on the world.

Du Bois boldly states that mass education in the United States is an outgrowth of black (self-)emancipation:

> They were consumed with desire for schools. The uprising of the black man, and the pouring of himself into organized effort for education, in those years between 1861 and 1871, was one of the marvelous occurrences of the modern world; almost without parallel in the history of civilization. The movement that was started was irresistible. It planted the free common school in a part of the nation, and in a part of the world, where it had never been known, and never been recognized before. Free, then, with a desire for land, a frenzy for schools, the Negro lurched into the new day.[35]

Du Bois's careful, inspiring diction indicates how much he wants to recontextualize learning in black culture. The problem is not simply that Jim Crow education has cultivated racism in its students and the general public. The deeper problem is that Jim Crow did not produce the public school in the first place. Jim Crow feeds parasitically on an institution not of its own making and latches on so convincingly that even radicals follow in Arendt's footsteps by mistaking public education for Jim Crow's brainchild. The public school belongs to a different tradition. Closely reading the above passage will clarify Du Bois's genealogy of the public school and reveal that several other black intellectuals elaborated a similar position, though in different ways.

Du Bois says a "frenzy" animates this founding movement. In *Souls of Black Folk*'s tenth chapter, "Of the Faiths of the Fathers," frenzy varies from "silent rapt countenance or the low murmur and moan to the mad abandon of physical fervor—the stamping, shrieking, and shouting, the rushing to and fro and wild waving of arms, the weeping and laughing, the vision and the trance." Du Bois says "many generations" of black folk "firmly believed that without this visible manifestation of the God there could be no true communion with the Invisible."[36] Even in *John Brown* and then in *Black Reconstruction*, Du Bois figures Emancipation in terms of the literal confrontation with God or the Christ for the (self-)emancipated. Thus, the radical texts assembled across these notebooks and from Du Bois's corpus identify a frenzy that leads to a transformative encounter "with the Invisible." The New Day belongs to this frenzy in black life, carrying a promise for collective learning and a threat to the Western tradition that, since Aristotle, has sought to expel poetic ecstasy from the polis.

Du Bois makes "frenzy" a theoretical and practical counter to Aristotle's principle of disengagement, associating it with a different grammar of being human, ethical, and empowered. The concept also registers thirty years of Du Bois's own intellectual development, reiterating the movement from *Souls of Black Folk* to *John Brown* to *Black Reconstruction* from the third notebook. In this intellectual evolution, Du Bois sought to make the freedpersons more than spectators, even in the classroom. Bruns would likely admire Du Bois's effort, considering how Bruns turns to Hans-Georg Gadamer to transform spectatorship into fascination:

The true being of the spectator, who belongs to the play of art, cannot be adequately understood in terms of subjectivity. . . . But this does not mean that the nature of the spectator cannot be described in terms of being present at something. . . . Being present has the character of being outside oneself. . . . In fact, being outside oneself is the positive possibility of being wholly with something else. This kind of being present is a self-forgetfulness. . . . Here, self-forgetfulness is anything but a privative condition, for it arises from devoting one's full attention to the matter at hand, and this is the spectator's own positive accomplishment.[37]

At this point in Bruns's argument, he finds himself on a parallel track with Du Bois and other black diasporic thinkers in the 1930s, including anthropologist, dance choreographer, and educator Katherine Dunham. In her notes on dance and education in "the movement of the *yonvalou*," Dunham associates fascination with "active wondering about the invisible." She calls *yonvalou* "fluid, involving spine, base of the head, chest, solar plexus, and pelvic girdle. The effect [of the dance] is complete relaxation. . . . The dance is decidedly soothing rather than exciting, and one is left in a state of complete receptivity. It is in this state that contact with the *loas* [the spirits] most often occurs." The transformation of spectatorship to fascination, for Dunham, requires fully embodied practice triggering a "release from emotional conflict" through a "complete externalization of one's ego in that of the essence or being with whom the communion is desired"—all characteristics of a different approach to learning that Jim Crow could never abide.[38]

Bruns's account of poetic communities converges with this theme in black thought, but not for long. By emphasizing the chance of being completely with another, Du Bois and Dunham, in their distinct ways, make ecstasy into a shared bodily comportment, an orientation resulting from a new sense of shared movement. If this comportment is disrupted, one cannot maximize the generativity found in giving oneself over to fascination. But even those disruptions do not necessarily extinguish the project. While Du Bois could sympathize with Bruns's account of short-lived poetic communities, he marvels at the freedperson's introduction of educational institutions to a place in the nation and world where it had never been acknowledged. The public school indicates that the ecstasy in Emancipation could inspire the production of viable, longstanding institutions under favorable or unfavorable conditions. A necessarily short-lived excitement for education would have done nothing to budge the majority of whites in the South, comprised of rich and poor who both considered education an elite luxury. Du Bois is saying that in the 1860s and 1870s, the dark proletariat's frenzy pushed against racial and class divisions that had made educational institutions for the masses unthinkable for virtually all Americans. Miseducation has worked so feverishly on an institutional level since the 1870s because, unchecked, this frenzied view of education would alter American society and politics, not just classroom conduct. No one can deny the historicity of institutions, which emerge and fade. Nevertheless, one can recognize that black life persists outside the terms of Western progress. This is partially attributable to the West's making blackness synonymous with ahistorical being—a *mis*recognition that means the West, on its own terms, has produced a historical object that it cannot historicize. This is also due to how blackness, on other terms, manifests itself through (a)rhythms freed from the constraints of conventional progress.

These broader claims on blackness and temporality help clarify the literal and metaphorical meanings of the "lurching" that characterizes the New Day. Lurching describes the performative character of this educational movement. The *Oxford English Dictionary* defines *lurch* as "to lean suddenly over to one side" like a ship or "to move suddenly, unsteadily, and without a purpose in any direction, as, e.g., a person staggering." As the title to Du Bois's magisterial volume indicates, the New Day sought to reconstruct American ideals on who should be educated and where and how they could be educated. This notebook takes the position that lurching remains characteristic of the founding and reconstruction of educational institutions that sustain black life. Identifying these temporal aspects of the lurching movement aids in distinguishing the effects of study from the effects of discipline. Granted, sometimes lurching may be the effect of both movements. Nevertheless, this modest exercise clarifies why Jim Crow's animus could not have founded the public school and why radically rethinking education today means turning to different traditions, including the black radical tradition, to find new terms for learning, teaching, and institution building.

Lurching occurs because the New Day inaugurates an underground activity establishing itself aboveground in American civil society. As Heather Andrea Williams has brilliantly shown, from the 1820s to the 1860s the enslaved attend "clandestine schools" to continue their study despite increasingly severe anti-literacy and anti-education laws being ratified across the

South. More significantly, the fugitive desire for education among the enslaved *precedes* the efforts among beneficent white slaveowners, business owners employing hired-out slaves or freedpersons, or ministers to educate for conversion missions. John Henry Hill's correspondence in *The Underground Railroad*, for instance, testifies to a broader, deeper, and still-evolving field of literacies within the labor for emancipation. The underground serves as a space for study. The same worklessness that enabled the general strike also enabled the slaves' attempts at studying, despite Southern society giving them over to endless work unto death. In the context of the New Day, that worklessness takes education beyond increasing the black body's utility for the market.

Granted, no education institution in the United States could ignore training for vocations. But the New Day's irruption from a frenzy occurring on the levels of the revolutionary and the mundane, encompassing everything from toppling slavery to erecting self-sufficient black townships to intimately sharing wonder tales suggests that it already knows "that there is as much dignity in tilling a field as in writing a poem." Booker T. Washington rightly challenges any who would dignify poetry and condescend against the black worker, although he follows that welcoming claim with the absolutely hierarchical claim that "it is at the bottom of life we must begin, and not at the top."[39] The class stratification that pits poetry against tillage is incompatible with the New Day. If the New Day is an outgrowth of clandestine schools where the enslaved envisioned freedom beyond labor, of the worklessness that allowed the enslaved to critique and shut down exploitative labor conditions, and of Emancipation's ecstasy, then purposelessness does not amount to upper-class leisure. Purposelessness refers to complete engagement in learning going in whatever direction it may. Purposelessness frees the New Day from the role of redeeming the black body through capitalist labor regimes and political passivity. These redemptive efforts are troubling because they never subdue the white supremacist logic influencing them. Nor can these efforts explain why the supposed *moral* redemption of the black requires their being instrumentalized for the *financial and libidinal* gain of whites. Vocation matters practically, without doubt. But the black radical tradition will not turn vocation into the salvation of black life, when said salvation is merely the conduit for another's voracious appetite for profits. Then and now, the New Day abandons this false transcendence.

Dunham's incisive comments on industrial capitalism's production and the body add another dimension to the discussion. The multiplicity in blackness's relation to itself and to industrialism's disharmony triggers this lurching movement. In "the most highly industrialized metropolitan centers," Dunham identifies "a pattern" over the "past century of rapidly changing mores, ethics, economics, and credos":

> The rhythm of the average metropolitan center is not one to induce integration—quite the contrary. Or perhaps as yet we human beings are still too cradled in the movement of the earth womb to adapt to the ever-increasing heterodoxy imposed upon us by our mode of life. Our pace is uneven, our boasting has lost the composure of its stature, and our spirit has no oneness with the air we breathe. We are dominated by a cross-current of rhythms and motions emanating from countless man-created machines and institutions, from fears, anxieties, and loss of faith. The rhythms of the human body itself—the beating of the heart, the motion of breathing, the delicate system of waves emanating from the brain centers, the flow of the blood stream, and the unconscious urging of the muscles are in constant competition with the cacophony and disharmony which are the fruits of the industrial age.[40]

With Dunham and Hughes being of the same generation and Du Bois coming of age a generation earlier, all three thinkers witnessed the racial compact that came with industrial capitalism. As the second notebook explored, the end of federally supported Reconstruction meant that white workers, North and South, would accept their economically exploited position so long as they remained on top of the hierarchy through Jim Crow at home and through imperialism abroad. Dunham concludes that for all the material gains that came from this compact, wholly submitting to industrialization's methods and objectives cannot lead to spiritual integration for anyone. Du Bois and Hughes concur, and all three thinkers, in their different ways, espouse alternative terms for an education that can affirm black life. Notably, in the above passage, Dunham does not counter industrialism's "cacophony and disharmony" with an ideal integrated spiritual self either. She describes a human body composed of multiple rhythms alongside the disharmony produced in the hubs of cultural and economic productivity. Rather than condemn the black body to fallenness and a path of redemption by the discipline that separates spirit from flesh, Dunham characterizes the black body by its polyrhythms. That multiplicity reiterates the significance of embodiment to learning and rebuts the argument that makes the flesh the locus of intellectual inadequacy or immoral lack. When ecstasy becomes a condition of possibility for education, the very basis for learning comes from enlivening the flesh, not stripping it away.

In sum, placing Du Bois, Dunham, and Hughes in conversation suggests that the New Day and United States industrialism stand in for two conflicting educational movements loaded with widely varying understandings of subjectivity, community, temporality, and embodiment. This means that the New Day cannot be a minority reaction to a preexisting industrial-era educational model in the United States. The conflict arises precisely because the New Day is no outgrowth of Western thought but sent from elsewhere. The New Day marks a different tradition of education that had been practiced before industrialism took root; before Lincoln even considered writing his executive order on behalf of the self-emancipated; and before white Southerners, rich or poor, had ever considered education for the masses. Beyond that, the New Day persisted despite Jim Crow parasitically clawing into and sabotaging opportunities for black education even as it consumed whatever black labor it could find. Black students and educators had to work across these conflicting grammars to build and sustain their schools, and it was the multiplicity within blackness that made this effort durable.

Therefore, Du Bois, Dunham, or Hughes would not understand the popular aim among today's academic laborers who hope to add diversity to their educational paradigms, which makes diversity an afterthought for public education. The New Day makes what is commonly called "diversity" the *forethought* of American education. Only Jim Crow would profit from this conceptual and historical confusion of terms. Speaking of adding diversity is, in itself, already an aftereffect of Jim Crow's work of violence. Three examples will serve to clarify this prior diversity's significance to the dark proletariat instituting public education. Two of these examples are historic instantiations of the New Day. The third example represents a primal scene of reaction against the New Day. The first instance comes from Savannah, Georgia:

It was decided to have the schools opened at once for all the colored people who should apply. A time was set for examination of teachers, and a number of colored men and women applied. The colored citizens of Savannah were greatly encouraged and assisted in their efforts by the Rev James Lynch of the AME Church, an educated colored man, who afterwards became Secretary of the State for Mississippi. Early in January, 1865, the Rev JW Alvord . . . and Mr Lynch examined the teachers. Ten colored persons were found competent. It was very difficult to find a building in which to locate the schools. The most available place was the "Old Bryan Slave Mart," which had recently served as the pen from which relatives of many of these Negroes had been sold. The bars which marked the slave stalls were knocked down to make more space for seating. To this and other places flocked the freed people of every age and shade, eager for that book learning which really seemed to them the key to their advance.[41]

The second instance comes from Little Rock, Arkansas:

Negroes themselves after 1865 established the first free schools in Arkansas. This they did at Little Rock, where after paying tuition for a short time, they formed themselves into an educational association, paid by subscription the salaries of teachers, and made the schools free.

In July, 1865, General Sprague appointed William M. Colby, General Superintendent of Refugees and Freedmen, to cooperate with the state authorities, and, if possible, work out a system of education for those classes. . . . Many Arkansas whites did not approve education under the Bureau because they feared it encouraged "social equality."

Under the Freedmen's bureau, Negroes built schoolhouses and sometimes furnished as much as 33% of the cost of instruction. The civil government did little toward the encouragement of Negro education.[42]

The third, reactive instance comes from Louisiana:

It was soon after the war that a white member of Johnson's restored Louisiana legislature passed one of the schools set up by the Freedmen's Bureau in New Orleans. The grounds were filled with children. He stopped and looked intently and then asked, "Is this a school?" "Yes" was the reply. "What, for niggers?" "Evidently." He threw up his hands. "Well, well," he said, "I have seen many an absurdity in my lifetime, but *this is the climax!*"[43]

Both dimensions of these passages deserve attention, because they confirm this notebook's emphasis on education emerging from an alternative tradition that makes ecstasy central to communal becoming. Those who are unwilling to countenance this tradition will not only misunderstand black efforts at education, they will reiterate Jim Crow's hallmark claims, all the while thinking that they are correcting a problem. Needless to say, Arendt's "Reflections on Little Rock" is a perfect example. She bases her entire article on the idea that Little Rock schools are a product of white sociality, when, twenty-five years earlier, Du Bois already claimed that Negroes themselves "established the first free schools in Arkansas," in Little Rock, and in the surrounding areas. Despite the anti-intellectualism that characterizes Jim Crow, it is utterly unfathomable to Arendt that American education is a product of black sociality, which means that, in her essay's own terms, the black people she dismisses would actually hold the power of discrimination over the white students at Central High School. Of course, Du Bois's historiography demonstrates that the dark proletariat sought to make social equality a reality and so they sought to establish schools that would not abide by a principle of discrimination in the first place. The point here is not that Arendt's theory is effective or that black folk should simply replace white folk in the same schema. Rather, the point is that Arendt's entire essay would fall apart, in her own eyes, if black people held this power of discrimination. She would likely have abandoned her claims if it meant granting black life that much power over the social order. Her fateful mistake falls completely in line with her overt mockery and rejection of black studies as an intellectual project. It also means that her role as mediator is disingenuous. A more effective version of "Reflections on Little Rock" would have entailed Arendt's *self*-reflections on her philosophical presuppositions that made her complicit with the very destructive forces she hoped to contain, so much so that she misrecognized them in the wrong place. More importantly, this would have entailed admitting the need to rethink philosophy as well as her place in it and the broader world by accepting that general education was a "Negro idea." Let it suffice that this notebook builds on this Du Boisian premise.

The freedpersons living in Savannah and Little Rock fostered an ecstatic joy to be wholly with another, fascinated and desiring knowledge and connection with an intensity beyond the privileges of any certification or vocation. Through such fascination, they escaped what Bruns calls a "privative condition," and amplified their second-sight.[44] This enabled them to view their conditions in multiple ways. Only second-sight would allow them to see that they could transform the dreaded slave mart into a school for their betterment. They are not after a Hegelian overcoming, which would contain the opposite. Rather, they are displacing a slave regime that wanted to teach only self-renunciation to the enslaved, nothing more. The physical transformation of Old Bryan Slave Mart into a school would involve the lurching Du Bois describes in *Black Reconstruction*. But that lurching motion would not completely obstruct the "complete receptivity" that Dunham describes in her ethnographic writings and teachings. One must consider the freedpersons' transforming Old Bryan Slave Mart into a school as partly a commemoration to ancestors. As Dunham herself once said, such commemoration offers "a spiritual key for survival today and the development of man."[45] That is to say, in ripping out the bars from the cells to create a more open classroom, the freedpersons had to recall the ancestors sold away, never to be seen again. In gathering or building the benches for students to occupy the classroom, they had to think of the parents, grandparents, and other loved ones who desired that future generations would have a space to read, unbothered by the overseer's lash. They must have remembered the teacher who suffered persecution for running clandestine schools before the Civil War. Concentrating fully on this work would help undo the knots that limited their potential to memories of belittlement and loss. They could now make the school a harbinger for future abolitions to come. The entire scene enacts a new orientation for black folk based not on hope's passivity but on the active transformation of material, physical, affective, and intellectual conditions.

An ecstasy linking commemoration to institution building in this manner expands who counts as students, as Du Bois says, "To this and other places flocked the freed people of every age and shade." The New Day is sustained by an eternal return to a prior diversity that never abided by Arendt's principle of exclusivity. Du Bois had this in mind when he chose the penultimate stanza of James Weldon Johnson's "O Black and Unknown Bards" to conclude the "Founding the Public School" chapter:

There is a wide, wide wonder in it all
That from degraded rest and servile toil
The fiery spirit of the seer should call

These simple children of the sun and soil.
O black slave singers, gone, forgot, unfamed,
You—you alone, of all the long, long line
Of those who've sung untaught, unknown, unnamed,
Have stretched out upward, seeking the divine.[46]

Earlier in the poem, the speaker longs to know who originally invented classic songs like "Swing Low, Sweet Chariot" and "Nobody Knows the Trouble I've Seen." By the penultimate stanza, the speaker learns to appreciate the collective creative act of "these simple children of the son and soil." Once again, black culture does not place the writing of poetry higher on a hierarchy than "tilling a field." Du Bois selects Johnson's verse because it makes the tillers of the soil essential members of a poetic community. These unknown bards are the prior diversity, the forethought to mass education in America, that allowed people of "every age and shade" to inhabit educational institutions for their betterment. Du Bois is saying that despite individual names disappearing from the rolls of those schools, and despite some of those institutions closing for many different reasons, the capacious *relation* they performed still survives.

The place of the "call" in Johnson's poem requires clarification. It must be distinguished from the fourth notebook's focus on Western sovereignty reducing call-and-response's polyvocality to a single sovereign figure initiating the call, as if that figure is the origin to which all others must bow. Mis-education counts among the many tactics Jim Crow uses to reduce call-and-response's complexity to serve the few at the expense of the many. This point recalls the third quotation from *Black Reconstruction*, when a Louisiana legislator outright denies black children's capability to learn, even when he stands in a schoolyard surrounded by black children learning and playing. On the one hand, the passage shows that young black children are not protected from racist attacks. Contrary to Arendt, black parents need not push their children into political frays, since Jim Crow's adherents cannot help but follow and stigmatize black children.

On the other hand, the example brings to mind the complexities of call-and-response as it initiates and echoes across the several materials explored in this notebook, including Johnson's poem, Du Bois's *Black Reconstruction*, Dunham's dance notes, Hughes's poetry, and Eckford's photographed resilience. As Stefano Harney says in *The Undercommons*, "In the call and response, the response is already there before the call goes out. You're already in something."[47] Call-and-response precedes any call to or from Western sovereignty. This also means that, despite unbelievable pressures, the culture performing this call-and-response may tap into a collective power that allows it to survive or even outlive Western sovereignty's onslaught. The call that Du Bois highlights in Johnson's poem, the call that his notebook tracks across several texts, "is always a call to dis-order" that often deranges the categories that enable Western sovereignty's operation.[48]

Halberstam's comment warns readers not to miss this detail of Du Bois's example. The children can play in the schoolyard despite the hostilities they face, because they respond to a call that could never be reduced to constitutionalism or Supreme Court decisions. The Louisiana legislator is upset precisely because his presence does not stop the children's learning experience or, more importantly, their frenzy to learn through play. The children do not suffer from "being unwanted" in this example, because they do not grant him the power to accept them in the first place. As the "Arkansas whites" said of the schools at Little Rock, they feared that these institutions founded by black people would produce "social equality." The Louisiana legislator knows this and needs to sabotage this possibility. If anything, the legislator throws a tantrum because *he* is unwanted. The children have denied the legislator the chance to deny them.[49] The legislator laments not being in the vaunted position so he can deny them social belonging. Although he occupies a political position of power over them, they have sabotaged his effort to devalue them socially, and the example suggests that this power to deny matters even more to him than whatever administrative sabotage he might accomplish to their institution.

Nearly one hundred years later and a few states westward, one finds the same derangements among the segregationists hurling their vitriol at Eckford and the other Little Rock Nine. Nothing in the image indicates that Eckford hopes to be wanted by the students spitting, yelling, cursing, and threatening her. One can hear the black community's songs and frenzied shouts cutting through the mob's vitriol at Eckford, as the photograph re-enacts the final lines of Johnson's poem that Du Bois so wisely selects, with Eckford surrounded by a mob, "alone, of all the long long line / Of those who've sung untaught, unknown, unnamed, / Have stretched out upward, seeking the divine." No one should deny that this is romance in a mine field. The second notebook makes it clear that administrative violence can be just as traumatic as physical violence and that administrative violence has become an optimal avenue for denying social equality. From this angle, Arendt's essay, which requires the social to be discriminatory, a claim that aligns perfectly with the "Arkansas whites" of the 1860s and the 1950s, helps justify the administrative violence of education after Jim Crow's partial unraveling. Nevertheless, these examples model the determination that comes from the dark proletariat hearing and responding to the call of those black and unknown bards. The dark proletariat is there with Eckford in that photograph. The mob does not threaten Eckford because she is a lone figure in the wrong place at the wrong time. They threaten her for announcing that the dark proletariat is reclaiming educational sites for the common, after being stolen and reprogrammed to make disengagement their highest virtue. Eckford's presence reasserts that such lowly principles fall short of her poetic community's frenzy that founded schools in the first place. Black poetry, then, responds to this call by inhabiting institutions of a conflicted making, torn between incommensurable grammars.

To be clear, this notebook values the critiques of mis-education occurring in academic, artistic, and activist circles today. However, to reduce black learning to spotting instances of mis-education is troubling. That reduction has become such a common shorthand that many have no clue of the New Day or the practices of black study that preceded it. Consequently, proponents of radical change in education may end up in a contorted position that can only count as defeat of the flesh. It is impossible to think, argue, and act with conviction when one has no historical traces in the educational system one seeks to transform. And yet, this section of the notebook returns us to the affects mentioned in Du Bois's famous essay "Criteria for Negro Art"—not the oft-discussed portion on art as propaganda but the passage that observes black writers looking back into their past, *feeling half-shamed that they ever felt ashamed about looking back in the first place*. Critiquing mis-education on its own terms will artificially curtail institutional change, whether that be transforming those institutions or altogether replacing some institutions with new ones, strategies that the New Day has consistently implemented. The unknown children from Louisiana as well as Eckford's bold presence in Little Rock remind readers that true revolution, in and through altering and creating educational institutions, would involve an instance where the "flesh triumphs (as well as the spirit)." This theme deserves further exploration, which can be achieved by returning to "Letter to the Academy," where Hughes first expresses it. This time, the poem must be placed alongside his poems in *Dear Lovely Death* (1931), *A New Song* (1938), and others from the 1930s to find insights on the role of students and the professoriate when frenzy becomes a condition of possibility for learning.

THE FLESH TRIUMPHS (AS WELL AS THE SPIRIT)

In "Letter to the Academy," the sarcastic tone of the first and second stanzas indicates Hughes's doubts about the professoriate's commitment to revolution. However, an earlier section of this notebook left open the possibility that Hughes may change his view later in the poem. Not only does the poem itself suggest that Hughes changes his mind later in the poem, the previous sections of this notebook can help explain what triggers his change. In the transition between its second and third stanzas, "Letter to the Academy" switches from sarcastic indictment to radical demand in response to the New Day, when the underground educational efforts of the dark proletariat went aboveground to found education based on a concept of frenzy. Between these stanzas, his doubts of reactionary faculty turn into an imperative that calls them to take a different political stand:

> I mean the gentlemen who wrote lovely books about the defeat of the flesh and the triumph of the spirit that sold in the hundreds of thousands and are studied in the high schools and read by the best people will kindly come forward and
>
> Speak about the Revolution—where the flesh triumphs (as well as the spirit) and the hungry belly eats, and there are no best people, and the poor are mighty and no longer poor, and the young by the hundreds of thousands are free from hunger to grow and study and love and propagate, bodies and souls unchained.[50]

This notebook wagers that the seemingly unimportant break in the line registers the force of the New Day. That break gets registered partly through the previously mentioned change in tone. But that is only the first indication of the New Day's power. The New Day is so forceful that one cannot decide between its being negation or surplus, since it at once undoes a "defeat of the flesh" and sustains a case in which "the flesh triumphs (as well as the spirit)." Just as Hughes's poem responds to this call from black and unknown bards before him, so the poem performs the opportunity the professoriate has to tap into this radical event. Hughes inverts the Pauline reference to spirit triumphing over the flesh. By saying "the flesh triumphs (as well as the spirit) and the hungry belly eats, and there are no best people, and/the poor are mighty and no longer poor," Hughes finds a flesh that survives discipline and, when reclaimed, it affirms the body as a site of transformation of self and world.[51]

The poem takes seriously the premise that the New Day's call cannot be answered with pessimism. Hughes is well aware of the wide range of difficulties the freedpersons faced to expand public education across the nation. Obviously Hughes knows the difficulties faced by the dark proletariat in the United States and around the world. And Hughes is not alone. When Du Bois calls their educational efforts "almost without parallel in the history of civilization," occurring in "a part of the nation," where it "had never been known" or "recognized before," he stands in awe because of the common-sense conclusion that the freedpersons would have no interest in learning, having been kept from formal education for so many generations. In contrast, the freedpersons relentlessly pursued education in ways that others with many more privileges never considered. Saying this does not amount to a naïve romanticist position that minimizes racial violence. The New Day's power persists directly in the face of overt hostilities and covert stratagems. Rather, the New Day calls into question those who are pessimistic of everything but their own pessimism and how that narcissistic remnant complicates a radical posture. This missed opportunity for self-criticism can sometimes send praxis in directions that are hard to distinguish from the docile dignity this notebook has taken to task.

Hughes's "Letter to the Academy" also changes tone because he agrees with one of the New Day's primary objectives: to undo the principle of disengagement by rethinking the relationship between flesh and spirit. Considering the subject of the poem, Hughes now ponders how the professoriate, as one class of academic laborers (with its own internal stratifications), could join in the frenzy. If professors are going to respond to the call as Hughes does, then this means a solid turn away from the nostalgia for the industrial era. Rather than wish for a return to precrisis conditions in the academy—which would amount to mere relief instead of reconstruction, restoring a sense of security to only a sliver of academic laborers—Hughes's

1930s poetry challenges scholars to embrace being part of the dark prole-tariat. He knows very well the scope of his demand, considering what he says about scholars in his poem "Ph.D." Hughes knows that such a change will involve a fight of affliction for a number of academics. But recall the introduction to *Thinking Through Crisis*, which quotes Langston Hughes's "Dear Lovely Death," in which the titular subject "taketh all things under wing . . . only to change / Into some other thing / This suffering flesh."[52] Hughes does not necessarily speak of actual death here, but of a death drive, a negativity informing collective and individual transformation. He is not calling an otherwise comfortable professoriate to endure unnecessary pain. In Hughes's estimation, the "flesh" is already vulnerable, already suffering, and already enduring something more than the suffering that institutional patterns perpetuate. He prompts academics to consider their fleshly exis-tence, to decide whether they will suffer for their privileges or experience the suffering that has "change" as its "other name."[53]

Deciding to maintain their privileges means staying the course that Hughes describes in "Ph.D." The fight to maintain privilege will not com-pletely stop the financial and libidinal returns from diminishing. Then again, this fight of affliction can also provide the circumstances for the pro-fessoriate renewing its intimacy with the dark proletariat. In light of the New Day, Hughes's "Letter to the Academy" takes the latter option seriously. For the same reason, this notebook concludes by taking that latter option seriously as well. Hughes's "Letter to the Academy" imagines the intellec-tual and ethical aims of a professoriate attuned to the call of the black and unknown bards. By building on those details in the final portion of "Letter to the Academy" and connecting them to several other of Hughes's 1930s poems, this concluding section locates the professoriate among the frenzy that displaces the principle of disengagement.

To attune itself to or even join the dark proletariat's frenzy, the profes-soriate would have to undergo a number of shifts in perspective and affect. "Dear Lovely Death" thinks of death as change through the medium of the flesh. Several other poems collected in *Dear Lovely Death* nuance the theme. Taken together, these poems help wrench the professor away from the af-fective entanglements characterized in "Ph.D." The flesh proves to be some-thing more than suffering when one connects "Dear Lovely Death" with another poem, "Demand." The latter poem begins with an exclamatory "Lis-ten!" In "Demand," the speaker's "body of utter death" feels touched by the "dream of utter aliveness."[54] The speaker demands that this dream identify its source. The question goes unanswered. What matters here is that this dream of utter aliveness incites a new questioning and exclamation at all. "Utter aliveness" transgresses the boundaries set by a death in life, by a death aiming to hold life hostage.

This same exclamatory "Listen" begins another poem, "Call to Creation." Therefore, both poems seek an adequate response to the life that they feel in spite of the death around them or even inside them. In "Demand," the speaker seeks a single transcendent answer to no avail. In "Call to Creation," the speaker looks at the surrounding world and its conflict:

> Listen!
> All you beauty-makers
> Give up beauty for a moment.
> Look at harshness, look at pain,
> Look at life again.
> Look at hungry babies crying,
> Listen to the rich men lying,
> Look at starving China dying.[55]

Hughes would place the conventional academic among the "beauty-makers," as "Letter to the Academy" and "Ph.D." indicate. Remember that the subject of "Ph.D." is ill-equipped to face a "human world . . . vast and strange despite" attending a school "where books were read and sums were proven true / And paper maps . . . / Were held up as the real world."[56] Both poems feature scholars deliberately turning away from difficult realities and using their social position to condescend to their critics.

With the opening lines of "Call to Creation," Hughes articulates the endpoint of this conventional academic role. The "beauty-makers" in the poem collude with the "greedy" who want a "thieving peace" that provides cover for their swindles. At the end of the poem, one can find Hughes calling that same group "futile beauty-makers," because they maintain allegiance to a social order that privileges beauty but produces so much ugliness and destruction. They produce a "thieving peace" based on the countless thefts that keep occurring under the guise of social harmony, all for the benefit of an imperialistic few and their adherents. That is to say, this beautiful realm does not save humanity from impoverishment. Impoverishment is an aftereffect of this beautiful realm. The poem's concluding lines demand that the

Futile-beauty makers—
Work for a while with the pattern breakers!
Come for a march with the new-world-makers:
Let beauty be!⁵⁷

By the poem's end, what has appeared to be a straightforward rejection of
beauty in the poem turns into a rejection of one concept of beauty. This
means the beauty-makers lack the authority to declare who is socially living or dead. This does not deny their attempt to make such declarations.
But this reading reveals the provincial, self-interested, purely subjective nature of the claim. More than that, this reading disabuses readers of the
sense that they must take such self-interested declarations as an *ontological
basis* for understanding black life. Hughes juxtaposes this view of life and
death with a different grammar, manifested in "Call to Creation's" choral
refrain, coming from the decolonizing areas of the world, which says "In
spite of all, / Life must not cease."⁵⁸ "Life" already exists, already persists. The
challenge is inhabiting and conceptualizing new worlds where that life can
be cherished in its heterogeneity. Hughes would have the professoriate align
itself with the "pattern breakers" who are also "new-world-makers," and that
new world, to be worthy of the name, would acknowledge a wider array of
forms of life that function under a sovereign ban.

These features of Hughes's 1930s poems effectively shift education out of
the "decent order" of the sonnet "Ph.D." and more into a realm of social reproduction. In heeding his own call to be a "new-world maker," Hughes
rephrases the famous command from Genesis for humans to be fruitful and
multiply ("free from hunger to grow and study and love and propagate"⁵⁹).
He refashions the original meaning of the proletariat—those who contribute to society only by populating it—to be the starting point of creation's
new mission. Hughes apparently agrees with Bruns in comparing poetry to
prophecy, to a condition of election and responsibility.⁶⁰ Redoubling the imperative in Genesis leads readers to a deconstructed notion of election and
responsibility that the Hurston of *Moses, Man of the Mountain* might have
affirmed, because it does not ensure the bombast or condescension that
comes with chosenness. The creaturely receive a charge that Hughes would
never grant exclusively to upper-class citizens, nor would they accept it.
Hughes reveals that the call to creation exists before, opposite of, quite often in surplus of, and as a threat to the narrow call to nationhood. It also

presses the professoriate to go even further beyond its monolithic under-standings of the human that, by the very operation of their categories, di-vorced from evidence, presuppose that the majority of humanity or life is impoverished, undervalued, and underprivileged and will find value only through being consumed by bourgeois social, politic, and economic processes.

Learning about and learning with life in this broader sense requires study. Notably, despite Hughes's harsh critiques of the professoriate and his chal-lenging claims about the transformations that class must undergo to speak of revolution, he does not give up on the idea of study. On this score, Hughes is of the same mind as Dunham, when she speaks of fascination, or Du Bois, who deems it glorious that the freedpersons "prayed," "worked," "danced and sang," and "studied to learn."[61] Richard Wright offers an interesting counterpoint to Hughes's idea of study, saying that "always ahead should be the sense of . . . problems to be framed, pondered, and solved; always in them should reside the sense of becoming."[62] Hughes shares the assumption that a sense of becoming prompts artistic and critical expression. Yet, Wright's phrasing may overstate the ever-forward-moving aspect of study. Hughes is more aligned with Du Bois's description of thought in *John Brown*, where he states that "human purposes grow slowly and in curious ways; thought by thought they build themselves until in their full panoplied vigor and defi-nite outline not even the thinker can tell the exact process of the growing, or say that here was the beginning or there the ending. Nor does this slow growth make the end less wonderful or the motive less praiseworthy."[63] This description complements the various flowing and lurching movements of study and institution building.

Though one could extract from this "panoplied vigor" a teleological pro-gression, it would terribly distort thought's vitality. The productivity of today's mis-education pales in comparison and significance to the econom-ically unproductive, socially reproductive element of study—unproductive because it responds to a debt too high to pay, too immense to be claimed by any single creditor, and offers no putative limit on when the project is com-pleted. Mis-education fetishizes individualist achievement and places re-search and teaching in an overly simplistic means-end schema. Learning becomes an instrument that can be set aside after reaching particular stages of achievement. Like Du Bois marveling at a thought process without de-tectable beginning or end, Stefano Harney and Fred Moten yearn for this "beyond of teaching," which "is really about not finishing oneself, not passing, not completing."[64]

Taken together, black study's critique of credentialing, emphasis on learning's heterogeneity and multiple paths, and focus on becoming instead of progress troubles the hierarchies that often impede learning in the Western tradition. For this reason, in "Letter to the Academy," Hughes describes the revolution as the moment when "there are no best people, and the poor are mighty and no longer poor." Hughes identifies an important distinction between Jim Crow's and the black radical tradition's views of equality and education. Social equality *threatens* learning in Jim Crow education, since that system must teach its students inequality and the abuses that always accompany it. The black radical tradition takes a very different attitude toward learning. In fact, *Black Reconstruction* consolidates this into a thesis: "This whole phantasmagoria has been built on the most miserable of human fictions: that in addition to the manifest differences between men there is a deep, awful and ineradicable cleft which condemns most men to eternal degradation. It is a cheap inheritance of the world's infancy, unworthy of grown folk. My rise does not involve your fall. No superior has interest in inferiority. Humanity is one and its vast variety is its glory and not its condemnation."[65] Jim Crow and the black radical tradition could not diverge more on this matter. Episodes from the mid-nineteenth century to the twentieth century and the present day illustrate that the principle of discrimination is inherent to Jim Crow and, beyond that, to mainstream notions of whiteness. This is a logical outcome of whiteness's defining itself by its accumulation and control of property. What counts as the basis for progress in white supremacy counts as a historical retrogression in the black radical tradition. Notably, Du Bois's claim to equality occurs through encountering difference with no prescription to consume, subsume, or transcend it for an eventual sameness.

This poses a particular challenge to the student-turned-academic, the Ph.D. whose entire educational path has been based on proving a superiority in terms of academic merit; social capital earned by joining the proper professional networks; and socioeconomic privileges determined by race, gender, sexual orientation, religion, alumni status, and other forms of legacy, sometimes more than they are determined by merit. Cultural and material wealth becomes a scare resource under mis-education's guidance. Only a privileged few can monopolize and leverage that scarcity. They hope to become stand-ins for the people, so that their exhaustion of resources can count as the people's progress. Indeed, the overrepresentation of these privileged academics' desires hopes to turn this theft into a virtue, such that they become models for others to mimic. Under such a regime, the "best" turns an artificial narrowing of social potentialities into an absolute. The Ph.D. has too often justified this theft, contributed to this overrepresentation, and crafted the very ethics that turns theft into fairly earned rewards. To heed the call to "speak about the revolution," as Hughes puts it in "Letter to the Academy," the Ph.D would have to rethink the conceptualization of wealth, who has access to it, and what ethics can question that relationship.

Yet Hughes's "dream of utter aliveness" carries so much significance in this notebook because its impact restores the physical comportments and libidinal attachments that so often impact thinking in and about the college or university. By extension, that dream touches the flesh to remind the student-turned-academic that other forms of wealth remain. The second notebook took note of this by quoting Marx's rhetorical questioning: "When the limited bourgeois form is stripped away, what is wealth other than the universality of individual needs, capacities, pleasures, productive forces, etc., created through universal exchange?" The second notebook also quoted Marx calling wealth "the absolute working-out" of humanity's "creative potentialities, with no presupposition other than the previous historical development, which makes this totality of development, i.e., the development of all human powers as such the end in itself, not as measured on a predetermined yardstick."[66] This process of becoming makes mis-education's version of the best students fall apart. And the Ph.D., the student-turned-academic, can stop justifying this violence.

In this "absolute movement of becoming," the professoriate grasps this other kind of wealth which, in Hughes's view, leads to a "might" that sustains entire educational institutions. Bearing and wielding this might changes the professoriate's role. As Du Bois says at the end of "Founding the Public School":

Had it not been for the Negro school and college, the Negro would, to all intents and purposes, have been driven back to slavery. . . . [The Negro's] economic foothold was too slight in ten years of turmoil to effect any defense or stability. [The Negro's] reconstruction leadership had

come from Negroes educated in the North, and white politicians, capitalists and philanthropic teachers. The counter-revolution of 1876 drove
most of these, *save the teachers*, away. But already, through establishing
public schools and private colleges, and by organizing the Negro church,
the Negro had acquired enough leadership and knowledge to thwart the
worst designs of the new slave drivers. They avoided the mistake of trying to meet force by force. They bent to the storm of beating, lynching
and murder, and kept their souls in spite of public and private insult of
every description; they built an inner culture which the world recognizes
in spite of the fact that it is still half-strangled and inarticulate.[67]

Du Bois's pacifism in the 1930s may lead him to understate how much black
folk met "force by force" in the New Day. Certainly, there are ways of linking armed self-defense and education to a broader effort to protect the dark
proletariat's inner culture. At the very least, this potential link can reveal
the lives put at risk in the pursuit of docile dignity. For now, what matters
is that the dark proletariat found the intellectual and practical strength to
withstand the worst of the hellish backlash they faced. The teachers joined
that effort. They found the courage to endure the counterrevolution alongside students and other academic laborers.

Once again, twenty-first century segregationists fear that social equality
can be achieved through education, based on several recent political, juridical, and demographic changes. The professoriate must consider its role.
There is always the opportunity to accommodate new reactionary strategies, find the contorted logics to defend them, and urge survivors of these
strategies to maintain docile dignity—and count all this as progress. Or the
professoriate can acknowledge the ethical difficulties of this structure, admit the ever-diminishing returns that come from enjoying this perverse predicament, and contribute to the inner culture that can survive this
backlash. Considering that all five notebooks have argued that the dark proletariat is comprised of the working classes as well as "the damned"—the
homeless, the politically free but legally rightless, the jailed (whether rightly
or wrongly), the mentally unstable, the flood survivor in labor, the survivor
of the relief camp itself, the lynching victim and their surviving loved ones—
that inner culture Du Bois speaks of is more expansive than the talented
tenth or other intellectual elites. These lives are often not associated with
the role of the student precisely because one cannot see how to restore them

to liberal paths of social mobility. However, this notebook refers to labor and resources professors can offer in developing an inner culture when returning to old routines is impossible or is the direct cause of misery.

Readers would do well to follow Harney and Moten in thinking of this topologically while holding on to the ecstatic subjectivity that this notebook has investigated. The college/university has its underground. Harney and Moten speak of "stealing to" and "stealing within" the college/university—a fugitive existence within the institution, putting it to other purposes. At times, these purposes are so at odds with the institution that one knows that a short-term strategy is in play. At other times, these purposes can signal impermanent transformations within the institution. No doubt the dark proletariat's traces are all over the grounds of the institution, which is why Jim Crow works so hard to hide or erase them. Look closely, however, and notice that some of those footsteps lead out of the university and return. That is to say, the fugitive effort inside the college/university can amplify what happens outside it and vice versa. The challenge is to create a linkage that frustrates Jim Crow's gentrifying impulse, which first cultivated the campus-community divides in order to stop black studies from transforming American education in the mid-twentieth century. Stealing to, within, and from educational institutions indicates that this ecstatic way of being can alter how intellectual and activist movements relate to the college/university and its nearby communities.

To conclude, the above passage from *Black Reconstruction* allows readers to contrast the dark proletariat's "inner culture" with Arendt's "untaught pride." No person or group can survive with a pride that is oblivious to the guilt, self-resignation, and hatred that Jim Crow cultivates. Nor will neutral confidence successfully *displace and correct* the countless stigmas projected onto black life. Whether on the grounds of the college or elsewhere, the professoriate that commits to this inner culture can join in displacing and correcting such stigmas. Du Bois praises students and educators who have done this work, though the expression he uses is "half-strangled and inarticulate." "Half-strangled" can refer to the literal violence terrorizing black life. Figuratively speaking, "half-strangled" refers to the stereotypes crowding out the black voices that are elaborating their own cultural evolution on their own terms. Nevertheless, inarticulacy need not refer simply to inadequacy based on external circumstances. Inarticulacy can also refer to the experimentation with new ways of speaking, new terms in speech, and new spaces to speak in. If blackness is not simply one genre among others but is the underground fount from which genres emerge and recede, then even this inarticulacy speaks to the act of becoming. It is precisely this experimentation with voice and embodiment that makes our conflicted educational institutions a matter for black poetry. It is precisely this collective experimentation with self and material world that makes the dark proletariat a poetic community. It is precisely this experimentation that gives learning no final end, such that poetry becomes a mode of study. Amid the storm and stress of a conflicted educational structure, black and unknown bards continue calling us to study in common, where the flesh may triumph as well as the spirit.

CONCLUSION

*From Being to Unrest, from Objectivity
to Motion—A Race for Theory*

Truly I say to you, this generation, will not pass away until all these things
take place. Heaven and earth will pass away, but My words will not pass
away. But of that day or hour no one knows, not even the angels in heaven,
nor the Son, but the Father *alone*. Take heed, keep on the alert; for you
do not know when the appointed time will come.

—MARK 13:32–33

ON SPIRITED SURVIVAL

Thinking Through Crisis critiques trauma theory for its dedication to the image of European Man. That dedication limits the theory's sensitivity to
epistemological and political complexities, especially racial difference.
"Unknowability" becomes the vehicle by which European catastrophe remains the standard for overwhelming experiences around the globe.
Otherwise, trauma theory would abandon this nostalgia for a revivified
European Man after Europe pulverized itself in world war. If trauma theory cannot face these limits within the European archive it claims, it is all
the more curbed in its approach to the suffering created by European Man's
colonial reach around the world.[1] Trauma theory can offer a liberal response that, at best, bears witness to suffering while offering few, if any, insights into altering the systemic factors perpetuating that suffering. Agency,
in this framework, remains limited to practices already recognized and

constrained by conventional liberal-democratic norms valorizing some forms of suffering and sufferers over many others. Nor can trauma theory fully account for how those living outside these norms are ignored and, when they are noticed, get punished for transgressing rules that were impossible to obey. *Thinking Through Crisis* stays with specific forms of life existing outside these norms, forms of life that consider transformation of material conditions indispensable to working through overwhelming experiences. That transformative effort has tremendous political consequences, although these forms of life are rarely granted the privileges and protections of Western politics.

While I have argued for the 1930s as a crucial instance of black writing that rethinks the agency irrupting from traumatization, I have also sought to recalibrate cultural theory's relation to the practical. Barbara Christian's "The Race for Theory" inspires this effort. As Christian puts it, the "new generation of professionals,"—that is, professional critics or "academics,"—have "subordinated" all interests "to one primary thrust—that moment when one creates a theory, thus fixing a constellation of ideas for a time at least, a fixing which no doubt will be replaced in another month or so by somebody else's competing theory as the race accelerates."[2] Christian chides her colleagues for reducing theory to an industry. Then Christian discusses the violence of one orientation to theory hardening into a norm by which scholars across fields must work: "Perhaps because those who have effected the takeover have the power (although they deny it) first of all to be published, and thereby to determine the ideas that are deemed valuable, some of our most daring and potentially radical critics (and by *our* I mean black, women, Third World) have been influenced, even co-opted, in speaking a language and defining their discussion in terms alien to and opposed to our needs and orientation."[3] Christian's critique cuts in two directions: in one direction, she challenges the fetishization of European philosophy as the model by which all American academics must work; in the other direction, she questions why scholars would succumb to this fetishism at the expense of the underrepresented groups they study. Theory can petrify the scholar, limiting one's critical vocabulary, methodology, expository modes, textual examples, canons, historical reference points, and conclusions. Black culture, under these conditions, can serve only as another object to be mentioned and left behind for supposedly more abstract, universal concerns.

Christian's essay exposes this false universality and the commercial rush behind it.

However, I am most interested in the second meaning of Christian's title. The second meaning allows me to consider the practical stakes for scholars moving from being to unrest, from objectivity to motion. Christian says:

> For people of color have always theorized—but in forms quite different from the Western form of abstract logic. And I am inclined to say that our theorizing (and I intentionally use the verb rather than the noun) is often in narrative forms, in the stories we create, in riddles and proverbs, in the play with language, *because dynamic rather than fixed ideas seem more to our liking. How else have we managed to survive with such spiritedness the assault on our bodies, social institutions, countries, our very humanity?* ... My folk, in other words, have always been a race for theory—though more in the form of the hieroglyph, a written figure that is both *sensual and abstract*, both beautiful and communicative.[4]

Christian's words remain a boon because she admonishes those who would try to dodge "theory" altogether, which may be the most extreme form of petrification, for it simply cedes the ground to the fashion of "fixed" theorizing that Christian finds so troubling. This would be even more problematic today considering the many bold advances in black critical theory since Christian's essay. Because of the curricular formation of today's rising professionals, I find this ceding of the ground less likely. The greater threat has to do with the "co-opted" scholars who take on the rigid orientation Christian protests, merely because it is the main currency through which social capital and professional opportunity circulates in the academy, at the expense of the artifacts they study and the cultures to which those artifacts belong.

This has a direct impact on theorizing trauma in the humanities. I have been troubled by the *kind* of turn scholars have made to Cathy Caruth's, Shoshana Felman's, and Giorgio Agamben's theories for framing and elucidating historically underrepresented literatures. Put too crudely, this scholarship has focused intently on what trauma theory can teach about historically underrepresented literatures. But Christian's argument says that black thinkers have often theorized in the hieroglyph, which means that the poem, the novel, the funk song, the jazz solo, and the hip-hop freestyle can each, in unique ways, serve as sites of theorizing. The implication here is that black literature already carries within it different theorizations of trauma, but hierarchies within the university, academic publishing, and conferences presuppose that theory must be happening elsewhere. No doubt this has changed somewhat in the past decade, but this recent shift merely confirms that a different pattern dominated for generations, and some are filled with sad passions as they see it fade away. Rather than assume that only trauma theory has something to teach about black literature, *Thinking Through Crisis* has braved the inverse route in the process of bringing low what was high (and what has been higher than "high theory" in the humanities?). Historically underrepresented literatures have much to teach trauma theory, as well as Marxist thought and political philosophy more broadly. Black radical writers have turned to the literary to theorize in the form of the hieroglyph—to theorize in ways that hold on to the sensual, the abstract, the beautiful, and the communicative.

My emphasis on "unrest" finds inspiration from Christian's emphasis on the "dynamic," seeing that both concepts counteract petrification in social theory. Christian associates dynamism with "intelligence":

> So my "method," to use a new "lit crit" word, is not fixed but relates to what I read and to the historical context of the writers I read *and* to the many critical activities in which I am engaged, which may or may not involve [academic] writing. It is a learning from the language of creative writers, which is one of surprise, that I might discover what language I might use. . . . I, therefore, have no set method, another prerequistite of the new theory, since for me every work suggests a new approach. As risky as that might seem, it is, I believe, *what intelligence means—a tuned sensitivity to that which is alive and therefore cannot be known until it is known.*[5]

More than two decades after its publication, Christian's definition of "intelligence" persuasively decries insensitivity "to that which is alive" in the humanities, where culturally specific artifacts are put to use by the most popular or convenient theories without considering the implications of this for criticism, the academy, or society. Placed within the materialist approach to trauma I have offered here, "intelligence" reveals the discrepancy between what mainstream American discourses and institutions count as known/

knowable and what *is living*. In this discrepancy, one finds an unremarked-on set of power structures making decisions on what can be known and who can know. One may also find the critic who enters this discrepancy in order to affirm life over institutional categorization. Following Christian, I speak of a poetics of relation that entails "risk": "For there is no reason, given who controls these institutions, for them to be anything other than threatened by these writers."[6] This remains true today, despite admirable efforts at digitizing black print archives or selecting contemporary black writers for literary awards. Christian's "critic" stands in league with such threatening and threatened intellectuals and, as a result, makes unrest another modality of intellectual inquiry.

Christian deconstructs the binary between safe academic work and threatening influences of the unknown outside the academy. My argument in the fifth notebook suggests my agreement with Christian's claim. Thus, the critic is not joining with other life out of a condescending benevolence but out of a mutual need for survival. Christian takes this need for collectivity so seriously that she offers readers a rhetorical question: "*How else have we managed to survive with such spiritedness the assault on our bodies, social institutions, countries, our very humanity?*"[7] Theorizing, for Christian, is crucial to a broad range of "critical activities" essential to mutual survival. Hortense Spillers says as much in a pointed study of the "overlapping theorizations" of the Frankfurt School and Du Boisian thought. "What they had in common . . . was the encounter with the extreme," Spillers says. "The tremor throughout every fiber and to feel it everyday is not the usual circumstance" of intellectual work, for they learned "to *write* and to *think* as though their very lives depended on it."[8] If the period from Hurricane Katrina and Barak Obama's presidency has not seen enough instances of institutionally sanctioned exploitation and injustice, recent surges in vigilante violence against people of color suggest black scholars are confronted with the extreme once again. There are unintended consequences to this unsettling of knowledge production. Deconstructing the line between the academic's common social role and forms of life without political recognition also alters the division between thought and its application. Against the binary of black intellectual / activist or, even worse, "talented tenth" / folk, in which one provides the ideas and the other simply acts, Christian and Spillers invite us to take on the broader task of being the living site of a significant intervention.

"TAKE HEED"; OR, BEING THE LIVING SITE
OF A SIGNIFICANT INTERVENTION

The cautionary phrase "take heed" evokes Hortense Spillers's exploration of a perennial question in black studies. "The 'real-concrete' question, then, that is posed to black creative intellectuals—what will you do to save your people?—and its thousand knee-jerk variations, is therefore misplaced." Spillers answers that there is no longer the activist who can do without theory (as if charisma takes the place of theorizing) or the intellectual who need not act (as if arriving at an idea already constitutes enacting it). The true question, the one "the intellectual can actually *use* is: To what extent do the 'conditions of theoretical practice' pass through him or her, as the *living site of a significant intervention*?" Theoretical practice may pass through an individual intellectual or through an "ensemble of efforts—the research center, the think tank, the thematic fellowship."[9]

Bringing Christian's and Spillers's formulations together helps explain the epigraph for this finale to *Thinking Through Crisis*. Cedric Robinson once claimed that "black radicalism cannot be understood within the particular context of its genesis."[10] In my closing ruminations on the relation between theory and practice, I am also suggesting that this redoubled concept of genesis problematizes teleologies attributed to black life. To put it another way, if theory is a matter of survival, then customary theorizations of the beginnings and endings of the black radical tradition must be upended. These theorizations play out through narratives that obstruct one's view of contemporary oppression and, most importantly, smudge the lens one uses to identify *where* black radicalism renews itself for current battles. Though commonly associated with predicting when social formations come to an end, the Bible verse used as the epigraph lends itself to an interpretation attuned to Christian's and Spillers's wisdom. This verse marks that difficult moment when a new generation finds its agency. Then, survival refers to a more robust relationship between theory and practical activity, precisely because the telos remains undetermined. I find the verse fascinating, because the would-be messiah refutes the claim that even he can calculate such endings and beginnings: "But of that day or hour no one knows, not even the angels in heaven, nor the Son, but the Father *alone*."

Granted, this epigraph could reinforce cultural-political gatekeeping and patronage structures in black culture, which get constructed to claim authority from certain political figures in the aftermath of the civil rights movement and decolonization. But that view contradicts the last line of the verse, which matters most to this conclusion: "for you do not know when the appointed time will come." The power of cultural-political gatekeepers depends on the assumption that they already know the appointed time, that they took their stand at that exact time, and that their timeliness grants them authority over future generations. The passage deconstructs the *possibility* of a single messianic hero dictating the time for political engagement, cultural renewal, and intellectual inquiry. In this deconstructed temporality— when grand narratives of black progress, of national redemption, and of successful integration are utterly failing; when the leaders who have grounded their power in these narratives flail in fear of waning influence— new intergenerational goals can emerge based on the honest assessment that black life has survived insurmountable odds. New hurdles and new possibilities remain, and every generation has something critical to offer to the others. Spillers calls this "cooperative antagonism," the moment when multiple generations converge on the same emancipatory outcomes, despite their different historical trajectories.[11]

Scholars committed to the black diaspora may "take heed" in many different ways, but one thing is for sure: across America's burgundy landscape, survival involves linking theorization and action. Practicality without theoretical contemplation betrays genuine effort; theoretical contemplation can only find its deepest nuances through committed practice. Being a race for theory, as Christian proposes, means testing how the practical and theoretical inform each other when the goal is collective survival. *Thinking Through Crisis* explores how racial difference, especially blackness, adds new layers of complexity to traumatic wounding. Understandably, such research may induce a profound pessimism about the world. But taking seriously Barbara Christian's concept of "intelligence" in these notebooks means addressing overwhelming experiences while finding my highest priority elsewhere. Insistent traumatization caused by imperial Europe's aim to subdue all life turns out to be of secondary importance. *Thinking Through Crisis*, at its most intense, studies the aesthetic, historical, and political components of making a way out of no way—the *conatus* by which blackness persists on fugitive terms.

NOTES

INTRODUCTION: FROM BEING TO UNREST, FROM OBJECTIVITY TO MOTION

1. Jared Sexton, "Ante-Anti-Blackness: Afterthoughts," *Lateral* 1 (Spring 2012), http://lateral.culturalstudiesassociation.org/issue1/content/sexton.html, accessed November 4, 2013.

2. For more on exorbitance and disciplinary formations in the human sciences, see Nahum Chandler, "Of Exorbitance," *Criticism* 50.3 (Summer 2008): 345–410; and Roderick Ferguson, *Aberrations in Black: Towards a Queer of Color Critique* (Minneapolis: University of Minnesota Press, 2004).

3. Louis Althusser, *Reading Capital* (London: Verso, 2009), 22.

4. Althusser, *Reading Capital*, 97.

5. If this provocative claim edges on exaggeration, consider the text of Louis Aragon's "Contre-Chant":

> In vain your image comes to meet me
> And does not enter me where I am who only shows it
> Turning towards you can find
> On the wall of my gaze only your dream of shadow
> I am that wretch comparable with mirrors
> That can reflect but cannot see
> Like them my eye is empty and like them inhabited
> By your absence which makes them blind.

Louis Aragon, "Contre-Chant," *Le fou d'Elsa* in *Oeuvres Poetiques Completes*, vol. 2 (France: Gallimard, 2007), 557. Compare "Contre-Chant" to Du Bois's "The Souls of White Folk":

> Of them I am singularly clairvoyant. I see in and through them. I view them from unusual points of vantage. Not as a foreigner do I come, for

I am native, not foreign, bone of their thought and flesh of their language. Mine is not knowledge of the traveler or the colonial composite of dear memories, words and wonder. . . . Rather I see these souls undressed and from the back and side. I see the working of their entrails. I know their thoughts and they know that I know. This knowledge makes them now embarrassed, now furious! They deny my right to live and be and call me misbirth! . . . And yet as they preach and strut and shout and threaten, crouching as they clutch at rags of facts and fancies to hide their nakedness, they go twisting, flying by my tired eyes and I see them ever stripped,—ugly, human.

W. E. B. Du Bois, *Darkwater: Voices from Within the Veil* (London: Verso, 2016), 15. Aragon's efforts operate along the outskirts of the surrealist movement and its influence on, say, Jacques Lacan, who uses the same poem to theorize misrecognition. What I find interesting about Du Bois's text, in comparison to Aragon's and Lacan's, is that in it one sees the haunting, denuding, degrading, even reconstituting, visceral force of the racialized gaze. The fact that Du Bois conceptualizes "second-sight" in 1903 and that his comments on whiteness are exactly contemporary with the Dadaists indicates the anticipatory nature of black life, in this case in relation to the surrealists. The images of the feminine body in *Minotaure* and *La Surrealism en la Service de Revolution* follow Du Bois's description of "white folk," "souls undressed," viewed "from the back and side," though these images don't amplify whether the viewer is raced. Perhaps this suggests that the surrealists offered a reduced application of anamorphosis in their work, compared to Du Bois. Suffice it to say that there is no need to think of the surreal as an invention of a single, white Parisian circle. Therefore, I am not as interested in the ethnographic aspects of the relationship between blackness and the canonical contributors to the surrealist movement. I am interested in the marvelous experience of seeing possibility where others strictly see impossibility, of locating overabundance in degradation, of finding new ways of being a collective force where one finds lone voices, of finding creative agency where others cannot even find human volition, and of finding the chance at social reconstruction where others can see only a rebuilding of the status quo.

6. Chandler, "Of Exorbitance," 346.

7. See Lewis Gordon, *Her Majesty's Other Children: Sketches of Racism from a Neocolonial Age* (Lanham, Md.: Rowman and Littlefield, 1997), 63.

8. Karl Marx, *Capital: A Critique of Political Economy*, vol. 1, trans. Ben Fowkes (New York: Vintage, 1977), 280.

9. Cedric Robinson, *Black Marxism: The Making of the Black Radical Tradition* (Chapel Hill: University of North Carolina Press, 2000), 168.

10. Robinson, *Black Marxism*, 126.

11. Marx, *Capital*, 303.

12. Marx, *Capital*, 1031.

13. Marx, *Capital*, 344.

14. Marx, *Capital*, 345.

15. Marx, *Capital*, 345.

16. Marx, *Capital*, 379.

17. Marx, *Capital*, 377.

18. Marx, *Capital*, 378.

19. Marx, *Capital*, 380.

20. Frederick Douglass, *My Bondage and My Freedom* (New York: Barnes and Noble Classics, 2005), 268–269.

21. Douglass, *My Bondage and My Freedom*, 269.

22. I am indebted to Moten's reading of this same passage from "Resistance of the Object: Aunt Hester's Scream." However, I diverge from his claim that "Marx comes down neither on the side of speech he produces nor on that of the speech of classical economists that he reproduces." Fred Moten, *In the Break: The Aesthetics of the Black Radical Tradition* (Minneapolis: University of Minnesota Press, 2003), 9. As I argue above, Marx accepts the terms of his classical economist foes to defeat them on their own terms. Nevertheless, Moten's *In the Break* and other writings remain the condition of possibility for much of my argument in this project.

23. Marx, *Capital*, 176–7.

24. Marx, *Capital*, 1033, 1034.

25. Marx, *Capital*, 167.

26. Marx, *Capital*, 296.

27. Marx, *Capital*, 304

28. Marx, *Capital*, 303–304.

29. Jacques Derrida, *Of Grammatology*, trans. Gayatri Spivak (Baltimore: Johns Hopkins University Press, 1997), 151.

30. Hortense Spillers's work inspires my reading:

Everywhere in this descriptive document, we are stunned by the simultaneity of disparate items in a grammatical series: "Slave" appears in the same context with beasts of burden, *all* and *any* animal(s), various livestock, and a virtually endless profusion of domestic content. . . . That imposed uniformity comprises the shock, that some this mix of things, live and inanimate, collapsed by contiguity to the same text of 'realism,' carries a disturbingly prominent item of misplacement: To that extent, the project of liberation for African-Americans has found urgency in two passionate motivations that are twinned—1) to break apart, to rupture violently the laws of American behavior that make such *syntax* possible; 2) to introduce a new *semantic* field/fold more appropriate to his/her own historic movement.

See Hortense Spillers, "Mama's Baby, Papa's Maybe: An American Grammar Book," *Diacritics* 17.2 (Summer 1987): 64–81, 79.

31. Giorgio Agamben, *State of Exception*, trans. Kevin Atell (Chicago: University of Chicago Press, 2005), 1.

32. Agamben, *State of Exception*, 50.

33. Agamben, *State of Exception*, 50.

34. Agamben, *State of Exception*, 59.

35. Agamben, *State of Exception*, 20.

36. Agamben, *State of Exception*, 20, 21.

37. For more on the complexity of decisionism, see David Marriott, "Whither Fanon," *Textual Practice* 25.1 (2011): 33–69.

38. W. E. B. Du Bois, *Black Reconstruction in America, 1860–1880* (New York: Free Press, 1998), 84, emphasis added.

39. Agamben, *State of Exception*, 29.

40. Shoshana Felman and Dori Laub, *Testimony: Crises in Witnessing in Literature, Psychoanalysis and History* (London: Routledge, 1992), xvii, 6, xi.

41. Antonio Gramsci, *Prison Notebooks*, vol. 2, trans. Joseph Buttigieg (New York: Columbia University Press, 1996), 32–33.

42. Felman and Laub, *Testimony*, 47.

43. Felman and Laub, *Testimony*, 5.

44. Felman and Laub, *Testimony*, 49, emphasis added.

45. Felman and Laub, *Testimony*, 52.

46. See "Of the Subject Who Is Supposed to Know, of the First Dyad and of the Good," in Jacques Lacan, *Four Fundamental Concepts of Psycho-analysis*, trans. Alan Sheridan (New York: W. W. Norton, 1976), 230–243.

47. Catherine Stewart, "'Crazy for this Democracy': Postwar Psychoanalysis, African American Blues Narratives, and the Lafargue Clinic," *American Quarterly* 65.2 (June 2013): 371–395.

48. Cathy Caruth, *Unclaimed Experience: Trauma, Narrative, History* (Baltimore: Johns Hopkins University Press, 1996), 92.

49. Caruth, *Unclaimed Experience*, 93.

50. Caruth, *Unclaimed Experience*, 104.

51. Ralph Ellison, Letter to Richard Wright, 3 November 1941, RWP, Box 97, Folder "Ralph Ellison," quoted in Michael Fabre, "From Native Son to Invisible Man: Some Notes on Ralph Ellison's Evolution in the 1950s," in *Speaking for You: The Vision of Ralph Ellison*, ed. Kimberly Benston (Washington D.C.: Howard University Press, 1987), 211.

52. Petar Ramadanovic points the way on this topic with the essay "Trauma and Crisis," which introduces a special issue on trauma in *Postmodern Culture*. He traces a genealogy of theoretical texts that inform Felman's "Education and Crisis" chapter in *Testimony*. Ramadanovic notes two lines of influence for

Felman's and Caruth's groundbreaking works on trauma in the humanities. The first comes from Paul de Man's "The Crisis of Contemporary Criticism." The second is Edmund Husserl's "The Crisis of European Humanity and Philosophy." The Husserlian line of trauma studies proves most useful for *Thinking Through Crisis* because of how directly it poses the question of the human into political, philosophical, and racial implications. See Edmund Husserl, "The Vienna Lecture" in *The Crisis of European Sciences and Transcendental Phemonenology*, trans. David Carr (Evanston, Ill.: Northwestern University Press, 1970), 269–299.

53. Reinhart Koselleck, "Crisis," trans. Michaela W Richter, *Journal of the History of Ideas* 67.2 (April 2006): 357–400.

54. Husserl, "The Vienna Lecture," 299.

55. Husserl, "The Vienna Lecture," 274, 275.

56. Husserl, "The Vienna Lecture," 275.

57. Warren Montag, "Martyrdom, Conversion, and the Imitation of the Affects: Spinoza and Marranismo" (unpublished manuscript, 2012), Microsoft Word file.

58. Montag, "Martyrdom, Conversion, and the Imitation of the Affects."

59. Husserl, "The Vienna Lecture," 270.

60. See sections two and four in Gilles Deleuze, *Nietzsche and Philosophy*, trans. Hugh Tomlinson (New York: Columbia Classics, 2006).

61. See Hortense Spillers, "The Crisis of the Negro Intellectual: A Post-Date," *Boundary* 2 21.3 (Autumn 1994): 65–116, 26.

62. Husserl, "The Vienna Lecture," 283.

63. See Alexander Weheliye, "After Man," *American Literary History* (Winter 2008): 321–336, 322.

64. Aimé Césaire, *Discourse on Colonialism*, trans. Joan Pinkham (New York: Monthly Review Press, 1972), 35–36.

65. Édouard Glissant, *Caribbean Discourse: Selected Essays*, trans. J. Michael Dash (Charlottesville: University Press of Virginia, 1999), 20.

66. See Gilles Deleuze, *Spinoza: Practical Philosophy*, trans. Robert Hurley (San Francisco: City Lights Books, 2001).

67. Césaire, *Discourse on Colonialism*, 21.

68. Husserl's work may also be translated as "hostile," but "inimical" speaks more directly to the political stakes of Husserl's argument as well as the argument of this notebook.

69. See Ian Baucom, "Cicero's Ghost: The Atlantic, The Enemy, and the Laws of War," in *States of Emergency: The Object of American Studies*, ed. Russ Castranovo and Susan Gilman (Chapel Hill: University of North Carolina Press, 2009), 140.

70. Cesaire, *Discourse on Colonialism*, 14.

71. Etienne Balibar, "The Relations Greece and Europe Need," http://www.versobooks.com/blogs/1987-etienne-balibar-the-relations-greece-and-europe-need, accessed June 18, 2016.

72. Frantz Fanon, *Wretched of the Earth*, trans. Richard Philcox (New York: Grove Press, 2004), 6.

73. Frantz Fanon, *Black Skin, White Masks*, trans. Charles Lam Markmann (New York: Grove Press, 1967), 10.

74. David Marriott, *Haunted Life: Black Culture and Visual Modernity* (New Brunswick, N.J.: Rutgers University Press, 2007), 273n9.

75. Etienne Balibar, "In Search of the Proletariat" in *Masses, Classes, Ideas* (New York: Routledge, 1994), 127.

76. Balibar, "In Search of the Proletariat," 133.

77. See Barbara Foley, *Radical Representations: Politics and Form in U.S. Proletarian Fiction, 1929–1941* (Durham, N.C.: Duke University Press, 1993); James Smethurst, *The New Red Negro: The Literary Left and African American Poetry, 1930–1946* (New York: Oxford University Press, 1999); Michael Denning, *The Cultural Front: The Laboring of American Culture in the Twentieth Century* (London: Verso, 1997).

78. Langston, Hughes, *The Collected Works of Langston Hughes, The Poems: 1921–1940.* (Columbia: University of Missouri Press, 2000), 121.

79. Hughes, *Collected Works*, 123.

80. Hughes, *Collected Works*, 147.

81. Du Bois, *Black Reconstruction*, 16, emphasis added.

82. See Michelle Stephens, *Black Empire: The Masculine Global Imaginary of Caribbean Intellectuals in the United States, 1941–1962* (Durham, N.C.: Duke University Press, 2005); and Brent Edwards, "The Autonomy of Black Radicalism," *Social Text* 19.2 (Summer 2001): 1–13, 2.

83. This project expands on Maxwell's thesis by demonstrating that some textual strategies employed in the 1930s can be found in 1920s (or earlier) black writing. I place greater stress on a break between 1920s and 1930s black writers because 1930s black writers were more dedicated to social reconstruction, not just offering minor tweaks to an otherwise structurally sound system. See William Maxwell, *New Negro, Old Left: African American Writing and Communism Between the Wars* (New York: Columbia University Press, 1999).

84. In this project, I refer to an extended version of Wright's canonical essay developed in the 1930s but published after the author's death. See Richard Wright, "Blueprint for Negro Literature," in *Amistad 2: Writings on Black History and Culture*, ed. John Williams and Charles Harris (New York: Random House, 1971), 12.

85. W. E. B. Du Bois, *The Correspondence of W. E. B. Du Bois*, vol. 1, ed. Herbert Aptheker (Amherst: University of Massachusetts Press, 1997), 480.

86. The phrase "labor for emancipation" comes from Du Bois's biography of John Brown and speaks to a lifetime commitment to overthrow slavery. "It was in 1839, when a Negro preacher named Fayette was visiting Brown, and bringing his story of persecution and injustice, that this great promise was made [by John Brown and his family]. . . . Brown told them of his purpose to make active war on slavery, and bound his family in solemn and secret compact to labor for emancipation. And then, instead of standing to pray, as was his wont, he fell upon his knees and implored God's blessing on his enterprise." W. E. B. Du Bois, *John Brown* (New York: Modern Library, 2001), 50. For me, the phrase marks an ongoing process of social reconstruction without a predetermined ending. Stressing single events or ideas at the expense of the larger process compromises the intellectual enterprise overall.

87. Deborah McDowell, "Lines of Descent/Dissenting Lines" in *Moses, Man of the Mountain*, by Zora Neale Hurston (New York: Harper Perennial Classics, 2008), 27.

88. Della Pollock, "Performative Writing" in *The Ends of Performance*, ed. Peggy Phelan and Jill Lane (New York: New York University Press, 1998), 81.

89. Pollock, "Performative Writing," 81.

90. Pollock, "Performative Writing," 97.

91. Henry Louis Gates, *Signifying Monkey: A Theory of African American Literary Criticism* (New York: Oxford University Press, 1988), 188.

92. See Antonio Gramsci, "How Many Forms of Grammars Can There Be?" in *The Gramsci Reader: Selected Writings, 1916–1935*, ed. David Forgacs (New York: New York University Press, 2000), 353–356.

93. Fanon, *Wretched of the Earth*, 2.

94. Roberto Esposito, *Third Person: Politics of Life and Philosophy of the Impersonal*, trans. Zakiya Hanafi (Cambridge: Polity Press, 2012), 108.

95. Emmanuel Levinas, *On Escape* (Stanford, Calif.: Stanford University Press, 2003), 50.

96. Pollock, "Performative Writing," 87.

97. Roy Pascal, *The Dual Voice* (Manchester: Manchester University Press, 1977), 10–11.

98. "La description faite plus haut du style indirect libre montre que cette form d'expression jouit d'une liberté syntaxique presque absolue." Charles Bally, "Le style indirect libre," *Germanich-Romanische Monatsschrift* (Biblioteque Geneva, 1912), 601, quoted in Pascal, *The Dual Voice*, 10.

99. Gerald Bruns, *On the Anarchy of Poetry and Philosophy: A Guide for the Unruly* (New York: Fordham University Press, 2007), 12.

100. Robin D. G. Kelley, *Freedom Dreams: The Black Radical Imagination* (Boston: Beacon Press, 2002), 5.

101. Pollock, "Performative Writing," 87.

102. The remix receives a new aesthetic-political conceptualization in Ivy Wilson, *Specters of Democracy: Blackness and the Aesthetics of Politics in the Antebellum U.S.* (London: Oxford University Press, 2011).

103. Robinson, *Black Marxism*, 246.

104. Ronald A. T. Judy, "The Threat to Islamic Humanity After 11 September 2001," *Critical Quarterly* 45.1–2 (2003): 105.

105. Harriet Jacobs, *Incidents in the Life of a Slave Girl*, ed. Nellie Y. Mckay and Frances Smith Foster (New York: Norton Critical Editions, 2000), 1.

106. Frank Wilderson, "Gramsci's Black Marx: Whither the Slave in Civil Society?," *Social Identities*, 9.2 (Fall 2003): 225–240, 237.

107. Joseph Buttigieg, introduction to *Prison Notebooks*, by Antonio Gramsci, ed. and trans. Joseph Buttigieg (New York: Columbia University Press, 2011), 49.

1. DOWN BY THE RIVERSIDE: RICHARD WRIGHT, THE 1927 FLOOD, AND THE CITIZEN-REFUGEE

1. William Howard, "Richard Wright's Flood Stories and the Great Mississippi River Flood of 1927: Social and Historical Backgrounds," *Southern Literary Journal* 16.2 (Spring 1984): 44–69; 48–49.

2. Wright is partly responsible for this mischaracterization due to his discussion of *Uncle Tom's Children* in his autobiography. See Richard Wright, *Black Boy* (New York: Harper Perennial Classics, 1998), 341.

3. Abdul R. JanMohammed, *The Death-Bound Subject: Richard Wright's Archaeology of Death* (Durham, N.C.: Duke University Press, 2006), 55.

4. Cheryl Higashida, "Aunt Sue's Children: Re-Viewing the Gendered Politics of Richard Wright's Radicalism," *American Literature* 75.2 (June 2003): 395–425; 400.

5. Richard Wright, "Blueprint for Negro Literature," in *Amistad 2: Writings on Black History and Culture*, ed. John Williams and Charles Harris (New York: Random House, 1971), 12.

6. Timothy Bewes, "The Novel Problematic," *Novel: Forum on Fiction,* 44.1 (Spring 2011): 17–19, 18.

7. Nancy Armstrong, "The Future In and Of the Novel," *Novel: Forum on Fiction*, 44.1 (Spring 2011): 8–10, 10.

8. J. K. Gibson-Graham, preface to *A Postcapitalist Politics* (Minneapolis: University of Minnesota Press, 2006), xxx.

9. Joseph Rebello, "The Economy of Joyful Passions: A Political Economic Ethics of the Virtual," *Rethinking Marxism* 18.2 (April 2006): 260–272, 261.

10. See Esposito's engagement with Deleuze in *The Third Person*:

Life, as such and in all its manifestations, is always real, even though it individuates itself into forms that, at each occurrence, actualize what is still virtual at an earlier stage. This does not mean that all reality is actual, or that the actual is the only mode of the real—this would mean locking the process of individuation into sclerotic, immobile forms. Indeed, like in Gilbert Simondon's ontogenetic theory (according to which every new individuation always preserves a pre-individual element that pushes the individual outside its confines), in Deleuze's theory, too, there always remains a portion of the virtual that precedes or exceeds the full actualization. There is no key moment at which something ceases to be possible in order to become real, because at all times the real retains a zone of virtuality.

Roberto Esposito, *Third Person: Politics of Life and Philosophy of the Impersonal*, trans. Zakiya Hanafi (Cambridge: Polity Press, 2012), 148.

11. Richard Wright, "Down by the Riverside" in *Uncle Tom's Children* (New York: Harper Perennial, 2004), 18.

12. Wright, "Down by the Riverside," 62.

13. H. L. Mencken, "The Mississippi Flood," *Evening Sun* (Baltimore), May 23, 1927, 17.

14. Mencken, "The Mississippi Flood," 17.

15. Nancy Armstrong and Warren Montag, "The Future of the Human: An Introduction," *Differences*. 20.2–3 (2009): 1–8, 2.

16. Wright, "Down by the Riverside," 63, 65, 74, 75, 97.

17. American Red Cross, *The Mississippi Valley Flood Disaster of 1927: Official Report of the Relief Operations* (Washington D.C.: American Red Cross, 1928), 67.

18. Karl Marx, *Capital: A Critique of Political Economy*, vol. 1, trans. Ben Fowkes (Vintage: New York, 1977), 895.

19. Saidiya Hartman, *Scenes of Subjection: Terror, Slavery and Self-Making in Nineteenth Century America*, (Oxford: Oxford University Press, 1997), 131.

20. Here I recall the distinction between "wealth," not just as material abundance but also as cultural development in all its fullness, and "dead labor," as that which reduces everything to the logic of exchange-value in Karl Marx, *Grundrisse: Foundations of the Critique of Political Economy* (New York: Vintage Press, 1973), 461, 487.

21. See Charles Lemert, "The Race of Time: W. E. B. Du Bois and Black Reconstruction," *Boundary 2* 27.3 (Fall 2000): 215–248.

22. Pete Daniels, *Deep'n As It Comes: The 1927 Mississippi River Flood* (New York: Oxford University Press, 1972), 3–6.

23. Maurizio Lazzarato, *The Making of the Indebted Man: An Essay on the Neoliberal Condition*, trans. Joshua David Jordan (Amsterdam: Semiotext(e), 2011), 42.

24. Lazzarato, *The Making of the Indebted Man*, 45.

25. Lazzarato, *The Making of the Indebted Man*, 45–46.

26. W. E. B. Du Bois, *John Brown* (New York: Library of America, 2001), 4. In this, his sole published biography, DuBois makes this memorable statement: "The price of repression is greater than the cost of liberty. The degradation of men costs something both to the degraded and those who degrade." The third notebook will devote great attention to this statement.

27. Find another exploration of the United States as a sharecropper's society in Ronald Judy, "Reflections on Straussism, Antimodernity, and Transition in the Age of American Force," *Boundary 2* 33.1 (Spring 2006): 37–59. Additionally, David Harvey notes that under neoliberalism, "state and international powers" carry "the cost of debt repayment no matter what the consequence for the livelihood and well-being of the local population." See David Harvey, *A Brief History of Neoliberalism* (Oxford: Oxford University Press, 2007), 29.

28. Wright, "Down by the Riverside," 64.

29. Wright, "Down by the Riverside," 64.

30. Wright, "Down by the Riverside," 69.

31. Wright, "Down by the Riverside," 73.

32. Abdul JanMohamed, *The Death-Bound-Subject: Richard Wright's Archaeology of Death* (Durham: Duke University Press, 2005), 53.

33. Wright, "Blueprint," 5–6.

34. Graham Hammill, *The Mosaic Constitution* (Chicago: University of Chicago Press, 2012), 68; Ashon Crawley, *Blackpentecostal Breath: The Aesthetics of Possibility* (New York: Fordham University Press, 2016), 4.

35. See William Percy, *Lanterns on the Levee: Recollections of a Planter's Son* (Baton Rouge: Louisiana State University Press, 2006).

36. Cedric Robinson, *Black Marxism: The Making of the Black Radical Tradition* (Chapel Hill: University of North Carolina Press, 2000), 291.

37. One may find this distinction between active and reactive forces in chapter 2 of the classic work Gilles Deleuze, *Nietzsche and Philosophy* (New York: Columbia University Press, 2006), 39–72.

38. Wright, "Down by the Riverside," 76.

39. Wright, "Down by the Riverside," 76.

40. Wright, "Down by the Riverside," 78–79.

41. Frantz Fanon, *Black Skin, White Masks*, trans. Charles Lam Markmann (New York: Grove Press, 1967), 155.

42. American Red Cross, *Mississippi Valley Flood Disaster*, 9.

43. Wright, "Down by the Riverside," 85–86, emphasis added.

44. Wright, "Down by the Riverside," 83–85.

45. Hortense Spillers, "Mama's Baby, Papa's Maybe: An American Grammar Book," *Diacritics* 17.2 (Summer 1987): 80.

46. Maurice Blanchot, *Infinite Conversation*, trans. Susan Hanson (Minneapolis: University of Minnesota Press, 1993), 386, 380.

47. Nancy Armstrong, "Darwin's Uncodable Difference" (unpublished manuscript, January 2013), Microsoft Word file.

48. Friedrich Nietzsche, *Twilight of the Idols*, in *The Portable Nietzsche*, ed. Walter Kaufman (New York: Viking Penguin, 1982), 463–563, 562.

49. In my analysis, I share Giorgio Agamben's apprehensiveness toward the camp but interrogate the complicated ways that social reconstruction, not just oppression, can emerge in this space, based on the urgent demands of the dark proletariat, not just the whims of the sovereign.

50. Robert Russa Moton, "Memorandum for the Committee," 3–4, n.d., folder 1, Papers of the 1927 Flood, Tuskegee University.

51. See Nikhil Pal Singh, *Black Is a Country: Race and the Unfinished Struggle for Democracy* (Cambridge, Mass.: Harvard University Press, 2004).

52. Etienne Balibar, "In Search of the Proletariat" in *Masses, Classes, Ideas* (New York: Routledge, 1994), 133.

53. Roderick Ferguson, "The Stratifications of Normativity," *Rhizomes* 10 (Spring 2005), http://www.rhizomes.net/issue10/ferguson.htm, accessed February 7, 2014.

54. Ryan McCormick, "The Parallax of Labor: Marx as a Moralist," *Rethinking Marxism* 23.1 (January 2011): 50–59.

55. T. M. Campbell, untitled, 1, n.d., folder 3, Papers of 1927 Flood.

56. Pete Daniels, *Shadows of Slavery* (Urbana: University of Illinois Press, 1972), 2.

57. T. M. Campbell, untitled, n.d., folder 3, Papers of 1927 Flood.

58. T. M. Campbell, untitled, n.d., folder 3, Papers of 1927 Flood.

59. Moton, "Memorandum," 4.

60. Ida B. Wells, *Chicago Defender*, July 30, 1927.

61. John Barry, *Rising Tide: The Great Mississippi Flood of 1927 and How It Changed America* (New York: Simon and Schuster, 1997), 378.

62. Robyn Spencer, "Contested Terrain: The Mississippi Flood of 1927 and the Struggle to Control Black Labor," *Journal of Negro History* 792 (1994): 170–181, 173.

63. Howard, "Flood Stories," 49.

64. Roderick Ferguson's *Aberrations in Black* guides my analysis with his assertion that "intellectual inquiry is always shaped out of heterogeneity." Roderick A. Ferguson, *Aberrations in Black: Toward a Queer of Color Critique* (Minneapolis: University of Minnesota Press, 2004), ix. He models this by interrogating how the regulation of sexuality and gender produces race, a process that cannot be explored without keeping this heterogeneity in mind. Ferguson's insight is illuminating in regard to the 1927 flood and Wright's novella.

65. American Red Cross, *Mississippi Valley Flood Disaster*, 38.

66. Wright, "Down by the Riverside," 87.

67. Michel Foucault, *The Archaeology of Knowledge and the Discourse on Language*, trans. A. M. Sheridan Smith (New York: Pantheon, 1972), 107.

68. Wright, "Down by the Riverside," 88–89.

69. American Red Cross, *Mississippi Valley Flood Disaster*, 41.

70. Walter White, "The Negro in the Flood," *Nation* 124 (1927): 688–689.

71. Wright, "Down by the Riverside," 97.

72. Wright, "Down by the Riverside," 117.

73. Wright, "Blueprint," 17.

74. Du Bois, *John Brown*, 50.

75. See Hortense Spillers, "The Crisis of the Negro Intellectual: A Post-Date," *Boundary 2* 21.3 (Autumn 1994).

76. See Esposito, *Third Person*, 144.

77. See Jacques Derrida, *Spectres of Marx: The State of the Debt, the Work of Mourning and the New International*, trans. Peggy Kamuf (London: Routledge, 1993); and Ivy Wilson, *Specters of Democracy: Blackness and the Aesthetics of Politics in the Antebellum U.S.* (New York: Oxford University Press, 2011).

78. Percy, *Lanterns on the Levee*, 267.

79. Wright, "Down by the Riverside," 267–268.

80. James Edward Ford, "An African Diasporic Critique of Violence: Walter Benjamin and Phillis Wheatley Reading the Niobe Legend," in *Systems of Life: Biopolitics, Economics, and Literature on the Cusp of Modernity*, ed. Richard A. Barney and Warren Montag (New York: Fordham University Press, 2018).

81. Percy, *Lanterns on the Levee*, 267.

82. Percy, *Lanterns on the Levee*, 257.

83. Higashida, "Aunt Sue's Children," 404.

84. JanMohamed, *The Death-Bound Subject*, 57.

85. André Pierre Columbat, "November 4, 1995: Deleuze's Death as an Event," *Man and World* 29 (1996): 235–249, 242.

86. Ida B. Wells-Barnett, "Flood Refugees Are Held as Slaves in Mississippi Camp." *Chicago Defender* (National Edition), July 30, 1927.

87. Wright, "Blueprint," 17.

2. "CRUSADE FOR JUSTICE": IDA B. WELLS AND THE POWER OF THE MULTITUDE

1. Cedric Robinson, *Black Marxism: The Making of the Black Radical Tradition* (Chapel Hill: University of North Carolina Press, 2000), 168.

2. James Ford, "Mob Rule in New Orleans: Anarchy, Governance, and Media Representation," *Biography* 33.1 (Winter 2010): 185–208.

3. Mia Bay confirms this claim by referencing biographer Patricia Schechter's attempt to place Wells in an activist tradition "when she lines Wells up next to

two individuals iconoclastic enough to stand alongside her—Maria Steward and Sojourner Truth." Bay explains that Schechter does so by "defining a tradition so tiny that it speaks more to the distinctiveness of these three women than to any cultural continuities they shared." See Mia Bay, "The Improbable Ida B. Wells," *Reviews in American History* 30.3 (September 2002): 439–444, 442. For a similar view, also see Thomas Holt, "Lonely Warrior: Ida B. Wells-Barnett and the Struggle for Black Leadership," in *Black Leaders of the Twentieth Century*, ed. John Hope Franklin and August Meier (Urbana: University of Illinois Press, 1982), 39–61.

4. Ida B. Wells, *Southern Horrors* in *The Light of Truth: The Writings of an Anti-Lynching Crusader*, ed. Mia Bay (New York: Penguin, 2014), 82.

5. Ovid, *Metamorphoses*, Book 10.586. "'Audentes Deus ipse iuvat!' dum talia secum."

6. "Hercules and the Waggoner," in *The Fables of Aesop*, ed. Joseph Jacobs (New York: Dover Publications, 2002), 145. As Sophocles says, "Heaven ne'er helps the men who will not act." Sophocles, *Tragedies and Fragments*, trans. E. H. Plumptre (Boston: D. C. Heath, 1902), 165.

7. While on trial, Sidney receives a letter from his nephew, who fears for his uncle's life. Sidney replies that he worries little for his own life but fears that the same lawlessness threatening his own life could endanger his nephew or anyone else that the government chooses, for whatever reason. Scott A. Nelson, *The Discourses of Algernon Sidney* (London and Ontario: Associated University Presses, 1993), 26.

8. Algernon Sidney, *Discourses Concerning Government* (London: Booksellers of London and Westminster, 1698), 15.

9. Cedric Robinson, *Terms of Order: Political Science and the Myth of Leadership* (New York: State University of New York Press, 1980), 1.

10. Robinson, *Terms of Order*, 17.

11. Warren Montag, *Bodies, Masses, Power: Spinoza and His Contemporaries* (London: Verso, 1999), 77.

12. That turn began decades earlier and involved several institutional changes, which all undermined the efforts of the Freedmen's Bureau and abandoned black workers to their most violent antagonists across the South. First, the Long Depression tested and revealed the nation's lack of commitment to restructuring the American polity to fulfill the hopes of Emancipation. Second, political leaders refused to support a strong multiracial working class, which left the black worker with limited political rights and economic power and left the white worker too weak to combat Southern oligarchy and Northern monopoly capital. Third, this turn involves a constitutionalism based on a legal metaphysics that renders the black worker naturally unfree and barbaric, so that any increase in the black worker's rights counts as barbarians dominating the civilized. Fourth, this turn

involves the counterrevolution of property, in which corporations use loopholes, legal precedents, and other methods to attain government protections for their enterprises through the rights granted to black workers. These factors coalesced to ensure that the American masses were disarmed before corporate powers, since the majority of those workers imagined they were junior partners in monopoly capital's expansion and equal owners of black workers' bodies, labor, affects, and even ideas. Lynching and other activities comprise a "system of anarchy and outlawry," that takes lives, steals resources, distorts historical fact, and twists the multitude's potential self-governance into self-resignation justifying state control and suppression. Thus, "the government instituted for the good of a nation" has now been "turned to its ruin," forsaking justice for black laborers, other laborers of color, the working class, indebted laborers, and the wageless to ensure its new place in monopoly capitalism's global expansion. Find the phrase "system of anarchy and outlawry" in Ida B. Wells, *A Red Record: Tabulated Statistics and Alleged Causes of Lynchings in the United States, 1892–1893–1894*, in *The Light of Truth: Writings of an Anti-Lynching Crusader*, ed. Mia Bay (New York: Penguin, 2014), 222.

13. Sidney, *Discourses Concerning Government*, 15.

14. Wells, *Southern Horrors*, 80.

15. I derive the concept of the vanishing point from Erica Edwards, *Charisma and the Fictions of Black Leadership* (Minneapolis: University of Minnesota Press, 2012).

16. Du Bois, *Black Reconstruction*, 166.

17. Jacques Derrida, *Without Alibi*, ed. and trans. Peggy Kamuf (Stanford, Calif.: Stanford University Press, 2002), 240.

18. Ida B. Wells, *Crusade for Justice* (Chicago: University of Chicago Press, 1972), 64.

19. Wells, *Southern Horrors*, 69.

20. G. W. F. Hegel, *The Phenomenology of Spirit*, trans. A. V. Miller (Oxford: Oxford University Press, 1977). See especially the sections "The Truth of Enlightenment," "Absolute Freedom and Terror," and "Conscience: The 'Beautiful Soul,' Evil and Its Forgiveness."

21. Etienne Balibar, *Violence and Civility: On the Limits of Political Anthropology*, trans. G. M. Goshgarian (New York: Columbia University Press, 2015), 60.

22. Wells, *Southern Horrors*, 75.

23. Wells, *Crusade*, 50–51.

24. Wells, *Crusade*, 52.

25. Wells, *Southern Horrors*, 78.

26. Wells, *Crusade*, 56.

27. Wells, *Crusade*, 45–46.

28. Wells, *Crusade*, 123.

29. Ronald Judy, "Provisional Note on Planetary Formations of Violence," *Boundary 2* 33.3 (Fall 2006): 141–150, 150.

30. Lindon Barrett, "Dead Men Printed," *Callaloo* 22.2 (1999): 309–326, 309.

31. Ida B. Wells, Frederick Douglass, Irvine Garland Penn, and Ferdinand L. Barnett, *The Reason Why the Colored American Is Not in The World's Columbian Exposition: The Afro-American's Contribution to Columbian Literature*, ed. Robert Rydell (Urbana: University of Illinois Press, 1999), 74.

32. Julian Ralph, *Harper's Chicago and the World's Fair* (New York: Harper and Brothers Publishers, 1893), 136.

33. Ralph, *Harper's Chicago and the World's Fair*, 134.

34. Russ Castronovo, *Beautiful Democracy* (Chicago: University of Chicago Press, 2007), 11.

35. Ralph, *Harper's Chicago and the World's Fair*, 135.

36. David F. Burg, *Chicago's White City of 1893* (Lexington: University Press of Kentucky, 1976), 119.

37. Burg, *Chicago's White City*, 115.

38. Burg, *Chicago's White City*, 115.

39. Ralph, *Harper's Chicago and the World's Fair*, 137.

40. Karl Marx, *Capital: A Critique of Political Economy*, vol. 1, trans. Ben Fowkes (New York: Vintage, 1977), 363.

41. Marx, *Capital*, 363.

42. Norman Bolotin and Christine Laing, *The World's Columbian Exposition: The Chicago World's Fair of 1893* (Urbana and Chicago: University of Illinois Press, 1993), 61.

43. "What to the Slave Is the Fourth of July" is the popular name of the speech "The Meaning of July Fourth for the Negro." Frederick Douglass, "The Meaning of July Fourth for the Negro," in *Frederick Douglass: Selected Speeches and Writings*, ed. Philip S. Foner (Chicago: Lawrence Hill Books, 1999): 188–208, 194.

44. Wells et al., *The Reason Why*, 9.

45. Wells et al., *The Reason Why*, 9.

46. Two conditions of the compromise have already been mentioned—namely, the alignment of the American government with monopoly capitalism and the abandonment of the Freedmen's Bureau. An effectively managed Freedmen's Bureau could have established a *multiracial* working class strong enough to contend with monopoly capitalism's threats to democracy. A white working class alone cannot counterbalance monopoly capital's power. Meanwhile, the US government's alignment with monopoly capital granted the nation access to global influence in collaboration and competition with Europe's own imperial misadventures.

47. Douglass, "The Meaning of July Fourth for the Negro," 194.

48. Paul Gilroy, *Black Atlantic: Modernity and Double Consciousness* (London: Verso, 1993), 71.

49. Wells et al., *The Reason Why*, 11.

50. Wells et al., *The Reason Why*, 17.

51. Wells et al., *The Reason Why*, 11.

52. For more on burial, read Maria Torok and Nicholas Abraham, *The Wolf Man's Magic Word: A Cryptonymy* (Minneapolis: University of Minnesota Press, 2005).

53. Douglass, "The Meaning of July Fourth for the Negro," 191.

54. Douglass, "The Meaning of July Fourth for the Negro," 196.

55. Wells, *Red Record*, 41.

56. Rebecca Comay and Joshua Nichols, "Missed Revolutions, Non-Revolutions, Revolutions to Come: An Encounter with *Mourning Sickness: Hegel and the French Revolution*," *PhaenEx* 7.1, (Spring/Summer 2012): 309–346.

57. After undergoing so much violence, abuse, starvation, rape, torture, misnaming, and deception, the black should have been reduced completely to an object of simple fear, or worse, mere amusement. The fact that this does not prove true after slavery suggests something unknowable and indeterminable stretching across the regions of anxiety and fright about black life. The murdered person in the lynching postcard is an attempt to reduce blackness to something knowable, determinable, controllable, and destructible. However excruciating it is to witness so many unjust deaths, one cannot forget that these postcards are a reaction to the failure of fully objectifying the black. Indeed, that forgetting is essential to their function.

58. Wells, *Southern Horrors*, 67–68.

59. Wells et al., *The Reason Why*, 18.

60. Ida B. Wells, *Lynch Law in Georgia* in *The Light of Truth: Writings of an Anti-Lynching Crusader*, ed. Mia Bay (New York: Penguin, 2014), 330–331.

61. Ida B. Wells, *The East St. Louis Massacre: The Greatest Outrage of the Century* in *The Light of Truth: Writings of an Anti-Lynching Crusader*, ed. Mia Bay (New York: Penguin, 2014), 466.

62. A few paragraphs earlier in the report, one finds proof of the report's claim, when a "nonresident of East St Louis" called "guardsmen" to stop "a boy" who had beaten a black woman with an "iron bar" "for several blocks"; the guardsmen "laughingly drove the boy off." This enjoyment shows up in how the mob set fires to forty-three black-owned or -rented homes on several blocks and threatened firefighters who would quell the flames or in how the mob threatened ambulance drivers who came to pick up bodies, so the dead would lay in the street "beside the street car tracks" for "passengers in every passing car" to see. Wells, *East St. Louis Massacre*, 469, 475.

63. Wells, *East St. Louis Massacre*, 472.

64. Wells, *East St. Louis Massacre*, 472.

65. Wells, *East St Louis Massacre*, 469.

66. Wells, *East St Louis Massacre*, 468.

67. Wells, *East St Louis Massacre*, 468.

68. Wells et al., *The Reason Why*, 37.

69. Wells, *Crusade*, 71.

70. Balibar, *Violence and Civility*, 60.

71. Balibar, *Violence and Civility*, 59.

72. George Washington Cable, *The Silent South: Together with the Freedman's Case in Equity* (New York: Scribner, 1889), 31.

73. Wells et al., *The Reason Why*, 26.

74. Wells et al., *The Reason Why*, 27.

75. Rizvana Bradley, "Reinventing Capacity: Black Feminity's Lyrical Surplus and the Cinematic Limits of *12 Years a Slave*," *Black Camera* 7.1 (Fall 2015): 162–178.

76. See especially "Seduction and the Ruses of Power" in Saidiya Hartman, *Scenes of Subjection: Terror, Slavery and Self-Making in the Nineteenth Century America* (London: Oxford University Press, 1997), 79–112.

77. See the discussion of "pornotroping" in Alexander Weheliye, *Habeas Viscus: Racializing Assemblages, Biopolitics, and Black Feminist Theories of the Human* (Durham, N.C.: Duke University Press, 2014), 97–99.

78. Olaudah Equiano, *The Interesting Narrative of the Life of Olaudah Equiano or Gustavas Vassa, the African, Written by Himself* in *The Classic Slave Narratives*, ed. Henry Louis Gates (New York: Signet, 2012), 181.

79. Harriet Jacobs, *Incidents in the Life of a Slave Girl*, ed. Nellie Y. Mckay and Frances Smith Foster (New York: Norton Critical Editions, 2000), 45.

80. Wells et al., *The Reason Why*, 26.

81. Talitha L. LeFlouria, *Chained in Silence: Black Women and Convict Labor in the New South* (Chapel Hill: University of North Carolina Press, 2015), 70.

82. See *Georgia Nigger*, originally published in 1932, in a new edition with a new title: John L. Spivak, *Hard Times on a Southern Chain Gang* (Columbia: University of South Carolina Press, 2012); and Sarah Haley, *No Mercy Here: Gender, Punishment, and the Making of Jim Crow Modernity* (Chapel Hill: University of North Carolina Press, 2016).

83. Wells et al., *The Reason Why*, 8.

84. Balibar, *Violence and Civility*, 64.

85. Ann V. Collins, *All Hell Broke Loose: American Race Riots from the Progressive Era Through World War II* (Santa Barbara, Calif.: Praeger, 2012), 110.

86. Ida B. Wells, *The Arkansas Race Riot* in *The Light of Truth: The Writings of an Anti-Lynchings Crusader*, ed. Mia Bay (New York: Penguin, 2014), 496–555, 501.

87. Wells, *Arkansas Race Riot*, 502.

88. W. E. B. Du Bois, *John Brown* (New York: Modern Library Classics, 2001), 51.

89. Karl Marx, *Grundrisse: Foundations of the Critique of Political Economy*, trans. Martin Nicolaus (New York: Vintage Press, 1973), 487.

90. Wells et al., *The Reason Why*, 62.

91. Gilles Deleuze and Felix Guattari, *A Thousand Plateaus*, trans. Brian Massumi (Minneapolis: University of Minnesota Press, 1985), 291.

92. Philip S. Foner, *History of the Labor Movement in the United States* (New York: International Publishers, 1955), 221.

93. Foner, *History of the Labor Movement*, 221.

94. Foner, *History of the Labor Movement*, 222. "Grand Army men" refers to former Union soldiers.

95. Foner, *History of the Labor Movement*, 221.

96. Foner, *History of the Labor Movement*, 224.

97. Foner, *History of the Labor Movement*, 224.

98. Foner, *History of the Labor Movement*, 224.

99. Joseph Young, "Phenomenology and Textual Power in Richard Wright's 'The Man Who Lived Underground,'" *MELUS* 26.4 (Winter 2001): 69–93, 71.

100. Foner, *History of the Labor Movement*, 228.

101. Wells, *Crusade*, xi.

102. Warren Montag, *Althusser and His Contemporaries* (Durham, N.C.: Duke University Press, 2013), 6.

103. Montag, *Althusser and His Contemporaries*, 7.

104. Wells, *Crusade*, 419.

3. W. E. B. DU BOIS'S *BLACK RECONSTRUCTION*: THEORIZING DIVINE VIOLENCE

1. Walter Benjamin, "Critique of Violence," in *Reflections: Essays, Aphorisms, Autobiographical Writings*, trans. Edmund Jephcott, ed. Peter Demetz (New York: Schocken Books, 1986): 277–300.

2. W. E. B. Du Bois, *Black Reconstruction in America, 1860–1880* (New York: Free Press, 1998), 83.

3. Ted A. Smith, "Reply to Angela Cowser," *Syndicate*, https://syndicate .network/symposia/theology/weird-john-brown/#working-divine-violence -exceptional-john-brown, accessed August 28, 2016.

4. W. E. B. Du Bois, *Souls of Black Folk* in *Writings* (New York: Modern Library Classics, 1996), 357–548, 501.

5. Du Bois, *Souls of Black Folk*, 501.

6. Du Bois, *Souls of Black Folk*, 373.

7. Du Bois, *Souls of Black Folk*, 375–376.

8. W. E. B. Du Bois, *John Brown* (New York: Modern Library Classics, 2001), 4.

9. Ted A. Smith, *Weird John Brown: Divine Violence and the Limits of Ethics* (Stanford, Calif.: Stanford University Press, 2015), 15–16.

10. Du Bois, *John Brown*, xxv.

11. Du Bois, *John Brown*, 40, emphasis added.

12. Smith, *Weird John Brown*, 91.

13. Ronald Judy, "Lohengrin's Swan and the Style of Interiority in 'Of the Coming of John.'" *CR: New Centennial Review* 15.2 (Fall 2015): 211–257, 246.

14. Miguel Mellino, "The *Langue* of the Damned: Fanon and the Remnants of Europe." *South Atlantic Quarterly* 112.1: 79–89, 81.

15. David Marriott, "On Racial Fetishism," *Qui Parle* 18.2 (Summer 2010): 215–248, 238.

16. Benjamin, "Critique of Violence," 250.

17. Smith, *Weird John Brown*, 41; Du Bois, *Black Reconstruction*, 9.

18. Smith, *Weird John Brown*, 83.

19. Smith, *Weird John Brown*, 83.

20. Hebrews 13:3 (King James Version).

21. Samira Kawash, "Terrorists and Vampires: Fanon's Spectral Violence of Decolonization," in *Frantz Fanon: Critical Perspectives*, ed. Anthony C. Alessandrini (London: Routledge, 1999), 235–257, 253; Du Bois, *John Brown*, 40.

22. Du Bois, *John Brown*, 41.

23. Frantz Fanon, *Black Skin, White Masks*, trans. Charles Lam Markmann (New York: Grove Press, 1967), 10.

24. Du Bois, *John Brown*, 75.

25. Langston Hughes, "Wait" in *The Collected Works of Langston Hughes: The Poems, 1921–1940* (Columbia: University of Missouri Press, 2001), 234; Zora Neale Hurston, *Moses, Man of the Mountain* (New York: Harper Perennial, 1991), 183.

26. David Marriott, *Haunted Life: Black Culture and Visual Modernity* (New Brunswick, N.J.: Rutgers University Press, 2007), 237.

27. Jacques Roumain, "Le Sale Negres," in *When the Tom-Tom Beats: Selected Prose and Poems*, trans. Joanne Fungaroli and Ronald Sauer (Washington, D.C.: Azul Editions, 1995), 94–97.

28. Du Bois, *John Brown*, 68.

29. Langston Hughes, *The Collected Works of Langston Hughes, The Poems: 1921–1940* (Columbia: University of Missouri Press, 2000), 235.

30. Roumain, "Le Sale Negres," 94–97.

31. Hughes, *The Collected Works*, 234. Note that this does not refer to the others who are being starved.

32. Benjamin, "Critique of Violence," 300.

33. Marriott, *Haunted Life*, 239–240.

34. Du Bois, *John Brown*, 68.

35. Kawash, "Terrorists and Vampires," 243.

36. Kawash, "Terrorists and Vampires, 240.

37. Du Bois, *John Brown*, 68.

38. Du Bois, *John Brown*, 63.

39. Du Bois, *John Brown*, 70.

40. Du Bois, *Black Reconstruction*, 36.

41. Du Bois, *Black Reconstruction*, 18.

42. Du Bois, *Black Reconstruction*, 19.

43. Benjamin, "Critique of Violence," 288.

44. Du Bois, *Black Reconstruction*, 7.

45. Du Bois, *John Brown*, 50.

46. Du Bois, *John Brown*, 59.

47. Du Bois, *John Brown*, 53.

48. Smith, *Weird John Brown*, 174.

49. Judy, "Lohengrin's Swan," 245.

50. Du Bois, *John Brown*, 152.

51. Smith, *Weird John Brown*, 174.

52. Smith, *Weird John Brown*, 175.

53. Du Bois, *John Brown*, 209.

54. Du Bois, *John Brown*, 117.

55. Du Bois, *Black Reconstruction*, 64, emphasis added.

56. Saidiya Hartman, *Scenes of Subjection: Terror, Slavery and Self-Making in Nineteenth Century America*, (Oxford: Oxford University Press, 1997), 66.

57. Hartman, *Scenes of Subjection*, 63.

58. Hartman, *Scenes of Subjection*, 60.

59. Du Bois, *Black Reconstruction*, 40.

60. Karl Marx, *Capital: A Critique of Political Economy*. vol. 1, trans. Ben Fowkes (Vintage: New York, 1977), 35.

61. Du Bois, *Black Reconstruction*, 40.

62. Du Bois, *Black Reconstruction*, 64, emphasis added.

63. Jean Luc Nancy, *Inoperative Community*, ed. Peter Connor, trans. Peter Connor, Lisa Garbus, Michael Holland, and Simona Sawhney (Minneapolis: University of Minnesota Press, 1991).

64. Cedric Robinson, *Black Marxism: The Making of the Black Radical Tradition* (Chapel Hill: University of North Carolina Press, 2000), 168.

65. For more on unproductive expenditure, see Georges Bataille, "Notions of Expenditure," in *Visions of Excess, 1929–1937* (Minneapolis: University of Minnesota Press, 1985).

66. Emmanuel Levinas, *On Escape* (Stanford, Calif.: Stanford University Press, 2003), 53.

67. Levinas, *On Escape*, 55.

68. Friedrich Nietzsche, *Twilight of the Idols*, in *The Portable Nietzsche*, ed. Walter Kaufman (New York: Viking Penguin, 1982), 530.

69. William Still, *The Underground Railroad* (New York: Arno Press, 1968), 68, 72, 73, 46.

70. Still, *Underground Railroad,* 1–2, 61, 68, 121, 123, 254; Fred Moten, "Taste Dissonance Flavor Escape," *Women in Performance: A Journal of Feminist Theory* 17.2 (Summer 2007): 217–246, 217.

71. Maurice Blanchot, *Infinite Conversation*, trans. Susan Hanson (Minneapolis: University of Minnesota Press, 1993), 380; Richard Wright, "Blueprint for Negro Literature," in *Amistad 2: Writings on Black History and Culture*, ed. John Williams and Charles Harris (New York: Random House, 1971), 17.

72. Still, *Underground Railroad*, 117.

73. Hortense Spillers, "Mama's Baby, Papa's Maybe: An American Grammar Book," *Diacritics* 17.2 (Summer 1987): 72.

74. Still, *Underground Railroad*, 133, 359.

75. Hebrews 10:32, 10:34 (King James Version).

76. Still, *Underground Railroad*, 117.

77. Still, *Underground Railroad*, 24.

78. Jesse Goldhammer, "Dare to Know, Dare to Sacrifice" in *Reading Bataille Now*, ed. Shannon Winnubst (Bloomington: Indiana University Press, 2007).

79. Still, *Underground Railroad*, 125.

80. Hartman, *Scenes of Subjection*, 67.

81. Du Bois, *John Brown*, 143.

82. Still, *Underground Railroad*, 185.

83. Du Bois, *John Brown*, 10.

84. Du Bois, *John Brown*, 148.

85. Hartman, *Scenes of Subjection*, 66.

86. Georges Sorel, "The Political General Strike," in *Reflections on Violence*, 5th ed. (Paris, 1919), 250, quoted in Benjamin, "Critique of Violence," 291.

87. Bataille, "Notions of Expenditure," 177.

88. Karl Marx, *Grundrisse: Foundations of the Critique of Political Economy*, trans. Martin Nicolaus (New York: Vintage Press, 1973), 487.

89. Du Bois, *Black Reconstruction*, 50.

90. Du Bois, *Black Reconstruction*, 61.

91. Some of Du Bois's radical contemporaries condemn him for misapplying Marxist orthodoxy in this passage. These naysayers fail to consider the fact that, by the 1930s, Marxism never established an orthodox use for the general strike. As early as the 1880s, Friedrich Engels says that only no well-organized party would need the general strike. He associated it with the most reckless, apocalyptic forms of anarchism. This view holds the day basically until Rosa Luxembourg begins to claim the mass strike for Marxism, by redefining the strike's spontaneity

as a sign of self-organization among the masses rather than misguidance by the elite. This is crucial considering that, in Western European radical movements, no general strike has occurred for which theorists envisioned them as top-down scenarios; on the other hand, successful general strikes have always developed from the bottom up, with the guidance of leaders attuned to the masses' political interests. In a way, Du Bois is asserting that the slaves in the Civil War have already demonstrated the most powerful general strike, which has fallen through the cracks of leftist theory and historiography.

92. Du Bois, *Black Reconstruction*, 67.

93. Benjamin, "Critique of Violence," 292.

94. Du Bois, *Black Reconstruction*, 61.

95. Du Bois, *Black Reconstruction*, 57.

96. Du Bois, *Black Reconstruction*, 65.

97. Du Bois, *Black Reconstruction*, 62.

98. Smith, *Weird John Brown*, 73, 74.

99. See "Divine Violence as the Relief of Law," in Smith, *Weird John Brown*, 59–84.

100. W. E. B. Du Bois, "Sociology Hesitant," *Boundary 2* 27.3 (Fall 2000): 37–44.

101. Du Bois, *John Brown*, 3.

102. Du Bois, *John Brown*, 67–68.

103. Smith, *Weird John Brown*, 76.

104. David Marriott, "Whither Fanon," *Textual Practice* 25.1 (2011): 34.

105. Marriott, "Whither Fanon," 63.

106. Michelle Stephens, *Black Empire: The Masculine Global Imaginary of Caribbean Intellectuals in the United States, 1941–1962* (Durham, N.C.: Duke University Press, 2005), 232.

107. Theodor W. Adorno, *Aesthetic Theory*, trans. Robert Hullot-Kentor (London: Continuum, 1997), 155.

108. Michael Gillespie, "Reckless Eyeballing: *Coonskin*, Film Blackness and the Racial Grotesque," in *Contemporary Black American Cinema: Race, Gender, and Sexuality at the Movies*, ed. Mia Mask (London: Routledge, 2012).

109. Clyde Woods, *Development Arrested* (London: Verso, 1998), 84.

110. Giorgio Agamben, *State of Exception*, trans. Kevin Atell (Chicago: University of Chicago Press, 2005), 154–155.

111. Agamben, *State of Exception*, 29.

112. Du Bois, *Black Reconstruction*, 267.

113. Allison Powers, "Tragedy Made Flesh: Constitutional Lawlessness in Du Bois's *Black Reconstruction*," *Comparative Studies of South Asia, Africa and the Middle East* 34.1 (2014): 106–125.

114. Du Bois, *Black Reconstruction*, 267.

115. Du Bois, *Black Reconstruction*, 268.

116. Alys Eve Weinbaum, "Interracial Romance and Black Internationalism," in *Next to the Color Line: Gender, Sexuality, and W. E. B. Du Bois*, ed. Susan Gillman and Alys Eve Weinbaum (Minneapolis: University of Minnesota Press, 2007), 96–123, 100.

117. John Eaton, *Grant, Lincoln, and the Freedmen: Reminisces of the Civil War* (New York: Longmans, Green, and Co., 1907), 2.

118. Du Bois, *Black Reconstruction*, 70.

119. Du Bois, *Black Reconstruction*, 71.

120. Du Bois, *Black Reconstruction*, 70–73.

121. Du Bois, *Black Reconstruction*, 70.

122. Agamben, *Homo Sacer: Sovereign Power and Bare Life* (Stanford, Calif.: Stanford University Press, 1998), 175.

123. Eaton, *Grant*, 165.

124. Eaton, *Grant*, 165.

125. Du Bois, *Black Reconstruction*, 66.

126. Du Bois, *Black Reconstruction*, 110.

127. Du Bois, *Black Reconstruction*, 104.

128. W. E. B. Du Bois, "Criteria for Negro Art," in *Writings* (New York: Modern Library Classics, 1996), 997.

129. Du Bois, *Black Reconstruction*, 66.

130. Du Bois, *Black Reconstruction*, 98–99.

131. Du Bois, *Black Reconstruction*, 90, 218, 91.

132. Du Bois, *Black Reconstruction*, 101.

133. Du Bois, *Black Reconstruction*, 102.

134. Du Bois, *Black Reconstruction*, 94.

135. Du Bois, *Black Reconstruction*, 108.

136. Du Bois, *Black Reconstruction*, 109.

137. Thavolia Glymph, "Du Bois's *Black Reconstruction* and Slave Women's War for Freedom," *South Atlantic Quarterly* 112.3 (Summer 2013): 489–505. This notebook diverges from Glymph's claim that Du Bois straightforwardly esteems John Eaton's account of reconstruction. Nevertheless, Glymph's insights add indispensable layers to the relationship of black fugitivity to gender, law, and divine violence.

138. Hegel meditates on this aspect of war: "Sacrifice on behalf of the individuality of the state is the substantial tie between the state and all its members and so is a universal duty. Since this tie is a single aspect of the ideality, as contrasted with the reality, of subsistent particulars, it becomes at the same time a particular tie, and those who are in it form a class of their own with the characteristic of courage." George Wilhelm Friedrich Hegel, "Third Part: Ethical Life" in *Elements of the Philosophy of Right*, https://www.marxists

.org/reference/archive/hegel/works/pr/prstate2.htm, paragraph 325, accessed May 5, 2016.

139. Du Bois, *Black Reconstruction*, 109.

140. Du Bois, *Souls of Black Folk*, 501.

141. Du Bois, *Black Reconstruction*, 107, emphasis added.

142. Du Bois, *Black Reconstruction*, 130, emphasis added.

143. Du Bois, *Black Reconstruction*, 144.

144. Du Bois, *Black Reconstruction*, 130.

145. Jim Downs, *Sick from Freedom: African-American Illness and Suffering During the Civil War and Reconstruction* (New York: Oxford University Press, 2012), 22.

146. Downs, *Sick from Freedom*, 42–43.

147. Vincent Brown, "Social Death and Political Life in the Study of Slavery," *American History Review* (December 2009): 1231–1249, 1247.

148. Agamben, *State of Exception*, 34.

149. Du Bois, *Black Reconstruction*, 122.

150. Gerald Bruns, *On the Anarchy of Poetry and Philosophy: A Guide for the Unruly* (New York: Fordham University Press, 2007), 81.

151. Blanchot, *Infinite Conversation*, 21.

152. Bruns, *On the Anarchy of Poetry and Philosophy*, 81.

153. Du Bois, *Souls of Black Folk*, 494.

154. Du Bois, *Souls of Black Folk*, 494.

155. Du Bois, *Souls of Black Folk*, 494–495.

156. Du Bois, *Black Reconstruction*, 123–124.

157. Du Bois, *Souls of Black Folk*, 541.

158. Nancy, *Inoperative Community*, 106.

159. Du Bois, *Black Reconstruction*, 30, emphasis added. Also consider Du Bois's quotation of the vice president of the Confederacy, who says their new government was based on the "great truth" of the black's natural inferiority, which makes them "fit" for enslavement, since God "has made one race to differ from another, as He has had 'one star to differ from another star in glory.'" Du Bois, *Black Reconstruction*, 50.

160. Bataille, "Notions of Expenditure," 144.

161. Du Bois, *Black Reconstruction*, 122.

162. Bradley Rizvana. "Reinventing Capacity: Black Femininity's Lyrical Surplus and the Cinematic Limits of *12 Years of Slave*," *Black Camera* 7.1 (Fall 2015): 162–178; Giorgio Agamben, *The Use of Bodies* (Stanford, Calif.: Stanford University Press, 2016), 208.

163. Du Bois, *Black Reconstruction*, 124.

164. Du Bois, *Black Reconstruction*, 124.

4. ZORA NEALE HURSTON'S *MOSES, MAN OF THE MOUNTAIN*: AN ANTHROPOLOGY OF POWER

1. Walter Benjamin, "Critique of Violence," in *Reflections: Essays, Aphorisms, Autobiographical Writings*, trans. Edmund Jephcott, ed. Peter Demetz (New York: Schocken Books, 1986), 295.

2. Zora Neale Hurston, "Crazy for This Democracy," in *Folklore, Memoires, and Other Writings* (New York: Library of America, 1995), 945–949, 947.

3. Zora Neale Hurston, "Characteristics of Negro Expression," in *Folklore, Memoires, and Other Writings* (New York: Library of America, 1995), 830–846, 830.

4. Ralph Ellison, "Recent Negro Fiction," *New Masses* 40.6 (August 5, 1941): 22–26; 24. For a reconsideration of the burlesque in 1930s writing, see Sonnet Retman's *Real Folks: Race and Genre in the Great Depression* (Durham, N.C.: Duke University Press, 2011).

5. Deborah McDowell, "Lines of Descent/Dissenting Lines," in *Moses, Man of the Mountain*, by Zora Neale Hurston (New York: Harper Perennial Classics, 1991), vii–xxii, xxii.

6. Blyden Jackson, "Introduction," in *Moses, Man of the Mountain* (Urbana: University of Illinois Press, 1984), xvi. Also see Mark Thompson, "National Socialism and Blood Sacrifice in Zora Neale Hurston's 'Moses, Man of the Mountain,'" *African American Review* 38.3 (Autumn 2004): 395.

7. Bernard Flynn, *The Philosophy of Claude Lefort: Interpreting the Political* (Evanston, Ill.: Northwestern University Press, 2005), 6.

8. Flynn, *The Philosophy of Claude Lefort*, 8.

9. Niccolo Machiavelli, *The Prince*, trans. Peter Bonadello (London: Oxford World Classics, 2005), 87.

10. Thompson, "Blood Sacrifice," 395.

11. Rudyard Kipling, *Recessional, with Numerous Original Illustrations by W. St. John Harper and George T. Tobin* (New York: Frederick A. Stokes, 1898), 94–95.

12. Michael Lackey, *The Modernist God State: A Literary Study of the Nazis' Third Reich* (London: Bloomsbury Academic, 2012), 156–157.

13. Lackey, *Modernist God State*, 157.

14. Michael Lackey, "Moses, Man of Oppression: A Twentieth-Century African American Critique of Western Theocracy," *African American Review* 43.4 (Winter 2009): 577–588, 578.

15. Zora Neale Hurston, *Zora Neale Hurston: A Life in Letters*, ed. Carla Kaplan (New York: Anchor Books, 2003), 532.

16. Hurston, *Life in Letters*, 531.

17. Lackey, *Modernist God State*, 251–253.

18. Zora Neale Hurston, *Dust Tracks on a Road: An Autobiography*, ed. Robert E. Hemenway (Urbana: University of Illinois Press, 1942), 285.

19. Deborah Plant, *Every Tub Must Sit on Its Own Bottom: The Philosophy and Politics of Zora Neale Hurston* (Urbana: University of Illinois Press, 1995), 56.

20. "Spinoza's doctrine of self-preservation and self-perfection reflected the wisdom Hurston found in the lore of the folk and in the teachings of Booker T. Washington. Spinoza's belief in the divinity of humankind and the power of reason is mirrored in Hurston's thought." Plant, *Every Tub*, 176–177.

21. Zora Neale Hurston, *Moses, Man of the Mountain* (New York: Harper Perennial, 1991), vii, viii.

22. Warren Montag, *Bodies, Masses, Power: Spinoza and His Contemporaries* (London: Verso, 1999), 77.

23. Susan Hegeman, *Patterns for America: Modernism and the Concept of Culture* (Princeton, N.J.: Princeton University Press, 1999), 45. Also cited in Retman, *Real Folks*, 154.

24. Retman, *Real Folks*, 154.

25. Zora Neale Hurston, *Their Eyes Were Watching God* (Urbana: University of Illinois Press, 1991), 86.

26. David Scott, "Archaeology of Black Memory," *Small Axe* 5 (March 2009): 80–150, 148, emphasis added.

27. Montag, *Bodies, Masses, Power*, 6.

28. Hurston, "Characteristics of Negro Expression," 822.

29. Baruch Spinoza, *The Theological-Political Treatise* in *Spinoza: The Complete Works*, trans. Samuel Shirley, ed. Michael L. Morgan (Indianapolis, Ind.: Hackett Publishing Company, 2002), 456.

30. Spinoza, *Theological-Political Treatise*, 456.

31. Graham Hammill, *The Mosaic Constitution: Political Theology and Imagination from Machiavelli to Milton* (Chicago: University of Chicago Press, 2012), 98.

32. Richard Wright, "Blueprint for Negro Literature," in *Amistad 2: Writings on Black History and Culture*, ed. John Williams and Charles Harris (New York: Random House, 1971), 16.

33. Hurston, *Life in Letters*, 532.

34. Hurston, *Life in Letters*, 529, emphasis added.

35. Friedrich Nietzsche, *The Anti-Christ*, trans. H. L. Mencken (Tucson, Ariz.: See Sharp Press, 1999), 40.

36. Nietzsche, *The Anti-Christ*, 43.

37. Hurston, *Moses, Man of the Mountain*, viii.

38. Hurston, *Moses, Man of the Mountain*, 1.

39. Hurston, *Moses, Man of the Mountain*, 2.

40. Hurston, *Moses, Man of the Mountain*, 15.

41. Thompson, "Blood Sacrifice," 401.

42. Hurston, *Moses, Man of the Mountain*, 1.

43. Hurston, *Moses, Man of the Mountain*, 1.

44. Baruch Spinoza, *Ethics*, trans. R. H. M. Elwes (London: Bell and Sons, 1887), pt. iii, 2.

45. Hurston, *Moses, Man of the Mountain*, 7, emphasis added.

46. Hurston, *Moses, Man of the Mountain*, 7.

47. Hurston, *Moses, Man of the Mountain*, 14.

48. Hurston, *Moses, Man of the Mountain*, 14.

49. Hurston, *Moses, Man of the Mountain*, 15.

50. Spinoza, *Ethics*, pt. iv, app. 13.

51. Hurston, *Moses, Man of the Mountain*, 15.

52. Cathy Caruth, *Unclaimed Experience: Trauma, Narrative, History* (Baltimore: Johns Hopkins University Press, 1996), 67.

53. Spinoza, *Theological-Political Treatise*, 418.

54. "The concept of guilt and punishment . . . [was] devised to destroy man's *sense of causality*: they are an attack upon the concept of cause and effect!" Nietzsche, *The Anti-Christ*, 50.

55. Thompson, "Blood Sacrifice," 407.

56. Hurston, *Moses, Man of the Mountain*, 18.

57. Hurston, Moses, *Man of the Mountain*, 18.

58. Hurston, *Moses, Man of the Mountain*, 21.

59. In *The Art of the Possible*, Kevern Verney calls Booker T. Washington the "Moses of his race" who made the South the "promised land" of the Negro. Kevern Verney, *The Art of the Possible: Booker T. Washington and Black Leadership in the United States, 1881–1925* (New York: Routledge, 2000), 50.

60. See Michael Rudolph West, *The Education of Booker T. Washington: American Democracy and the Idea of Race Relations* (New York: Columbia University Press, 2006), 70.

61. Booker T. Washington, "Booker T. Washington Delivers the 1895 Atlanta Compromise Speech," in *The Booker T. Washington Papers*, ed. Louis R. Harlan, vol. 3 (Urbana: University of Illinois Press, 1974), 585.

62. Washington, "Atlanta Compromise Speech," 585.

63. Washington, "Atlanta Compromise Speech," 586.

64. Roderick Ferguson, "The Stratification of Normativity," *Rhizomes* 10 (Spring 2005), http://www.rhizomes.net/issue10/ferguson.htm, accessed January 10, 2014.

65. Hurston, *Moses, Man of the Mountain*, 56, 57.

66. Hurston, *Moses, Man of the Mountain*, 62.

67. Washington, "Atlanta Compromise Speech," 586, emphasis added.

68. Washington, "Atlanta Compromise Speech," 586.

69. Charles Chesnutt, *Marrow of Tradition* (New York: Dover, 2003), 61.

70. Hurston, *Life in Letters*, 532.

71. Hurston, *Life in Letters*, 530.

72. Nietzsche, *The Anti-Christ*, 42.

73. Spinoza, *Theological-Political Treatise*, 469.

74. Erica Edwards, "Gendered Violence in Black Leadership's Gothic Tale," *Callaloo* 31.4 (Fall 2008): 1084–1102.

75. W. E. B. Du Bois, *Black Reconstruction in America, 1860–1880* (New York: Free Press, 1998), 322.

76. Hurston, *Moses, Man of the Mountain*, 76.

77. Spinoza, *Theological-Political Treatise*, 11.

78. Hurston, *Moses, Man of the Mountain*, 61.

79. Hurston, *Moses, Man of the Mountain*, 59.

80. Flynn, *The Philosophy of Claude Lefort*, 7–13.

81. Hurston, *Moses, Man of the Mountain*, 95.

82. Hurston, *Moses, Man of the Mountain*, 80.

83. Spinoza, *Ethics*, pt. iv, 325.

84. Hurston, *Moses, Man of the Mountain*, 80.

85. Hurston, *Moses, Man of the Mountain*, 75.

86. Hurston, *Moses, Man of the Mountain*, 105.

87. Hurston, *Moses, Man of the Mountain*, 121.

88. Hurston, *Moses, Man of the Mountain*, 123.

89. Hurston, *Moses, Man of the Mountain*, 112.

90. Hurston, *Moses, Man of the Mountain*, 127.

91. Zora Neale Hurston, "Conversions and Visions," in *Folklore, Memoires, and Other Writings* (New York: Library of America, 1995), 846–849, 846.

92. Hurston, "Conversions and Visions," 848.

93. Hurston, "Conversions and Visions," 848.

94. Hurston, "Conversions and Visions," 837.

95. Exodus 3:14 (King James Version).

96. Louis Althusser, "Ideological State Apparatus," in *Lenin and Philosophy and Other Essays*, trans. Ben Brewster (New York: Monthly Review Press, 1971), 127–186, 179.

97. Joseph Rebello, "The Economy of Joyful Passions: A Political Economic Ethics of the Virtual," *Rethinking Marxism* 18.2 (April 2006): 261.

98. Hurston, *Moses, Man of the Mountain*, 129.

99. Hurston, *Moses, Man of the Mountain*, 130.

100. Hurston, *Moses, Man of the Mountain*, 89.

101. Hurston, *Moses, Man of the Mountain*, 127.

102. Nietzsche, *The Anti-Christ*, 40.

103. Hurston, *Moses, Man of the Mountain*, 137.

104. Hurston, *Moses, Man of the Mountain*, 133.

105. Hurston, *Moses, Man of the Mountain*, 138.

106. Hurston, *Moses, Man of the Mountain*, 138.

107. Spinoza, *Ethics,* pt. III, prop. 50, Scholia: "Anything whatever can be, accidentally, a cause of hope or fear."

108. I find several examples of this in Hurston's novel, like when the Hebrews protested to Pharaoh and "some rolled over and over in a wallow of hope and scratched their backs with wishes. These men were afraid to think." Hurston, *Moses, Man of the Mountain*, 19. But passivity does not always mean paralysis in the novel, like when Moses, still Egypt's general, felt he could not die before reading the Book of Thoth and became "reckless in his daring. The huge hope of audacity spurred him . . . and [he] won because his men had come to believe that he could not fail, so they fought like fiends from hell." Hurston, *Moses, Man of the Mountain*, 58. But even in this second example, the audacity of hope leads to the belief that a single leader is all-powerful, and paradoxically, the soldiers must throw their own less powerful bodies into harm's way so the all-powerful attains more power.

109. In Spinoza's psychology, "emotion towards a thing which we know not to exist in the present, and which we imagine to be possible" garners greater emotion than a "contingent thing." Spinoza, *Ethics*, part IV, prop. 12.

110. Hurston, *Moses, Man of the Mountain*, 139.

111. Yahya M. Madra, "Questions of Communism: Ethics, Ontology, Subjectivity," *Rethinking Marxism: A Journal of Economics, Culture and Society* 18.2 (2006): 205–224, 217, 218.

112. Hurston, *Moses, Man of the Mountain*, 144.

113. Hurston, *Moses, Man of the Mountain*, 147.

114. Hurston, *Moses, Man of the Mountain*, 145, 146.

115. Erica Edwards, *Charisma and the Fictions of Black Leadership* (Minneapolis: University of Minnesota Press, 2012), 89.

116. Edwards, *Charisma*, 96.

117. Edwards, *Charisma*, 11.

118. Hurston, *Moses, Man of the Mountain*, 262.

119. Hurston, *Moses, Man of the Mountain*, 263.

120. Hurston, *Moses, Man of the Mountain*, 244.

121. Carl Schmitt, *Political Theology: Four Chapters on the Concept of Sovereignty*, trans. George Schwab (Chicago: University of Chicago Press, 2005), 36.

122. Thompson, "Blood Sacrifice," 398.

123. Spinoza, *Theological-Political Treatise*, 446.

124. Spinoza, *Theological-Political Treatise*, 450.

125. Hurston, *Moses, Man of the Mountain*, 59.

126. Hurston, *Moses, Man of the Mountain*, 252.

127. Hurston, *Moses, Man of the Mountain*, 274, emphasis added.

5. THE NEW DAY: NOTES ON EDUCATION AND THE DARK PROLETARIAT

1. W. E. B. Du Bois, *Souls of Black Folk* in *Writings* (New York: Modern Library Classics, 1996), 541; Zora Neale Hurston, "Spirituals and Neo-spirituals," in *Folklore, Memoirs, and Other Writings* (New York: Library of America, 1995), 872.

2. Gerald Bruns, *On the Anarchy of Poetry and Philosophy: A Guide for the Unruly* (New York: Fordham University Press, 2007), 79–80.

3. Bruns, *On the Anarchy of Poetry and Philosophy*, 83.

4. Indeed, thinking of Felman's "Education and Crisis," who else but a professor in the academy would have the opportunity to take students from normality to trauma *and back again*, class after class? Far from a critique of academic freedom, this is actually a worry as to why that freedom gets secured by the return to normality and not as an opportunity to construct something that normality would treat only with contempt.

5. Langston Hughes, "Letter to the Academy," in *The Collected Works of Langston Hughes: The Poems: 1921–1940*, ed. Arnold Rampersad (Columbia: University of Missouri Press, 2001), 231–232.

6. Antonin Artaud, "Letter to the Chancellors of European Universities," *La Revolution Surrealiste* 3 (April 1925): 4.

7. Langston Hughes, "Advertisement for the Waldorf-Astoria," in *The Collected Works of Langston Hughes: The Poems: 1921–1940*, ed. Arnold Rampersad (Columbia: University of Missouri Press, 2001), 208–209, 139.

8. Warren Montag, "Martyrdom, Conversion, and the Imitation of the Affects: Spinoza and Marranismo" (unpublished manuscript, 2012, Microsoft Word file).

9. Langston Hughes, "Ph.D.," in *The Collected Works of Langston Hughes: The Poems: 1921–1940*, ed. Arnold Rampersad (Columbia: University of Missouri Press, 2001), 224.

10. Langston Hughes, "Good Morning Revolution," in *The Collected Works of Langston Hughes: The Poems: 1921–1940*, ed. Arnold Rampersad (Columbia: University of Missouri Press, 2001), 225.

11. Langston Hughes, "Goodbye Christ," in *The Collected Works of Langston Hughes: The Poems: 1921–1940*, ed. Arnold Rampersad (Columbia: University of Missouri Press, 2001), 228.

12. Langston Hughes, "Cowards from the Colleges," *The Collected Works of Langston Hughes*: Fight for Freedom *and Other Writings on Civil Rights*, ed. Christopher C. De Santis (Columbia: University of Missouri Press, 2001): 213–221, 216.

13. Hughes, "Cowards from the Colleges," 214.

14. Ashon Crawley, "Lonely Letters: Letters to Moth, II" *artseverywhere*, https://artseverywhere.ca/roundtables/lonely-letters/, accessed August 7, 2018.

15. Hughes, "Cowards from the Colleges," 216–217.

16. See the brilliant work *On Being Included: Racism and Diversity in Institutional Life*. In it, Sara Ahmed makes the following point based on interviews with several diversity workers: "The institution can be experienced by practitioners *as* resistance. One expression that came up in a number of my interviews was 'banging your head against a brick wall.' Indeed, this experience of the brick wall was often described as an intrinsic part of diversity work. . . . The official desire to institutionalize diversity does not mean the institution is opened up; indeed, the wall might become all the more apparent, all the more a sign of immobility, the more the institution presents itself as being opened up." Sara Ahmed, *On Being Included: Racism and Diversity in Institutional Life* (Durham, N.C.: Duke University Press, 2012), 26.

17. Hughes, "Letter to the Academy," 232.

18. Hughes, "Cowards from the Colleges," 220–221.

19. Hannah Arendt, "Crisis in Education," in *Between Past and Future*, ed. Jerome Kohn (New York: Penguin, 2006), 170–193; 193.

20. Hannah Arendt, "Reflections on Little Rock," in *The Portable Hannah Arendt*, ed. Peter Baehr (New York: Penguin Books, 2003), 233.

21. Du Bois, *Souls of Black Folk*, 359.

22. Arendt, "Reflections on Little Rock," 235.

23. Arendt, "Reflections on Little Rock," 246.

24. Arendt, "Reflections on Little Rock," 235.

25. Arendt, "Reflections on Little Rock," 236.

26. "The moment social discrimination is legally enforced it becomes persecution. . . . The moment social discrimination is legally abolished, the freedom of society is violated." Arendt, "Reflections on Little Rock," 240.

27. Kathryn Gines, "Hannah Arendt, Liberalism, and Racism: Controversies Concerning Violence, Segregation, and Education," *The Southern Journal of Philosophy* 67 (2009): 53–76, emphasis added.

28. Arendt, "Reflections on Little Rock," 237.

29. Arendt, "Reflections on Little Rock," 234.

30. Arendt, "Reflections on Little Rock," 242.

31. Arendt, "Reflections on Little Rock," 243.

32. Arendt, "Reflections on Little Rock," 244.

33. In an interview with Robert Penn Warren, Ralph Ellison says Arendt

has absolutely no conception of what goes on in the minds of Negro parents when they send their kids through those lines of hostile people [to school]. Yet they are aware of the overtones of a rite of initiation . . . of the terrors of social life. . . . And in the outlook of many of these parents (who wish that the problem didn't exist), the child is expected to face the terror and contain his fear and anger *precisely* because he is a Negro American. Thus, he is required to master the inner tensions created by his racial situation, and if he gets hurt—then his is one more sacrifice. It is a harsh requirement, but if he fails the basic test, his life will be even harsher.

Robert Penn Warren, "Leadership from the Periphery," in *Who Speaks for the Negro* (New Haven, Conn.: Yale University Press, 2014), 344. After reading this interview, Arendt writes a letter to Ellison, explaining that her experiences as a Jewish schoolgirl made her aware of these issues. Her private gesture of sympathy, rather than an engagement with Ellison's *thought*, recalls a pattern of triangulation among newcomers entering mainstream American life. They hope to join the mainstream by critiquing black culture, though they expect some recognition (and not criticism) from black people because they, too, have suffered under white supremacy. See Gines, "Arendt, Liberalism, and Racism," 67.

34. W. E. B. Du Bois, *Black Reconstruction in America, 1860–1880* (New York: Free Press, 1998), 123.

35. Du Bois, *Black Reconstruction*, 123.

36. Du Bois, *Souls of Black Folk*, 494–495.

37. Bruns, *On the Anarchy of Poetry and Philosophy*, 222n16.

38. Katherine Dunham, "Form and Function in Primitive Dance," in *Kaiso!: Writings by and about Katherine Dunham*, ed. VèVè A. Clark and Sara E. Johnson (Madison: University of Wisconsin Press, 2005), 505.

39. Booker T. Washington, "Booker T. Washington Delivers the 1895 Atlanta Compromise Speech," in *The Booker T. Washington Papers*, ed. Louis R. Harlan, vol. 3 (Urbana: University of Illinois Press, 1974), 584.

40. Katherine Dunham, "Notes on the Dance," in *Kaiso!: Writings by and about Katherine Dunham*, ed. VèVè A. Clark and Sara E. Johnson (Madison: University of Wisconsin Press, 2005), 516.

41. Du Bois, *Black Reconstruction*, 645.

42. Du Bois, *Black Reconstruction*, 658.

43. Du Bois, *Black Reconstruction*, 637.

44. Bruns, *On the Anarchy of Poetry and Philosophy*, 40.

45. Gwen Mazer, "Katherine Dunham," in *Kaiso: Writings by and about Katherine Dunham*, ed. VèVè A. Clark and Sara E. Johnson (Madison: University of Wisconsin Press, 2005), 419–426, 424. On the theme of commemoration, also see Vincent Brown, "Social Death and Political Life in the Study of Slavery," *American Historical Review* 114.5 (December 2009): 1231–1249.

46. Du Bois, *Black Reconstruction*, 667.

47. Stefano Harney and Fred Moten, "The General Antagonism," in *The Undercommons: Fugitive Planning and Black Study* (New York: Minor Compositions, 2013), 100–159, 134. Harney and Moten build on a longstanding refrain in

black thought. It may be productive to think about the alternate path by which European phenomenology has recently examined call-and-response. See Jean-Louis-Chretien, *The Call and the Response*, trans. Anne A. Davenport (New York: Fordham University Press, 2004), 5.

48. Jack Halberstam, "The Wild Beyond" in *The Undercommons: Fugitive Planning and Black Study* (New York: Minor Compositions, 2013), 5–12, 7.

49. What Arendt labels the desire for acceptance/humiliation is actually Eckford claiming "the right to refuse what has been refused to" her. See Halberstam, "The Wild Beyond," 8.

50. Hughes, "Letter to the Academy," 232.

51. Hughes, "Letter to the Academy," 232. The most influential engagement with "the flesh" in black studies is Hortense Spillers, "Mama's Baby, Papa's Maybe: An American Grammar Book," *Diacritics* 17.2 (Summer 1987): 64–81.

52. Hughes, "Dear Lovely Death," in *The Collected Works of Langston Hughes: The Poems: 1921–1940*, ed. Arnold Rampersad (Columbia: University of Missouri Press, 2001), 121.

53. In addition to Hughes, see Achille Mbembe, "And power is what was able to escape death and return from among the dead. For it is only in escaping death and returning from the dead that one acquires to make oneself into the other side of the absolute." Achille Mbembe, *Critique of Black Reason* (Durham, N.C.: Duke University Press, 2017), 133.

54. Langston Hughes, "Demand," in *The Collected Works of Langston Hughes: The Poems: 1921–1940*, ed. Arnold Rampersad (Columbia: University of Missouri Press, 2001), 123.

55. Langston Hughes, "Call to Creation," in *The Collected Works of Langston Hughes: The Poems: 1921–1940*, ed. Arnold Rampersad (Columbia: University of Missouri Press, 2001), 203–204.

56. Hughes, "Ph.D.," 224.

57. Hughes, "Call to Creation," 204.

58. Hughes, "Call to Creation," 203.

59. Hughes, "Letter to the Academy," 232.

60. Bruns, *On the Anarchy of Poetry and Philosophy*, 80.

61. Du Bois, *Black Reconstruction*, 122.

62. Richard Wright, "Blueprint for Negro Literature," in *Amistad 2: Writings on Black History and Culture*, ed. John Williams and Charles Harris (New York: Random House, 1971), 17.

63. W. E. B. Du Bois, *John Brown* (New York: Modern Library Classics, 2001), 51.

64. Harney and Moten, *The Undercommons*, 27.

65. Du Bois, *Black Reconstruction*, 705–706.

66. Karl Marx, *Grundrisse: Foundations of the Critique of Political Economy*, trans. Martin Nicolaus (New York: Vintage Press, 1973), 487.

67. Du Bois, *Black Reconstruction*, 667, emphasis added.

CONCLUSION: FROM BEING TO UNREST, FROM OBJECTIVITY TO MOTION—A RACE FOR THEORY

1. Alexander Weheliye's recent work offers a powerful instance of this critique by noting how Agamben's commitment to a theory of bare life inherently tied to jurisprudence mistranslates Walter Benjamin and the testimony of so-called *muselmanner*, among other things. My larger point is that Agamben produces the sort of "fixed" theory that Christian critiques. Meanwhile, Weheliye employs a black feminist perspective in order to read more effectively the same European textual archive as Agamben. I have tried to go further in this direction by noting how Agamben's antiquarianism yields his greatest epiphanies while, somehow, never leading to a more comprehensive analysis of colonialism, slavery, or racial difference. Trauma theory has also faltered in capturing this unrest which, during the Holocaust, involved escapes, sabotage, hunger strikes, and outright rebellions in the camps. If this is how today's dedication to European Man elides forms of life *within* Europe, then I find little gain in exporting this figure to other fields yet again. See Alexander Weheliye, *Habeas Viscus: Racializing Assemblages, Biopolitics, and Black Feminist Theories of the Human* (Durham, N.C.: Duke University Press, 2014). Also see James Edward Ford, "On Black Study and Political Theology," *Cultural Critique* 100 (March 2018).

2. Barbara Christian, "The Race for Theory," *Cultural Critique* 6 (Spring 1987): 51–63, 52.

3. Christian, "Race for Theory," 51–63, 52.

4. Christian, "Race for Theory," 52.

5. Christian, "Race for Theory," 62.

6. Christian, "Race for Theory," 62.

7. Christian, "Race for Theory," 52.

8. Hortense Spillers, "The Idea of Black Culture," *The New Centennial Review* 6.3 (Winter 2006): 7–28, 15.

9. Hortense Spillers, "The Crisis of the Negro Intellectual: A Post-Date," *Boundary 2* 21.3 (Autumn 1994): 100.

10. Cedric Robinson, *Black Marxism: The Making of the Black Radical Tradition* (Chapel Hill: University of North Carolina Press, 2000), 73.

11. Hortense Spillers, "Long Time: Last Daughters and the New 'New South,'" *Boundary 2* 36.1 (Spring 2009): 149–182, 171.

INDEX

1927 Mississippi River Flood, 35–73, 221

Aaron (character in Hurston, *Moses*), 236, 237, 239, 242
abandonment, politics of, 31, 36, 78, 79, 249
abolished time, 96, 112
abolition, 6–7, 11–13, 75, 77, 79–80, 112–120, 137
academic labor, 33, 250–251
academic laborers, 246, 248, 272, 280
accommodationism, 216, 218
accountability, 254–255, 261
acquiescence, 228, 231, 265
actual death, 37, 71–72, 85–86, 155
"Advertisement for the Waldorf-Astoria" (Hughes), 249
Aesop, 76
affect, 18–19, 98, 209, 214, 215, 263. *See also* imitation of affects
affective regimes, 69, 103, 216–217; challenging, 31, 68, 202, 212, 228, 237, 242
affirmation of life, 212–213, 271
African diaspora, 138, 162
Agamben, Giorgio, 3, 10–13, 164, 172–173, 186, 187, 293, 309n49, 332n1
Ahmed, Sara, 329n16

Althusser, Louis, 230–231
"Always the Same" (Hughes), 26
American Crisis Biographies, 128
American Red Cross, 41, 52, 60, 69
American Revolution, 76, 165
American War of Independence, 176
Amram (fictional character in Hurston's *Moses*), 210–212, 215
analogies, 10–11
anamorphosis, 223, 300n5
anarchism, 77, 319n91
ancestors, commemorations to, 275
Andrews, Sidney, 182
"Ante-Bellum Sermon, An" (Dunbar), 198
anthropology, 202
Aragon, Louis, 299n5
archives. *See* records
Arendt, Hannah, 10, 256–265, 274, 275, 278, 288, 329n33, 331n49
Aristotle, 245, 249, 250, 256, 264, 267
Arkansas race riot, 113–115
Arkansas Race Riot, The (Wells), 80, 101, 113–115
armed prophet, 225, 235
Artaud, Antonin, 248–249
articulation, 15, 136
asceticism, 253

asserted spirit of slavery, 93–98, 108, 120
assimilation, 87
asymmetry, 83, 203
"Atlanta Compromise" speech
  (Washington), 216–221
authentic upheaval, 24, 132
autocolonization, 23–24
autonomy, 18, 26

Bacchae of Euripides, The (Soyinka), 244
Baldwin, James, 199
Balibar, Etienne, 23, 25, 83
Banquo's ghost (fictional character in
  Shakespeare's *Macbeth*), 88, 91, 95, 111
barbarism, 72, 104, 165, 168, 258, 311n12
bare life, 10, 11–12, 41, 118, 208
Barnett, Ferdinand, 90
Barrett, Lindon, 89–90
Bassett, Chauncey J., 178
Bataille, Georges, 156
Batiste, Stephanie Leigh, 25
"Battle Hymn of the Republic, The,"
  123–126, 129, 137, 142, 143, 174, 186–187
Bay, Mia, 76, 310n3
beautiful soul, 80–84, 87, 90–91, 98,
  99, 105–112
beauty, 91–92, 249, 282–283
becoming, 80, 115–116, 120–121, 136,
  148–150, 152, 191, 274, 284, 286, 289
becoming-minoritarian, 116
being completely with another, 268, 274
being present, 268
being to unrest, objectivity to motion,
  4, 8–9, 28, 72, 164–165, 293
being unwanted, 262–263, 277
Benjamin, Walter: divine violence, 124,
  125, 136; general strike, 144–145, 153,
  156, 158–159; great criminal, 131–132;
  lawmaking violence, 140; mythic
  violence, 69, 125. *See also* "Critique
  of Violence, A" (Benjamin)

Bethel A.M.E. Church, Chicago, 89
Bible, 200, 203–206, 222–223
biography, 128, 129
biological life, 173
birth and labor/nationhood, 41, 108,
  172–173, 207, 208
Birth of the Clinic, The (Foucault), 60
black(s), black people: barbarism,
  72, 165, 168; beautiful soul and,
  83–85, 87; chosenness, 217; in
  European theory, 24; inner
  development, 129, 168, 185; naturally
  inferior, 322n159; sick body, 24–25;
  threat of, 50
black activity, 84, 106, 108, 113, 180
black agency, 126–130, 171, 194
black bodies: capacity, 110; control of,
  117; convict leasing and, 108; loss of,
  180–181; multiplicity, 271–272; New
  Day and, 270; pathology, 253;
  slavery and, 139; social devaluation,
  102; violence against, 44
Black Boy (Wright), 36
black collective, 70–71, 127, 147
black culture, 116, 136, 292; exodus and,
  155; learning, 267; minor position,
  116; nationhood, 195; pathology,
  24; patronage structures, 296–297;
  persistence, 87; poetry, 276; responses
  to suffering, 24; second-sight, 136;
  state and, 79; theology, 189; theory
  and, 292; writing, 28
black diaspora, 203, 204, 297
black females, 53, 63, 64, 109, 111, 178
black insurgency, 168, 174
black intellectuals, 55, 66, 72, 219, 253
black labor, 72, 110, 174
black laborers. *See* black workers
black life: antagonisms with whiteness,
  173; anticipatory nature, 300n5;
  conatus, 1; devaluing, 97; dissonant

character, 34, 258; ecstasy, 191, 246; education, 271–272, 288; frenzy, 267; illusions of political messiah, 195; joining, 24; misreadings, 72; obstacles, 133; persistence outside Western progress, 269; presumptions about, 13, 176, 177; productivity, 172; romance, 170, 175; self-governance, 172; self-organization, 79; slavery's end and, 97; surplus, 4, 45; survival, 71, 296–297; threat of, 314n57; understanding, 283; vocation, 270; Western theology and, 148

black males, 53, 64

black movement, 122, 203

black phalanx, 142, 143

black radicalism, 1, 3–4, 17, 20, 24, 26, 70, 124–126, 147, 196–204, 285, 296

Black Reconstruction in America, 1860–1880 (Du Bois), 26, 32, 110, 123–192, 194, 221, 224, 235, 247, 266, 267, 275, 285

black soldiers in Civil War, 126, 174–180, 186–187

black thought, 20, 24, 26, 75–81, 124, 268, 331n47

black townships, 168, 172

black workers: barbarism, 311n12; captive, 60, 63, 69, 109–112, 117, 119; convict leasing and, 116; critical intelligence, 31; disposability, 63, 64–65; drive for citizenship, 42; European class system and, 87; free, 26, 97, 140–141, 171; general strike, 161; interchangeability, 63; labor for emancipation, 114; liberal state and, 78–79, 98, 311n12; mythic violence and, 47; NAACP and, 167–168; plantation owners and,

59–60, 139; post-Reconstruction, 84; productivity, 110, 173, 216; progress prized over justice for, 115; race riots, 114–115; resentment against, 110; self-defense, 104; sharecropping, 63–64; state and, 311n12; *vogelfrei*, 41; Washington and, 216–221, 270; white supremacy and, 110; white workers and, 181–182, 183

black writing, 2–3, 24–28, 244–245, 265, 278, 292, 294–295, 304n83

blackness, 30, 75, 80, 113, 120, 121, 124, 150, 174; ahistorical being, 269; attempt to reduce, 314n57; barbarism, 258; collective power, 127; *conatus*, 297; conventional progress and, 269; fears about, 84; frenzy, 188; genres and, 163, 289; humanity in a "minor" key, 75, 121, 124; its own adequate cause, 192; modernism and, 30; multiplicity, 271, 272; nonvalue, 2, 3; ontological totality and, 80, 113, 119; pathology, 25, 26, 134; persistence, 26, 297; suffering, 2–3; traumatic wounding and, 297; Western gender scripts and, 235; Western imperialism and, 174; Western theology and, 148, 245; West's concepts of, 2, 3, 84, 174, 235, 258, 269

blamelessness, 70, 214

Blanchot, Maurice, 53, 188

Bleeding Kansas, 138, 140

bloodshed, 91, 105, 128, 174–175

"Blueprint for Negro Literature" (Wright), 27, 44, 66

blues, 164

body, 20, 209–10, 249, 280. *See also* black bodies

bodily practices, 218

bounty hunters, 140, 141
Bradley, Rizvana, 110
Brawley, Benjamin, 197
Brent, Linda. *See* Jacobs, Harriet
    (pseud. Linda Brent)
Brother Mann (fictional character in
    Wright's "Down by the Riverside"),
    36, 38–40, 43–52, 54, 60–66, 71–72,
    156, 235, 242
Brown, John, 125–133, 136–138, 141–145,
    152–155, 160, 168, 175, 180–181, 185–187,
    235, 305n86
Brown, Major (faculty representative),
    254
Bruns, Gerald, 30, 187–188, 245–246,
    250, 267, 268, 274
Buchanan, Buck, 117, 118, 119
Burrows, Trigant, 36

Cable, George Washington, 107
CAC (Colored Advisory Commission),
    55, 56–59, 66
caesura, 126, 157–162
Caleb (fictional character in Hurston's
    Moses), 210–211
call-and-response, 276–277, 330n47
call from black and unknown bards,
    275–276, 278, 280, 281, 289
call to creation, 283
"Call to Creation" (Hughes), 282
call to preach, 229–230, 231, 232
Campbell, T. M., 57–58
camps, 72, 164–165, 168, 172–173,
    206–208, 309n49. *See also* convict
    camps; relief camps (1927 flood);
    Union: camps
Capital (Marx), 3–10
capitalism, 5–6, 8, 92–93, 139–140, 157,
    174, 249, 251, 271–272; emancipation
    and, 97, 108, 164, 168
Carnegie, Andrew, 216, 221

Caruth, Cathy, 213, 214, 215, 293, 303n52.
    See also *Unclaimed Experiences*
    (Caruth)
categorical imperative, 2, 144
causality, 214, 217, 218, 325n54
ceremonies, 233–234
Césaire, Aimé, 20–24, 25
chain gangs, 109, 111
chance as primary rhythm of
    temporality, 160–161
change, 55, 93, 95, 113, 210, 213,
    265, 281
charismatic leaders, 32, 75, 102–103,
    124, 132, 142, 169, 194–195, 203,
    221–243, 327n108
Chase-Riboud, Barbara, 244
Chesnutt, Charles, 221
Chicago, 88–89
Chicago Defender, 55, 59, 60, 63, 66,
    68–69, 72
Chicago Herald, 102, 103–104
children, 258, 260–262, 276, 329n33
chivalry, 99, 100, 262
chosenness, 32, 195, 199, 206, 213–221,
    232, 283
Christian, Barbara, 292–297
Christian idealism, 200, 201
Christianity, 44, 130, 142, 200–201, 222,
    229, 252
church, 126–127, 188–189
citizen-refugees, 35–73
citizens, 35–36, 81
citizenship, 36, 38, 39–41, 81; black, 42,
    54–55, 95, 175, 177, 181–182
City Beautiful movement, 91
civil war, 10, 11
Civil War (US), 11–12, 96, 126, 127,
    157–158, 161, 165–174, 177; aftermath,
    82, 83, 97; black involvement, 158,
    180, 191, 320n91
civilization, 104, 165, 181–182

claimed experiences, 16, 17
clandestine schools, 269–270, 275
class legislation, 90
Coal Creek rebellion, 80, 116–120
collective consciousness, 31, 33–34
collective power, 78–79, 127, 144, 194, 277
collectivity, 70–71, 129, 133, 295
colleges/universities, 246, 249, 252–255, 286, 288
Collins, Ann V., 114
colonial gaze, 92
colonialism, 18, 257, 291
colonization, 18, 21–24
color problem. *See* race problem
Colored Advisory Commission (CAC), 55, 56–59, 66
Coming of the Lord, 32, 96, 124–128, 157–192, 245
commemorations to ancestors, 275
commodities, 7–8, 10
common world, 256, 257
community, 143, 147, 156, 161; black, 71–73, 142, 177, 203
compromise, 25, 55, 135, 140–141, 216–221
conatus, 1, 297
conceptual translation, 124–126
Confederacy, 12, 41–42, 158, 161, 170, 177–179, 182–183, 217–219, 260
Confiscation Acts of 1861, 179
connectivity, black, 67
consciousness, 8, 16, 17, 62, 209–210. *See also* collective consciousness
conservatism, 113, 126
Constitution, 165, 262, 264
consumption, 5, 105, 110
contingency, 38, 48, 164, 203–204, 234
"Contre-Chant" (Aragon), 299n5
conversion, 229–230
"Conversions and Visions" (Hurston), 229–230

convict camps, 108–111
convict labor, 107, 117
convict leasing, 80, 106–112, 116–120
Coolidge, Calvin, 60
cooperative antagonism, 297
counterrevolutions, 95–96, 99, 176, 221, 271, 286
"Cowards from the Colleges" (Hughes), 253, 255
creation, call to, 283
crimes: being black, 84; Brown's, 132; capitalism's, 227; civic authorities', 259; of the enslaved, 132, 144; Eurocentric position, 22–23; parrhesiastes', 81; poor people's, 47, 50, 51; selective judgment of, 100, 114
crisis, 1–2, 11, 13–17, 20, 24
"Crisis in Education" (Arendt), 256, 260
Crisis magazine, 59, 60, 167, 253
crisis notebooks, 33
"Crisis of European Humanity and Philosophy, The" (Husserl), 17–20, 22, 23, 25, 303n52
"Criteria for Negro Art" (Du Bois), 175, 278
critical consciousness, 7–8, 34
critical narrative, 3, 28–34
critics, professional, 292–295
"Critique of Violence, A" (Benjamin), 43, 45–46, 144–145, 158–159
cruelty, 80–81, 120
Crusade for Justice (Wells), 31, 74–122
Cruse, Harold, 26
cry, 73, 209, 217
cultural patterns, 229–230
cultural-political gatekeeping, 296–297
culture workers, 137

damnation, 130, 132, 133, 136
damned, 130–144, 148, 287

dark proletariat, 24–28, 30–34;
   alternate subjectivity, 3; anarchist
   tendency, 147; Brown's place in,
   125–126, 129, 132, 136; charismatic
   leader and, 194–195, 216, 238, 243;
   ecstasy, 187–188; education,
   244–289; Emancipation and, 189,
   191–192; ethics, 137, 157; Event, 37;
   force, 32, 124; group-centered
   leadership, 159, 169, 238; minor
   position, 121; poetic community,
   246; politics in general strike and
   Civil War, 158–192; revolution, 157;
   state and, 135; transformation in,
   157; trauma and, 28; West and, 202
Darkening Mirrors (Batiste), 25
darkness, 48, 64, 65, 130, 207
Darwin, Charles, 143
Davis, Angela, 110
Davis Bend, Mississippi, 172, 173, 175
dead labor, 42, 307n20
Dear Lovely Death (Hughes), 279, 281
"Dear Lovely Death" (Hughes), 26, 281
death, 281–282, 283; absolute and,
   331n53; overcoming fear of, 37,
   71–72, 155; as passage, 72
death-bound subjectivity, 37, 45
decadence, 205, 232, 233, 238, 249
decent order, 250–251, 252, 283
decisions: crisis and, 14; to die, 71–72;
   free, 231; informed by passive
   thinking, 49–52; political, 3;
   sovereign, 10, 11, 12, 186, 187; space of,
   38; in undecidable moments, 1, 48
decomposition, 21, 25, 140, 164
"defeat of the flesh and the triumph of
   the spirit," 247–256, 257, 265, 271,
   272, 279
degenerate aristocrat, 221
degradation, 118, 128–131, 133, 136,
   156–157, 164, 285, 308n26

Deleuze, Gilles, 116, 306n10
"Demand" (Hughes), 26, 281–282
democracy, 67, 195, 256, 262, 266
Denning, Michael, 25
denunciation: of life, 238; of multitude,
   205, 206
departure, 40, 41, 43, 65, 155, 237
Derrida, Jacques, 81
desegregation in public schools,
   256–266
detour, politics of, 21, 43
dictators, 11–12, 240
difference, 49, 188, 285, 291, 297
dignity, 254, 255, 270
disavowals: black humanity, 98;
   Confederacy's, 178; critical
   consciousness, 8; dark proletariat's
   agency, 137; freedperson's activity,
   98; between "John Brown's Body"
   and "The Battle Hymn of the
   Republic," 145; historical
   conditions, 257, 259–260; multitude
   and, 87; slave agency, 6–7; in
   truth-telling, 81; white crimes, 106
discipline: educational, 269, 252–255;
   in Pauline scripture, 249, 252
Discourse on Colonialism (Césaire),
   20–24, 25
Discourses Concerning Government
   (Sidney), 74, 76
discrimination, 257, 260, 261, 264, 265,
   274, 278, 285
disengagement, 245–246, 249–250,
   252–253, 256–257, 265, 267, 278,
   280–281
disidentification, 212–213
disposability of black people, 63,
   64–65, 72
dispossession, 58–59, 146
dissemblance, 119
diversity, 265, 272, 275, 276

diversity work, 329n16

divine violence, 46, 48, 123–192, 235, 245

docile dignity, 254, 255, 256, 265, 280, 287

docility, 72, 254

domestic realism, 38–39

domestic space, 150

domination, 21, 199, 232, 253

Douglass, Frederick, 3, 6–9, 46, 90, 93–96, 113, 128, 137, 158, 177. See also *Reason Why the Colored American Is Not Part of the World's Columbian Exposition of 1893, The* (Wells et al.)

"Down by the Riverside" (Wright), 31, 35–73, 85–86, 207, 208, 221, 235, 242

"dream of utter aliveness," 282, 286

Du Bois, W. E. B., 31–32, 123–192, 295, 319n91; black workers, 26; Civil War's aftermath, 80; "Criteria for Negro Art," 175, 278; economic exploitation, 43; equality, 285; free indirect style, 32; human purposes, 115, 284; on Lincoln, 13; Negro Spirituals, 245; New Day, 247, 266–278, 280, 284, 286–287, 288; plantation owners, 110, 221; "problem of the color line," 258; protest and construction, 27; relief project (1927 flood), 55, 66; "Sociology Hesitant," 160; "The Souls of White Folk," 299n5; transubstantiation, 224. See also *Black Reconstruction in America, 1860–1880* (Du Bois); "Founding the Public School" (Du Bois); *John Brown* (Du Bois); *Souls of Black Folk* (Du Bois)

Dunbar, Paul Laurence, 198

Dunham, Katherine, 247, 268, 271–272, 275, 284

Dunning School of Reconstruction, 165

Dust Tracks on a Road (Hurston), 200

Duster, Alfreda, 121–122

Dvorak, Antonin, 116

East St. Louis affair, 102–104, 314n62

East St. Louis Massacre, The (Wells), 80, 101, 102

Eaton, John, 168–174, 183

ecclesiastical authority, 223

Eckford, Elizabeth, 262, 277–278, 331n49

ecstasy, 33, 244–247, 253, 265, 267, 272, 274, 275, 288; black life, 191, 246; dark proletariat, 187–188; Emancipation, 186–188, 268, 270; freedpersons, 148

ecstasy-belonging of sovereign, 186

ecstatic overwriting of society, 164, 165, 185–192

education, 14–15, 20, 33, 244–289

educational decline narratives, 32–33, 247, 252–253

Edwards, Brent, 26

Edwards, Erica, 223, 238

election, 245, 283

Ellison, Ralph, 17, 197, 329n33

Elysium, 123, 125, 186, 187, 189

emancipation, 11–13, 26, 30, 97, 108, 164, 168, 174–175. *See also* Emancipation (South); labor for emancipation

Emancipation (South), 32, 126, 147; black agency, 127–128, 190; complications, 181–182; Confederacy and, 41–42; as confrontation with God, 267; Dunning School, 165; ecstasy, 186, 268, 270; Europe, 202; liberalism, 113–115, 174–175; mass education, 266; messianism, 32; montage and, 162–192; new song, 191–192; nonevent, 180, 182, 184, 186; revolutionary meaning, 189; violence leading to, 174–175, 186–187

Emancipation Proclamation (Lincoln), 3, 12, 13, 179

embodiment, 49, 272

emotions, 227

Engels, Friedrich, 145, 319n91
enjoyment: loss of power, 252; as
  political factor, 94, 95, 96; privileges,
  96; punishment, 150, 215–216; racist,
  105, 111–112, 314n62; white supremacy,
  103
epistemology, 115, 214, 215
equality, 50, 104, 181–183, 274; in
  education, 257, 259, 260, 262, 264,
  265, 285. *See also* social equality
Equiano, Olaudah, 110
escape, 71, 145, 148–156, 188, 189
eschatology, 148
Esposito, Roberto, 29, 306n10
ethical demands, 16
ethical relationality, 15–16, 62, 191
ethics, 56, 133, 137, 143, 157
Ethics (Spinoza), 225, 227
Eurocentrism, 3–4, 18, 23–25
Europe, 17–24, 202, 257, 291, 292, 297
European Man, 2, 13, 17–24, 42, 53,
  291, 332n1
Europeanization, 18, 19, 21–22, 25
Event, 31, 33, 37, 71–73, 180, 211
Every Tub Must Sit on Its Own Bottom
  (Plant), 200, 201, 222
"Everytime a Knot Is Undone, a God Is
  Released" (Chase-Riboud), 244
exception, 13, 236, 240, 242. *See also*
  state of exception
exchange-value, 7, 42, 50
exclusivity, 257, 261, 264, 265, 275
exile, 86, 205. *See also* exile to exodus
exile to exodus, 79, 81–88, 147
exodus, 86, 245; from Egypt, 205, 235,
  238; Eurocentric narratives of,
  155–56, 177, 199; from Memphis,
  86–87, 88; Underground Railroad,
  153; from United States, 141, 155;
  Western narratives of, 197–198, 235.
  See also exile to exodus

expenditure, 126, 144, 147, 152, 156,
  176, 191
experimentation, 30, 163, 288–289
exploitation, 4, 7, 23, 43, 56, 58, 72,
  107–108, 248

false burial, 98, 105, 128
Fanon, Frantz, 20, 29, 46, 50, 133, 162
fantasy, 30, 89–91, 194, 238
fascination, 267–268, 274, 284
Fayette (preacher who visited Brown),
  141, 305n86
fear, 50, 71–72, 84, 234, 235, 240, 241, 242
federal government. *See* US
  government
Felman, Shoshana, 293, 302n52, 328n4.
  See also *Testimony* (Felman and
  Laub)
females, black, 53, 63, 64, 109, 111, 178
feminine logic of "non-all," 236, 240
Ferguson, Roderick, 56, 219
feudal production, 108, 110, 111
fight of affliction, 151–52, 171, 183–184,
  237, 281
Fleming, J. L., 81
flesh, 281; spirit and, 247–256, 257, 265,
  271, 272, 279–289
flight, 71, 188, 189. *See also* escape
Flint, Dr. (in Jacobs's *Incidents in the
  Life of a Slave Girl*), 110–111
Flood, 1927 Mississippi River, 35–73, 221
Foley, Barbara, 25
footnotes, slaves in, 4, 9
force, 1; absolute, 234; active, 49; affect,
  18–19; black collectives', 70–71, 127,
  147; black freedom, 13; causing
  unrest that leads to thinking,
  137–138; dark proletariat's, 32, 124;
  defense and, 74, 78; external, 223,
  228, 234; of life, 54; multitude's,
  124; passive, 49, 66, 73; passive

emotions, 227; private man's, 74, 78; revolutionary, 166; state and, 40; students and, 250. *See also* divine violence; mythic violence; power

Foucault, Michel, 60, 81, 86

"Founding the Public School" (Du Bois), 247, 266, 275–276, 286–287

Four Fundamental Concepts of Psycho-analysis, The (Lacan), 15–16

fragments, 33, 34

Frankfurt School, 295

Franklin, Benjamin, 76

Franklin, John Hope, 121

free indirect discourse, 28–30, 32, 40, 44, 53, 66, 226–227

Free Soilers, 141

free speech, 79, 81, 82

free workers, 3–9

Freedmen's Bureau, 79, 311n12, 313n46

freedom, 26, 112, 115, 126, 128, 152, 189–191, 308n26, 328n4

freedpersons: Coming of the Lord, 127; drive for education, 266, 280, 284; ecstasy, 148; founding public schools, 33, 268, 274–275, 280; freed through own efforts, 13, 32, 114, 126, 178, 191; indebtedness, 42; joy, 189–190; mourning, 183, 185, 186; objectification, 95–98; overwriting of society, 163–192; racial discrimination against, 95–96; racial resentment against, 78; standards for, 150; Western theology and, 148. *See also* Emancipation: montage and

frenzy, 68, 70–72, 188–189, 203, 266–267, 269–270, 278–281

Freud, Sigmund, 15–16, 62, 67, 202, 213

fugitive discourse, 6–8, 20, 41

Fugitive Slave Law of 1850, 138, 140

fugitive slaves, 127, 145, 148–150, 154, 157, 168–170, 186–187

fugitivity, 188, 189

fusion, 156

futurity, 38, 42, 96, 120, 121

Gadamer, Hans-Georg, 267

Garrison, William Lloyd, 8, 29, 76

Gates, Henry Louis, Jr., 28–29

gaze of the damned, 136, 137. *See also* vision of the damned

gender, 52, 155, 235

general strike, 124–127, 144–149, 153, 157–192, 319n91

generalization, 34

Genesis (book of), 283

gentrification, 288

German East Africa, 175

German idealism, 8

German intellectuals, 82–83

Giddings, Paula, 76

glory, 190, 284

Glymph, Thavolia, 179, 321n137

God, 137, 138, 160–161, 189, 223, 230, 267; in Hurston's *Moses*, 228–229, 231

"gods help those who help themselves," 74, 76, 78, 85, 89, 116, 121

"Good Morning Revolution" (Hughes), 251–252

"Goodbye Christ" (Hughes), 252

Gramsci, Antonio, 14, 34, 226

Grannie (fictional character in Wright's "Down by the Riverside"), 36, 61

Grant, Lincoln, and the Freedman (Eaton), 168–174, 183

Grant, Ulysses S., 173, 174

great criminal, 131–132

Great Depression, 3, 36, 72, 75, 79, 126

Great Hurricane of 1928, 196

Greek imaginary, 187, 188

Green, Shields, 152, 180–181

group fantasies, 90, 91

Guattari, Felix, 116
guilt: causality and, 325n54; chosenness, 214–15; damned, 131, 208; liberal subjects, 46, 186; metaphysical, 32, 245; mythic violence, 68, 69–70, 131, 194–195; sharecropping, indebtedness and, 38–43

Haitian Revolution, 129–130, 132
Halberstam, Jack, 277
Hall, Romulus, 151, 152
Harlem Renaissance, 196
Harney, Stefano, 276–277, 284, 288, 331n47
Harper, Frances E. W., 193
Harper's Chicago and the World's Fair (Ralph), 91–92
Harper's Ferry, raid at, 125, 144, 180–181, 198
Harrison, Benjamin, 90
Hartman, Saidiya, 41–42, 110, 146, 153
Harvey, David, 308n27
Hatch, Edward, 182
hatred, 19, 105, 219
Heartfield (fictional character in Wright's "Down by the Riverside"), 44, 49–50
Hebrews (characters in Hurston's *Moses*), 206–212, 215–216, 220, 226–229, 231–242
Hebrews (historical people), 205, 214. *See also* Israel (historical people)
Hebrews (letter to), 151
Hegel, G. W. F., 82–83, 96–97, 137–138, 321n138
hegemony, 34, 69, 132
Henson, Josiah, 154
"Hercules and the Waggoner" (Aesop), 76
Herod the Great (Hurston), 199
heterogeneity, 88, 115, 131, 237, 283, 309n64

hierarchies, 49, 270, 271, 276, 285, 294
hieroglyph, theorizing in the, 293–294
Higashida, Cheryl, 37, 71
Higginson, Thomas Wentworth, 145
Hill, John Henry, 149, 153, 270
Hill, Robert L., 114, 202
historically underrepresented literatures, 293–294
history, 13, 31, 222–223. *See also* records
Hitler, Adolf, 200
Holocaust, 332n1
homes, 260–261
Hoover, Herbert, 56, 59, 69
hope, 56–57, 59, 233–235, 327nn108–109
Hose, Sam, 101–102
hospitals, 60–63
Huffman, Ernest, 230, 231
Hughes, Langston, 26, 33, 133, 135, 136, 247–256, 271, 272, 278–286
human bodies, 271–272
human purposes, 115, 284
humanities, 247, 265, 293, 294
Hunter, David, 178
Hurd, Carlos F., 102
Hurricane Katrina, 35, 39, 43, 72
Hurston, Zora Neale, 32, 133, 193–243, 245, 324n20
Husserl, Edmund, 14, 17–20, 22, 23, 25, 303n52
hypermasculine logic of "all," 236

"I am what I am," 229, 230–231, 232, 233
"I Have Been to the Mountaintop" (King), 198
"I-you" positioning, 29–30
idealism, 8, 49, 77, 200, 201
identification with oppressor, 19, 208, 211–212, 215, 219
identity, 83, 98, 119, 149, 250, 252, 263
illumination, 151
imagery, 99–100, 262–263, 277, 314n57

imagining of general strike, 168–174
imitation of affects, 18–19, 211–212, 217
immanence, 143, 144, 148, 191
imperialism, 21, 56, 90, 92, 93, 95,
    219–221, 257–258
impersonal flows, 67
impoverishment, 282
improvisation, 9
inaction, 233, 234, 242
inarticulacy, 288–89
Incidents in the Life of a Slave Girl
    (Jacobs), 33–34, 110–111
incorporation, 98, 105, 128
Indebted Man, 38–43
indebtedness, 42, 55, 64
individual postures, 89–90
individuation, 7, 46, 90, 122, 306n10
industrial capitalism, 139, 176, 271–272
industrial-era education, 32–33, 247,
    256, 265, 280
industrialism, 264, 271–272
inequality, 56, 60, 260, 261, 264, 285
inferiority, 182, 261, 263–64, 285, 322n159
inimicus, 22
inner culture, 287–288
Inoperative Community (Nancy), 147
insecurity, 25, 33, 252
inside state, 202, 203, 242
institution building, 31, 33, 113, 167,
    275, 284
institutional religion, 214
institutions, 33, 67, 167, 195, 252–255,
    329n16
insurrection, 10–11, 158, 164, 178, 179, 181
integration, 87, 175, 181–182, 260, 261,
    263, 271
intellectual engagement, 253
intellectual inquiry, 295, 309n64
intellectuals, 55, 66, 72, 82–83, 222
intelligence, 294–295, 297
interchangeability of black workers, 63

internalization, 69, 194, 210, 213, 230, 251
international solidarities, 175, 176
interpellation, 51, 60, 230–231
Interpretation of Dreams (Freud),
    15–16, 62
interpretation of scripture, 203–206, 223
intervals, irregular, 33–34
inverse movement of revolution, 13, 164
inversion, 2, 8–9, 13, 96, 112, 164–165,
    280, 294
involuntary vision, 229
irony, scorching, 98, 100–101, 107
irregular intervals, 33–34
Israel (historical people), 197–98, 205,
    222. *See also* Hebrews (historical
    people)
Italy, 197–198
iustitium, 11

Jackson, Blyden, 197, 199, 201
Jacobs, Harriet (pseud. Linda Brent),
    33–34, 110–111
James, Joy, 76
JanMohammed, Abdul R., 37, 45, 71
Jesus, 200
Jethro (character in Hurston's *Moses*),
    228–229, 231–232, 236
Jewish culture, 199, 200
Jewish priesthood, 205
Jews, 199–201, 213, 221
Jochebed (fictional character in
    Hurston's *Moses*), 210–212
John Brown (Du Bois), 126–30, 132–33,
    135–40, 143, 153–54, 156, 160, 162,
    267, 284, 305n86
"John Brown's Body" (song), 32, 125,
    128–29, 137, 142, 143, 185–187, 192
Johnson, Andrew, 154, 155, 224
Johnson, James Weldon, 275–276
joy, 143, 211, 244, 274
justice, 74, 85, 115, 140, 186, 218, 312n12

Kansas, 139, 140–141
Kant, Immanuel, 144, 200
Kawash, Samira, 132, 138
King, Martin Luther, Jr., 198
Kingdom of God, 160
Kipling, Rudyard, 198–199
knot of desire, 252
knowledge, 49, 225, 241

labor (work), 26, 91–92, 140, 161, 171;
    birth and, 41, 108, 173, 207, 208;
    process of, 8–9, 14–15. See also
    reproductive labor (biological)
labor exploitation, 119, 150, 207–208
labor for emancipation, 27, 32, 66, 112,
    129, 141, 147, 191, 242, 270, 305n86
Lacan, Jacques, 15–16, 236, 300n5
Lackey, Michael, 198, 199–201
Laub, Dori. See Testimony (Felman
    and Laub)
law, 11–13, 56, 59, 74, 78–79, 115, 125,
    140, 160–161, 164–168
laziness, 69, 146, 156, 173
Lazzarato, Maurizio, 23, 42
Le Vin, Louis P., 101
leadership: black, 79, 119, 125, 129,
    152–156, 286–287; confused with god,
    233–235, 239, 242; conservative, 56;
    dead labor, 242, 243; group-centered,
    159, 169, 238; of mobs, 101–103, 115;
    political, 221, 223, 242, 311n12;
    religious, 204–206; talented tenth,
    132, 133; transference and, 194–195.
    See also charismatic leaders; priestly
    class
learning, 16, 284–285, 289
LeFlouria, Talitha, 111
legal metaphysics, 165, 258–259, 311n12
"Let My People Go" (song), 198
"Letter to the Academy" (Hughes),
    248–249, 278–282, 285

"Letter to the Chancellors of European
    Universities" (Artaud), 248–249
Levites, 222
liberalism, 29, 40, 46, 96–97, 113–115,
    174–175, 291–292
liberty. See freedom
libidinal economy, 81, 108, 111, 139, 162,
    164, 181, 183
life, 54, 62, 72, 173, 241, 242, 283–284,
    306n10. See also bare life
light, 49–50, 51, 60, 130, 207
Lincoln, Abraham, 3, 11–13, 32, 164, 177,
    179, 186, 187
Little Rock, Arkansas: public school,
    262–263, 273–274, 277, 278
Little Rock Nine, 258, 277
Locke, Alain, 197
Long Depression, 42, 79, 311n12
Louisiana: public school, 273, 276,
    277, 278
Lulu Mann (fictional character in
    Wright's "Down by the Riverside"),
    36, 37, 48, 52–54, 60–62, 65, 235
lurching, 266, 269, 271, 275
Luxembourg, Rosa, 145, 319n91
"Lynch Law in All Its Phases" (Wells), 88
Lynch Law in Georgia (Wells), 101, 102
lynching, 31, 80, 82, 83–85, 98–107, 111,
    115, 231, 259, 312n12
lynching at the Curve, 82, 85, 87

Macbeth (Shakespeare), 88, 91, 95,
    105, 111
Machiavelli, Niccolò, 197–198, 225
majority/minority perspectives, 75, 114,
    116, 121, 259
"make a way out of no way," 1, 297
males, black, 53, 64
Mann, Brother. See Brother Mann
    (fictional character in Wright's
    "Down by the Riverside")

Mann, Lulu. *See* Lulu Mann (fictional character in Wright's "Down by the Riverside")

Mark (gospel of), 291, 296–297

Marriott, David, 1, 15, 131, 137

martyrs, 142, 238, 239

Marx, Karl, 3–10, 25, 41, 92–93, 97, 115–116, 176–177, 286, 301n22

Marxism, 145, 319n91

masculine imaginary, 175, 176–177, 235

mass education, 266, 269, 276

mass labor, 92–93

massacres, 104, 106

master-slave dialectic, 96–97

material economy, 139

Maxwell, William, 25

McClellan, George B., 177

McCormick, Ryan, 56

McDowell, Calvin, 82

McDowell, Deborah, 197, 199, 201, 219

Memphis Commercial, 104–105

Memphis Free Speech, 81, 85, 86, 87, 105

Mencken, H. L., 39, 40

Mentu (fictional character in Hurston's *Moses*), 224, 225

messianism, 32, 193–196

Metamorphosis (Ovid), 69, 76

method, 49, 294

Mexico, 139

Middle Ages, 222, 223

middle class, 79–80, 176

migration, black, 66, 71. *See also under* exodus

military and property, 103–104, 117–18

Militia Act of 1862, 179

Miller, C. J., 99

Milliken's Bend, battle of, 179

mind/body dichotomy, 209–210

minority/majority perspectives, 75, 114, 116, 121, 259

Minotaure, 300n5

miracles, 32, 190, 191, 195, 206, 235–243

Miriam (character in Hurston's *Moses*), 236, 238–239, 242

mis-education, 32–33, 247–266, 269, 276, 278, 284–286

Mis-Education of the Negro (Woodson), 247

misrecognition, 168–69, 189, 269, 300n5

Mississippi delta reconstruction, 37, 54–59, 66, 73

Mississippi River Flood (1927), 35–73, 221

Mississippi Valley Flood Disaster of 1927, The (American Red Cross), 41, 52, 60, 69

Missouri, 139

mistranslation, 32, 125

Mob Rule in New Orleans (Wells), 80

mobs, 102–103, 258, 259, 314n62

modernism, 30

modernity, 7–8, 77, 113, 172–173

monopoly capitalism, 96, 98, 312n12, 313n46

Montag, Warren, 78, 249

montage and emancipation, 162–192

monuments, 239–240

moral evasions, 254, 255

moralism, 100, 105, 253–255

morality, 95, 201, 219

Moses (biblical character), 155–156, 169, 201, 202, 205, 213; Lincoln as, 177; Tubman called, 153–156, 235; Washington as, 216, 221, 325n59; white man as, 199

Moses (character in Hurston's *Moses*), 219–20, 223–229, 231–243

Moses (Harper), 193

Moses, Man of the Mountain (Hurston), 32, 206–243

Moses and Monotheism (Freud), 202, 213

Moss, Thomas, 82, 85–86

Moten, Fred, 7, 226, 284, 288, 301n22, 331n47

Moton, Robert Russa, 55, 56, 57, 59

mourning, 46, 62, 180–181, 185, 261

Mullen, Bill, 25

multiplicity, 67, 83, 271, 272

multitude, 133, 193–196, 201, 203–206, 221–223, 244, 311n12; black thought and, 75–81; power of, 74–122, 124, 226

mutual decomposition, 21, 140

My Bondage and My Freedom (Douglass), 6–7, 8, 9

mystical experience, 160–161

mythic violence, 32, 46–48, 69–70, 80–81, 125, 131, 156, 162, 187, 209, 214–215, 223

NAACP (National Association for the Advancement of Colored People), 55, 59, 64, 68–69, 124, 167–168

Nancy, Jean-Luc, 147

Nation, 59, 60

nation-state-empires, 22–23

nation-states, 78, 125, 133, 164, 166, 185, 195, 239–240

"nation within a nation" thesis, 195

nationhood, 195; birth and, 41, 108, 172–173

National Association for the Advancement of Colored People (NAACP), 55, 59, 64, 68–69, 124, 167–168

nationalism, 137, 187, 258

Native Son (Wright), 36–37, 54, 61–62

naturalism, 38, 71, 250

Nature, 224–225

Nazism, 22, 200–201

negative attitude, 145, 147–149, 161

Negri, Antonio, 77

negrophobogensis, 50, 84

neoliberalism, 43, 252, 308n27

New Day, 33, 244–289

new humanity, 20, 23

New Orleans, 39

New Song, A (Hughes), 279

New South, 87, 108, 206, 219

Nietzsche, Friedrich, 54, 200, 201, 204–206, 214, 215, 222–223

Nightingale, Taylor, 81

Niobe (Greek mythological character), 46, 69

nonevent of Emancipation, 180, 182, 184, 186

nonidentity, 119, 149, 150, 163, 250, 258

normality, return to, 14–15, 16, 17, 55, 246, 280, 328n4

North (US), 140, 158

nostalgia, 3, 14, 17, 32–33, 217, 247, 256, 265, 280

notebooks, 28, 33–34

"O Black and Unknown Bards" (J. W. Johnson), 275–276

objectification, 4, 8–9, 38, 95–98

observation, 60–61

"Ode to Joy" (Schiller), 32, 123, 125, 186, 187, 191

oedipal triangle, 67

Olmsted, Frederick L., 9, 146

On Being Included (Ahmed), 329n16

On the Anarchy of Poetry and Philosophy (Bruns), 187–188, 245–246

ontogenetic theory, 307n10

ontological totality, 4, 76, 77, 80, 112–13, 115, 120, 147; preservation of, 31, 75, 150

ontology, 264

"Open Letter to the South" (Hughes), 26

oppressed, 19, 129, 201; identification with oppressor, 211, 215, 218, 220, 233

oppression, 45, 69–70, 83, 152, 206, 207, 227, 258, 296

otherness, 83, 120

overwhelming experiences, 1, 291–292, 297

overwriting of society, 126, 162–192

Ovid, 69, 76

Oxford English Dictionary, 269

Palmetto, Georgia, 101–102

parents and desegregation in schools, 260, 261, 329n33

parodic overwriting of society, 163–168

parrhesia, 79, 81

parrhesiastes, 81, 86

passivity, 208, 232, 234, 241, 255, 261–262, 327n108

pathologization, 22, 24–25, 47, 58, 137, 253

Paul (Biblical character), 206

Pauline rhetoric, 249, 252

peace, 74, 221, 230, 231, 282

pedagogy. *See* education

People's Grocery Company, Memphis, 82, 105, 113

Percy, William, 47, 67–71, 72

performative writing, 28–29, 33

persecution, 32, 213–221, 240, 263, 329n26

pessimism, 280, 297

petrification, 37, 46, 47, 69, 292, 293, 294

Pharaoh (character in Hurston's *Moses*), 207–12, 215–216, 220, 223–226, 236

"Ph.D." (Hughes), 250–251, 254, 255, 281, 282, 283

Phenomenology of Spirit, The (Hegel), 82

Phillips, Wendell, 153–154

Philosophy of History (Hegel), 138

photographic imagery, 99–100, 262–263, 277, 314n57

Plant, Deborah, 200, 201, 222

plantation owners, 221; black workers and, 42, 140; Civil War, 182–183; general strike, 145, 147; imperial plot, 138–139; logic for slavery, 190; relief camps (1927 flood), 59–60, 64;

sexual violence, 110–111; slaves' rebellion, 146–147, 157–158; white workers and, 168, 182–183

plantations, 5–6, 42, 108–111, 139, 147–149, 153, 156, 158–159, 173, 176

planters. *See* plantation owners

poetic communities, 246–247, 268, 276, 289

poetry, 244–247, 265, 267, 270, 276, 278, 283, 289

polis, 245

political, 27–28, 32, 77–78, 194, 197–198

political decision, 3

political leadership, 221, 223, 242, 311n12

political miracles, 240–241, 242

political movement, 31, 203, 213–214, 235, 236, 259

political organization, 136

political power, 29, 157, 183, 197

political sphere, 257, 261, 262, 264

political suppression, 138

politics of detour, 21, 43

politics with improper locus, 144–157

Pollock, Della, 28, 29

possibility, 1, 28, 36–38, 47–48, 55, 156, 231, 245, 257, 279; in education, 247, 272; Wright as theorist of, 31, 45

post-Reconstruction era, 84, 91, 92, 98–99

Postmodern Culture, 302n52

power, 193–243; alternative forms, 75, 110; balances, 204, 218; collective, 78–79, 127, 144, 194, 277; to deny, 277; documentation, 223; guilt and, 214–215; horizontal, 136; institutional religion, 214; knowledge, 294–295; loss of, 252; miracles, 206; multitude's, 74–122, 124, 226; New Day, 279, 280; political, 29, 157, 183, 197; reactive, 205; rod of, 235–243;

power (cont.)
    state's, 240; theory and, 292;
    transfer to state, 110. *See also* force
Powers, Allison, 165
practice and theory, 296–297
preach, call to, 229–230, 231, 232
preservation of ontological totality, 31,
    75, 150
presidential office, 224
pride, 31, 263, 288
priestly class, 203, 204–206, 224, 232, 236
priests (characters in Hurston's *Moses*),
    221–222, 225, 232, 236–237, 241
Prince, The (Machiavelli), 197–198
prison-industrial complex, 106–107
private man, 74, 78
private schools, 265
private sphere, 257, 260, 263, 264
production, 5, 108, 110, 111, 139–140, 173
productive expenditure, 147, 176
productivity, 90, 147, 156, 172, 207, 216
professoriate, 246, 248–249, 252–253,
    279–289, 328n4
progress: black, 82, 85, 89, 108; liberal,
    80, 93, 113, 115, 116, 120, 121, 150, 152;
    national/US, 93, 115, 116, 136, 157,
    168; war leading to, 179–180; white
    supremacy's concept of, 285, 287
Progressive Farmers and Household
    Union of America, 114
proletarianization of professoriate,
    248, 252
proletariat, 25–26, 283. *See also* dark
    proletariat
proletarius, 25
property: black people as, 108, 117;
    counterrevolution of, 312n12;
    freedpersons as, 6, 7, 97, 103–104;
    military and, 103–104, 117–118;
    realism grounded in, 38–39, 47;
    refugees and, 50; second-sight, 136;

slaves as, 3, 97, 175–176; Western
    concept of, 147; whiteness and, 50
property ownership, 104
property relations, 46, 47, 98
prophecy, 245, 283
protections, 40, 46, 74, 78, 79
protest, 215–216, 254
psychoanalysis, 80–81
public schools, 33, 256–279, 287
public sphere, 55, 59
punishment, 111, 115, 161, 205, 207,
    214–215, 223, 230, 238, 239, 325n54
purposelessness, 270

race for theory, 291–297
"Race for Theory, The" (Christian),
    292–297
race problem, 88, 91, 95, 111, 257–258
race riots, 102–104, 113–115
racial difference, 110, 257, 291, 297
racial oppression, 69, 206
racial violence, 31, 37, 75, 80, 98, 99, 106
racialization, 46, 90, 260
racism, 110, 164, 167, 170, 190, 200,
    261–263, 267
radical subjectivity, 129
raid at Harper's Ferry, 125, 144, 180–181,
    198
Ralph, Julian, 91–92
Ramadanovic, Petar, 17, 302n52
reading, 1–2, 204
Real Folks (Retman), 25, 202
realism, 38–39, 47
reality, 30, 38, 306n10
*Reason Why the Colored American Is
    Not Part of the World's Columbian
    Exposition of 1893, The* (Wells et al.),
    79–80, 87, 89–100, 104–120
recapture, 97, 108, 111, 164
Recessional (Kipling), 198–99
reconciliation, 87

reconstruction. *See* social reconstruction
records, 174–81, 222–223
Red Record, A (Wells), 80, 105
redemption, 96, 128, 180–181, 185–186, 270
redemptive critique, 96–97
"Reflections on Little Rock" (Arendt), 256–257, 261, 262, 264, 265, 274, 275, 278
refugees, 35–36, 50, 57–58. *See also* citizen-refugees
rejection, 263
relief camps (1927 flood), 51–71, 108
relief project (1927 flood), 31, 37, 39, 51–71
religion, 45, 200, 214, 222, 225
renunciation of fear, 71–72
repression, price of, 128, 131, 132, 137, 308n26
reproductive labor (biological), 37, 47, 52–53, 54, 207, 209
resentment, 80, 82, 97–103, 118, 217, 219
resistance, 8–9, 11, 37, 66, 67, 164, 329n16
responsibility, 161, 245, 283
restoration of Mississippi delta's debtor's economy, 31, 37, 54–55, 60, 64, 65
Retman, Sonnet, 25, 202
retrogression, 285
return to normality, 14–15, 16, 17, 55, 246, 280, 328n4
revelation, 205, 252, 255
revisionist history, 215, 222
revolution, 13, 191, 252, 278, 279, 285, 286
Revolution Surréaliste, La, 248
rhythms of temporalities, 160–161
Richardson, Detective (Walker lynching), 104
risk, 42, 45, 184, 261, 295
ritual, 234
Robinson, Cedric, 47, 296. *See also* ontological totality
rod of power, 235–243

romantic overwriting of society, 163–164, 165, 168–180
romanticization of mass labor, 92–93
Rome, 202
Rony, Fatimah Tobing, 202
rough-draft character of humanity, 120, 121
Roumain, Jacques, 133–136

sacrifice, 32, 142–144, 161, 175, 206, 216, 235, 237–238, 321n138
sadism, 110–111
sadness, 19, 206, 211, 212
"Sales Nègres" (Roumain), 133–136
Savannah, Georgia: public school, 272–275
Scenes of Subjection (Hartman), 146, 153
Schechter, Patricia, 310n3
Schiller, Friedrich, 32, 123, 125, 186, 187, 191
Schmitt, Carl, 10, 11, 186, 240, 242
Schurz, Carl, 103
scorching irony, 98, 100–101, 107
scripture, 200, 203–206, 222–223
second Great Depression, 3, 72, 111
second-sight, 2, 30, 99, 112, 130, 136–137, 145, 212, 223, 275
segregation, 59, 60, 64, 98, 256–266, 287
self-colonization, Europe's, 21, 22–23
self-defense, 104, 287
self-destruction, 106, 182, 206
self-determination, 70, 113–114, 195
self-forgetfulness, 268
self-governance, 112, 121, 172, 174, 312n12
self-hatred, 19
self-perfection, 240–241
self-renunciation, 32, 206, 211, 213, 216, 235, 242
self-resignation, 312n12
self-sufficiency, 142, 168, 173, 270
servile insurrection, 158, 181

Shakespeare, William, 88, 91, 95, 105, 111
shaming, 253
sharecroppers, 55, 63, 64, 65, 114
sharecropping, 38–43, 46, 59–60
shared desire, 55
Shaw, Robert Gould, 178
sheltering children from racism, 260, 261–262
Ship of State (World's Columbian Exposition, 1893), 93
sick body metaphor, 14–16, 18, 22, 24–25
Sidney, Algernon, 74, 76, 77, 121, 311n7
sight, 2, 9. *See also* second-sight
Signifying Monkey (Gates), 28–29
"Silent One, The" (Hughes), 133, 135
Simondon, Gilbert, 307n10
slaves, slavery, 4, 6, 157–158, 201, 269–270, 301n30; Agamben on, 11–13; Douglass and Wells on, 94–98; Du Bois on, 125–132, 138–146; Marx on, 3–10. *See also* Emancipation; fugitive slaves; general strike
Small Axe, 202
Smalls, Robert, 235
Smethurst, James, 25
Smith, Ted. See *Weird John Brown* (Smith)
Snead, W. T., 89
Social Basis of Human Consciousness, The (Burrows), 36
social contract, 218, 220
social-death, 71–72, 86
social discrimination, 329n26
social equality, 220, 265, 273, 274, 277, 278, 285, 287
social order, 138, 161–162, 163, 265, 282
social reconstruction, 26–27, 33, 280, 309n49; of Mississippi delta, 37, 52–59, 66, 72–73
social sphere, 257, 260, 261, 263, 264
social upheaval, 31, 33, 52, 132, 161, 194

socialism, 113, 172
socialization, 208–209
"Sociology Hesitant" (Du Bois), 160
Solid South, 80, 99–107, 113
solidarities, international, 175, 176
Sorel, Georges, 145, 156
Souls of Black Folk (Du Bois), 126–130, 133, 137, 142, 180, 187–189, 191, 267
"Souls of White Folk, The" (Du Bois), 299n5
South. *See* Solid South
Southern Horrors (Wells), 74, 76, 83, 85, 113
sovereign miracles, 240–41
sovereignty, 32, 186–188, 191, 208–209, 213, 235, 240–242, 264, 276–277
Soyinka, Wole, 244
speaking commodities, 4, 6, 8, 157
spectatorship, 267–268
spectrality, 53–54, 62–63, 67, 207
spell of Africa, 137, 138, 160–161
Spillers, Hortense, 53, 295, 296, 297, 301n30
Spinoza, Baruch: belief and the political, 32; chosenness, 213; ecclesiastical authority, 223; *Ethics*, 225, 227; hope, 327n109; Hurston and, 200–201, 324n20; imitation of affects, 18–19, 211–212; interpretation of scripture, 203–204; mind/body dichotomy, 210; mutual decomposition, 21; social contract, 218, 220; sovereign miracles, 240–241; state and multitude, 77; *Theological-Political Treatise*, 213, 214, 233–234, 240; thought, 225; *Treatise on the Emendation of the Intellect*, 225
spirit and flesh. *See* flesh: spirit and
Spirit of God, 137, 138, 160–161
spirited survival, 291–297

spiritual fulfillment, 249
St. Louis Dispatch, 102
stagism, 209
state: care of biological life, 173; infrastructure, 108, 109; miracles, 240; multitude and, 75, 77, 78; power, 110, 240; redemptive tendencies, 180–181, 185–186, 297; refusal to mourn, 180–181, 185; relationship between citizens, refugees and, 36; war, 321n138
state forms, compromise with and use of, 25, 55, 135
state of exception, 10–13, 164, 165, 187, 254
State of Exception (Agamben), 10–13, 164, 187
stealing away, 146, 149–153, 161, 188
stealing to, within, and from educational institutions, 288
Stephens, Michelle, 26, 162
stereotypes, 25, 169
Stewart, Henry, 82
Still, William. See Underground Railroad (Still)
strikes, 145, 153. See also general strike
students, 14–16, 245–257, 261–262, 265, 267, 272, 275, 278, 280–281, 287–288
subaltern activity, 79, 142
subjection, 45, 146, 153, 231
subjectivity, 3, 15, 17, 46, 53, 76, 129, 130, 133, 189, 245, 250, 368; death-bound, 37, 45
suffering, 2–3, 19, 201, 213–214, 219, 237–238, 281, 291–292
Sumner, Charles, 76, 224
superiority, 18, 100, 263, 285
superstition, 234, 235, 240, 242
supranationality, Europe as, 19
surplus, 4, 45, 148, 191
surrealism, 27–28, 30, 300n5

Surréalisme au Service de la Révolution, Le, 300n5
surrealist texts, 27–28
survival, 291–297
sympathy, 60–62

Ta-Phar (fictional character in Hurston's Moses), 219–220, 236–237
"take heed," 291, 296–297
talented tenth, 132, 133, 137
teaching, beyond of, 285
temporalities, 42, 75, 77, 80, 160–161, 297
Tennessee Coal, Iron, and Railway Company, 117
tense talk and whispers, 67, 149
Testimony (Felman and Laub), 13–15, 16, 17, 19, 246
textual supplements, 4, 9
Their Eyes Were Watching God (Hurston), 196, 202
theological imaginary, 44–45, 126, 130, 148, 187, 194–195, 216–217, 237, 249
Theological-Political Treatise (Spinoza), 213, 214, 233–234, 240
theology, 148, 189, 204, 206, 245
theorizing, 292–297
theory and practice, 296–297
third person, 29–30, 141, 149
Third Person, The (Esposito), 306n10
Thompson, Mark Christian, 198, 208
thought, 33, 49, 51, 137–138, 224–225, 284. See also black thought
Toussaint Louverture, 129
tragic artistry, 148, 152
tragic overwriting of society, 164, 165, 180–186
transcendence, 32, 144, 148, 191, 245, 246, 249
transference, 194–195, 226, 239, 242
transformation, 280, 281, 292
transindividuality, 40

translation, 124–126

translation and displacement, 203–206, 230, 234

transubstantiation, 224

"Trauma and Crisis" (Ramadanovic), 302n52

trauma theory, 1, 3, 13–20, 291–294, 332n1

traumatic awakening, 15–16

travail, 151

Treatise on the Emendation of the Intellect (Spinoza), 225

triangulation of newcomers to mainstream American life, 330n33

Tripp, Colonel (East St. Louis affair), 104

Truth, Sojourner, 137

truth-tellers, 81, 86

Tubman, Harriet, 153–156, 235

Turner, Nat, 128

Tuskegee Institute, 55, 56, 216

twin infamies, 80, 91, 98–112

unclaimed experiences, 16–17

Unclaimed Experiences (Caruth), 13, 15–16, 17, 19, 62

Uncle Tom's Children (Wright), 31, 36–38. *See also* "Down by the Riverside" (Wright)

Undercommons, The (Harney), 276–277, 284, 288, 331n47

underground, 20, 33, 67, 118–119, 216, 244–245, 269–270, 279, 288

Underground Railroad, 66–67, 126, 144–158, 161, 185

Underground Railroad (Still), 148–149, 151, 154–156, 171, 183, 237, 270

Union, 165–174, 184; armies, 125, 145, 174–180; camps, 164, 168–174, 181, 183–184

United States, 23–24, 90, 93–98, 257–258

unity, 163, 181

University of Chicago, 91

universities. *See* colleges/universities

unknowability, 213, 291

unproductive expenditure, 147, 156, 191

unrest, 4, 8–10, 14–15, 28, 38, 54, 137–138, 174, 294, 295, 332n1

uplift ideology, 137, 238

US government, 56–57, 59, 99, 113, 121, 165–168, 173, 184, 260–262

use-value, 7, 50

utility, 176

Van Vechten, Carl: Hurston's letter to, 199, 204–206

vanishing point, 79, 122, 142, 312n15

Varro, Marcus Terentius, 4

vernacular writing, 206

Verney, Kevern, 325n59

versatility, 8, 9

Vicksburg, Mississippi: Civil War campaign, 168–174; relief camp (1927 flood), 67–68

Vienna lecture (Husserl), 17–20, 22, 23, 25, 303n52

vigilantism, 112

violence: administrative, 277–278; critique of, 43–46, 71; college/ university's on students, 254–255; sexual, 110–111. *See also* convict leasing; divine violence; lynching; mythic violence

virtuality, 307n10

vision of the damned, 136–144

vocation, 270

vogelfrei, 41, 97

wage laborers, 3–9

"Wait" (Hughes), 133, 135–136, 249

Wald, Alan, 25

Walker, Lee, 99, 104–105

war, 141–142, 175–176, 321n138

Washington, Booker T., 32, 56, 75, 128, 201, 270, 324n20; "Atlanta Compromise" speech, 216–221; as Moses, 216, 221, 325n59

"we," 18, 21, 260

wealth, 115–116, 156, 285, 286, 307n20

Weheliye, Alexander, 20, 110, 332n1

Weird John Brown (Smith), 125, 130–131, 142–144, 152, 157, 159–164, 185–186, 191

Wells, Ida B., 31, 55, 59, 66, 72–122, 130, 221, 235, 310n3

"What to the Slave Is the Fourth of July?" (Douglass), 94–95, 96

Wheatley, Phillis, 70

whipping bosses, 111

White, Walter, 55, 64

white abolitionists, 116, 194

White City (World's Columbian Exposition, 1893), 88–100, 106–112, 116, 128

white culture, 181–182

white man: Hitler's crime against, 22–23; in Moses's position, 199; power to save or condemn black man, 230–231

"White Man's Burden" (Kipling), 198–199

white people: Emancipation and, 78; fears about black people, 114, 263; innocence, 46; insurrection against, 158; lynching, 82–83, 99; property, 97; resentment, 217; as saviors, 32, 126; segregation in schools and, 258–265, 273–274, 277

white soldiers in Civil War, 170, 177–178, 191

white supremacists, white supremacy, 89–90, 101–105, 110, 113, 133, 259, 262, 263, 270, 285

white workers, 12, 96, 116, 168, 181–185, 217, 219, 271, 311n12

whiteness, 19, 83, 99–100, 108, 110, 183, 258, 261, 262, 285; law, 100–101, 114–115, 258, 259; property, 50, 108, 285

Wilderson, Frank, 34

Williams, Heather Andrea, 269

witnessing trauma, 15–16, 17, 54, 62, 132, 141

Witsen, Jake, 119

Woodson, Carter G., 32–33, 247

working class, 77, 118, 176, 287, 311n12, 313n46

Workingmen's Association (England), 176, 177

worklessness, 147, 148, 149, 156, 161, 171, 270

World's Columbian Exposition, 1893, 87–98, 109, 113, 115, 120. *See also* White City (World's Columbian Exposition, 1893)

Wretched of the Earth (Fanon), 29, 162

Wright, Richard, 27, 31, 130, 199, 204–205, 284. *See also* "Down by the Riverside" (Wright)

writing, performative, 28–29, 33. *See also* black writing

Wynter, Sylvia, 20

yonvalou, 268

James Edward Ford III, Associate Professor of English at Occidental College, has published widely on cultural and political theory. His writings on the aesthetics of black radicalism, black popular culture, and political theory have appeared in the journals *Novel: A Forum on Fiction*; *Biography: An Interdisciplinary Quarterly*; *Cultural Critique*; *College Literature: A Journal of Critical Literary Studies*; *New Centennial Review*; *ASAP Journal*; and multiple edited collections. He is currently working on "Phillis, the Black Swan: Disheveling the Origins" and "Hip-Hop's Late Style: Disheveling the Origins," two projects that rethink the origins and ends of black American cultural production.

Roberto Esposito, *Terms of the Political: Community, Immunity, Biopolitics.* Translated by Rhiannon Noel Welch. Introduction by Vanessa Lemm.

Maurizio Ferraris, *Documentality: Why It Is Necessary to Leave Traces.* Translated by Richard Davies.

Dimitris Vardoulakis, *Sovereignty and Its Other: Toward the Dejustification of Violence.*

Anne Emmanuelle Berger, *The Queer Turn in Feminism: Identities, Sexualities, and the Theater of Gender.* Translated by Catherine Porter.

James D. Lilley, *Common Things: Romance and the Aesthetics of Belonging in Atlantic Modernity.*

Jean-Luc Nancy, *Identity: Fragments, Frankness.* Translated by François Raffoul.

Miguel Vatter, *Between Form and Event: Machiavelli's Theory of Political Freedom.*

Miguel Vatter, *The Republic of the Living: Biopolitics and the Critique of Civil Society.*

Maurizio Ferraris, *Where Are You? An Ontology of the Cell Phone.* Translated by Sarah De Sanctis.

Irving Goh, *The Reject: Community, Politics, and Religion after the Subject.*

Kevin Attell, *Giorgio Agamben: Beyond the Threshold of Deconstruction.*

J. Hillis Miller, *Communities in Fiction*.

Remo Bodei, *The Life of Things, the Love of Things*. Translated by Murtha Baca.

Gabriela Basterra, *The Subject of Freedom: Kant, Levinas*.

Roberto Esposito, *Categories of the Impolitical*. Translated by Connal Parsley.

Roberto Esposito, *Two: The Machine of Political Theology and the Place of Thought*. Translated by Zakiya Hanafi.

Akiba Lerner, *Redemptive Hope: From the Age of Enlightenment to the Age of Obama*.

Adriana Cavarero and Angelo Scola, *Thou Shalt Not Kill: A Political and Theological Dialogue*. Translated by Margaret Adams Groesbeck and Adam Sitze.

Massimo Cacciari, *Europe and Empire: On the Political Forms of Globalization*. Edited by Alessandro Carrera, Translated by Massimo Verdicchio.

Emanuele Coccia, *Sensible Life: A Micro-ontology of the Image*. Translated by Scott Stuart, Introduction by Kevin Attell.

Timothy C. Campbell, *The Techne of Giving: Cinema and the Generous Forms of Life*.

Étienne Balibar, *Citizen Subject: Foundations for Philosophical Anthropology*. Translated by Steven Miller, Foreword by Emily Apter.

Ashon T. Crawley, *Blackpentecostal Breath: The Aesthetics of Possibility*.

Terrion L. Williamson, *Scandalize My Name: Black Feminist Practice and the Making of Black Social Life*.

Jean-Luc Nancy, *The Disavowed Community*. Translated by Philip Armstrong.

Roberto Esposito, *The Origin of the Political: Hannah Arendt or Simone Weil?* Translated by Vincenzo Binetti and Gareth Williams.

Dimitris Vardoulakis, *Stasis before the State: Nine Theses on Agonistic Democracy*.

Nicholas Heron, *Liturgical Power: Between Economic and Political Theology*.

Emanuele Coccia, *Goods: Advertising, Urban Space, and the Moral Law of the Image*. Translated by Marissa Gemma.

James Edward Ford III, *Thinking Through Crisis: Depression-Era Black Literature, Theory, and Politics*.

www.ingramcontent.com/pod-product-compliance
Lightning Source LLC
Chambersburg PA
CBHW022133020426
42334CB00015B/879